THE
BROTHERS OF BAGHDAD

TARA NAJIM

For the true "Kadhim" and "Mohammed": It was your courage in the face of danger that first inspired—indeed, necessitated—the writing of this book, and it is your humility and honesty that continue to inspire me today. *The Brothers of Baghdad* was written for your children and grandchildren, that they may know the Iraq that you knew. May your tragedies and triumphs never be lost.

NOTE FROM THE AUTHOR

The inspiration for *The Brothers of Baghdad* came about as I was conducting my Master's thesis research. I was interviewing Iraqis about their experiences as refugees and became, inevitably, more interested in their experiences in Iraq. There were two brothers in particular whose stories stood out as so unbelievable and shocking that I knew that their narratives needed to be recorded.

When I approached the brothers about writing a book, I feared that they would have reservations. To my delight, they were generously open and honest, sharing everything from their most embarrassing accounts to their most raw and painful memories. I am grateful to both of them for their incredible openness and vulnerability in the sharing of their experiences.

I conducted countless recorded interviews with both brothers over the course of more than a year. I was also able to interview their parents, family members, and some of their closest friends (who are also characters in the book). The brothers shared with me all of their photographs from childhood, medical school, and working with the U.S. Forces, as well as documents establishing the veracity of their stories whenever available, including awards, certificates, medals, transcripts and letters. I kept copies, but chose not to publish these records in order to protect the brothers' identities. I also changed all of the names (the brothers included), and for one or two of the very minor characters I combined two actual people into one for the sake of simplicity.

Memory is fallible, and as with any memoir, some elements may have grown fuzzy with time. Fortunately, I found that the brothers generally remembered their experiences in surprising detail, and it helped that many of the events were in their recent past at the time of the interviews. I also fact-checked as much of their stories as possible. Many of the conversations in the book are transcribed exactly as relayed in the interviews, particularly for the more traumatic events which they remembered in great detail.

If there is something to take away from this author's note, it is that these are *true* stories about *real* people. Perhaps that is the most incredible fact of all.

ACKNOWLEDGEMENTS

First and foremost, I want to once again emphasize how indebted I am to Kadhim and Mohammed for their willingness to share the highs and lows of their lives in such full detail. I am amazed and so grateful to you both!

To my mother, Sylvi Koso, and my sister, Deirdre Hess: I could not have written this book without your help. Both of you have been such incredible pillars of support, from editing, financing and website creating to simply reawakening my passion for the project when I had all but given up hope. Thank you, thank you, thank you!

And finally, a special thanks to my husband, Amjad, whose love for me and pride in my work keep me smiling.

FORWARD

As a rural family physician and military medical officer in the Ohio Army National Guard, I have often felt frustrated dealing with the numerous rules and regulations that intrude daily into my work. However, when I arrived in Iraq, that frustration was replaced with a sense of horror at the absence of structured laws and a dictatorship that had no respect for human dignity and individual freedom.

I have practiced rural medicine in the Appalachian region of Ohio since 1981, and have been a member of the Ohio Army National Guard since 1987. I served as the State Surgeon of the Ohio Army National Guard from 1999 through 2010. In these roles, I have taught medical students, taken care of a wide range of rural patients and helped plan the medical aspects of the Ohio National Guard deployments. I also deployed twice to Iraq.

During my two tours of Iraq, I was overwhelmed by the beauty of the country as I flew above it. I had hoped to meet more of the Iraqi people, but due to the nature of my assignments, I had limited contact with the local communities. We did, however, often treat local Iraqis and other Arabic speaking patients in our military clinic.

In February 2007, I was delighted to hear that we were going to have an Iraqi physician as an interpreter at our clinic outside of Baghdad. It was hard enough discussing medical subjects with English speaking patients, let alone trying to understand a patient from a different culture while he communicated through an unknown interpreter whom he may not trust. I felt that now we could at least get the story straight.

I expected that the interpreter would not be up on the latest medical technical knowledge and would have some cultural issues understanding western medicine. It was a typical American attitude of smugness. However, I quickly realized that Kadhim Al Baghdadi was a very bright, well-educated young physician. His English was excellent and his medical knowledge and common sense really impressed me. I was a little less smug for the experience.

Kadhim rapidly made friends with the younger soldier medics and became a part of our team. We shared our stories and found that we both had some aspect of rural living in our histories. After knowing him for only a few weeks, he approached me requesting a letter supporting his immigration to the United States. Taken aback, I tried to sidestep the question by pointing out that Iraq needed young professionals like himself who had skills, common sense and respect for life and human freedom to rebuild the country. In return, he pointed out that if he were killed for those same strengths, he would not be much use to his country dead. I had to admit that he made a pretty compelling argument.

I wrote the letter not feeling totally comfortable with it and not sure of the ultimate outcome. However, as I came to know Kadhim I became increasingly convinced that I had made the right decision. The stories he shared of his family's struggle for survival in the chaos made me realize that I needed to know more about this ancient land, its politics and its people, but I was limited to my contact with Kadhim and not allowed to travel outside of the base. And for good reason, I might add.

It was soon afterward that Kadhim Al Baghdadi met the author of this book. Like me, Tara Najim was impressed with his story. She had a background in Arabic and refugee studies, and having once been exiled from Syria by Assad's dictatorial regime, she was both intrigued by and sympathetic to Kadhim's story. She began working on a series of interviews with both Kadhim and his brother, Mohammed. With her Arabic language skills, she was able to interview Kadhim's parents and relatives to obtain details and knowledge that would otherwise have been hard to come by.

Because of my friendship with Kadhim and my role in his journey, Tara interviewed me as part of her research, sharing the book with me at times as she continued to edit. As it turned out, her telling of the story gave me the answers I was seeking from the beginning, and it brought aspects of Iraqi people, culture, and history to life in a way that I had not been able to access from the military base.

What resulted is a true story that tells the chilling yet uplifting account of two young men struggling to find their way in a world turned upside down. It gives the reader insight into Iraq, from the regimented power structure of Saddam Hussein's rule intruding into every aspect of Iraqi life, to the complicated turmoil that was unleashed with the American invasion of Iraq. It is a tale of caution for us in Western civilization to consider the individual humanity of our Arab brothers as they struggle to find a stable form of government that will protect people while respecting their human rights.

I have never regretted writing that letter.

- Stephen C. Ulrich COL MC FS, Ohio Army National Guard

PART I:
GROWTH HORMONES

THE BEGINNING

In the beginning, it was only the three of them: Kadhim, Mohammed, and the corpse.

Two of the three were sweaty, out of breath, and had hearts that were beating faster than they thought possible. Overhead, the Iraqi sun beat down through the palm trees, making wavy patterns on the sand-gritted path where the boys had been playing just moments before. That is, until their soccer ball was stopped by an elbow.

It was odd, how an elbow became almost unrecognizable when it was all by itself.

Then they noticed a dismembered hand... then a foot... then a bloody mess of intestines... and there, next to the bush, sending a breathless chill down their spines, was the severed head.

It was the first dead body the two brothers had ever seen, but Kadhim, staring in morbid curiosity, knew that it was not the work of an animal. The body had been hacked to pieces the way Mama chopped mutton, and although covered with flies, the blood around it was still fresh. Whoever this was, it had not been long since his murderer had walked the very path on which they now stood.

Ten-year-old Kadhim and his twelve-year-old brother stared at their discovery in shock; the hair rising in unbidden chills on the backs of their necks. Something felt wrong, a fear in the pit of Kadhim's stomach that grew quickly into nausea. He was beginning to taste the bile in his throat when Mohammed grabbed his hand.

"Let's go. Now!"

Steeling his nerves, the boy defiantly snatched his ball from the corpse and ran after his brother. The dismembered body remained behind, an unwelcome stranger in a children's park, a premonition of the horror to come.

When Kadhim awoke, it was raining. Rain rarely came to the desert city of Hilla, but when it did, it was as though God, who had forgotten to water the city all year, had suddenly remembered and decided to douse it with a quick, heavy, very cold bucket of water. With every drop, the layer of sand that dusted the city was turning to mud, and Kadhim thought pityingly of the people waiting in two long lines at the gas station (one for men, another for women, as was proper) to buy gas and kerosene.

Sixteen-year-old Ali was still snoring next door, but Mohammed's bed was already empty and in other parts of the house, his grandparents, aunts, and uncles would soon be getting up. Kadhim wasn't used to the presence of so many relatives, whose homes, apparently, were no longer safe. He flicked the light switch out of habit, but there hadn't been any electricity for months. So he made his way down the hall, hopping from rug to rug in an attempt to avoid the cold marble floor.

In the kitchen, Mama had lit the gas stove with a match and was making tea, eggs, and warm bread while two-year old Salih played on the floor next to her. She smiled as Kadhim sat at the table.

"Good morning, *habibi,* my sweetheart. How would you like your eggs?"

"Sunny-side up—without the yellow."

She laughed. "Without the yellow, huh?"

As she cooked, Baba entered the kitchen, kissed the top of Kadhim's head, and ruffled little Salih's hair. "I'm going out to meet with the other teachers to see if there's any news."

"Again? Why don't you just listen to the radio?" Even as Kadhim spoke, he could hear news broadcasts in the living room. Their beautiful mahogany radio enjoyed a prime spot in a room which was normally lit by a stunning chandelier but now had only kerosene lamps and candles.

Mama pulled Salih up on her hip in one practiced swoop. "Sometimes you learn more by talking to people directly."

With that, Baba was out the door. Kadhim never thought to say goodbye. His father would be back in a few hours, surely.

Kadhim waited for the rain to stop before grabbing Mohammed. The tub on the roof caught rainwater, but with the number of people in their house, it was never enough. The hunt for water had become a necessity for all of Hilla, but for Kadhim and Mohammed, it was their daily dose of adventure. They gathered the empty jugs and were out the door and riding their bicycles before their oldest brother, Ali, had even woken up.

"Are we going to that cracked water pipe again?" Kadhim asked as they pedaled down the street.

"No. It's empty, remember? Let's just bring water from the Euphrates until they break open another tank. It's cleaner than rain water anyways." Mohammed grinned and sped up. "But first let's race to that pole."

"You started before me!" Kadhim shouted, but he laughed and pedaled as fast as he could nonetheless.

They flew past date palms and pomegranate trees, long out of season, but even in the winter, oranges could be found in many backyards, so Mohammed and Kadhim helped themselves. They stopped to stare in awe at the ruined house of a neighbor who had dared to fire at an American helicopter. They passed their school, where they used to go Saturday through Thursday to learn about Arabic, math, and Baba Saddam's many feats for the good of the Iraqi nation.

But the school had sat dark and empty for many months now. Ever since the Americans had come to Iraq.

Kadhim's ten years had afforded him, he felt, a wealth of useful knowledge. The Americans had come from... wherever Americans came from, to get Iraq out of Kuwait and to fight Saddam. Baba said they were bombing Iraqi infrastructure. Kadhim wasn't sure what that meant, but electricity and water had been gone since that January, 1991, and the schools had closed as well. And so he'd learned that war meant using kerosene lamps, taking a vacation from his studies, and running inside whenever he heard a loud BOOM.

But that evening, when Baba didn't come home, war started to mean something else.

Fear.

Baba didn't come home the next day either, or the day after that, and with each passing day, the fear grew, until it became an electric current that ran through every member of the crowded household. Each day, Kadhim—like his brothers—questioned Mama even more.

"Where's Baba? Is he coming home?"

"He'll be home soon, *habibi*, don't worry." Her eyes were red and puffy. Something was definitely wrong.

"But *when*?" Kadhim knew the truth. It pounded in every beat of his heart.

He's dead.
He's dead.
He's dead.

THE REBELLION

Mama shoved a few bills in her boys' hands and pushed them out the door with bribes of sweets from the corner store. She put two-year-old Salih down for a nap, and with all four of her boys finally out of sight, the feeling of panic she'd been holding at bay overtook her. Her breath came in wheezy gasps, her throat constricted, and she slid to the floor, her head in her hands, her body wracked with sobs. She looked up to find her aging mother gazing down at her in pity.

"It's been a week since he disappeared," Mama said beseechingly through her tears. "One of the neighbors thinks that he went to fight with the regime's popular army. But that can't be. The United Nations brokered a ceasefire a week ago. The war is over. Iraq has pulled out of Kuwait, and the American troops are withdrawing. What could the army possibly need him for?"

Something else was going on, a current of unrest was spreading throughout Iraq, and it frightened and unsettled her.

Her mother's eyes were sympathetic. "Dear, you have to face the possibility that he may have been in the wrong place at the wrong time. A few weeks ago the Americans bombed a gas station, killing dozens of innocent bystanders. Perhaps it was something like that."

"Maybe not. Maybe he's out there somewhere and can't contact me. The phone lines have been down since the Americans bombed the..."

Her panicked voice trailed off as her mother put a gentle hand on her shoulder and shook her head.

"If he were alive, he'd come home. I'm sorry my darling, but he's gone. And now you need to be strong for your children."

Then the aging woman knelt on the floor and embraced her weeping daughter.

An hour passed as Mama collected herself. It seemed she had no sooner dried her tears than her sons burst into the house, shouting with excitement. And as Ali's breathless words sank in, Mama felt her head spin.

"The intifada! It's happening!"

The world would not let her catch her breath.

In an instant, the family gathered around the radio. Kadhim joined them, listening intently, sensing the momentousness of the occasion but unsure as to what it meant. Uncle Ehab was pacing in a circle, eyes wide.

"The Shiites in the South are rebelling against the regime! The Kurds in the North have joined, too."

"How? Where?" Fear played with the shadows on Mama's face, and Kadhim looked from her to Uncle Ehab, trying to determine whether this news was good or bad.

"It's *The Voice of Free Iraq*," Uncle Ehab answered. "It's been broadcasting from Saudi Arabia, encouraging Iraqis to overthrow Saddam. Even the American president has been encouraging a coup! It's only been a few days since the rebels took Basra and already the rebellion is spreading like wildfire! The regime is weakened by war, and with the Americans on our side, we could finally—"

He stopped abruptly, silenced by a sharp look from Mama. Then he continued slowly. "The rebels have seized Basra, Najaf, Amarah... This uprising will come to Hilla soon."

"Enough." Mama turned to her boys. "Ali, Mohammed, Kadhim: listen to me. You be careful of those rebels. They're bad men and troublemakers."

Kadhim, wide-eyed, nodded solemnly. *So we're on the side of Baba Saddam. He is Iraq's savior, isn't he?*

Within days, the rebels reached Hilla. Despite being kept inside by Mama, Kadhim could see that all the shops had closed and the streets were filled with people, though he couldn't tell whether their shouts were of anger or joy.

Over the following days, he overheard Mama, Uncle Ehab and the other adults sharing news whenever they came back in the house from a trip outside. The rebels had raided the school and burned the Ba'athi headquarters. They were visiting all the houses of known party officials, killing and driving out Ba'athis like rabbits. For the most part,

Kadhim paid little attention to the commotion. He was far more interesting in playing jacks with Mohammed. He and his brother did discover the mutilated body in the park, but other than that, there seemed to be far less fighting than Kadhim had expected. When he put this question to Uncle Ehab, his answer seemed oddly pensive.

"They have killed some Ba'athis. And some of the government officials have switched sides and joined the rebels. But it seems that mostly, there's just no one left in Hilla for the rebels to fight. The Ba'athis have vanished."

Just like Baba.

BODIES

It was dark, wet, and miserably cold. Pangs of hunger growled in Baba's stomach, and his army fatigues were drenched. With a grimace at his aching feet, he shook off the mud that caked his boots, and the same thought that had been plaguing him for weeks nagged him once again.

Of all the places in the world, this is the last place I should be.

Baba had been exchanging news with other teachers when the government vehicles arrived.

"Everyone needs to wear army fatigues and get into the trucks, now!"

There was no time to go home. Baba, like the rest of them, had been forced long ago to become a low-level Ba'athi. Refusing to do so would not only have vastly limited his career options, it would also have put his life in danger. Now, with all Ba'ath party members called upon to do their part for the regime, he and some two hundred other teachers were loaded into trucks and shipped two hundred kilometers away to Samawa without so much as a note to their wives.

With a ceasefire between the UN and Iraq, there was little to do in Samawa besides cook, eat, and hang out with the others. Their boredom was relieved only with the arrival of the Intifada a few days later. The irony of it was painful: Baba, a 41-year-old high school English teacher, fighting on the side of a regime he detested. The rest of the regime's Popular Army was similarly half-hearted, and within two days, the city fell to the rebels. Confusion followed among the remaining teachers as the Popular Army disbanded and scattered.

"The rebels say their problem isn't with us. They know we were brought here against our will."

"Where should we go then? All of Iraq is falling to the rebels, and Saddam's Republican Guard is slaughtering any male old enough to hold a weapon."

"Some of the men are hiding in palm trees to escape the Guard."

"What about you, Abu Ali? What will you do?"

Baba was resolute. "I'm going to Hilla to protect my wife and children."

One of the teachers laughed. "We'd all like to do that, but Hilla is nearly two hundred kilometers away and we have no transportation."

"I'll walk."

The man's laughter stopped abruptly. "It's too dangerous, Abu Ali. The other day a group of disbanded soldiers just like us was caught by the rebels and killed. In fact, one of the men committed suicide just so he wouldn't have to die by another's hand. Look at us! We're still in our fatigues! If you aren't killed by rebels who think you're with the regime, then you'll be executed by the Republican Guard, who will think you've defected. The Intifada is on its way to Hilla, the Republican Guard will be there to take it back, and both sides are dangerous."

Baba met the man's gaze head-on. "Then I'd better walk fast."

Now, fourteen rainy kilometers later, Baba was soaked, exhausted, and hungry. He was walking with nine other men; some he knew, others he didn't. Daylight had long since disappeared, and still they had not reached Rumaythah, the first town en route to Hilla. They were stranded.

"Ali! Mohammed! Kadhim! Come inside! *Now!*" Fear echoed in Mama's voice, and for once they did not question her. They ran into the house and locked the door.

Within two weeks, most of Iraq had fallen to rebel forces. Now, only four of the eighteen provinces remained in the hands of the regime: Baghdad—the seat of Ba'athi power—and the three provinces known as the Sunni Triangle. Uncle Ehab said that most Sunnis stood to gain from the Ba'ath party remaining in power, but if they did join, then perhaps even Saddam Hussein himself would be unable to withstand the force of an entire nation.

That was before the Republican Guard came to Hilla to reclaim it from the rebels. Now, even Kadhim could not ignore the war outside his doorstep.

Heart pounding, he stood close to Mohammed as they watched out the window. Across the street, two guards entered the home of Hayder, one of Ali's closest friends.

The Republican Guard had arrived like a plague, killing everything in its path. Suddenly, the chopped-up corpse in the park became the first of many. On their daily hunt for water, Kadhim and Mohammed were careful to step around the unclaimed bodies that littered the streets, some of whom they recognized. They made sure to be home by the state-mandated nine o'clock curfew and watched together in horror as helicopters shot at their city right in front of them, always running home as quickly as they could. But for Kadhim, the most terrifying part was still the thought that Baba was dead. Mama insisted their father would be home soon, but her tone grew less convincing with each day that passed.

"Boys! Get away from the window!"

The two brothers pulled the curtain shut and peered through the crack, unable to tear their eyes away.

Over the past week, they had watched as men were taken by the Guard, never to be seen again, and others were executed in the street. This time, the Republican Guard reappeared with a young boy in their grip, and Ali let out a blood-curdling scream.

"*Hayder!*"

Mama rushed to Ali's side and held him as they watched the scene unfold.

Hayder's mother was on her knees in the street, pleading and sobbing, "Please, let him be! He's only sixteen! He hasn't even finished school yet!"

"The *mukhtar* has informed us that your son is a traitor to the regime. The punishment for joining the rebels is execution."

It was the job of the *mukhtar*, the malicious party official, to know and report the intimate details of every soul in his neighborhood. Behind the curtain, Kadhim's pulse quickened, and he felt Mohammed's grip on his hand tighten.

This can't be real.

"Please, have mercy on him! He's just a boy!" Hayder's mother clung to the guard's pant leg as he raised his Kalashnikov. He kicked her away and trained the barrel at Hayder's skull. The boy was crying and shaking.

Mama gasped and pulled Ali close to her, trying to shield her son's eyes as a shot rang out and Hayder's mother screamed. Mohammed and Kadhim could only stare in wide-eyed shock as the boy's lifeless form fell to the ground.

The farmer took one look at the nine hungry, dirty men who crowded his doorstep, and without asking who they were or where they were going, invited them in for dinner and a free place to sleep. In the tradition of true Arab hospitality, it was the guest's right to stay for three days—no questions asked—but Baba had no intention of making such an

11

imposition on their host.

"I'll have to leave you here," the farmer said the next morning, after giving them a ride to the outskirts of Rumaythah. "The fighting is still ongoing within the city, and I don't want to get mixed up in it. Besides, you're still wearing your Ba'athi uniforms." He looked at them gravely. "We've been hearing rumors that Saddam's thugs are capturing unarmed civilians and burying them alive."

The men looked at each other in somber silence. This sounded exactly like something Saddam and his Republican Guard would do.

That day, several of them decided to discontinue their journey, looking for a safe place to wait out the fighting. But for Baba, the fear wasn't for himself. His wife and four boys were alone in a city that would soon fill with violence as the Republican Guard weeded out the rebels. So, dirty and weary, he and the remaining men began to walk to the next city en route to Hilla: Diwaniya, a city still in the hands of the Ba'ath.

They spent the night in the small town of Hamza about halfway to Diwaniya, and continued their endless walk the next day, choosing small side roads in an attempt to stay out of sight. As they walked the dirt road, an old pickup truck pulled up beside them, and a young man with a Kalashnikov eyed them suspiciously from the driver's seat. "Where are you headed?"

"Diwaniya." Even as he said it, Baba was frighteningly aware of the fact that they were walking, unarmed, in full Ba'athi garb, toward one of the regime's remaining cities. He and his companions stopped warily, and he felt a chill as the rebel and his passenger exchanged looks, grabbed their weapons, and jumped out of the truck, encircling the group like a large cat circles its prey.

"I see." The rebel peered at Baba, head cocked, a strange look in his eyes. "Where are you from?"

"Hilla." Something about the young man's look made Baba nervous, and he tensed himself to run. Then the tips of the young rebel's mouth twisted into an ominous smile.

"Don't you recognize me, teacher?"

The pounding came at their door at nearly ten o'clock at night, and almost before they knew what was happening, two armed guards burst into the entranceway. At the sound of his aunt and mother's screams, Mohammed ran into the living room with Kadhim close behind.

"Where is the young man who was just outside?" The guard's shout made Kadhim tremble.

Grandfather raised his hands in protest. "No one was outside. All of us were here, inside, before curfew."

"Don't lie to me. We saw someone in the street, and he entered *this* house. Where are you hiding him?"

He raised his gun and pointed it at Grandfather's head. Kadhim heard someone gasp and turned to see the color drain from his mother's face.

"It was me!" Uncle Ehab stepped out of the hallway's shadows. "Please, don't hurt him!"

Instantly, two long Kalashnikovs were pointed at the young man.

Kadhim froze, but he could not look away. A voiceless prayer formed itself in his heart. *Baba, Baba, we need you! Baba, help us!*

Mohammed put a protective arm around Kadhim, and they braced themselves as they heard the clicks of weapons being readied.

"Don't you recognize me, teacher?" The words rang in Baba's head, and he stared, uncomprehending, at the young rebel.

"I'm afraid not."

The young man grinned. "I was one of your students in Hilla. One of many, I guess. Look, if you guys keep walking around dressed like Ba'athis, you're going to get yourselves killed! Get in the truck and I'll take you to my place for the night."

The men hesitated for only a second before jumping in the back of the pickup.

"I'll have to get you a change of clothes," the rebel shouted to them as they drove away. "And it's way too dangerous to go to Hilla. I'm taking you to Baghdad."

Baba's heart sank. What about his wife and sons? Were they okay? *Were they alive?* It seemed that the more he tried to reach them, the farther away he ended up.

"Please, *please* don't kill him!" Mama's hands shook as she found herself in the same position as so many others.

"Only enemies and those hostile to the Ba'ath are out past curfew."

"But we're not enemies!" Mama cried. "Look at the pictures!" Fear had seeped so deeply into their personal lives that they, like everyone else, had long ago hung pictures of the dictator on their living room walls as if he were a beloved uncle. They never knew when to expect a visit from the *mukhtar* or another unknown informant. "Besides, he wasn't out—"

"I was, I was outside," Uncle Ehab interrupted. "But I'm not an enemy. I'm loyal to the regime, I swear."

"I don't believe you," a guard growled.

"I shouldn't have gone out, I know! But I heard a shot, and I went outside just for a minute, just to see what it was!"

"You went out to take part in the rebellion, traitor."

"No! I swear I was only outside for a second! I'm sorry!" Ehab's voice cracked. "I'll never do it again!"

For a moment, as Uncle Ehab teetered on the thin line between life and death, time stood still. The Republican Guard had been shooting suspects on the spot, rounding up any men old enough to fire a gun and executing them on the mere suspicion that they might join the rebellion. Mohammed and Kadhim watched, frozen in place, as the Republican Guard's guns remained trained on their uncle. Only Mama's tears cut through the silence.

"Please," Uncle Ehab pleaded softly. "It was a mistake. I'm loyal to Saddam, may Allah keep him safe and raise him high. I'll never be out past curfew again."

The guards exchanged looks, then lowered their weapons.

"You've been warned," one snarled, and they stomped out the door.

A week had passed, and the atmosphere in the Al Baghdadi house remained somber. In the flickering light of an oil lamp, Kadhim and Mohammed were attempting an evening game of cards, repeatedly frustrated by little Salih's efforts to play with them. Meanwhile, bits of the adults' conversation floated in from the living room.

"...It's over. It only took three weeks for the Republican Guard to crush the uprisings."

"I need to go back to the farm." That was Grandfather. "I have crops and animals that need to be cared for, and we've all heard that government forces have sprayed toxins over Iraq's landscape, drained southern marshlands and felled thousands of palm trees in order to flush out the rebels. God only knows what shape my farm is in."

His voice was drowned by protests from the others that it was too soon, too dangerous.

"Over one hundred thousand killed, raped, and 'disappeared'... Refugees fleeing... Land mines everywhere..."

Then Uncle Ehab's voice, loud and angry: "Where are the Americans? For all its rhetoric, America did *nothing* to stop this bloodshed. But what really boils my blood is the lack of support from Sunnis. With their support, the rebellion might have succeeded. Instead, they just stood by and watched as Shiites and Kurds were slaughtered by the thousands. How could they *do* that to us? Our Sunni 'brothers'." He spat the last word out angrily.

Although Kadhim did not know it then, beneath the surface, born of a regime that favored one sect over the other, the fault line separating Sunnis and Shiites was widening. A far more destructive eruption brewed below, lying in wait for his own generation.

A pounding at the door brought the conversation to an abrupt standstill.

"Come on!" Mohammed whispered, and he and Kadhim dashed into the living room.

"Boys, stay out of the way!" Mama ordered.

"Ali, go get my gun." Uncle Ehab made his way to the front door and cautiously undid the lock, opening the door just a crack. Then he emitted a gasp and flung the door open.

There, under Hilla's starry night skies, stood Baba.

The house erupted into trills, cheers, and tears of joy as each fought for their turn to embrace the man who had been presumed dead for four long weeks. But Kadhim was first, throwing himself into his father's arms, breathing in his familiar smell and taking in the comfort of his strong embrace. Mohammed was right behind him, then Salih and Ali and Mama.

"Thank Allah a thousand times for your safety!" She kissed him repeatedly on both cheeks. "Where have you *been*?"

"It took me about a week, but I finally borrowed a car and drove home from Baghdad."

"*What?*"

Baba laughed. "Give me a cup of tea and I'll tell you the whole story."

15

HUNGRY

No one said anything when, for the sixth night in a row, they dined on bread and fried tomatoes. The bread tasted funny and they never had eggs anymore, but the boys knew not to complain. Perhaps Kadhim and Salih were still too young to fully understand why their dinners of hamburger or kabaab had been replaced by potato sandwiches, or why their breakfast was now just bread and tea, if they had breakfast at all. But Mohammed knew why.

Shortly after the rebellion, Baba had pulled every string he had to circumvent Saddam's edict that no one from the rebelling districts was permitted to move to Baghdad. They sold their home in Hilla and moved to the capital, looking to start afresh. They were met with the grim face of an economic embargo.

Mama's part-time teaching job brought in 2,000 Iraqi dinars per month, and Baba's full-time position as an English teacher brought 12,000 to 15,000 dinars. Between the two of them, their total monthly income was no more than $20. With the cost of two kilograms of meat at seven dollars, feeding their family of growing boys was quickly becoming impossible.

A lot of staples, in fact, were in short supply. Eggs, cooking oil, milk, and butter were rare. Flour was nowhere to be found, and much to the boys' disgust, Mama now baked bread using a crude brown flower that a dishonest salesman had mixed with plaster. They ate the very substance their walls were made of.

The boys watched as their home was gradually stripped bare. Their good Ukrainian furniture, chandeliers, paintings, all three A.C. units, and even their camera were all sold for less than they were worth. Baba began to stay at school until nine o'clock every night to teach private lessons to more affluent students, which earned an extra hundred dollars or two every month. And Ali—in his final year of high school— began to drive a taxi in the evenings. Anything to make ends meet.

Still, for all the stress of poverty, it was the birth of Firas that pained Mohammed's parents the most.

There could be no doubt about it. Firas was a blessing, a delight, and a complete surprise. He was their fifth and final son, and he came to them in 1993, in the midst of the embargo. Without access to prenatal testing, their new baby brought with him a few extra surprises.

The first came within a few days of his birth, when the doctor sat down with the parents and informed them that their son had been born with a congenital heart defect. Extra precautions would have to be taken his entire life. They came home that night stricken, fatigued, and fearing for the life of their newborn.

When Firas was three months old and still did not have the strength to hold up his head, they took him to the doctors once again. Tests were run, and the physician's look was grave as he revealed the news.

At first, Mama and Baba didn't believe it. "But how could that be? He looks completely normal!" *Surely there was some mistake.*

"Not everyone with this condition looks the same. The results, however, are conclusive." The doctor set down the papers, and his eyes met those of the stricken parents. "This condition varies from individual to individual, and while it will affect his I.Q., he may still be able to maintain a good quality of life. He will be prone to many health problems, however, such as hearing loss, vision loss, and obesity. For those with a heart defect, like Firas, there is only a fifty percent chance of living to the age of thirty."

Mama and Baba were stunned. When Mohammed saw them that evening, they seemed to have aged a decade. Mama couldn't stop crying, and Baba looked heartbroken. Their four other sons crowded around them, concerned and frightened.

"Mama, what's wrong?"

Baba answered in her stead. "Your little brother Firas is Mongoloid."

"What is that?" Salih was only five years old and didn't understand, despite the fact that this would be the only term used in Iraq until the medical schools finally received new textbooks around the turn of the millennium. But Mohammed knew.

Firas had Down Syndrome.

With this twist of fate, baby Firas transformed their lives. On that day, all the calculations their father had made for his own life and the lives of his children were changed. The fear that he might live to see his son's premature death haunted him every day. Though they ached for the loss of what could have been, they accepted that their son would always need extra care, for they had all fallen completely and irreversibly in love with the warm, cheerful spirit that now lived amongst them.

With the addition of their seventh family member—not to mention frequent visits from relatives—the household budget became even tighter. It was through careful saving and great sacrifice that they celebrated every Ramadan, as they thanked Allah for His many blessings and enjoyed festive evening meals with family and friends. As was tradition, they shared what they had with those less fortunate. Even with the assistance of governmental welfare, there were those around them who were dying of starvation. The Al Baghdadi family had much to be thankful for.

During the summers, they went to Grandfather's date farm. There the children played with cousins, fished, harassed the livestock, swam in the Euphrates, and ate an inordinate amount of dates.

In his third year, Firas learned to walk. He was gradually learning to talk and understand them as well, although as time passed, his tongue thickened and it became increasingly difficult to understand his speech. His eyesight was poor, and he often held objects very close to his face in order to see them properly, but he was loving and playful, and his innocence endeared him to the entire neighborhood. The family settled into a new normal. There was nothing they could do to change Firas's fate or their own, so they accepted life as it was, and thanked Allah for it all, the good and the bad.

"Do you ever go to the Shurja Market?"

His peer's whisper came at the end of the school day, just as their teacher was detailing their evening assignment.

"Sometimes, I guess. Why?"

"Teacher Haitham sells socks there in the evenings." The boy smirked.

Mohammed looked at his teacher's worn pants and outdated shirt and felt a flush of embarrassment for him. So what if the man sold socks or drove a taxi in the evenings? It was better than the neighbors who received $300 a month from Saudi Arabia to convert to the extremist Sunni offshoot of Wahhabism. This was so much money that even Shiites left their sect, discarded their Western clothes for short dishdashas, and grew long and unkempt beards. The offense was punishable by death, and Saddam's guards came quickly for such men.

Mohammed was saved from responding to his friend's remark by the sudden screeching of chairs as the bell rang. In the hallway the younger students ran gleefully for the doorway, and although Mohammed felt the same sense of relief, he was in tenth grade and was too cool for such antics. He was gathering his books when a familiar shout stopped him in his tracks.

It was Kadhim, whose cries filled the hallway as a teacher beat him.

The sight of his slight little brother being beaten by a man three times his size incensed Mohammed, and rage took over. He charged at the teacher, nearly knocking him down as he hit him, and began punching him as hard as he could. Mohammed was one of the tallest, strongest boys in his class, and his blows came as a painful shock to the older man.

"*What the hell do you think you're doing, beating my brother?*"

"Your brother?" The teacher tried unsuccessfully to fend off Mohammed's punches. "Stop! Look, I'm sorry!"

"You're sorry? He's only in seventh grade!"

"He was running in the hallway!"

"So *what* if he was running in the hallway?" Mohammed pummeled the teacher with another series of painful blows. "*All* the seventh graders run in the hallway! Why do you have to pick on *him*?"

"I'm sorry!" The teacher gasped. "I didn't know he was your brother!"

"MOHAMMED! What are you *doing*?" The shout came from behind him, as the principal ran to the scene. Kadhim, meanwhile, watched in awe of his older brother as he wiped the tears from his eyes and checked his fresh bruises.

"You wait till we tell your father!" The principal pulled a struggling Mohammed away from the teacher. "We could have you expelled for this!"

Baba's look was no less angry as he faced Mohammed that evening. "Perhaps that teacher should not have beaten Kadhim, but Mohammed, your actions were inexcusable. They're talking about expelling you!"

Mohammed crossed his arms and stared defiantly at his father. "*Nobody* hurts my family! I don't care *what* the consequences are!"

GROWING PAINS

"I can never tell if they like me or if they're laughing at me." Kadhim glanced at the threesome of giggling girls who were staring at him from a few seats away. Next to him, Anwar shrugged.

"Who knows what girls think."

The schools had been segregated since middle school; the only time that boys and girls mixed was on the bus. As he started high school, it seemed that the more Kadhim's interest in girls grew, the more unapproachable they became. Luckily, Mohammed, who had never been shy, had given him a few pointers:

"Some guys stand in the street and make comments as the girls walk past. Don't. You're better than that.

"If you find a pretty girl, just tell her that you like her eyes or something. If she smiles, it means she likes you.

"Be careful when you call her house. If a man answers the phone, hang up immediately."

As the bus pulled to a stop and the girls filed out, one of the gigglers dropped a piece of paper in Kadhim's lap. On it was scribbled her name, phone number, and a short note: "*Call me tonight at 8:00.*"

Sometimes, the bolder girls made it easy.

After lining up in the schoolyard for a recitation of the national anthem, Kadhim and his classmates—all around sixteen years old—were called to their first lesson of the day: Nationalism. Usually, they read from a Ba'athi textbook extolling Saddam's many feats. There was nothing that could put Kadhim to sleep quite like Saddam's implementation of the first state welfare system in the Arab world, the best healthcare in the Middle East, the National Campaign for the Eradication of Illiteracy, and mandatory education funded entirely by the government through graduate school.

Today, however, they were taken outside to train on Kalashnikovs, and Kadhim found himself standing in a field with an assault rifle resting awkwardly in his hands.

"Now, take the butt of the gun and rest it against your shoulder."

"Like this?" Learning to shoot a gun was a standard part of the boys' curriculum, and Kadhim was so excited that he barely noticed as the regime's fingers reached into his life and slowly tightened their grip.

"No, a bit more like this."

At the age of twelve, he and the other boys had been offered the chance to join "Saddam's Cubs," the Ba'athi version of boy scouts, which gave young boys extreme physical training and groomed them to join the ranks of Saddam's Special Forces. There were parents who were proud to have their children join. At the age of sixteen, he was forced to become a party member, albeit the lowest level of "loyal."

"Now when you have the rifle properly positioned, aim at the target, and shoot."

Feigning confidence, Kadhim squinted his eyes and pulled the trigger. The force of the assault rifle flung him backward, and in his shock he was unable to remove his finger. The Kalashnikov, set to fully automatic, sprung up and hit him in the face as it sprayed bullets in the air.

As soon as the other boys overcame their surprise, a wave of laughter rippled through the group, and Kadhim's face reddened. A faint but growing divide had begun to split the boys who aspired to climb the Ba'athi ladder, who bragged about their increasing rank, the rank of their fathers, and their connections to Saddam's hometown of Tikrit, from the boys who did not. They were annoying and haughty, but Mohammed had warned Kadhim about them.

Mohammed, with his bullheadedness and hot temper, rarely had good advice when it came to fights, but in this case, his words were solid. "Stay away from those Ba'athis. Whatever you do, DON'T pick a fight!"

"I have a new assignment for you boys today." It was the last class of the day, Islam, which had recently been taken over by a new professor, who was apparently an imam himself and far more religious than his predecessor. "Your assignment is to attend the Friday prayer every week, write a report on what was said, and turn it in the next day."

Kadhim cringed. He never attended Friday prayers. No one in his family did, although he wasn't sure why. For a moment, he envied Christian students, who weren't required to attend the class. He had learned all he wanted to know about Islam from his mother, who taught religion in elementary school.

The Quran was the third and final installment of three holy books, preceded by the Torah and the Bible. In fact, it maintained that Judaism, Christianity, and Islam all worshipped the same God and that

Moses, Jesus and others had all been God's prophets. The Prophet Mohammed, peace be upon him, had come simply to complete the divine message. The word "Allah," which seemed so divisive, simply meant "God," and was the same word used by Arabic-speaking Christians. Why did so many think that "Allah" was a different god entirely?

Whatever. Kadhim refocused his thoughts on the assignment, feeling rebellious.

He brought it up with Baba that evening.

"Tell him you don't attend Friday prayers." Baba's response was short, his smile oddly cryptic. "He'll understand."

"That's it? What if he asks why?"

"Don't worry, he'll know what it means."

"Know what what means?" Uncle Ehab walked in on the end of their conversation, grabbed a handful of nuts from a bowl on the table, flung himself on the couch, and changed the topic before they had time to respond. "Did you hear about the Al Shuwairi boy down the street?"

Baba glanced at Kadhim out of the corner of his eye and seemed to hesitate for a moment. "What happened?"

"Not too long ago, he was out and had too much to drink, and started to curse the Ba'ath, apparently in front of the wrong people. So yesterday, some Ba'athi police came to his house and dragged him, his parents, and all of his siblings out onto the street. Then, right in front of the whole neighborhood, they cut off his tongue."

"God help him."

"And the worst part? They forced the father to clap and the mother to trill while they did it by threatening to kill the other children too."

Trilling was a sound of joy, saved for engagements and weddings. The image of parents being forced to cheer as they watched their son's tongue cut from his mouth was chilling.

Baba looked at Kadhim pointedly. "He got off lightly. He's lucky he isn't dead."

Kadhim thought of the boys at school who bragged about their fathers' high rank in the party, and his father continued gravely. "Kadhim, you should understand that anything that's said in this home should never *ever* be repeated."

Gone were the days when, fearing the words that might slip from their children's mouths, his parents had praised the Ba'ath and referred to the leader as "Baba Saddam." Slowly, a new picture of his government was beginning to form, and a new lesson was internalized for Kadhim, as it had for those before him.

Hide your true feelings; fake your love.

22

It was evening before Kadhim remembered the slip of paper in his pocket. He couldn't remember if the girl who had passed it to him was cute, or even which of the three had tossed it, but who cared? She was a girl, and she was interested in him. Tentatively, he picked up the phone and dialed, praying not to hear a male voice.

"Hello?" She sounded just as nervous as he.

"Is this Maryam?"

"Yes, it is."

"Hi, I'm Kadhim..." He wasn't sure what to say, and Maryam seemed a lot less confident without the presence of her friends, but they managed some awkward conversation and agreed to meet for a few minutes the next day after school. When Kadhim at last returned the phone to its receiver, it was with a sigh of relief and a heady flush of excitement and embarrassment.

He had a girlfriend.

Friday was Kadhim's only day off, and it came and went without a visit to the mosque, which his teacher was quick to point out the next day.

"Kadhim, where's your report of the Friday sermon?"

"I didn't go this week, sir."

"Next week then."

Next week came and went, and several weeks after that, and still Kadhim did not attend the Friday prayer. Much to the amusement of their friends, Kadhim and Maryam had several brief, innocent meetings after school, which was as far as a high school relationship ever went. They confessed their feelings for one another, made plans to attend the same university, and eventually, the relationship fizzled out. They both knew that their futures would largely be determined by their score on the final baccalaureate exams at the end of high school.

The assignment, however, could not be ignored forever. Things came to a head the day Kadhim dared to ask a certain question in Islam class.

"Sir, why is it that Muslims can't eat pork?"

"Because it's *haram*."

The answer was frustratingly uninformative. In a world where extremism came and went like waves, Baba—though a devout Muslim himself—had warned his sons: "If something doesn't make sense, *question* it. Don't just accept it blindly like sheep."

"But sir, *why* is it *haram*?"

"Because it says in the Quran that pork is forbidden."

The professor turned to change the subject, but Kadhim's hand was still raised. "Sir, I read that during the Prophet's time, pigs had diseases that made people sick. Could that be the reason?"

A look of annoyance grew on the professor's face. "If the Quran says that pork is *haram*, then Allah Himself has forbidden it. Who are you to question Allah?"

"You don't know why pork is forbidden, do you?" The words slipped from Kadhim's mouth before he had time to filter them, and the professor's look of annoyance quickly turned to anger.

"Kadhim, you will stop talking and stay after class."

Kadhim stayed in the classroom as the students filed out and cringed under the professor's reprimand, but to his relief the professor soon changed the subject.

"Kadhim, in the past month I haven't received any Friday sermon reports from you. Why is that?"

"Sir, my father sends his regards, and says to tell you that we don't attend Friday prayers."

"Ah. You're Shiite."

"That's what I hear, sir." Kadhim wasn't trying to be flippant. The truth was, he had only just learned that he *was* Shiite. "I barely know the difference between Sunnis and Shiites," Kadhim confessed, his cheeks reddening slightly. "I've heard that Sunnis don't visit the shrines of saints like we do, but that's all I know."

"I'll tell you the difference. Don't worry about the homework. You're exempt. As for the Friday sermon..." He paused and raised a finger. "By the way, this conversation is just between you and me. People can be killed for these words."

"Yes, sir."

"The reason that you, as a Shiite, don't attend the Friday sermon is because Shiites hold to the principle that as long as the leader is unjust, the Friday prayer must be shunned."

The implications of this knowledge were a revelation to Kadhim, and he felt a swell of pride. In a land where opposition was quickly muted and destroyed, they had a code, a way of speaking out against the regime without using words. They would abstain from Friday prayers until their voices were heard and their needs justly addressed.

And suddenly he knew.
Shiites would not go to Friday prayer until Saddam was gone.

PART II:
MEDICAL SCHOOL

SCHOOL ENROLLMENT

His future, or his principles.

He could keep one or the other, but not both.

Kadhim stared at the form on the desk with dread as the assistant dean's words echoed in his mind. *"Look, there's no getting around it. You want to get into medical school? You need to increase your commitment to the Ba'ath Party."*

And to think that he had believed, only twenty minutes ago, that his acceptance letter to Al Kindy Medical School would suffice.

"Kadhim Al Baghdadi?"

"Yes, sir." Kadhim took a nervous step forward from the door.

"Have a seat, son." The dean waved him in and pointed distractedly at the chair in front of his desk. "I've taken a look at your baccalaureate scores. Excellent." He looked up from the paper and peered at Kadhim through his glasses. "Can you tell me more about why you're interested in medicine?"

Kadhim stumbled through an answer that he hoped would suffice. He wasn't sure why he was so nervous. He had already been officially accepted into Al Kindy Medical School. The interview was only a formality, surely.

"Well, it seems you're an excellent student and will do well here," the dean said. "Any idea what you would like to specialize in?"

"Hopefully surgery, sir."

"I see. And are you Ba'athi, son?"

"I carry the rank of 'loyal to the Ba'ath,' sir."

"Loyal? That's it? Hmm." The dean looked at him sharply for a moment. "I'm shocked that you were even accepted into medical school at this rank. How strange that you haven't risen to the second level yet, a victor for the Ba'ath. Why is that?"

"My brother is a victor, and my father a comrade. I come from a Ba'athi family, sir, praise be to God, and I didn't see any need to increase my rank. I mean, we as a family have no problem with rising in the Ba'ath; we love the Ba'ath."

Kadhim started to sweat. He had been lying his whole life about his love and loyalty to Saddam and the Ba'ath party. Why should it cause panic now? "I may officially have the rank of 'loyal,' but I'm a victor for the Ba'ath at heart."

This was getting ridiculous.

The dean eyed him for a long moment. "Wait here a second." He got up and left the room, the door closing with a resounding thud.

Kadhim sat in silence, heart pounding, listening to the whir of the air conditioner. A nervous sweat glistened on his forehead and palms. Minutes ticked by, and he began to shake. It was going to be taken from him, all his hard work, his whole future as a doctor, gone because he had not risen in the ruling party. Like everyone else, if he wanted a successful career in Iraq, he had to rise in the ranks of the Ba'ath.

The door opened at last, and in returned the dean followed by the assistant dean, Abu Zaman, Head of Student and Ba'athi Affairs. The assistant dean had obtained his elite position by rising high in the Ba'athi ranks, and had never even completed high school.

"Hello, Kadhim. Welcome." He shook Kadhim's hand. "I've been speaking with the dean, and it seems that you're an excellent student from a good family. Where are you from?"

"I'm from Karrada."

"And why don't you want to join the Ba'ath party, Kadhim?"

"But I have joined. I'm a loyal."

"Being loyal isn't really joining the Ba'ath party. You know that. Being a loyal is for children. We need you to prove your loyalty to the Ba'ath party and to the regime."

"I am one-hundred percent loyal to the Ba'ath and to the leader of Iraq. My whole family is Ba'athi. My father, my brother, my uncles... I have twelve uncles and at least half of them are in the army. I don't know how to prove my loyalty more than that!"

"You need to become a victor."

"I would love to become a victor for the Ba'ath. It's my dream to become a victor." Kadhim felt the panic rising in his voice. "But the problem is that right now I'm just too busy. Between study and classes and exams... I just don't have the time to commit to the Ba'ath meetings and activities."

Deep down he knew he would have to give in to their demands if he wanted to become a doctor. The mandatory Ba'ath activities meant nothing to him; it was all lies and posturing for the government. But something inside him fought against involving himself deeper in the despotic party.

The mere presence of the regime had silenced his cynical tongue from a young age, had forced a perjured love of government, had enveloped him and his family members within its ranks against their wills. He could be a Ba'athi by name—that's all "loyal" was, after all, the title of Ba'athi, but none of the duties—but the notion of increasing his participation and rising in the party's ranks went against everything he believed in, and he had no way to fight it but with lies.

"I promise you," he pleaded, "by the second or third year of school, if I haven't become a victor for the Ba'ath, you can come find me!"

Abu Zaman remained silent for a minute, then shook his head. "No. I'm not convinced. You need to become a victor now."

"What, has the Ba'ath party become compulsory?" Kadhim laughed nervously, trying to pass off his dangerous question as a joke. He put his shaking hands on his knees to steady them.

"No, it's not compulsory. But you still have not proven your loyalty."

"How can I prove my loyalty more than I already have? My whole family is Ba'athi!"

"No, Kadhim. This has nothing to do with your family. We want you to prove your loyalty to the homeland, and to the leader Saddam Hussein, may God keep him safe and raise him high." Abu Zaman's voice was rising dangerously.

Kadhim could tell that the Head of Ba'athi Affairs was not backing down. He felt the freedom of choice slipping through his fingers. It was either acquiesce to the Ba'athi's demands, or lose his future as a doctor. There he was, only eighteen years old, forced to either betray his principles and identity, or sacrifice his dream of becoming a surgeon.

"What is it you want me to do?" He felt a crushing weight on his chest.

"You need to sign this." Abu Zaman pushed a form toward him and Kadhim stared at it for a moment, arms crossed.

"Look, there's no getting around it." Abu Zaman's eyes locked with his. "You want to get into medical school? You need to increase your commitment to the Ba'ath."

Kadhim knew it was true. If he refused now, not only would he lose his spot at this medical school, but he would face closed doors at all the other Iraqi medical schools as well. All it took was a simple note from Abu Zaman, Head of Ba'athi Affairs, saying that he was not loyal to the regime, and his future was over.

"And if I don't have time to attend the meetings, what then?"

Abu Zaman regarded the stubborn teenager for a moment and his

31

hard eyes softened.

"Look, I swear to you on this mustache," he said as he pulled on his mustache, which was very long indeed, "if you find yourself in a fix where you absolutely do not have the time to attend one of our meetings, then you come let me know. I will excuse you from the meeting, and I personally will mark you as in attendance."

"Really?"

"Really." Abu Zaman seemed sincere, and his promise left Kadhim no room for excuses. He scribbled his name at the bottom of the form and handed it back, hating himself for it. At long last, the dean stood up and spoke.

"Thank you," he said, reaching out to shake Kadhim's hand, "and welcome to Al Kindy Medical School."

ANATOMY

Chatter filled the Anatomy lecture hall as students found their seats, and Kadhim took a deep breath to calm his nerves. It was his first day of class, and he had been so excited the night before that he had barely slept.

The professor entered the room, and in an instant the hall fell silent.

"My name is Professor Ali Al Barradi. Welcome to Basic Anatomy. This course, just like all others at Al Kindy Medical School, will take place in English, with English textbooks. I recommend that those with weak English bring their language skills up to par quickly if they mean to keep up with the pace of the class."

He turned and set a box on the table in front of him.

"As a treat, for your first day of class, we will be performing a dissection." He opened the box and pulled out a dead frog. A few of the girls let out small shrieks.

"Now, I am going to need a volunteer to be the first one to dissect this frog in front of the class as an example for his or her peers."

The hall was dead silent. Kadhim looked at the nervous faces around him and stood.

"I will do it, sir." He was surprised that no one else had volunteered. He had always loved dissecting animals in high school.

"Excellent. You can borrow one of the school's dissection kits from that room at the back."

"No need, sir," Kadhim said, holding up a small box. "I brought my own."

The professor broke into a laugh. "Now *this* is a student who has come prepared!"

Within a week, the students were divided into small groups to act as lab and study partners, and to complete their rotations in clinics that did not have the capacity to handle an entire class. Through his group, Kadhim quickly became friends with Mahjoub, a tall, slim boy with a large personality and a larger interest in girls; Malik, a stocky student with a voracious appetite; and Farouq, who was short, skinny, very serious and somewhat dour. There were also two girls in the group, and the boys were immediately intrigued by Hind, who wore her long dark hair uncovered, and had beautiful eyes and a gentle smile. She and Fatma, the other girl in the group, quickly became inseparable, and where Hind was shy and reserved, Fatma was loud, outspoken and very religious.

Kadhim and his buddies enjoyed a great deal more freedom than their female counterparts. While the girls tended to have early curfews and strict rules, the boys were free to roam the city as much and as late as they wished.

They often took advantage of this freedom, usually at the expense of their studies, frequenting hookah bars and restaurants, and crashing weddings and any other event that caught their interest. Alcohol-serving bars were rare in Baghdad, but when they found one, they went there as well. Only Kadhim seemed able to keep up his grades after such late nights, and more than once Malik and Farouq teased him in mock anger.

"Are you sneaking around behind our backs and studying without telling us? We all go out together, waste the same amount of time drinking and smoking hookah, and then you turn around and ace your exams while we're barely pulling passing grades!"

"It's called studying for a few hours. Maybe you guys should try it." Kadhim grinned wickedly, ducking as they chucked wadded-up paper in his direction.

It was not that they didn't invite the girls. The girls simply wished to avoid the damaged reputations that would be wrought by late outings with single, unrelated men. Even if one had wanted to join them, her parents would have forbidden it to protect the girl's reputation, thereby protecting the family's honor. A man could also bring shame to his family, but his reputation was not nearly as fragile as a woman's, who had no more than to be seen with a strange man than to be thought of poorly.

Nevertheless, they often went as a mixed group of guys and girls to study at cafés or restaurants near the university during their lunch hour or shortly after classes, and—not having any luck with Hind or Fatma—the boys soon turned their attentions to other girls.

Medical school girls were notoriously reserved, pious, and difficult to date. There were more girls at Al Kindy than boys, which should have been to the boys' advantage. However, a certain small percentage of these girls had enrolled and would complete their medical training with the sole purpose of finding a husband and living comfortably as his housewife, without ever practicing a day of medicine. Having gone through the training themselves, they would accept no one less than a doctor as a husband. The majority of the girls, however, were very serious about their studies. For both types, dating was out of the question.

Kadhim would learn this the hard way.

"Who are you looking at?" Mahjoub's pointed question interrupted Kadhim's thoughts amidst the furious chatter of the college cafeteria.

"That girl over there. She's been looking over here and making eye contact with me for the past fifteen minutes." Kadhim nodded toward a table where a group of girls were sitting, and Mahjoub glanced over.

"The brunette? She's cute, man. You should go talk to her."

"I don't know."

"Come on. At least you're not like Malik and Farouq, who can't string two words together in front of a girl. Look, she just smiled at you. What more do you need?"

"All right, all right, I'm going." Kadhim stood and sauntered over to the brunette. He introduced himself, asked her name, and wondered if she wouldn't mind if he joined her and her friends. She invited him to do so, and they spent the better part of their lunch hour making small talk before Kadhim at last ventured to ask, "I was wondering if you might join me for lunch sometime at Moonlight Café?"

"And I would go with you as your... what, exactly?" The brunette's head tilted coquettishly to one side.

"Well, I guess, not as my anything," Kadhim replied, taken aback. "I just wanted to get to know you better."

She shook her head. "I'm afraid that won't work. First you have to propose to me and make our engagement official in front of our parents; *then* perhaps you can take me out to lunch."

Kadhim couldn't get out of there fast enough.

"You should see these girls, Mohammed!" he complained that evening. "You can't approach them! They all seem to think that if you're not prepared to take that long march towards death with them, then you shouldn't be talking to them at all!"

"Let *me* try," Mohammed winked. "I bet *I* could—"

"Oh no, no way am I letting you come back! The one time you visited my school you brought a DJ, organized a party in the cafeteria, and almost got me expelled!"

Mohammed laughed heartily and put a struggling Kadhim in a chokehold. "Fine. If it's girls you want, you should visit *my* university!"

"You're not skipping the Ba'ath meeting, are you?"

Kadhim gave a wry laugh at Mahjoub's question. "I wish. Come on, let's get this over with."

"Where do you want to sit?"

"Where we always do," Kadhim grinned. "At the very back!"

As if lectures six days a week weren't enough, it was time for their mandatory monthly Ba'ath meeting. Kadhim and Mahjoub shuffled with the rest of the students into a large hall, sat themselves as far out of sight as possible, and prepared themselves for the usual tedious speeches. Today, a Ba'athi official invited by Abu Zaman was droning on ad nauseum about one of the "Wise Leadership's" latest decisions. It was always the same. Their great leader had done everything right. He could do no wrong.

It was a terrible waste of time, and Kadhim hated it. They were just a flock of sheep holding meetings to lie to each other about how great the regime was and how much they loved their wise ruler. Occasionally, when he had an important exam coming up, he went to Abu Zaman and ask to be excused, and Abu Zaman, true to his word, marked Kadhim as in attendance and permitted his absence. For the majority of the meetings, however, Kadhim was required to be present.

By the end of the first year, Kadhim and Mahjoub had become fast friends. Between daily study sessions and frequent outings, Mahjoub had become not only Kadhim's closest friend in the group, but also the most trusted. In fact, if Kadhim had not been one hundred percent certain of Mahjoub's attitude toward the regime, he would not have joked around with him the way he did. When reluctantly dragged to a Ba'ath meeting, the pair snickered at students higher up in the party's ranks who sat in the front of the hall hoping to curry favor. They themselves sat way in the back, quietly cracking jokes to pass the time.

"Did you hear the one about a man from Nasiriyah who felt like having some fun?" Mahjoub whispered. The people of Nasiriyah had gained an unearned reputation amongst Iraqis as being particularly malicious, and were often the butt of Mahjoub's jokes.

"No," Kadhim replied.

"He went to a thief and said, 'I'd like to become a thief. Will you show me how to steal?' The thief said, 'Sure, it's easy. Just watch.' And he went and stole a wallet from a passerby's pocket. Returning to the Nasiriyan, the thief asked, 'Since you're from Nasiriyah, can you show me how to be malicious?' 'Sure, it's easy. Just watch,' replied the man from Nasiriyah. Then he turned toward the people on the street and, pointing at his companion, shouted at the top of his lungs, 'THIEF! THIEF!'"

The two friends chuckled, prompting Fatma, who was sitting in front of them, to turn around and glare.

"Saddam and his top party commander Ezad Dury go on a trip to Europe," Kadhim said to Mahjoub quietly. "They visit a brothel, and Saddam sleeps with a sexy blonde prostitute. When he's finished, Ezad Dury asks, 'How was she?' 'Oday's mother was better,' Saddam replies, referring to his own wife. Then Ezad sleeps with a prostitute, and Saddam asks, 'How was she?' So Ezad replies, 'Oday's mother was better.'"

Kadhim suddenly felt a sharp pinch on his arm from a wide-eyed Mahjoub.

"*Holy shit, Kadhim, shut up! Are you trying to get us killed?*"

"Relax, no one can hear us."

"But can you imagine what would happen if they overheard you? In a Ba'athi meeting no less? We'd be dead!" Mahjoub hissed, "You keep telling jokes like that and I'll never sit next to you again!"

Then, much to Kadhim's amusement, his friend huffed and moved several seats away.

STEROIDS

It was another clear-cut case of misused steroids. Kadhim and his group were rounding with a physician in the clinic, and as he regarded the humpbacked patient with her bloated torso, skinny, stick-like arms and legs, and round face, Kadhim found himself contemplating the extremes to which so many would go for some arbitrary standard of beauty. For some, it was Botox, implants, and various forms of cosmetic surgery. In Iraq, men and women alike frequently turned to the use of steroids.

To most Iraqis, being attractive meant having a nice full body: not fat, but well-built and (for women), curvy, feminine and lightly padded. Those who suffered from skinniness, whether male or female, often strove to gain weight. On the other hand, many overweight Iraqis tried to lose a bit, each striving for a mildly plump "full-bodied" look. The beautifully round "moon face" was particularly desirable, and some would stop at no lengths to obtain it.

The moon face had been a symbol of beauty in the Middle East for hundreds, perhaps thousands of years. While in parts of the Middle East the concept of beauty was changing, in Iraq it was still common for women in particular to try to alter the shapes of their faces, although many men were guilty as well, and in recent years they had done so through the use of a drug nicknamed "Dikon."

The catabolic steroid dexamethasone had gained widespread use in the streets of Baghdad. Whereas an anabolic steroid increased muscle mass (and was popular among athletes and body builders), catabolic or corticosteroids did the opposite, weakening muscles in the arms and legs, and increasing fat deposits around the torso and upper back and, happily for its Iraqi customers, the face.

It was for this reason that the woman sitting on the exam table today had used it in such excess. Not so long ago, she'd had a slim face and rather skinny figure. Now, no matter how round her face became with increasing doses of dexamethasone, it was never round enough. Her growing addiction had led not only to a round face with oddly translucent, shiny, thinly-stretched skin, but also a chubby, slightly hunchbacked torso from which sprouted skinny arms and legs whose muscles had been depleted by the drug. It was a look the doctors jokingly called "apple on a stick," and was so common in Iraq that even some of the medical students themselves took "Dikon."

Hind had mentioned to Kadhim that she had considered taking the drug while in high school, feeling pressure from older students, but in the end had decided against it. Kadhim teased her mercilessly. "Just what we need—another apple on a stick. Actually, you're so little you'd be more like a grape on a toothpick! Come on, Hind—what were you thinking?"

"Well, I didn't do it!"

"Yeah, and you don't need to. You're beautiful the way you are."

She blushed furiously, too shy to answer. Kadhim simply laughed.

"Based on your results, it looks as though you're suffering from high blood pressure. You may also be developing diabetes, so we'll need to run further tests," the doctor was saying. "But the first step is to taper off the steroids."

"What?" The patient laughed nervously. "I don't take any steroids!"

She was a terrible liar. The doctor stopped to glare at her for a moment as her laughter subsided awkwardly, then continued his speech.

"Already, the health problems you are experiencing are a direct result of your misuse of this drug: muscle loss, weight gain, hypertension, hunchback, possible diabetes... And it will only get worse from here." He turned to the group of students. "Can anyone tell me other possible side effects from corticosteroids?"

"Increased appetite, changes in mood, water retention," said Farouq.

"Also increased risk of infection, osteoporosis, and even cataracts," added Kadhim.

"See?" resumed the doctor. "You're going down a very unhealthy path. You need to quit taking 'Dikon' immediately. I'm going to give you a prescription for your hypertension, and we'll schedule another appointment to follow up on the diabetes."

The woman looked around in fright and stood to collect her jacket and purse. Then she turned to face the doctor, hunchbacked, with her lumpy, shapeless breasts, stomach and buttocks, and her "apple-on-a-stick" legs, and said with all the desperation and determination that her shiny moon face could muster, "But I'm finally beautiful!"

"Trust me, Ali, you don't want to do this."

"I have to, Kadhim. I'm eating a lot, I'm working out constantly, and I can't seem to gain any weight!" Kadhim's oldest brother Ali rubbed his brow in frustration. He had come to Kadhim for advice a few days ago, and was insistent upon taking anabolic steroids to gain muscle.

"Look at me!" He raised a scrawny arm. "No matter what I do, I'm skin and bone! I'm like a starved chicken who's been plucked!"

"It's not that bad," Kadhim soothed, but he knew the source of Ali's frustration. Ali had been skinny his entire life, and now, having graduated from college, he wanted to find a wife and settle down. He had never been fully comfortable in his own skin, but the prospect of finding and courting a girl had brought out his insecurities in full bloom.

"But it *is* that bad," he groaned. "What woman is going to look at me twice?"

"A true, quality woman will see past that to your personality and accomplishments."

"A true, quality woman will have her pick of men who are not only accomplished but also good-looking! Look, all the guys I know are doing this, and they've had great results. I've decided that I'm going to go to a nurse tomorrow and get a testosterone shot, and that's final."

"Do you know what kind of steroid?"

"What do you mean?"

"Well, in terms of anabolic steroids—the type that builds muscle—there are two kinds: testosterone derivatives, and full-on testosterone, which is the stronger of the two and has more side effects. If you take it in excess, it can cause increased hair growth, deepened voice, and hepatitis. It can even shrink your testicles, if you're not careful."

"What?" Ali shrieked. "I was going to take the full testosterone, but how much of it can I take safely?"

"Most of the side effects only come with long-term usage, but since people can have different reactions to any drug, it's best to be careful. I don't recommend you do this at all, because who knows what you'll get yourself into. But if you absolutely insist on taking steroids, then you could probably safely have several shots over a period of time. However, start with just one and see how it goes."

Ali nodded, sufficiently scared by the testicles remark to take his brother's advice.

A couple weeks had gone by when Kadhim began to notice the changes in his brother's body.

"You're really building some muscle!" he said one day as Ali was changing out of his sweaty gym shirt.

"I know!" Ali proudly flexed an arm that had expanded visibly from previous weeks. "I've been working out everyday, and for once I'm seeing results."

"You're eating twice as much, too!" Mama added. "I can barely cook enough to keep you all fed with the way you're eating now, Ali. Which reminds me—dinner will be ready in half an hour, so don't go out." She disappeared and delicious smells began to waft from the kitchen.

"Trust me, I'm not going anywhere!" Ali laughed. No one in their right mind would skip one of Mama's home-cooked meals.

As the months went by, much to his family's astonishment, Ali expanded to nearly twice his size. Within six months of daily visits to the gym, he gained over 100 pounds of muscle. He didn't even look like the same person.

The topic came up on a rare rainy day when the family was sitting around the living room in their pajamas, snacking on nuts and watching television. They chanced upon a movie starring Arnold Schwarzenegger, and young Salih laughed.

"He looks like you, Ali!"

They all began to tease him. "Show us your new muscles, Ali! Show us!"

Ali obliged, pulling off his t-shirt and flexing a bulging bicep. It had been a while since Kadhim had seen his oldest brother without the cloak of clothing, and he was astounded. His arms and legs had not just doubled but tripled in size, and his thighs and biceps were covered with pink stretch marks that betrayed their rapid growth. Ali's scrawny chicken neck had disappeared, and his head now rested on a short, tree-trunk of a post. He seemed to have gained a slight layer of fat as well, as his appetite grew to enormous proportions. The overall effect of such drastic change in such a short period of time left them speechless.

"Oh my God," Mama breathed at last.

"Ali, be honest," Kadhim said. "Are you sure you only took one shot of steroids?"

"I swear by the Holy Quran, I only took one! I've been working with new trainers, and now the changes are coming so rapidly, I never felt the need for more steroids. Look at me!"

He needn't have told them to look at him. None of them could look away. Even giant Mohammed felt smaller than him. Kadhim knew his brother was telling the truth, but he could not figure out how a single shot could have caused such a drastic transformation. Had it been a bad batch, perhaps more concentrated than usual? Was his brother's body particularly sensitive to the drug? Were the trainers really that good? Kadhim had never before seen or even heard of anyone achieving such enormous success—if it could be called that—from a single shot. In fact, he had seen men take two doses per day of the same drug for lengthy periods of time in order to achieve similar results.

Salih hit the nail on the head when he said with a grin, "It looks as though you just keep inflating and inflating until eventually you're going to explode!"

Everyone burst into laughter, and little Firas cackled along with them and warbled loudly.

But Ali's physical changes did not stop there. After eight months of religious trips to the gym, he grew bored. There was only so much he could take of the same regimen day in and day out, and he lost interest in exercising. His appetite, on the other hand, continued to increase. He had never had a small appetite, but by the time a year had gone by, his appetite had more than tripled.

Mama struggled to keep up with the growing demands of her eldest son's ferocious cravings. Whereas the other men of the family would content themselves with reasonable though hearty meals, Ali would devour three heaping plates of rice, a full plate or two of meat, and a veritable stack of hot bread, in addition to his soup and hummus and post-meal baklava and chocolates. Eventually, Mama was forced to set up a small table where Ali ate dinner by himself, as his endless plates of food no longer fit at the dinner table with the rest of the family.

Ali attacked all of his meals with the same raging appetite, and it was not long before his once spectacular "Arnold Schwarzenegger" muscles softened, his stomach grew to an enormous potbelly, and his face rounded out. By some freakish trick of nature, scrawny "plucked-chicken" Ali had transformed from stick-figure to body builder to plump and round within a period of two years.

And all through the unusual influence of a single dose of steroids.

RENAL FAILURE

Kadhim ran into Hind in the hallway shortly after one of the insufferable Ba'ath meetings.

"Hind! How are you?"

She turned around and her face broke into a smile. "Hi, Kadhim. What's up?"

"The guys and I are planning to study for a while at Moonlight Café. Would you and Fatma like to join us whenever you're finished with classes?"

"Well, I'm finished now, actually. Let me call Fatma and see if she'd like to share a taxi."

"Why don't you just ride with me? I'm about to drive there now." Kadhim smiled. "I promise I won't charge for the trip."

Hind hesitated. When she first met Kadhim and the other men in her group, she had been so shy that a conversation with any of them had been difficult for her. Fatma, who came from a family of boys, had done most of the talking. By now, in her third year of seeing her male colleagues almost every day, Hind had finally started to come out of her shell. Still, the thought of riding alone with Kadhim made her flush.

"No," she said at last. "I'll go with Fatma. See you there!"

When Kadhim arrived at Moonlight Café, only Malik was there. Kadhim sighed and tried to prepare himself for an unproductive evening. Whenever Malik came out to study, he always made a big show of groaning loudly over a textbook, but in fact rarely accomplished much more than eating his way through half of the menu. There he was now, munching on fries and staring blankly at his closed textbook. He brightened as soon as he noticed Kadhim.

"Hey, there you are! I've been poring over that chapter in the Pathology textbook and was just about to take a break."

"Oh really?" Kadhim eyed the closed textbook. Malik appeared not to notice his sarcasm.

"Want some coffee? I was about to get a fresh cup."

"Sounds great. Thanks."

Malik returned with two coffees and a tray full of food. "Just a light snack to help me study."

But as Kadhim had expected, they didn't get any studying done. Instead, Malik launched into a long anecdote about his uncle, all the while shoveling food into his mouth as if he didn't even notice he was eating. Forty-five fruitless minutes went by before a text message interrupted Malik's long-winded story.

"Got to go!"

"So soon? We haven't even started studying yet!" Kadhim tried to hide his relief.

"Sorry man, but dinner's ready, and I'm starving! Haven't eaten all day!" Within seconds, Malik was out the foor and Kadhim returned to his textbook.

"Hey, where is everyone?"

Kadhim looked up to see Hind standing in front of him, looking confused.

"Well, Malik just left, and I presume the others are on their way. Where's Fatma?"

"I couldn't find her on campus and she didn't answer my calls, so I thought she was already here." She remained standing, looking hesitant.

"Would you like to sit down?"

"I don't know... I really should go home..." She was clearly anxious that Fatma had not arrived, and she didn't want to be seen in public alone with an unrelated male.

"It's up to you," Kadhim replied nonchalantly. He returned to reading his textbook.

Hind was still standing there.

"Actually," she ventured at last, "I wanted to ask you something about this chapter before I go. Have you reached the part about Reed-Sternberg cells yet?"

"Just getting to that now."

"I guess I'll wait a moment then." She sat down with an exaggerated sigh, pulled out her book, and started reading in companionable silence.

When at last they broke the silence to discuss an upcoming exam, the topic somehow turned to professors whom they equally loathed and the antics of other students. Conversation came so easily that they forgot social boundaries, and it wasn't long before minutes had turned into two hours, several cups of coffee, and many good laughs.

"Another cup of coffee?" Kadhim asked as he stoof up and stretched his stiff legs.

"I've had too many already." Hind looked at her watch and jumped up, her eyes widened. "It's so late! I should have left ages ago!"

"Well, at least we got some good studying in."

"It's a shame I missed Malik, though. I'm sure he could have explained it much better."

Kadhim looked up at her sharply, just in time to see a gentle smile at her quip transform her worried features into something lovely and delicate. Her doe-like eyes that had always seemed so distant were suddenly warm and gentle. He laughed with her, and suddenly, before he realized what he was saying, the sentence slipped from his lips.

"You're beautiful when you smile, Hind."

Her laughter stopped abruptly and she flushed as she turned away. They suddenly became aware of how near they were to each other, and Hind quickly turned and put on her jacket.

"I'd better go find a taxi."

"It's dark out, Hind. Let me give you a ride."

"Thanks for the kind offer, but no. I don't even want to *think* about what my parents would say if they saw me ride home with a man. I'm late as it is."

"Let me help you find a cab then." Kadhim couldn't let a young lady go out into the dark street alone; etiquette required that he accompany her home or at least to a taxi. She consented and they walked out together.

It felt nice to be next to her in those twilight hours, there to protect her should she need it. Although nothing was said between them, Kadhim felt an electric sensation—perhaps excitement, perhaps nerves, perhaps sheer awkwardness. He wondered if she felt anything other than embarrassment. She seemed to stand very close to him, but perhaps she was just anxious about being out so late.

A taxi arrived all too quickly, and the moment was over. Kadhim drove home and tried to study by oil lamp, since the electricity was out again, but he had difficulty concentrating. The look in Hind's eyes when she smiled kept resurfacing between the words.

Two weeks passed without a chance to speak with Hind alone, and it was driving him crazy. Their evening together at Moonlight Café had, it seemed, been a strange and unrepeatable fluke, and since then, there was always someone else with them when Kadhim saw her. For the most part, Hind avoided looking at him, and even the most banal conversation with her seemed rife with discomfort. Yet Kadhim found himself searching for her in the halls after class and was excited every time she joined their group to study in the library or for a lesson in the lab. He wondered if she was avoiding him on purpose, and if she felt uncomfortable, or worse yet, insulted by the comment he had made. But then he thought of the hours they had spent talking and laughing. How could she possibly be upset with him? Could she perhaps feel the same way he did? Nothing, it seemed, could take Kadhim's mind off her. Nothing, that is, until his morning with Dr. Al Qazzaz.

Kadhim had been hearing stories about Dr. Al Qazzaz since he entered medical school.

"*He's a genius.*"

"*He's a pompous asshole. You should see how he treats the students.*"

"*You should see how he treats the **doctors**.*"

"*He acts like he knows everything.*"

"*He. Knows. **Everything**.*"

"*He's completely antisocial. No bedside manner at all.*"

"*Brilliant. Asshole or no, we're lucky to have him.*"

Everything Kadhim had heard had been proven accurate. At once terrified and in awe of the renowned internist, Kadhim listened in rapt attention as he and a small group of students walked with Dr. Al Qazzaz through campus on their way to morning rounds of the clinic. The physician was discussing a complex case when he suddenly stopped and interrupted himself mid-sentence.

"You see that man on the bench?"

The students turned to see a man in his late thirties enjoying a morning cigarette some ten yards away. There did not appear to be anything remarkable about him whatsoever.

"What about him, sir?"

"Renal failure. I guarantee it."

The students looked in astonishment at the man once again. He had a slight potbelly, perhaps, and a cigarette between his lips, but otherwise looked healthy.

"Doctor, that's not a patient. That's our bus driver," one of the students pointed out. Although no one dared to say anything, a wave of doubt washed over them. It seemed that Dr. Al Qazzaz had finally overestimated his own brilliance.

"Just go ask him if he suffers from high blood pressure."

The students looked at their teacher doubtfully. It was embarrassing enough to approach someone who was not a patient and ask him outright about possible medical conditions. It was even more embarrassing that everything they asked was clearly going to be wrong. Dr. Al Qazzaz, however, was thoroughly unperturbed by social protocol. Accusing people of hosting a disease had never bothered him in the least. It was only the diagnosis that mattered.

"Likely he has uncontrolled high blood pressure. Go ask, and then have him come here." Dr. Al Qazzaz peered at his hesitant students, then snapped in annoyance, "Go!"

Kadhim and the others hurried over to the driver.

"Good morning, uncle." They addressed him with as much respect as they could muster. The bus driver looked up at them in surprise.

"Morning."

"We're sorry to bother you, but one of the hospital's physicians has sent us to inquire as to whether you have renal failure."

The bus driver looked astonished. "No. Why would I have renal failure?"

That was it then. Dr. Al Qazzaz was finally wrong. Although they had expected it, Kadhim felt surprisingly disappointed that the renowned physician's cross-campus diagnosis had proven incorrect. They were turning to leave when Kadhim stopped suddenly and asked, "Do you suffer from high blood pressure?"

The driver looked even more astonished. "I do. I've had high blood pressure for years now."

"Do you take medicine for it?"

"I've been taking meds, but they don't seem to do any good. It seems like no matter what I do, I can't get my blood pressure under control."

The students looked at each other.

"Would you come with us? The doctor would like to speak with you."

The driver tossed his cigarette and stood. He couldn't understand what was going on, but he was curious, and the doctor's odd diagnosis made him anxious.

"I suspect you have renal failure," Dr. Al Qazzaz said without introduction as the driver approached. "I'm going to have my students run some tests and then I'll get back to you."

"Okay," the driver said hesitantly. The physician's instructions didn't seem to be optional. They did a blood test to confirm and soon the results were back: renal failure.

"How did you know, sir?" Kadhim asked, as an unsurprised Dr. Al Qazzaz read their findings.

"The man was earth-colored. Classic sign of renal failure."

The students stared at their professor, then looked at one another in astonishment. They were all Arabs, their skin various shades of brown.

"But we're *all* earth-colored!"

"When you've seen hundreds of cases, you will know the color. Even on Middle Eastern skin."

When the students examined the patient again, even *knowing* that he had renal failure, they could not for the life of them see any distinguishable difference in the color of his skin. And they certainly could not fathom how—with a brief glance from afar—Dr. Al Qazzaz had detected his condition and its cause without so much as the foreknowledge that the man on the park bench was sick. It only further cemented their belief that Dr. Al Qazzaz was, indeed, a genius.

Kadhim was just about to leave campus that evening when he heard someone call his name.

"Kadhim, wait!"

It was Hind. Her long brown hair reflected waves of sunlight, and she smiled as she waved at him to slow down.

"How have you been?" She was slightly breathless as she caught up with him.

"I was going to ask you the same! I haven't seen you in a while." *Not since that night at Moonlight Café*, he thought. He wished he could ask how she felt, and if she had been upset or secretly pleased by his comment, but he couldn't. "Hind, you should hear what happened today with Dr. Al Qazzaz!"

She listened in amazement to his story, and it was as though all the awkwardness that had grown between them since his comment two weeks ago suddenly dissipated. She was gazing into his eyes in rapt attention, laughing, and the smile that so transformed her features had returned. Kadhim felt an unmistakable warmth between them, an attraction that seemed to emanate from the way they looked and spoke to each other. He could not—*would not*—let this opportunity pass him by.

"Hind, would you like to go out with me sometime? For lunch, maybe? We can go as a group..."

He let his words trail off as he watched her face falter. The smile vanished abruptly and a look of consternation made small lines on her forehead.

"Kadhim, I'm sorry if I gave you the wrong impression, but I just don't feel that way about you." Her cheeks grew slightly pink and she walked away quickly.

Kadhim's chest burned with an odd feeling of rejection as he watched her leave. He felt like an idiot.

How could he have misread her actions so drastically, when all Dr. Al Qazzaz had to do was glance at a person in order to see right through them?

MANURE & SCABIES

"This is absolute *bullshit!*" Kadhim had to hold the phone away from his ear in order to tolerate the blast of his friend's furious voice. Other students in the library looked up at him in shock and annoyance.

"What's wrong? What's going on?" Kadhim kept his voice low, hoping that Anwar would get the hint.

"I fucking hate this country. If I could leave, I would!"

"Hold on, hold on. Let me find somewhere private, and you can tell me what happened." *Before you say something you regret.* Kadhim was already afraid that students loyal to the Ba'ath had overheard the last sentence, and he wanted to get out of earshot before his friend's temper landed them both in trouble. He found an empty lab and shut the door. "What is it, Anwar?"

"They're forcing me to leave my university. Fucking bastards!"

"You can't be serious! You're one of their best students!" It didn't make sense. Kadhim had known Anwar since secondary school, and he was a model student: perfect grades, impeccable behavior, and a good personality to boot. The two of them had been close friends throughout school, despite the fact that Anwar was a year ahead of him. After graduation, Anwar had gone on to get his Bachelor's degree in engineering, and was now in his fourth and final year.

"I'm not just *one* of their best students; I *am* their best student," Anwar replied bitterly. "I ranked number one out of one hundred and fifty students in my class for three years running. And this year they started to fail me."

"What do you mean, fail you?" Kadhim had a sinking feeling in his stomach.

"I mean, I turn in a perfect exam, and they give me a zero. Labs, papers, homework, quizzes, in *all* of my classes, have been given failing grades! And I *know* that my work is accurate. I went to one professor after another, asking them why I got a zero on this exam or that quiz. You know what they said? That I hadn't turned it in! *Bullshit!*" He spat the word out again. "I work harder than any student here! After a few months of this, one professor finally had the decency to tell me what was going on."

"And?"

"He told me, 'Son, get the hint. They don't want you here. You need to leave this university and go somewhere else.' He said I could try to change my major, but that really I should just forget my dreams and goals for the future and focus on something else entirely."

"What the hell does that mean? What was your major?"

"I was specializing in lasers for military technology and intelligence."

"Oh hell. It's never going to happen, is it?"

"That's what they're telling me, by failing me like this. I can't believe I ever dreamed that I, as a Shiite, could even get into that field." Anwar sounded miserable. His anger was giving way to disappointment and heartbreak. "I don't know how my parents could have kept supporting and encouraging me in this specialty, when they should have known all along that it was never going to happen. They were just so proud of how well I was doing. Maybe they actually thought I had a chance, especially after I got into the top public school for engineering."

In Iraq, public universities, whose students were fully funded by the Iraqi government and thus obtained their degrees for free, were generally considered to be better than private universities, which often took students not accepted elsewhere. However, the discrimination inherent in the Ba'ath regime gave Sunni students and those high in the ruling party priority among the ranks of the accepted. Shiites and Kurds, whose communities were generally less enthusiastic about the government, were less likely to gain acceptance into public universities and had to work far harder when they did.

Whether or not a student was eligible for a certain specialty or university was determined by exams at the end of high school known as the baccalaureate. However, whereas a given university might only require an above average grade of "Good" for entrance, when it came to Shiites and Kurds, they often unofficially demanded "Very Good" or even "Excellent." The result was that in a country where Shiites constituted nearly two-thirds of the population, the majority of those with university degrees were Arab Sunnis.

Anwar, despite being Shiite, had been accepted into his school of choice. His problem was that he had chosen the wrong specialty. Kadhim knew it, Anwar's professors knew it, and deep down, even Anwar knew it. But he had hoped against hope that, despite his sect, being the best would make him a desirable asset to his country.

He had been wrong.

Kadhim let him vent and silently prayed that his friend was in a private place with a secure line.

"You know, you look at the rest of the world and you see societies advancing everywhere. Women and minorities as presidents and prime ministers. Equal rights for everyone. Hell, even gays can get married in certain parts of the world. And here in Iraq, there's a thick black ceiling that cuts you off if you try to climb too high.

"Military security, technology, or intelligence? A high-up government position like a minister? You can forget it unless you're a Sunni from the 'right' family. Or the son of a Shiite who's *really* high up in the Ba'ath. And the only way to get there is to climb up others' backs. Write reports full of lies about your neighbors to ingratiate yourself with the government. Be ready to have innocent people convicted and executed, just to rise in the ranks.

"You do things like that, become the head of a unit or higher, and all of a sudden it's: '*How many cars do you want? Two? Three? How many houses would you like? What universities do you want to send your idiot children to? Want to get rid of the neighbor you don't care for? Done.*' They're given free reign, unchecked privileges from the great leader himself. It's fucking bullshit."

"Speaking of reports," Kadhim inserted nervously, "I hope for both of our sakes that no one can overhear this conversation."

He couldn't believe the words spilling so blatantly from his friend's mouth, words only spoken in the privacy and security of one's own home, if at all. Words like these could spell a death sentence, granted by the very opportunists whom Anwar described. It was all Kadhim could do to prevent himself from hanging up out of sheer anxiety.

"Don't worry. I rigged it. No one's listening."

Trust Anwar to be able to do something like that. Kadhim was tense nevertheless. He wanted to be supportive of his friend, but the longer the topic went in this direction, the more likely it would be *his* head on the chopping block.

"So what are you going to do now?" He tried to redirect the conversation.

"I'm going to finish my Bachelor's degree at another university. I have no choice." Anwar sighed. "And I'm going to forget about lasers."

"I'm sorry, man. Let me know if there's anything I can do."

There was nothing either of them could do, and they both knew it.

"Thanks, brother. I'll let you know how it goes."

As Kadhim ended the call, he heard one last sentence from his old friend before the line when dead.

"It's fucking horseshit."

The stench was absolutely unbearable. It had assailed Kadhim's nostrils from the second he walked in, and for the life of him, he could not figure out why the university outpatient clinic smelled like... what was that? *Was that shit?* He and the other third-year students with whom he was rounding were completely baffled.

Kadhim, Hind, Malik and Mahjoub had just finished seeing a patient with the attending and, as the physician had gone to lunch, they were looking to join another doctor. Nearly a month had gone by since Kadhim had asked Hind out to lunch and been turned down, and although his feelings for her had not yet faded, the awkwardness was gradually dissipating. They were all nervously awaiting the results of a major exam that would be available later that day, so to pass the time as they looked for another case the four of them jokingly debated the possible sources of the terrible stink that filled the clinic. They stopped suddenly and stared as the smell walked right past them and into a neighboring exam room. It was a middle-aged man and woman in rural clothing, with their necks, chests, arms, and legs lathered liberally in a thick brown goop that could only be one thing.

Feces.

The odd couple was followed by a physician who spoke softly to the two, shut their exam room door, and turned to the group of students.

"Would anyone care to join me in exam room?" He glanced at the confused look on their faces and added, "They're from a rural farming community, and they have scabies. They were told by others in the community that the cure for scabies is the application of animal dung. Apparently it's a common home remedy there. Would one of you like to conduct the physical exam?"

There was a brief moment of silence, filled only by the overwhelming stench of manure. Then one by one, the medical students shook their heads. The physician sighed with resignation, took a deep breath, and entered the room.

At the end of the day, with bated breath, Kadhim finally obtained his results for the Hematology exam. It was a standardized test taken by all of Iraq's medical students, and although he didn't like to jinx his luck, he had a good feeling about it. He was hoping to rank among the top ten percent in the country, perhaps among the top five percent, if he was lucky. It was the nature of this exam, as with a few others, that he would be privy to the exact number of students ranked above and below him.

Nervously, Kadhim took a deep breath and read the results.

Wow.

He shook his head, blinked, and looked again. That couldn't possibly be right.

He had ranked first in the nation. He was the highest scoring student in all of Iraq.

A warmth of happiness burst aflame in his chest, spreading through his arms and legs and growing into a huge smile until Kadhim was laughing with amazement. He knew he had done well on the exam, but to be *first*? He couldn't believe it. A feeling of accomplishment washed over him, and he thought of how happy Mama and Baba would be when they heard the news. He was overjoyed.

"What are you giggling about?" The rude voice of Ala Al-Tikriti interrupted Kadhim's blissful daydream and brought him back to reality.

"I just received my results," Kadhim replied cautiously, lowering the paper in his hands. He didn't want to appear a braggart, particularly in front of this student.

Ala was from the Sunni area of Tikrit, Saddam's hometown. He had made it well-known that his father and uncle were among the upper echelons of the Ba'ath party, and that due to familial ties to Saddam they enjoyed special privileges. His boastful statements, although irritating, were not claims made in vain. In fact, he had gained entry to one of Iraq's top medical schools through Ba'athi connections, despite the fact that he had—according to rumors—only obtained a "Below Average" on his baccalaureate exams. It was common knowledge that without Ba'athis exerting pressure on the professors to pass him, Ala would not have advanced with his peers to the third year of medical school. He was not the only Ba'athi student who haughtily lectured others in the university, and Kadhim tried to avoid them like vermin.

"You're giggling like a girl over a score? Let me see." Ala reached out and snatched the paper, and Kadhim watched as his classmate's eyes scanned the page, registering first shock, then annoyance.

"First, huh? Congratulations." His tone was flat.

"Thanks." Kadhim's smile had vanished, his voice quiet. It was okay for Kadhim to be annoyed by Ala Al-Tikriti. It was not okay for Ala Al-Tikriti to be annoyed by Kadhim. He waited, nervously, for a good time to leave. Ala was still holding his exam results, and he couldn't leave without them.

"I don't know why you're so happy, Kadhim," Ala said slowly, a smirk forming on his face. "Work as hard as you want; *be* the top. It doesn't matter. You're still just going to end up in some shit hospital. Meanwhile I can sit back and relax without learning a thing and I will *still* be more successful, better paid, and with a higher position than you because I'm Tikriti. And you? You're just a low-life Shiite with no connections. Even rising in the ranks of the Ba'ath won't get you far, because you'll hit a ceiling." He laughed. "No matter how hard you work, I will *always* be better than you."

He let the document fall from his hand and stepped on it with a malicious smile. "Oops."

Kadhim was silent. He hoped that the venom he felt was not seeping through his scowl. There was nothing he could say to stick up for himself, and they both knew it. He hated the fact that every word his pompous classmate uttered was true. He hated that this idiot was less qualified, less intelligent, and still far more powerful than he. He hated that voicing the stinging retort that had formed in his mind could lead to Ala complaining to his father, who could then submit a poorly written report that would lead to Kadhim losing his spot at the university, being arrested, or even being executed for "conspiring against the state" or some other concocted crime. He hated the fact that he both hated Ala and feared him.

So he remained silent, as close to submission as he could stand.

Ala Al-Tikriti, satisfied that there would be no retort, turned and walked away, leaving a dirty footprint on Kadhim's exam results. Kadhim picked the paper up quickly and tried to brush it off, but it was too late. The perfect score had been marred.

Anwar was right. It *was* bullshit.

"Kadhim, what's wrong? Are you okay?"

Kadhim was still standing frozen in the hallway when Hind approached him, her question bringing him out of a trance of despair and anger. Kadhim quickly put the results away among his books.

"I'm fine."

"Are you sure? You look upset."

"It's nothing. Just a mix-up." He tried, unsuccessfully, to put a normal smile on his face as they started walking toward the campus gates. He didn't trust her enough to divulge what had just happened. It was too close to criticizing the regime, and he had the feeling that she wouldn't understand.

"Are you still moaning about me turning down your offer of lunch a few weeks ago?" she asked with a laugh. It wasn't the first time that she had teased him about that evening, and it was starting to get old. He tried to joke along.

"Yeah, maybe that's it."

"Well, you haven't asked me out lately, so I'm not sure why you're still upset. Maybe you should try again."

"Why? Do you *want* to go out to lunch with me?"

"No." She giggled.

Kadhim turned to face her in exasperation, and snapped, "Then why do you keep teasing me about it, Hind?" He hadn't meant to lash out at her, but he'd had enough for one day.

Instantly the impish smile vanished from her lips and her cheeks grew pink.

"I'm sorry, Kadhim. I didn't mean to upset you."

"It's fine." He turned and kept walking.

"Kadhim, wait!"

He stopped and looked at her impatiently. If she didn't want him, then the least she could do was stop taunting him.

"I know I shouldn't tease you like this. I guess what I'm trying to say is..." she paused nervously and looked at some invisible speck on the ground. "...I guess I'm just trying to say that I've reconsidered my feelings for you."

The words tumbled out in a rush, and her cheeks grew bright red.

Kadhim took several steps closer to her, hoping he'd understood. "Hind, are you telling me that you like me?"

She looked up at last and her bright, doe-like eyes met his.

"Yes, I like you."

PULL YOUR PANTS DOWN!

It was clear, as they stood in uncomfortable silence, that the small group in the exam room had come to an impasse.

"Well?" Dr. Al Qazzaz snapped, "What are you waiting for? Do the physical exam!"

Fatma had just finished explaining the causes, treatment and possible complications of hernias in adults and had presented the case of the fifty-six year old male standing before them. She, Kadhim, Farouq and Hind were to take turns examining him in preparation for their year-end exam, where they would have to demonstrate the correct way to examine and diagnose hernias, among other tasks.

When it came to sensitive male parts, many female students preferred to practice conducting exams on pediatric patients rather than adults, as much for the patient's sake as for their own. And it was clear in this case that the middle-aged man standing before them was just as reluctant to have the hijab-wearing student examine his private area as she was reluctant to examine it.

He must have come directly from the office, as he was still wearing a suit and tie and a look of hardened dignity when he allowed Kadhim and Farouq to examine the inguinal hernia in his groin. Upon seeing the girls, however, he had promptly pulled his pants back up into position and zipped them up tightly.

And that was where they stood now, in uncomfortable silence, as Fatma tried awkwardly to make a gloved feel of the man's abdomen, far above the site of the hernia. Dr. Al Qazzaz had no time for slow students or prideful patients.

"What are you doing?" he yelled. "*Examine him!*"

"He won't pull down his pants!" Fatma's small voice trembled with anxiety.

Dr. Al Qazzaz turned to the suited businessman in full rage and screamed at the top of his lungs,

"PULL YOUR PANTS DOWN!"

There was nothing to be done. Fumbling and red-faced, the businessman hurriedly dropped his trousers.

"Wow! Well, that was awkward!" Hind and Kadhim laughed as they left the clinic.

"Dr. Al Qazzaz was so convincing, I almost pulled down my *own* pants!" Kadhim joked. She giggled and pushed him away.

"Don't be vulgar, Kadhim!"

He wanted to reach out and grab the hand that playfully pushed him, maybe even put his arm around her, but she never would have permitted it.

Several weeks had gone by since she had announced her feelings for him, and the two had become a "couple" insomuch as their culture would allow. They kept their relationship secret from most of their peers and, more importantly, from their families.

Kadhim's family might have been more understanding, but if any of Hind's relatives were to learn of the relationship, no matter how innocent, her honor would be tarnished and so, too, would that of her family. She was particularly afraid of her younger brother, who was in his first year of college and far more aware of the technology used by youth to conduct secret relationships. While he himself was not against the occasional clandestine relationship, he adamantly opposed anyone pursuing such a venture with his sister and had appointed himself her moral guardian.

Hind was careful to delete any incriminating messages on her phone, which her brother liked to confiscate and peruse from time to time. She also insisted on going out in groups, so as not to raise suspicions should anyone see her. If she and Kadhim wanted private time, they had to content themselves with whispered conversations over the phone when her family thought she was asleep. It was typical of underground relationships but frustrating for Kadhim nonetheless.

"Why don't you let me take you to lunch sometime at Moonlight Café—just you and me?"

"Come on, you know we can't do that."

"Who will see us, Hind? Who will care? I just want to spend some time with you. Alone."

She glared.

"No, I didn't mean anything like *that*. It's just that I want to get to know you better, and I feel like we barely have time to talk to each other here at school."

"Invite at least two others, and I'll go."

They found a couple of friends to go along with them, and just as Kadhim had feared, the presence of others made it impossible to have any private conversation, so he tried again as they left the restaurant.

"Hind, let me give you a ride home."

"Just the two of us?"

"Just you and me."

"Give Zara a ride too, and I'll go."

He laughed. "All right, let's go."

He made record time to Zara's neighborhood, and soon Hind sat next to him in the passenger seat.

Alone at last.

"Kadhim, I live in Adhimiyya!"

"I know."

"But you're going the wrong direction!"

"I didn't say I would take you the most direct route."

"Would you at least speed up, please?"

"Safety first, Hind."

She laughed in spite of herself. "Don't you have better things to do than drive me in circles around Baghdad?"

"I do, in fact. I have important documents to send to Britain. But I would rather drive you in circles first." He grinned.

"What documents? Are you joking or do you really have paperwork to send?"

"I really do."

"For what?"

"I've been corresponding with some medical schools in London... I'd like to see if there's any way I could finish my training there."

"Seriously? How long have you been doing this?" She seemed suddenly pouty. "And what's wrong with being here?"

"I started contacting them around the beginning of the year, so it's been over six months now. And there's nothing wrong with being here. It's just that London has some of the best medical training this side of the Atlantic."

"Would you really leave Iraq in the middle of your medical training?"

"I would if it worked out that way. It's a long shot, Hind. Even if I somehow gained acceptance into one of London's schools, I don't know how much of my completed education would be given credit there, despite the fact that Iraq's medical curriculum is based on a British system. Also, I'd have to get a scholarship of some type, because I don't know how I'd pay for it myself."

London was a distant dream, a paradise of advanced techniques and world-class doctors. He thought of Baba's measly $25 per month salary as a high school English instructor. Mama's part-time teaching salary was even less. Where would they find the funds to pay tens of thousands of dollars in tuition, living, and travel expenses if he *did* get in? He said something to that effect.

"True." Hind seemed momentarily mollified. "Besides, let's say the Brits gave you a visa... it *still* wouldn't be easy to get out of Iraq. The Ba'ath could easily block your exit; they do it all the time."

"Or they'll keep harassing my family about my whereabouts in a Western country," Kadhim added. "They'll send Ba'athis to my parents' home, asking what I'm doing in an enemy land."

"That's right!" Her tone was triumphant. "So you'd better just stay here. Iraq has some of the best medical training in the Middle East anyway, and we're in one of Iraq's top schools. Kadhim, you're lucky to be here. Arabs from all over the region come to Baghdad for medical education."

"I know, I know. You're right."

He dropped the subject, but the more he thought about how the Ba'ath regime wanted to thwart his efforts to better himself as a doctor and fulfill his life's dreams, the more London grew in his mind as a beacon of hope, enlightenment, and freedom.

He decided to write more letters that evening, giving information about himself and his accomplishments as a student, and requesting further information about their application process. But first, he wanted to see if Hind would let him hold her hand.

◇ ◆ ◇

"Kadhim, you need to go to Abu Zaman's office." Ala Al-Tikriti's tone was officious as he poked his head into the lab.

"Okay, let me finish up with these slides and I'll be there."

"No, he says come now."

"All right, all right, I'm coming." Kadhim put down the slides, shared an apprehensive glance with Mahjoub, and hurried down the hallway, trying to quickly leave Ala behind in order to avoid his pompous questioning. He had no idea what this sudden meeting could pertain to, and he couldn't stop an uneasy feeling from creeping up his spine. Abu Zaman may not be the scariest of officials, but with Ba'athis there was no way of knowing. The basic rule of thumb was that if a Ba'athi wanted to talk to you, it was bad news.

He knocked on the door to Abu Zaman's office and heard a voice from the other side. "Come in."

He entered. Abu Zaman did not look pleased.

"Shut the door behind you."

"Yes, sir." Kadhim obliged and took a seat. *What was going to happen that Abu Zaman didn't want others to see?*

Abu Zaman came around to the front of his desk, threw down a stack of papers in front of Kadhim, and crossed his arms. "What are these?"

Kadhim leaned forward and peered at the papers.

He noted, with no small measure of trepidation, that the brochures were addressed to him. Individual houses didn't receive mail, so he'd had the brochures sent to the medical school, an act that he now sincerely regretted.

"They're brochures, sir."

"I can see that." Abu Zaman's eyes grew narrow, and his annoyance at having to spell out the problem seemed to multiply. "And do you want to explain to me what they say, and what you're doing receiving brochures from Britain? Don't you know that Britain has been an official enemy of the state ever since their involvement against our country in the 1991 Gulf War?"

Kadhim suddenly realized that the Head of Student and Ba'athi Affairs, possessing only a high school education that had grown dusty from lack of use, could make neither head nor tail of the stack of English-language pamphlets sitting on his desk. He had gleaned that they were from Britain, but the rest was beyond him. His humiliation at having a mere student translate them only angered him further.

"Sir, they're just informational brochures from medical schools. I've been learning about their training programs and comparing them with ours. It's a completely innocent correspondence; there's nothing political in it whatsoever." Kadhim felt himself break into a sweat. "If you want to see the emails, I'll also open those up and read them to you."

"That won't be necessary. I want you to immediately cut off all contact with these and *any* foreign schools you may be corresponding with, or else you will make yourself the target of suspicion."

He grabbed Kadhim's scattered stack of dreams and threw them into the trash.

"If we suspect, for *any* reason, that you are conspiring with the enemy against the regime, it will be over for you and your family, understand?"

"I understand, sir."

"You may go."

Kadhim stood and reached for the door with a shaky hand, relieved that the meeting was over.

"And Kadhim?"

He turned to see Abu Zaman's eyes trained on him like a snake. "We'll be watching you."

Kadhim was still shaking when he returned to the lab. It had been such a simple correspondence, such basic information. It was ludicrous that he and his family could have lost everything. And over what? A few medical school pamphlets?

As his fear ebbed, his anger surged.

For many months, he had been living daydreams of studying and practicing medicine in some of the world's most advanced centers, in a free society. It was a dream that no matter how distant, no matter how expensive or difficult to obtain, he had never given up on. It was simply too beautiful a future to release.

And now, an uneducated man who could barely read English had the right to sift through his mind, find his dreams, and extinguish them. If Kadhim continued to strive for them in secret, he could be criminalized as a conspirator against the state. If by some miracle he obtained a British visa, they could forbid his departure, making him a prisoner in his own country. And if he tried to struggle his way up the ranks of medicine and prestige within his own country, there too he would hit a ceiling, as his own classmate had recently pointed out.

The hernia patient who had graced their clinic only a few weeks prior suddenly came to mind.

"Pull down your pants" indeed, Kadhim thought ironically, *and bend over.*

THE PROTESTS

In the summer of 2002, during the break between his third and fourth year of medical school, Kadhim and fourteen other classmates were chosen to attend two months of training with the Jerusalem Army. Unassociated with the Iranian army of the same name, the Jerusalem Army was called into creation by Saddam in 2001. It was the Iraqi contribution to freeing Jerusalem from Zionist elements, a purpose loudly touted in the Ba'ath-controlled media.

The Iraqis, however, knew the Jerusalem Army for what it was: a joke.

Kadhim and his classmates had been selected the same way the rest of its constituents had—without pay or a choice in the matter, through the dictates of various deans doing their duty for the party via "donations." They were not given physical training nor were they schooled in the use of weaponry; being required to march daily formations at the training site under the scorching 115° heat of a Baghdad summer was considered enough.

During their third week, Kadhim and several others befriended an officer of particularly modest circumstances and for ten dollars each, they convinced him to record them as present and went on a week-long trip to Kurdistan. Most of their time, however, was spent hanging out, smoking with the officers and posing for pictures that would appear on television as proof of Saddam's power... until the arrival of Officer Basheer.

"I can't take any more of this!" groaned Saleem, a stick-like dental student, who was panting and dripping with sweat. The rest of the small unit was in equally bad shape.

"I can't believe he takes this shit so seriously!" Mahjoub, who had been "volunteered" as well, took a moment to rest his hands on his knees in an exhausted pant. "He's been making us run and do push-ups and sit-ups all week!"

"What does he think he's doing? None of the other officers cared what we did." Kadhim shook his head. "I'm done. I'm not doing this anymore."

"I'm with you," added Mahjoub.

"I don't think I could do any more even if I wanted to!" The others laughed at Saleem's desperate look. Soon, the entire group had united in a miniature rebellion, calling the dean of Al Kindy Medical School to complain.

"He's treating us like we're an actual army!"

"We're dying out here in this heat!"

"Don't worry, I'll take care of it." The dean made a phone call to the offending officer. "Look, Basheer, these are kids volunteering their summers. They're not soldiers. Go easy on them, for heaven's sake."

Officer Basheer's only response was to push them even harder, and the students felt the anger of his power-trip. They had just returned from a two-mile run in 119° heat when Basheer greeted them with a glare.

"Fifty push-ups. Now!"

"No." Kadhim did not get down. Several others remained standing as well.

"What do you mean, 'no'? Get down now and give me fifty!"

"No, I won't do it."

"I'm your commanding officer! You *have* to!"

"I don't give a damn if you are an officer." Kadhim was too exhausted to care anymore. "This is the Jerusalem Army. It's all posturing. We're here as volunteers for the President, may God keep him safe and raise him high. We're all Ba'athis here; when you insult us, you insult the Ba'ath party."

Others who had started doing push-ups suddenly stopped, watching in nervous silence as the scene unfolded. The officer's face grew red.

"I *demand* that you complete your exercises!"

"Look, me doing push-ups? You can forget it."

"Me too." Mahjoub stepped forward.

The other students stood up as well, and a standoff formed between students and officer.

"*That's it!*" Basheer screamed. "I'm bringing my commanding officer, and *he* will bring you to order!" He stormed off, hands balled into fists and teeth gritted.

It wasn't long before an apologetic head officer appeared before the students. "Look guys, he's kind of upset. Be nice to him, okay?" He looked beseechingly at the upset young men around him. "For my sake, would you at least *try* to follow his commands?"

"We respect you, sir, but we're done. He's being unreasonable. No more exercises."

There was nothing else to do but imprison the entire unit, but without an actual jail on site, the young men had to be provided beds, food, and drink for the evening. What was meant to be an overnight imprisonment quickly turned into a social gathering at the government's expense. Between cigarettes and stories, the students called their various universities, and late in the night several tired and harassed deans arrived on site.

"Look, officers, we're all in the Ba'ath, and we all know that this entire thing is a charade to ingratiate Iraq with other Arab countries. These students have given up their summers and come here in the middle of the heat so that the media can photograph them. Either respect yourselves and stop pretending that this is a real army, or we're going to take our students back. It's up to you."

Officer Basheer was quickly transferred out of the Jerusalem Army.

The summer flew by under the shade of the training site's palm trees, and Kadhim soon returned for his fourth of six years of medical school. In spite of the mounting American pressure on Iraq and rumors hinting of war, it was still inconceivable to him and his classmates that Saddam and his indomitable regime might not survive the year.

They had been doomed since the moment a Ba'athi official poked his head into the lecture hall and, as usual, it was all Mahjoub's fault.

"Everyone needs to pick up their books and get going. Your presence is required for a protest against the United States in Freedom Square. There are buses waiting for you outside."

The lecturer tried to hide her annoyance at this last minute interruption, as her students stood up with muted groans.

"Here we go again," Kadhim said as they left the lecture hall. "We were due for another mandatory protest. With all this pressure from America, I'm surprised we haven't been called out sooner."

"Well, this time I call the 'Down With America' sign," Mahjoub smirked. "Just can't resist the opportunity to take down 'The Great Devil' with one of our handy-dandy pieces of cardboard."

They joined over a hundred other students on the buses and soon arrived in Freedom Square.

"Wow, it seems like they're sending the entire school this time."

"Abu Zaman didn't want to lose face." Farouq rolled his eyes. "You know they compete over how many people they bring to these things, right? If one Ba'athi brings a hundred and Abu Zaman only brings twenty, it makes him look bad."

"Lucky for him, he's got a whole school of 'willing volunteers' at his disposal," Kadhim said with a snort of ironic laughter as he and the others grabbed pre-made signs and joined the protest.

No, no America.

Little Blair.

Reckless Bush.

They 'protested' for a few moments in front of the cameras, then Mahjoub turned to the others. "That's it, the heat is killing me. Let's get out of here."

"And do what?" Farouq looked around nervously. "What if Abu Zaman comes out to check attendance?"

"Not in this heat he won't. Come on! We'll get something to drink to cool us off, catch a movie, and be back in time for the end of the protest. Where's the harm?"

If there was one thing Kadhim couldn't stand, it was a mandated protest in the heat of the unforgiving Iraq sun. Mahjoub's idea was a bad one—Mahjoub's ideas usually were—but right now it sounded perfect. "I'm in."

"Me too." Malik's round cheeks glistened and he was drenched in a comical amount of sweat.

Farouq gazed around anxiously. "Fine, fine. I'll come."

"Great. We're all set then." Mahjoub led the way. "I'm glad you've decided to protest the protest with us, Malik, but dear *God* you cannot come with us looking like that."

"Malik, Mahjoub, Farouq, and Kadhim: Abu Zaman would like to see you in his office."

Hind looked at Kadhim questioningly as the official left the classroom. Kadhim shrugged, but he had a feeling he knew what it was about. He joined the other boys as they walked down the hall to meet their fate.

"How do they know that we skipped the protest? What are we going to *do*?" Farouq's voice was practically a squeak.

"Just tell him we were there and he didn't see us."

Kadhim shook his head, "That's not going to work, Mahjoub. If he was there taking attendance you don't want to start by insulting him. Tell him you went to the bathroom."

"All of us? *Together?*" Farouq's voice rose several more octaves.

"You have a better idea?"

His question was met with silence.

"We were in the bathroom then. Good luck, guys."

Abu Zaman separated the boys and interrogated them one by one, his muffled shouts seeping through the closed door. Farouq came out looking positively green. Even Mahjoub looked frightened. Kadhim entered last, his heart pounding.

"I suppose you're going to tell me that you went to the bathroom with the rest of your girlfriends."

"Yes, sir."

"I don't believe a word of it, Kadhim. It's a shame. You come from a good family and you risk smearing their good name. Have you no respect for authority?"

His voice rose with every word until Kadhim cringed from the volume.

"That's it. There's an "X" next to each of your names now, for skipping the protest and lying about it! I've been nice to you so far, but I've had enough!"

A vein protruded angrily from the Head of Student and Ba'athi Affairs' forehead and spit flew from his lips.

"Another stunt like this, and I'll have you arrested!"

TROUBLE

Mohammed watched in horror as silent tears rolled down his father's cheeks, and his mother, sobbing, frantically packed her son's clothes into a bag in the hopes that he would flee the country. Fear gripped his chest, and an unbearable wave of guilt and regret washed over him. *If only I could have kept my cool, the way Kadhim would have. If only I could have been diplomatic, like Ali. If only the Ba'athis weren't such assholes.* But no, on that day, several months ago, he had been one hundred percent Mohammed: bullheaded, brash and outspoken. And because of that, now his parents would have to be tortured, and he would have to die.

Mohammed took a satisfied drag on his cigarette and observed contentedly that things at the university could not be going better. He had his pick of some of Iraq's prettiest (and easiest) girls—which was why he had chosen this private liberal arts school in the first place—and his studies were going well. Much to his parents' chagrin, he had purposely failed multiple times in order to avoid the mandatory military service that came after college. Well, maybe not entirely on purpose... he had never cared much for studying. However, it looked certain that this time around he would finally graduate with a BA in English Literature. He would miss college life when it was over, but seven years was long enough.

"What are you smiling about?" Professor Qasim approached him with a grin, taking a seat next to him in the shade of the Language Hall.

"Why don't you just ask for the cigarette instead of pretending you want to make small talk?" Mohammed retorted with a laugh, tossing his professor a cigarette.

Over the years, Professor Qasim had become more of a friend than a teacher. Only slightly older than Mohammed and his cohort, they had a lot in common. Despite the fact that he was fairly high up in the Ba'ath, he didn't mind talking politics, nor was he quick to leap to the regime's defense. In a world with so little trust, it was refreshing to find someone like him. Professor Qasim practiced his own form of Ba'athism.

It wasn't a political philosophy that he took to heart, nor a regime that he felt any real loyalty to; it was simply a way to get to the top.

"I was thinking," Professor Qasim said languidly after exhaling a long stream of smoke, "maybe we could go to Louie Café tonight. It's been a while since I had hookah and *arak*."

Nearly the entire group of friends showed up that evening at Louie Café: Mohammed, Salam, Saif, Hashim, and the professor. They had been smoking hookah, drinking potent *arak*, and talking about girls, school, and politics for nearly an hour when Professor Qasim changed the subject.

"Hey, why don't you guys increase your rank in the Ba'ath?"

The guys looked at each other hesitantly. It wasn't the first time the professor had asked them this, and as their friend they had let it slide, but they didn't want to be pushed. Mohammed was the first to respond.

"I was thinking I'd let that wait until after I graduate," he said, trying to find a diplomatic way to sidestep the question. "I'm pretty busy right now."

"You mean busy with the girls!" Salam joked.

"Yeah, and that's *if* you ever graduate!" Hashim added with a roar of laughter. Mohammed glared at him, and he shut up instantly.

"I don't think now is really the right time for any of us, Professor," Saif said.

"Well, you boys should consider it. In my opinion, now is the *perfect* time. You're about to graduate—well, that's if you get your grades up, Hashim—"

The boys laughed, and it was Hashim's turn to flush.

"And once you get out of here, you're going to have to get real jobs. You know that the only way to get the job you want is by raising your rank. In fact, if you let me help you raise your rank, maybe I'll put in a good word for you. I have a lot of great contacts; it might be time to start pulling some strings, and thinking about long-term careers."

When Mohammed had first entered college, his rank had been mandatorily increased, both against his will and without his knowledge. He was furious when they told him that he had become a 'victor' for the Ba'ath.

"Since when? I never signed anything! I never asked to raise my rank!"

"Doesn't matter," came the reply, and the papers documenting his new rank were thrown in his face. The dean had mandatorily raised the political ranks of the entire student body in hopes of ingratiating himself with the regime. *Look!* they said, *The whole university is Ba'athi! Isn't that fantastic!*

Professor Qasim was a friend. They smoked together, drank together, joked about politics together. Hell, Mohammed and his friends had not only attended their professor's wedding, they had helped *fund* it. The professor's government wage was barely enough to live on, and certainly not enough to pay for a wedding to a woman with no parents and no assets. They had been glad to help.

Yet despite their friendship, Mohammed knew the real reason behind Professor Qasim's request. The more people he enlisted, the higher his own rank would become. He was hungry to gain status, and this was one venture where Mohammed did not feel like helping him.

The professor brought up the issue again a week later. It was approaching 5:30 in the evening, and the temperature was starting to dip and the sky turn grey with the possibility of a winter rain. Mohammed was about to head home when he heard a shout behind him. "Mohammed! Hey!"

Mohammed wished he were far enough away to pretend he hadn't heard. He knew what the professor wanted.

"Hey, wait a second! How've you been? I haven't seen you around in a while."

It's because I've been avoiding you. "Hey, Professor. How are you?"

Professor Qasim didn't bother to exchange pleasantries.

"Good. Look, I've been meaning to ask you. What did you decide about raising your rank?"

"I've decided not to," Mohammed replied flatly.

"Really?" He was obviously annoyed. "You know, both Hashim and Salam raised theirs. Why won't you?"

"Why should Hashim and Salam's rank concern me?" Mohammed was cold, hungry, and tired of being hounded on the issue. He was hoping to end the conversation as quickly as he could.

The professor seemed taken aback by Mohammed's curtness, but he regained his composure and replied coldly, "I just thought you might want to do something for your friends."

"You mean you want me to do something for *you*."

"For God's sake, Mohammed, what's the big deal? What does it matter to you if you're a victor or a low-level comrade? I only need *one* more and I..." He faltered.

"You only need one more and then what, Qasim? You get a promotion? You know how I feel about the Ba'ath. I've said that I don't have the time for the increased commitments, and I just don't want to, plain and simple."

"Just one more and I become the head of a unit, Mohammed! Why are you holding me back?"

"Are you kidding me? *I'm* holding you back? This isn't my responsibility! Who gives a shit about you or the Ba'ath Party? After all our years of friendship you just want to use me as a stepping stone in your political game."

Mohammed's temper suddenly slipped out of his control, and before he realized it, insults to Saddam and to Professor Qasim's *'aradh*—his mother and wife—had escaped from his lips unfiltered.

In an instant, Professor Qasim went from anger to a cold, steely look of pure hatred.

"I swear by Allah, Mohammed, if I don't rise in the ranks by stepping on *you* specifically, then my name isn't Qasim Al-Askari."

"To hell with you. Do whatever you want. I have nothing to do with it anymore." Mohammed turned and left campus, his blood boiling.

He was trying desperately to keep his eyes open in Professor Maya's English class the next day, as the middle-aged Palestinian droned on about the uses of inversion in dependent clauses, when, without knocking, several uniformed soldiers burst through the door, causing the tiny professor to take a startled hop backwards.

"Mohammed Al Baghdadi—where is he?"

Shit.

Mohammed stood up, and they walked him out into the hallway.

"What's going on?"

"You've been requested."

"What do you mean I've been requested? Where are you taking me?"

"It's more a question of *who* we're taking you to."

"Yeah? Who then? What do they want? I'm not going to let you walk me to my death!"

"They just want to ask you some questions," a soldier replied, exasperated.

"In that case, screw them. I'm going back to class. I've got some English grammar to learn, if you don't mind." Mohammed marched back into class and planted himself firmly in his seat.

The soldiers reentered the room.

"Hey!" shouted Professor Maya, with another tiny jump.

Ignoring the professor, they walked up to Mohammed and to the shock of the entire class and to Mohammed's humiliation, forcibly

71

dragged him from his chair into the hallway as he shouted at them, at his teacher, and at no one in particular. They then marched him to a conference room, threw him inside, and shut the door.

Mohammed looked around. There sat a veritable display of full Ba'athi power, from Unit Head to Branch Head, people who could decide whether he lived or died. At the end of the table, looking small and petty, sat Professor Qasim.

"So," sneered one of the most important among them, "why do you think you're too good for the Ba'ath?"

The interrogation had begun.

Over two agonizing hours passed in that small, hot room, as the high-up Ba'athis kept repeating the same questions over and over.

"Why don't you raise your rank in the Ba'ath? You think you're too good for us?"

"The timing's not right! I don't want to!" Mohammed was exhausted and his nerves jangled. His responses only seemed to anger them more.

"Why aren't you attending the mandatory Ba'ath meetings and lectures?"

"I'm busy! I'm not even a Ba'ath party member! I shouldn't have to attend if I'm not Ba'athi!"

"But you are Ba'athi. You're a victor."

"Yeah, *you* guys made me a victor, remember? What does it even mean, being a victor? All of Iraq is a victor by now!" He could tell that his slippery tongue was only exacerbating the situation. "This is all because of *him*." He pointed at Professor Qasim. "He's been pushing me to become a comrade. He just wants a promotion."

"So what if he does? Why don't you just raise your rank?"

"I already *told* you why! Why do you keep asking the same questions?"

"How about this one: Why haven't you participated in a rotation with the Jerusalem Army?"

"Because I don't have to! If you've looked through my documents, then you'll know that I failed last year when I was supposed to graduate! I need to focus on my studies so I can complete my schooling! As for participating in the Jerusalem Army, Saddam Hussein himself said that final year students don't have to—"

"*How dare you.*" The man's tone silenced Mohammed instantly. The Branch Head didn't look angry. He looked *furious*. "How dare you say it like that, without saying Sir Saddam Hussein, Esteemed President, may God keep him safe and raise him high."

Allah. It was the kind of mistake that no one would make at a table with this type of guests. Never—*ever*—say Saddam's name without adding one of the many epithets of praise.

"I'm sorry. I meant the Leader of Iraq, Companion to the Warrior, may God keep him safe and raise him high."

"You think you're funny, don't you?"

"Well, which do you want then? Should I say Saddam Hussein or 'The Prime Leader'?"

"Traitor. Agent for Iran." The words cut deep, like death threats. They were among the worst accusations one could hear from the regime. Mohammed broke into a cold sweat and his hands started to shake.

"See this dog, how he acts?" Professor Qasim spat from the corner.

"I'm the dog? The one who always gave you cigarettes, hung out with you, went to your wedding, and you call *me* a dog?" Mohammed felt his face burning with anger. Two hours of this was enough. Where was it all going?

"Well, it's not *your* fault you're a traitor," the Branch Head said slowly, nastily. "How can you help it when your father's a traitor, just like the rest of your family."

Fire suddenly flared through his veins. To insult Mohammed was one thing. To insult his father and his family was enough to send him off the deep end. He opened his mouth to reply when the man's next sentence stopped him cold.

"Where's your aunt?"

"*Who?*" He couldn't believe his ears.

"You know, your dear auntie Fatuma."

The question had hit a new nerve, deep, raw, in a place where one doesn't go. The family's honor was by far one's most valuable possession, and the seat of a family's honor was in its women. As a male, bringing up the issue of someone's female family member, even in passing, was such a taboo that Iraqis went to great lengths to avoid it. Often, they didn't even look directly at others' female relatives, avoiding eye contact out of respect. When possible, it was more polite not to address the woman, but her male companion instead, and when enquiring about the health of a colleague's sickly wife, they would ask, "How's your family?" The meaning was implied. They *never* referred directly to someone's *'aradh*—their female relatives—and when they did so

73

maliciously, it was the worst insult imaginable.

In this case, the Branch Head had not only referred *by name* to Mohammed's aunt, he had referred to an aunt who had been executed by the regime.

How had he known?

Suddenly, a feverish rage took over and the words that would get him killed flew uncontrollably from Mohammed's mouth.

"Fuck the Ba'athi meetings, fuck the Jerusalem Army, and isn't Jerusalem the house of God? Then to hell with Jerusalem and the whole of Palestine as well! To hell with you and your dog of a father! Fuck Saddam Hussein and the whole damn regime!"

For a moment, they stared at Mohammed in wide-eyed shock as he panted in rage. People had been killed for far less.

"That'll do it," the Branch Head said at last. They had extracted what they came for.

"Take him!" screamed Professor Qasim, once he had recovered from his shock. "Didn't you hear what he said? *Arrest him!*"

The soldiers grabbed Mohammed and were pulling him out of the conference room when Professor Najim, Head of the English Department, saw them from afar and rushed over as quickly as his seventy-year-old legs would carry him. He had been around long enough, and knew Mohammed well enough, to have an inkling of what was about to happen.

"You can't do this!" he shouted, mustering up all the authority his seniority at the college could bring. "This is a college campus, *our* territory. You know the Ba'ath Party is not allowed to arrest students while on campus. It's illegal! Please respect our laws!"

He turned to Mohammed. "Son, as long as you're on this campus, no one can touch a hair on your head."

"Let me talk to you for a second." One of the Ba'athis pulled Professor Najim into a nearby office as Mohammed waited nervously, grateful for the old professor's intervention.

After what seemed like ages, the men opened the door... and the sight of Professor Najim, his tie askew, his aged and bloodshot eyes bright purple and puffy where they had punched him, threw a shock of fear into Mohammed's stomach. *He had **really** messed up if they wanted him this badly.*

"Mohammed, my son." The old professor grasped Mohammed's hand and squeezed it. "I am sorry, I'm so sorry, but there's nothing more I can do. The matter is out of my hands."

He walked away with a limp, broken as much by the humiliation as the pain.

Mohammed was pulled to the college gates, where the university guards kept their daily watch.

"Keep him here," one of the Ba'athis ordered. "We'll send someone for him shortly."

"Dude, what did you *do*?" one of the guards asked when the Ba'athis left. "Those aren't the kind of guys you want to piss off!"

The guards knew Mohammed well—he had, after all, been passing their gates everyday for nearly seven years—and they listened with growing astonishment and gravity as he explained the situation. When he finished, the guards looked at each other.

"Mohammed, habibi, we've known you for a long time. You're like a brother to us. You know what? Go. Leave."

"What?"

"Go. Don't worry about us. Just go before they get back."

"Thanks, guys. I won't forget this." Mohammed worried about the consequences they might face on his behalf, but he had a feeling he would regret it if he didn't take their advice. He turned to leave... and stopped dead at the sight of Professor Qasim, who, arm extended, was pointing a pistol directly at his face.

"If you leave, I'll shoot you." His voice was high and shaky.

A female student stopped and screamed. Other students quickly took notice and started shouting.

"*Professor! Put that down! What are you doing?*" Some of the bigger boys considered knocking him down and taking the gun, but thought better of it when Professor Qasim released the safety and repeated, "If you try to leave, I swear to Allah I'll shoot."

"If you really have the guts to do it, then do it," Mohammed replied angrily.

"Professor, stop it! Put that down!" screamed a female student. A small crowd had formed, and Professor Qasim looked around nervously.

"You really think you'll get away with shooting a student on campus in front of the world?" Mohammed pushed him. "Go ahead! If you're man enough to do it, then *do it!*"

His hand shaking, the professor raised the gun higher and pointed it straight at Mohammed's forehead. The pitch of screams and shouted warnings around them rose. Other professors started to hurry to the scene. Mohammed held his breath.

Professor Qasim lowered his gun with a hiss of exasperation.

"You're dead either way," he snarled, and he took off as the crowd quickly parted to make way for him.

"In the name of Allah and all that is holy! What the hell were you doing, Mohammed? Is there anyone crazy enough to talk this way to the *government*?"

It was Mohammed's second day at home. He had told his father the story as soon as he got there, and Baba had listened, dry-mouthed, and then without responding, stood up and started making phone calls. It was way too late to reprimand his son; it was time to try to find a way to save his life.

Abu Hameed, who was sitting across the table from them, had no such attitude.

"By God, Mohammed, you've really gone and done it now! Who the hell *does* this kind of thing? You shouted slurs against the Ba'ath and the government and the house of Allah and even Saddam Hussein himself, right in front of these guys? Even *I* might not be able to help you!"

Abu Hameed was one of Baba's oldest friends, and they had maintained a firm friendship even as Abu Hameed reached the upper echelons of the Ba'ath party. If Abu Hameed couldn't help Mohammed, then no one could.

"I know, I know. I'm an idiot. I couldn't control myself. But you heard what they said about Aunt Fatuma." Mohammed was red with embarrassment and fear. Even *he* couldn't believe that he had gotten himself into this mess.

"Please, see what you can do." Baba's voice was strained.

"For you, I'll try." Abu Hameed drained his tea and stood. "But for now, Mohammed, stay home. I'll call when I have an update."

Mohammed nodded. His mother, anxiety written all over her face, waited for Abu Hameed to leave before bringing the full force of her wrath upon her son.

They received a phone call a few days later.

"You can go back to school," came Abu Hameed's voice over the line. "Your file has been burned. They can't do anything to you now."

When Mohammed returned to college, everything had changed.

Saif, Salam, Hashim—none of his friends would talk to him. In fact, the story had circulated around the school, and suddenly the entire student body was terrified of being associated with him. Even Professor Maya seemed nervous when he apologized for his shouting that fateful day. He had become a pariah.

Months went by.

Every neighborhood had its own *mukhtar*, a little mayor responsible for the area. Behind the façade of paperwork, his true duties included spying on the neighborhood's residents and reporting untoward behavior to the government, like a fly in the Ba'ath intelligence services. Many *mukhtars* were known to take advantage of their meager posts to exploit and harm the locals, but there was one *mukhtar* who was an oddity in a group of bad apples.

He was a good man who truly cared about his neighborhood, despite being Sunni from Saddam's hometown of Tikrit, whereas the neighborhood was Shiite, a combination that in many places would have been particularly volatile. Generally, Tikritis enjoyed special privileges due to their link to Saddam, and often saw themselves as superior to the rest of the population. For many Tikritis, it was only too easy to take advantage of their special position to lord over and terrorize others, for which they were hated and feared.

Rather than report his constituents to the regime for arrest, torture and possible death, however, this *mukhtar* was known to turn a blind eye to their mild activities, and, on occasion, went out of his way to protect them. In a rare twist, the neighborhood loved and respected their *mukhtar*, and it was this *mukhtar*, along with Abu Hameed, who knocked on the door one evening.

"Is your father home?" Abu Hameed asked as Mohammed greeted him. Mohammed called out for his father, who arrived at the door looking worried.

"Why don't you go back inside," the *mukhtar* said. "We need to speak to your father in private."

Mohammed acquiesced. In all likelihood, this had nothing to do with him. After all, he had been back at school for nearly two months without incident.

Fifteen minutes passed before his father reentered the house. He seemed to have aged drastically. His eyes were red, and he looked about to cry. Mohammed was more than startled; he was downright frightened. He had never seen Baba like this.

"Um Ali," his father called, "I need to talk to you."

77

Mohammed watched as Mama entered the room and shut the door. What was going on? He heard voices rise, but he couldn't make out what they were saying. Mama burst from the room in great heaving sobs and walked straight into Mohammed's room.

"Mama?"

To his astonishment, she strode purposefully to his dresser and began gathering his clothing by the armful.

"Mama? What's wrong? Why are you crying?"

Her sobs only grew louder as she shoved his clothes into a duffle bag in frustration.

"Mama, what are you doing with my clothes?"

"You're leaving!" she cried. Baba came and stood in the doorway, his face adorned with a look of grief and—*was that fear*?

"What do you mean I'm leaving? Why?" Mohammed couldn't believe what was going on around him.

"You have to leave now! There's no time!"

"Don't you think you should tell me what's going on?"

"You need to leave Iraq immediately! Go to Kurdistan, go anywhere! Just leave Iraq!"

"Why, Mama? Why won't you tell me what's going on?"

Mama burst into a fresh wave of tears. "*Fidayee* Saddam are on their way to take you!"

Mohammed froze.

It was a death sentence.

The *fidayeen* were members of a paramilitary organization composed of Saddam's extreme loyalists. Rumor had it they were trained by being released unarmed into a pack of hungry wolves, and to save themselves, they had to rip the wolves apart with their bare hands. In fact, their very name said it all: *Those who sacrifice themselves for Saddam.*

For a simple arrest, the police would have been sent. *Fidayee* Saddam did not arrest. They executed. When the *fidayeen* came, the end result was always the same: someone would be put to death. Most frequently, the event took place in the person's own home or on his street, where it could be witnessed by his family and neighbors. They would make an example of him, a chilling reminder to the public of what happened when one dared to speak out against the regime.

Mohammed was stunned.

He would be executed.

It seemed that not quite *all* of his papers had been burned.

Mama was packing his bags, preparing him to flee the country.

Baba was standing in the doorway, tears of pain at the thought of his son's inevitable death flowing silently down his cheeks.

Leave? He couldn't leave them! Mohammed started ripping his clothes out of the duffel bag as his mother frantically packed.

"What are you doing?" she screamed, desperately reaching to put more clothes in as he in turn threw them out.

"Do you really think I'm going to leave? Let the *fidayeen* come here and find you guys, arrest you, torture you until you tell them where I am? Maybe kill you in the end? Do you really think I could so selfishly just leave and let them do that to you on my account?" Shock, fear, panic, and anger all expressed themselves in Mohammed's roar. Clothing flew around the room.

"You don't understand! *They're going to kill you!*" T-shirts, magazines, and empty wrappers flew from Mama's hands to the abused duffle bag in a blind panic.

"I can't! I'm not going! Mama, you don't know what they do to women in the prisons here!" *They rape them,* Mohammed thought in a sickening wave of dread. *They rape them in front of their brothers, sons, and husbands.* It was their way of drawing out the wanted criminal— raping one of his beloved female family members until he could stand it no more and came to offer them his own head. It had happened to one of Mohammed's friends, whose sister had been raped in front of him.

Never. He could *never* let that happen to Mama. He would die first.

He had brought this upon them. His own wild and unruly tongue had brought down the full wrath of Saddam's brutal regime, and now it was time to pay. He knew that his parents loved him, that they would do anything to save his life, but he would rather die in front of them than let them make the sacrifice that they were preparing to make.

"I'm not leaving! I swear to God, I'm not leaving!" Mohammed shouted. The whirlwind of clothing, trash, and unknown articles continued their trajectory around the room. The *mukhtar* and Abu Hameed entered the room. Even the neighbor came over to find out what was going on, and she too began to plead with Mohammed.

"Leave, son! Leave now, before they come!"

The neighbor's husband soon appeared, bewildered by the pandemonium. He turned to Baba and got the gist of the story.

"Mohammed," the neighbor shouted over the din. "You can come with me. I own a company where you can hide safely. Come, before it's too late. I'll help find someplace safe for your family as well."

It was that final sentence that caused the last article of clothing to drop. Of course. Hide the family. It wasn't a long-term solution, but for now it might work.

Within less than an hour, he was bunkered up in the neighbor's workshop. His parents, Firas in tow, had also left the house to hide. His other brothers would sleep elsewhere for the night.

For months, Mohammed slept in a different place every night. He spent most of his time far from Baghdad, his studies put on hold. His parents had stayed away from home for as long as they could, but eventually returned. Mohammed's visits were brief, and he was never allowed to stay.

As the weeks passed, they nervously wondered, *Where are the fidayeen?* It was not until Baba spoke with Abu Hameed that he found out what had happened.

The *mukhtar* had returned to his office after warning the family of the pending arrival of the *fidayeen*, then picked up his phone to make a call.

"The family's left," he said to one of the *fidayeen* commanders. "The entire family has fled; we can't find them anywhere. We got there and the house was emptied of everything; you can go check for yourself, if you want. It looks like they're going to be gone for a while. I'll let you know when they come back."

The commander hung up. There was no point in wasting his time if no one was there. He would wait until they returned.

It was February 2003. Although the commander did not realize it, events were about to take place that would soon make this recalcitrant student the last thing on his mind.

WAR

The pulse of Baghdad was still as alive as it had always been. The streets were filled with dust, honking cars, dirty children selling packets of tissues, and street vendors boasting wares from falafel and cell phones to ladies lingerie. But they knew the war was coming. News and rumors raced hot and thick throughout the city. On March 17, 2003, American President George W. Bush had issued an ultimatum: *"All the decades of deceit and cruelty have now reached an end. Saddam Hussein and his sons must leave Iraq within 48 hours. Their refusal to do so will result in military conflict, commenced at a time of our choosing..."* Saddam would never back down. The Americans were coming. It wouldn't be long now.

On TV there were clips of Saddam, once brutally against any extremism, now calling for Wahhabis and other terrorists to come fight the occupier. There were interviews with bearded men who arrived in droves from other Arab countries, promising to destroy the infidels, should they occupy Iraq.

The atmosphere at Al Kindy Medical School was tense. One day, Hind—like many others—stopped coming to class. Kadhim called to check on her. She was fine, she said, just staying home for a few days, to be safe. Kadhim made his way home after classes on Tuesday evening, March 18th. The hours of the ultimatum were slowly ticking away, and he noticed en route that fully packed cars were starting to leave the city.

Mama had outdone herself at dinner that night. Parents, brothers, aunts, uncles, cousins; all of three or four worried families had come to the Al Baghdadi house to discuss what was to be done, and to simply be together. Baba was the eldest, and they needed his opinion and consent. Should they flee to Karbala? Basra? Where did they have relatives who could take them in? Should they stay?

That night, hotel Al Baghdadi was full. Kadhim shared his room with Firas and two cousins. Mohammed also was sharing his small bedroom with several men. Ali had been kicked out of his bedroom entirely, which was now occupied by the women. He and others were forced to sleep on cots in the kitchen and living room. Sleep did not come easily for any of them.

In Kadhim's room, only young Firas seemed able to sleep, and his small snores from the corner of the room were comforting compared to the tossing and turning of their cousins. Kadhim himself slept only in fits and starts, and was troubled by strange dreams.

A dismembered arm lay in the park, next to his soccer ball. He wanted just to pick up the ball and run, but slowly the arm was reattaching itself to a body, a leg inching its way over. He was alone with the corpse, his legs frozen to the ground in terror as he watched the head—its eyes open and staring—roll over to reattach itself to its core. The body was coming alive...

Stop. Breathe.

Put a finger on the pulse of the city. It's holding its breath. All is silent; the streets are empty. Citizens, thieves, murderers, they're all inside. People sit at kitchen tables, in living rooms, in bedrooms, staying close to loved ones. No one speaks. Hearts racing, they wait.

BOOM.

At approximately 5:30 in the morning on Wednesday March 19, 2003, as if struck by a terrible crack of lightening, the sky lit up, the city began the quake, and several windows of the Al Baghdadi house instantly shattered.

The day of shock and awe had begun.

On the following Saturday, some twenty students returned to Al Kindy Medical School, where the dean and several doctors were waiting to tell them that classes had been canceled indefinitely. Abu Zaman, Head of Student and Ba'athi Affairs, was mysteriously absent.

They did not know how long the fighting would last, nor when they might be able to safely hold classes again. Though no one spoke of the matter, it was not known whether their regime, political system, and way of life for over thirty years would survive this war, although it was difficult to imagine life any other way. For now, they had to focus on the matters at hand.

"I recommend that you go home to your parents and stay safe," the dean was saying. "We will contact everyone once the school reopens. In the meantime, Al Kindy Hospital, Saddam Medical City, Nu'man Hospital and many others will remain open during the war. They will need help, if you are willing to volunteer. Please know that if you choose to volunteer, we cannot guarantee your safety. Only Allah knows what is in store for us. Stay safe, everyone. We'll see you all when this war is over."

The meeting disbanded. There were many whom they would never see again.

"Look, I just don't think that volunteering at Saddam Medical City is a good idea." Lines of stress and fatigue had begun to appear on his father's face. Ten days had gone by since the start of the war, and restaurants, schools, universities, and governmental agencies were all closed and empty. Fear was circulating amongst Iraqis that if Saddam really went crazy, he would hit his own people with chemical weapons as he had done to the Kurdish town of Halabja in the eighties. Over half of Baghdad—some two million residents—packed their homes and fled the city during those first few days. It felt as though the lively metropolis was becoming a ghost town. Nevertheless, after much debate, the Al Baghdadi family decided to stay. Rumor had it that the Americans were attacking other cities anyway—Nasiriya, Najaf, Basra and others were all currently taking the blow. Hotel Al Baghdadi was still fully booked, and the running and crying children, the constant mess, and the lack of privacy were beginning to wear on them all.

For several days, Kadhim had been trying to convince his parents to let him volunteer at the closest hospital, Baghdad Medical Complex. Formally known as Saddam Medical City, it was the largest medical complex in Iraq—so large that it did indeed constitute a small city, comprised of eight hospitals and countless clinics. His parents were reluctant, to say the least.

"I want you to stay here," Mama insisted. "I would worry too much about you out in the middle of a war."

"The war isn't even in Baghdad right now. The hospital is close by, and I can call and keep you updated. It'll be fine." Kadhim was glad that his father hadn't forbidden his volunteering outright, because he could never disrespect his father enough to go directly against his wishes.

"The American forces may be elsewhere right now," Baba said, "but they'll be back, and it will be chaos. Last week they only hit military and intelligence bases and some other strategic points. They're trying to weaken the Iraqi regime, Kadhim, and before long they'll come to the capital to finish the job. You should be somewhere safe when that happens."

"I understand, but the hospital is well-known and won't be a military target. This is an opportunity for me to learn, Baba, to gain hands-on experience. If I truly want to be a great surgeon, then I shouldn't turn down *any* opportunities, and this could be a great one!"

His father did not answer.

"Furthermore, if the Americans occupy Baghdad, then surely civilians will also need medical care. If I can help save lives, then don't I have a moral obligation to do so? Won't the hospital need all the help it can get?"

His father sighed, and his mother regarded her husband anxiously.

"Kadhim," he said slowly, "your heart is in the right place. If you really want to go, I won't stop you. But please, be careful."

Elated, Kadhim threw clothes and a few basic items into his duffel bag. He meant what he had said to his father. He wanted to help and learn, but there was more to it than that. The truth was, he wanted to *see* the war, be right in the thick of it. He wanted to live the events, not hear of them later from the relative safety of his living room. Besides, he thought, as he heard two of his cousins get into a screaming match over a toy, he *had* to get out of the house.

Duffel bag in hand, he rushed down the stairs, where Mama was waiting with a small feast wrapped in various containers.

"At least take some food with you."

"Mama, I can't possibly take all this!" It made Kadhim laugh to see the copious amounts of food that she had prepared. He grabbed a couple of chocolate bars. "These should be enough."

"But what if you get hungry?"

"In Baghdad Medical City?" Kadhim laughed. "There are five or six cafeterias in the Baghdad Teaching Hospital alone. They could feed a small army! I'll be fine, Mama, trust me. There'll be more than enough food."

He said goodbye to his family and relatives, and Baba accompanied him to the door.

"Kadhim, you were not in Iraq during the war with Iran, and you were young during the revolution of '91 and the war with Kuwait. We did our best to protect our sons from the horrors of those events, so you do not yet know the ugliness that war can bring. But I fear you will see it now. Just remember to hold tight to your faith, and never forget the values and morals on which you were raised. I hope you're ready."

Nervous and excited, Kadhim made his way through the nearly empty streets to the hospital. The city felt oddly quiet, and for the most part the only cars around were those fleeing the city. He thought back to his father's words and hoped that he was ready.

But nothing could have prepared him for what was to come.

"Have you seen Dr. Abbas, sir?"

"The surgical resident? No, I haven't." The surgeon's response was curt. He was busy, and the presence of the two volunteers annoyed him.

"I apologize for the intrusion," Kadhim persisted. "It's just that we were supposed to round with Dr. Abbas this morning and he's three hours late."

"Round with someone else."

"But do you know where he is, sir?" Kadhim's colleague spoke up, a fourth year medical student whom Kadhim recognized vaguely from some other medical school—Sami was it? Or Fadi?

"Look, if he's not here by now, it means he's not coming."

"But he said – "

The doctor turned and glared. "Dr. Abbas is not coming. In all likelihood, he has packed up his wife and child and fled the city like the others. Now, you can either make yourselves useful, or you can be like Dr. Abbas and get out of here."

Kadhim and his friend gratefully chose the latter. They had begun to notice the disappearance of doctors and staff from the initially fully staffed hospital. Sometimes a doctor would announce his intent to leave, but more often it was a silent departure. One day there, the next day gone, without a word spoken to anyone. Despite it all, the hospital was still functioning as normal, and between rounding with various residents and doing menial tasks, Kadhim had grown accustomed to monitoring the news around the clock. TV, radio, word of mouth – they all followed intently.

April 5: "Occupation forces have taken over the Baghdad airport." A whole wave of physicians and staff disappeared overnight.

April 6: "The occupier is in Saddam's presidential complex— they've overtaken one of Saddam's palaces." Yet more disappearances. The blood in their veins began to pump faster. *Here it comes.*

April 7: "The American forces are in Saddam's palaces in the south of Baghdad. They're taking them over one by one. Looters are everywhere."

It was as though a dam had suddenly burst. Twenty, thirty, forty, fifty... a deluge of patients began to flood the ER, their numbers increasing by the hour. All were trauma patients, primarily bullet wounds and shrapnel. Many were high-ranking Ba'athis or *fidayee* Saddam, targeted by Americans and Iraqis with vendettas.

They discovered that upon x-ray, it could be determined whether the bullet was American or Iraqi. While a bullet from the average AK-47 was slow and would usually lodge somewhere in the body, the larger, faster American bullet would pass straight through, creating a vortex of destruction in its wake, as the impact pulverized tissue, organs and bone. Bullets did not make a clean entry through the skin, but blew a large hole upon impact that closed nearly instantly, swallowing with it clothing, dirt and any other foreign objects that happened to be in the way, including shrapnel from an occasional cell phone.

Those remaining at the hospital suddenly found their hands full. All with the necessary know-how took an OR, performing a stream of emergency surgeries. Kadhim, Fadi, and the first-year residents stayed in the ER to triage the incoming waves of trauma patients. Nurses, having limited medical training in Iraq, brought medicines, anesthetics, blood and other basics, and a group of European volunteers, who had arrived in the hospital about a week before, did their best to make themselves useful. They had no medical training but were courageous and worked tirelessly, bringing clean sheets and mopping blood off the floor.

Kadhim took blood, inserted IVs, cleaned wounds, performed transfusions, and directed patients either to immediate surgery or to another ward to heal. Hour after exhausting hour went by, and he, like the rest, became soaked in blood and sweat. The ER was packed. When his legs and hands began to tremble from low blood sugar, he rushed to the cafeteria and grabbed a couple sandwiches, noticing that the patient cafeteria was nearly out of food. He stopped to watch the news on the cafeteria TV as he wolfed down a sandwich.

"*As we speak, Saddam's palaces are being ransacked and stripped. Rumors that even the faucets are made of gold have brought looters in droves.*" Thick swarms of looters and thieves were shown running in and out of a palace like wasps to a nest.

"*It is apparent that the American occupier will do nothing to prevent them. President Saddam Hussein's whereabouts are still unknown, as other Ba'athis flee the country en masse.*"

Kadhim threw his wrapper at a trashcan, where it bounced off the overflowing mound of garbage and fell to the floor. He ran back to the emergency department. Day turned into evening, and evening to night, and still Kadhim worked.

He had no idea what time it was when he felt a hand on his shoulder, startling him from the wound he was cleaning. A senior resident was gazing down at him, the fatigue apparent in her features.

"Go. You're done for the day."

Kadhim looked around. The ER had calmed considerably. Stretching his sore back and legs, he asked, "What about this patient?"

"The patient will be fine." The resident noticed his uncertainty and repeated, "Look, I'm not asking you, I'm telling you. Get some sleep while you can. Tomorrow's going to be rough."

Kadhim wiped the sweat off his brow with a sleeve and looked at his watch. It was nearly three o'clock in the morning. "How much rougher can it get?" he asked with a wry chuckle as he peeled off his gloves.

The resident didn't laugh.

"Judging by the rate at which we've been losing doctors and staff, by tomorrow, less than ten percent will be left." She looked at Kadhim gravely. "The ER can hold up to two hundred patients. Today, we received one hundred and ninety-six. Tomorrow, we're going to overflow."

TRAUMA & TRIAGE

On April 8th, the hospital began its descent into chaos.

Neighborhood by neighborhood, street by street, the Americans tightened their grip around the city, flushing out Ba'athis and *fidayee* Saddam. The more control they gained over Baghdad, the more the waves of incoming patients at the hospital swelled.

When Kadhim awoke just before six A.M., the ER had already reached maximum capacity. He pulled on a fresh pair of scrubs, ate his last chocolate bar, and prepared himself for another long day and an excess of trauma patients.

As it turned out, the overflow of patients would only be one problem of many. They were about to be hit by a perfect storm, and nearly everything that could go wrong, would.

The resident's prediction that very little of their staff would remain by the next day was spot on. Looking around the ER that morning, Kadhim saw only five medical professionals—including himself and Fadi—to take on two hundred patients and counting. At times throughout the day, they would be even fewer. There were still several surgeons left in the operating rooms, but administrative, cafeteria, janitorial, and nearly all the nursing staff were gone.

In the ER, their job was triage: identify the cases who might live—from most critical to least—and stabilize them before sending them off to surgery or to heal. This required mitigating any life-threatening conditions: restart the heart, stop the bleeding, open the airways, regulate extremes in blood pressure, and perform a transfusion if the patient was losing too much blood. Those who were on the brink of death? Leave them to die. Others would die who might have lived had they not wasted precious minutes on a lost cause. Kadhim quickly learned to identify such cases. They were the ones whose lungs bubbled with blood as they tried to inhale, the ones who did not have the energy to shout for the doctor or fight for their lives. They were the ones who were fading fast in front of him. Such patients quickly formed inert piles on the floor of the ER, pushed to the side in the hopes that someone would eventually transport them to the morgue.

No, the patients whom Kadhim focused on were the critical cases who still fought for their lives, who shouted desperately for his help. He tried to save as many as he could, sprinting from one to the next, treating them in beds, on floors and leaning up against walls. Many died nonetheless, some in his hands, some as he carted them to surgery. Bullet wounds and x-rays showed collapsed lungs, pulverized organs, hearts that didn't stand a chance. He was fighting an uphill battle; very few of these patients could be saved, particularly with limited equipment.

Within the first hour, Kadhim learned how to place catheters, NG tubes, angiotubes, endotracheal tubes and basically anything else involving a tube and an orifice, although normally he would not have been trained on such procedures for another two or three years, as an intern. It was what the circumstances required; there was no one else left to do the job. He would repeat these procedures hundreds of times over the next 72 hours, until they became second nature.

When there was time, he arranged the transfer of patients to another ward, making room in the ER for new arrivals. He saw to the patients with less critical injuries, and for each patient he took a quick mental inventory of the damage.

Male, unconscious, multiple bullet wounds to the chest and stomach, possible shrapnel, hemorrhaging fiercely. Blood pressure... non-existent. Heart... Kadhim put his stethoscope to the man's chest, expecting nothing, preparing to move onto the next patient, but there it was, a faint heartbeat. The man was still alive, but he needed an immediate blood transfusion and would be dead by the time they had tested for blood type. Kadhim searched for a vein, knowing the next best thing was to insert an IV of saline, any fluid to raise the blood pressure from its fatal low.

"I can't find a vein!" he shouted desperately to an attending, who was seeing to a patient next to him.

"Check the antecubital vein in the crook of the elbow," the doctor called back.

"Already did! I also checked the great saphenous vein in the upper inside of the thigh—nothing!"

"Extreme blood loss has put him in a state of shock. All of his blood has gone to his brain, heart, lungs, kidneys, and other vital organs. You won't find a vein."

"So what do I do?" Kadhim was bordering on desperation. He considered leaving the man, frightened that others would die unnecessarily because he was wasting time.

The doctor glanced over at him. "What year are you? Sixth year med student? Intern?"

"I'm a fourth year medical student, sir."

"God help us. You just started rounding on patients last year, didn't you? Listen, your patient is probably going to die anyway, and I can't leave my patient or he'll die too. You'll have to follow my instructions to the letter. Can you do that?"

"Yes."

"Good. I'm going to teach you how to do a venous cutdown."

Kadhim had heard of it, an emergency procedure that required severing major veins. He had once watched a Youtube video of it; he hoped that would suffice.

"Grab some silk suture and a mosquito clamp, if you have it. Quickly disinfect the inside of the ankle just above the medial malleolus."

"Okay."

"Now use your blade to make a two centimeter cut horizontally across the ankle. You need to penetrate the skin and subcutaneous tissues, but be careful not to go too deep. We need the vein intact."

Kadhim took a deep breath and made the cut. It was his first surgical procedure, and the attending—who was shouting out instructions as he worked desperately on his own patient—was barely watching.

"Okay, now use your clamps to widen the opening, and once you've located the vein, use the tips of your clamps to draw the vein up through the opening. About two centimeters of vein should be pulled through the flesh and completely exposed."

Kadhim pulled the noodle-like vein out until it was clear of skin and created a small loop. "Okay."

"Now I want you to tie off the distal end of the vein—the end going to the ankle—with the silk suture."

"Done."

"If we had more time you would leave a small portion of the vein intact, but under these circumstances, you'll have to sever it completely to quicken access. Using your blade, I need you to cut all the way through the end of the vein that goes to the heart." He glanced at Kadhim. "Excellent." He returned to his patient and resumed the shouted instructions while Kadhim grabbed the opportunity to do a quick blood draw for testing.

"Okay, now insert a small sterile cannula directly into the open end of the vein, and connect it to the IV. You need to pump fluids as fast as possible." He paused for a while, focusing on his own patient, then turned, sweating, to check on Kadhim.

"Let me see... excellent job for a first time. See how the vein is distended all the way up the leg? That's how you know the fluids are pumping through it. You'd better remember this procedure. You're going to be using it a lot. Now do the same to the other ankle as quickly as you can and send him to surgery."

By noon Kadhim was drenched in sweat and blood. He left the ER to wash up, and as he entered the restroom he saw with dismay that all of the toilets were backed up. A man was just leaving a stall when he noticed Kadhim's look of dread.

"I hope you're not looking for a clean bathroom. I've looked throughout the hospital, and whole sections of plumbing are down. I heard there are still a few wards with functioning facilities, but I haven't found them yet."

What could he do? Getting a plumber in the midst of the war was out of the question. In the hall, a doctor and volunteer passed by with trays filled with enough food and drink to feed dozens, and Kadhim realized he was starving. The volunteer saw him eyeing the tray and answered his unspoken question in broken English.

"The patient cafeteria is no more food. We take this from doctors' cafeteria, we give to patients." She offered him a sandwich. "You are hungry?"

Kadhim accepted gratefully as the doctor raised an eyebrow.

"Enjoy it while you can. That's about all that's left. Looks like admin stockpiled food for the doctors but didn't think to do the same for the patients. Maybe they didn't realize that we would have such a large volume."

Soon, Kadhim himself was distributing small meals from the doctors' cafeteria as he checked on post-operative patients. They were so low on food that to a patient who needed blood infusions and high caloric intake to regain strength, Kadhim would hand a small milk box. He wondered if there was more stored somewhere, but there was no one to ask. The cafeteria workers and administrative staff were gone, and the few doctors who remained had no idea themselves. They could either feed the patients and let the doctors starve, or vice versa. The doctors barely had the time to eat as it was, so they did their best to share what they had. There wasn't much more to give.

Hours flew by like minutes under the heavy rush of trauma patients. There were a million urgent tasks that all needed to be done at once and only three or four doctors available in the ER at any given time, approximately one doctor to every 75 patients. Their workload was further quadrupled by the lack of auxiliary staff for the small but necessary details. The foreign volunteers helped by exchanging dirty linens with clean sheets and scrubs, but the few remaining doctors did not just treat patients. They replaced bed sheets, changed IV bags, and desperately mopped blood off the floor in the midst of the madness.

Kadhim was delivering a patient for emergency surgery to the cardiothoracic ward on the seventh floor when he heard a shout.

"Hey! You!..." A surgeon peeked his head out of one of the operating rooms. "I've been alone up here for the past five or six hours. Scrub in, would you? I need some help!"

Kadhim quickly joined the operation. The surgeon was repairing damage to the kidneys, spleen, and rib cage where an American bullet had passed through.

"I can't tell you what a relief it is to have some help. Will you direct that light so that it shines directly on the spleen? Now get your hand in there and push aside the intestines so that I have some room to work. Perfect."

Kadhim recognized him as Dr. Abdulqasim, cardiothoracic surgeon. He had been alone in the OR for hours on end, performing surgeries as quickly as his hands would allow. Dr. Abdulqasim was considered one of the best, not just for his skill, but because of the way he put everything he had into surgery. His relentless passion for the profession was inspiring. It was apparent, however, that a day and a half of non-stop surgeries was taking its toll. Black bags had begun to form under his eyes, his cap was soaked, and rivulets of sweat ran down his face and neck.

When they were finished, the surgeon turned to Kadhim. "Can you close for me? I need to sit down. Oh, and when you're finished, get me a bite to eat and some coffee, would you? I haven't eaten since three o'clock this morning and I'm famished."

"I'm afraid we're running out of food, sir," Kadhim said as he began to close the incision. He saw exhaustion turn to alarm in the doctor's eyes. "But I'll try to find something for you."

"Thanks. I'm afraid I'm going to run out of energy soon. Surgery was never meant to be a one-man job." Even as he sat, Dr. Abdulqasim's legs were trembling. "By the way, I need you to pass a message to the ER when you get back down there. Our supply of general anesthesia is almost completely depleted. Any remaining anesthetic will be used for surgeries on vital organs only. Before sending patients to the OR, ask them if they are willing to undergo surgery without anesthesia. If they're not, don't fill up my ward with them. Just get them out of the way to die in peace and send me the ones that are ready."

The exhaustion in his voice and his bloodshot eyes underscored the severity of his message. "Oh, and watch your use of local anesthesia—we're nearly out of that too."

Kadhim grabbed an empty gurney to take back to the ER, but not before stopping to glance out the window. The sight from the seventh floor of Baghdad Teaching Hospital was stunning. The setting sun cast a red glow over the city, making snaky reflections in the Tigris River and playing with the swaying silhouettes of palm trees. Meanwhile, American armored vehicles advanced through the streets of Baghdad, as Iraqi soldiers, *fidayee* Saddam, and others fled before them like action figures. They ran into houses, jumped into rivers, hiding wherever they could. He watched as several dropped motionless in the streets. The Americans continued until they had nearly reached the hospital, and then, just across the bridge from Saddam Medical City, they stopped. Night was about to fall, and they would go no farther.

The ER had become even more chaotic by the time Kadhim returned. It was filled with patients, dead bodies, family members and, when they could squeeze their way through the throng, a few medical staff. A cacophony of shouting, screaming, and crying made it difficult to concentrate. Kadhim found some juice and gave it to one of the foreign volunteers to pass along to Dr. Abdulqasim. It was the last bit of hospital food he would see. One after another, all of tens of cafeterias throughout Saddam Medical City had been stripped clean of food and drink.

Meanwhile, Kadhim cleaned wounds, cut away dead tissue, and stitched gashes, at times holding the patients down as they cursed him and cried out in pain. Where 5 milliliters of local anesthetic was standard, he used 1 ml. When his supplies diminished even more, he dropped down to half a milliliter, then to no local anesthetic at all. He apologized to patients and asked the same blunt question of them all: "Can you handle surgery without anesthesia or can't you?"

He was about to check a patient with a bullet to the leg when an odd flash of color in the crowd caught his eye.

The chai-chi?

Kadhim couldn't remember the boy's name, but he recognized him instantly. It was the boy who dressed in traditional Arabic garb and carried an enormous teapot on his back, selling tea for a few cents a cup outside the hospital.

"What are you doing here?" Kadhim called out to him over the crowd. "Are you hurt?"

"No, I'm fine, praise be to God," the chai-chi shouted back. "There's just too much violence outside. If I stayed out there, I'd either be shot or hit by a flying air conditioner. Please, don't let me interrupt your work."

"Do you have any tea left?" Kadhim shouted up to him, as he kneeled to check a patient in the midst of the melee.

"Just a little." The boy was already pouring him a cup.

"Thank you." Kadhim drained his lukewarm dinner gratefully, then stopped. "Wait—what do you mean you might get hit by a flying air conditioner?"

"The looters, doctor. They're here."

From a window at the back of the hospital, Kadhim watched in equal parts amazement and disgust as looters swarmed the Ministry of Health like flies over a carcass. They were people of all social classes, wearing pajamas, Iraqi Army fatigues, and dress-shirts. They ran from the building carrying everything from office furniture and pipes to porcelain toilets, which were later dumped in the streets when they realized they had no use for them. It didn't matter what they took; they had been infected with a need to steal.

"There goes my money."

Kadhim jumped. Another doctor had also been watching beside him.

"What do you mean?"

"The Ministry of Health holds millions of Iraqi dinars in cash; that's where we receive our pay. Now it's gone."

Paychecks and online banking were unheard of; the entire medical city received their wages directly in cash. Any cash the looters did not find that night was destroyed when they burned the Ministry of Health to the ground, along with seven or eight other ministries looted and burned that night. Having stripped Saddam's palaces of every last item, valuable or otherwise, looters had moved to the ministerial buildings. Then, noticing that the Americans did nothing to stop them, they came for the hospitals.

It was a sight that Kadhim would never have believed if he had not seen it with his own eyes. As he peered out of the ER window, his jaw dropped. Undisturbed by the Americans across the bridge, looters found deserted clinics and empty wards, and stripped them of TVs, desks, chairs, medical equipment, and even, as the chai-chi had said, enormous AC units, so heavy that a single man couldn't carry one by himself. Three men would tear it from the wall and drop it out a window into shopping carts. In front of the window, one man, sweating and red-faced, tried to push a cart laden with three AC units. Realizing that the cart would not budge, he pushed one of the units out with extraordinary effort, letting it shatter on the ground.

Armed looters stole heart monitors, thinking that they were TVs, then broke them in the streets when they realized that they "didn't work." They stole a gamma knife from the hospital of neurology, a machine costing hundreds of thousands of dollars, which they later resold on the black market for $20, having no idea what it was. The hospital hunted it down and bought it back. These people were destroying their own hospitals and clinics in a craze of looting. *How could they do this? And why didn't the Americans stop them?*

The few remaining medical staff were unarmed; there would be nothing they could do to stop the looters when they came for the emergency room itself.

THE INTERPRETER

"There's something going on at Adal Square." Uncle Ehab shut the door behind him, looking decidedly relieved to be home.

"What is it?" Mohammed's curiosity was instantly piqued.

"The Americans are there, and they're firing shots."

"Why? At who?"

"I don't know. It looked like they were firing into the air. I couldn't really understand them, so I got out of there as quickly as I could." Uncle Ehab sat down and reached for a snack, then glanced up to see Mohammed pulling on a shirt and heading for the door. "Hey! Where are you going?"

"I want to see what's going on."

"Are you crazy? I just told you they're shooting…!" Uncle Ehab's voice disappeared as Mohammed shut the door behind him.

Mohammed was not the kind of person to sit at home and wait as the world passed him by, and the past several weeks of being shut in the house like a caged bird had driven him crazy. With a twinge of jealousy, he thought of Kadhim, who had been at the hospital for nearly two weeks now. They hadn't heard from him except for the odd thirty-second phone call, but Mohammed was sure that his brother was having the time of his life.

If there was something going on, Mohammed wanted to be there. If there was a battle, he wanted to see it, maybe even participate. Young, strong, and confident in his ability to take care of himself, Mohammed walked the short distance from his house to Adal Square, armed only with his curiosity, to see what the Americans wanted.

Adal Square was a major intersection that connected several large neighborhoods. Despite a lull at the beginning of the war, its busy streets had, by necessity, returned to their former life, as the people's homes had run out of food, drink, and other basic needs. At the head of the street sat Ahmed Chalabi's flour factory, and it was there that the Americans had stationed themselves, one of many units stationed throughout the city.

Mohammed walked right up to them, even as they fired a few shots into the air. Other Iraqis approached the Americans as well, curious about the stranger's presence so close to their homes. Those who could speak English exchanged a few words with the Americans, answered the

Americans' questions to the best of their ability, and went on their way.

"Hello." Even in the midst of a war, basic manners required a civil greeting.

The soldier looked at him cautiously.

"Hi."

"Why are you shooting?"

"Look around you. Hundreds of people are walking toward us. We're just trying to get them to back off." The soldier seemed relieved to find someone who spoke English.

Mohammed looked at the pedestrians and laughed.

"These people aren't walking toward you. You're sitting at a major intersection, and they're just walking past to do their business. Look at them—they're unarmed civilians. If they wanted to fight you, they'd fight you. The buses and taxis aren't running, so if they need anything, they have to walk. They come in peace—all of them."

The soldier looked around and lowered his gun slightly. The commander of the unit had joined them and was listening closely.

"These people see something strange and want to check it out," Mohammed continued, "so they're coming up to ask you questions and see what you're doing, but they're not trying to harm you."

"Well, we don't have an interpreter and we didn't have any way of communicating with them," the commander replied. "What do you think of interpreting for us... fulltime?"

Mohammed hesitated for a moment, as the possible implications of working with the American forces swirled through his mind. Excitement, strange people, danger, action... he felt himself instinctively drawn to the job. But it was not a decision to be made lightly, and certainly not without first discussing it with Baba.

"I'll think about it," he said.

A few days later, with his parents' reluctant consent, Mohammed made his way to the rich area that housed Saddam's palaces, and which was now being called the International Zone, or IZ, by those who occupied it. It would soon be nicknamed the Green Zone.

The checkpoint was no more than a few thin wires stretched across the road. After taking his I.D., the Americans let Mohammed through, and he was hired by KBR, a large US construction company, to act as an interpreter and security detail for the KBR headquarters, where he would check badges at night.

He was one of the very first local contractors hired by KBR to work with the Coalition Forces, and it began as a way to get out of the house, meet some new people, and maybe have some fun.

What it would turn into, however, was a whirlwind of sex, danger, betrayal, mistrust, life-threatening chaos and eventually a life that even Mohammed had never dreamed of.

PANDEMONIUM

"Look at me! Can you handle the surgery without anesthesia?"

Kadhim was shouting over the din, trying to get a response from the patient. It was useless; the man was in complete shock. A bullet had ripped through his calf and shattered his tibia, part of which was now protruding through his skin. Another bullet had torn through muscle on the meaty interior of his thigh. The young man sat staring at his wounds, uncomprehending, as Kadhim did his best to clean and dress them. He needed surgery to tag and close arteries, stitch up muscle, and address the break and fracturing in the bone, but there would be no general anesthesia. At best, there might a bit of local anesthetic, but at this stage it would do little good.

Despite the tourniquet, his thigh and lower limb were bleeding profusely, and Kadhim suspected that major veins or arteries had been severed. "Listen to me! If you don't go into surgery soon, you could die of blood loss! Can you do it without anesthesia, or can't you? Nod if you understand what I'm saying!"

There was no response. Frustrated, Kadhim moved the patient to the side and went on to the next. Perhaps the man would recover from his shock and change his mind before it was too late. Already, many had turned away potentially life-saving surgeries with fear and desperation in their eyes as they contemplated whether to choose torturous agony or death.

"I can't," one of the patients had told him. "I'll wait. Maybe you'll get more anesthesia, or maybe someone will take me to another hospital." An hour later, the man was still waiting where Kadhim had left him, cold and lifeless on the floor.

There were those who consented to surgery without anesthetia in order to save their lives, and Kadhim pitied them as well. Many passed out from the agony, only to be reawakened by it. Others simply died from pain. The doctors did their best with what they had on hand, and they sent volunteers to break the windows of pharmacies, scouring them for medications and all types of painkillers.

The next patient, with a bullet wound through her upper back, was willing to try surgery. Kadhim took her up to the seventh floor, where he assisted in a surgery, checked on post-op patients, and was about to return to the ER when the doctor shouted out to him, "Look out the window! The acting Head of the Hospital is going to ask for the Americans' help!"

The sun had set, but a faint rim of light still made the scene visible. The actual Head of the Hospital was a high-ranking Ba'athi and had fled when the war began. The man who now stood in for him had watched as the hospital fell into pandemonium. He was even more alarmed to see looters stripping Saddam Medical City of expensive and vital equipment. When the Americans had done nothing to stop them, the acting head had decided to take matters into his own hands.

As Kadhim watched from high up in the hospital, the man drove through the looters and across the bridge to the American armored vehicles. He stepped out of the car cautiously, waving a white flag. The Americans fired warning shots into the air, but the Head braced himself, waved his flag, and held up his hands to show them that he was unarmed.

When at last they allowed him to approach, Kadhim knew the conversation without hearing it. *The hospital's situation was dire. Just protect it from the looting. That's all he asked.* At his request, the Americans drove their armored vehicles across the bridge and prevented looters from entering the hospital until early the next morning.

"Does anyone speak English here?"

At first, Kadhim did not notice the American who entered the hospital around midnight. His voice was lost in the din of the ER, and one patient in particular had been screaming nonstop, scaring other patients, annoying the doctors, and giving everyone a splitting headache.

"Anyone speak English?" His American accent was out of place in the Iraqi ER, but his height, huge build, and marine uniform made him stand out even more.

"I speak English," Kadhim volunteered. "How can I help you?"

"I'm a Marine Staff Sergeant, and the head of your hospital requested our assistance in protecting the medical complex from looters."

"Yes, I realize that. Thank you for your help."

"The thing is, we need somewhere to sleep. We've set up sleeping stations outside our humvees on the banks of the Tigris River, but it isn't safe. We saw a place over there that looks perfect." He pointed to the building containing the Saddam Medical Conference Center. "But we didn't want to break any windows. Would you mind asking someone in charge if they could open the doors for us?"

Kadhim was ready to go ask the Head of the Hospital, but the sergeant rushed on, as if afraid that Kadhim would refuse his request.

"It's your Head of Hospital that invited us to come, by the way.

We're protecting the hospital, and we came to help you guys. We came to liberate Iraq."

Kadhim was amused. "Yes, of course. I'll go talk to him."

He hurried out of the ER, relieved to leave the ear-splitting screamer behind. His shoes squeaked with blood as he rushed through the hallways to reach the Head's office. He found him in a worried conference with another doctor.

"Sorry for the interruption, Doctor, but I have a couple requests."

"What is it, son?"

"I have a screamer down in the ER; I need to find him some painkiller."

"You know that we're nearly out. We can't just give it to him for being loud."

"Well, he's really in pain, sir. But worse, he's driving us all crazy. Please, we can't concentrate down there!"

"Alright, give him this." The Head unlocked a tiny cabinet and pulled a syringe of morphine from a dwindling supply.

"And the second thing, sir. The Americans need a place to sleep, and they would like to use the conference center."

"Let them sleep."

"They want the key."

"There is no key. Let them break the windows and enter." He waved Kadhim away; he had more than enough insane problems as it was.

That night, the marines respectfully broke and entered their way into the richly decorated conference center. Meanwhile, the screamer, having been dosed with morphine, calmed down at last. It was difficult to say who was more relieved; the marines, the screamer, or the hundreds who were trying to soothe their splitting headaches.

It occurred to Kadhim, as he worked without sleep, food, functioning toilets or anesthetics, that he may have made a mistake in coming to volunteer at the hospital. It was too late. There was no way to leave. There were no taxis to be found, and many of the staff who had fled that day in their cars returned to the hospital shortly thereafter in body bags. He was stuck.

April 9, 2003. It was light out before Kadhim realized that he had worked through the night. Many more doctors and nurses had disappeared, and Kadhim wondered how many of them had survived their escape. The remaining hospital staff was now but a few scattered bones, buried alive under a swarming mass of patients.

Blood covered the ER floor, not in spots or puddles, but in one solid sheet, from wall to wall, soaking through tennis shoes and socks to the point that when Kadhim walked to another ward, his toes squished through the blood and left a trail of crimson footprints. Desperately, he and the few remaining doctors and volunteers made futile attempts to mop away the blood of over four hundred patients.

The Americans who had protected the hospital from looters had left to continue their overthrow of Baghdad, with the exception of a mobile unit that stayed behind as one of many stations to secure the city. Two American marines stationed by the hospital doors were showing pictures of their girlfriends to the Iraqis, who considered it hilariously odd. In Iraq, the privacy and respect of one's daughters, sisters, mothers, fiancées, and wives were considered paramount to and representative of the honor of their men and their entire family. In an effort to protect his honor and theirs, an Iraqi man would not dream of showing their pictures to another male. The Americans, on the other hand, showed off pictures of their girlfriends as if they were movie stars. Who were these people who did not seem to care about their honor or respect their women? Without a solid concept for "girlfriend," the Iraqis assumed the pictures to be of fiancées or wives, or possibly prostitutes. The Americans' actions were so shocking that they became a source of hilarity. "Look at this guy!" They would say to each other in laughter. "He keeps showing off pictures of his fiancée!"

However, even the American presence could not prevent the looters that day. They had discovered an even bigger prize. Hundreds of brand new, top-of-the-line cars had been purchased by the regime and secretly stored in hidden garages below the hospital. They were Toyota Cedrics and Land Cruisers, and the cheapest one among them could not have been worth less than $70,000. Without keys, the thieves hotwired the cars or stripped them down and carried away the parts. Looters arrived en masse, armed with AK-47s and revolvers, and drove away with millions of dollars worth of vehicles.

"Move aside! Make way!" More American voices cut through the Arabic shouts in the hospital. Kadhim looked up to see two American medics carrying in an injured marine, and he ran over.

"What's going on?"

"He's been shot by a looter," someone answered.

The marine had taken a bullet to the neck, and it was clear that the injury was critical. Dr. Abdulqasim came quickly and offered his help, but the American medics waved him away and kept working. Kadhim felt the smart of insult. *What could these two young medics do compared to an expert cardiothoracic surgeon with decades of experience? Was that how little regard they had for Iraqi medicine, or how little they trusted an Iraqi doctor, that they would rather their colleague die?* Perhaps, he realized slowly, this is just the way of war.

They respected the Americans' decision and let them work. Eventually, the medics called time of death and zipped up the body bag.

The Marines had lost one of their own, and they were furious. They went back out with a vengeance, and within an hour, looters riddled with American bullets flooded the ER. Kadhim overheard a second-year resident berating them.

"See? This is what you get when you loot! Now you might die of blood loss all because you were trying to steal a car! Was it really worth it?"

The thief, it appeared, was in too much pain to answer.

However, it was not only injured looters who flooded the ER. Saddened to have missed out on car theft and ministry looting, uninjured looters also showed up in the ER in droves, desperate to steal anything they could find, regardless of whether they could obtain any money or use from it. Kadhim watched in disbelief as entire armed families appeared: uncle, father, son, and child! Nine-year-old boys were running around the ER, instructed to steal anything they could find. Half of the adults were barefoot, in too much of a hurry to steal something, *anything*, before it was all gone. They had not even bothered to put on shoes before they ran out of the house. They stole medications, IV bags, stands that held the IV bags, and heart monitors; anything and everything was fair game.

Kadhim watched in desperation, yelling at them as he inserted a chest tube into a struggling patient. *Damn this lack of anesthetic!* A pimply teenager with an AK-47 attempted to take his IV bag.

"Hey, I need that! Leave it alone!" Kadhim screamed, pulling the bag from his hands.

The boy dropped it immediately. He did not even appear to notice Kadhim, his eyes glazed over in a fever of looting. *Steal. Steal. Steal.* He raced to a cabinet and started pulling open the drawers one by one and stuffing gauze, disinfectants, empty needles, IV tubing and gloves into his pockets.

"Stop it!" Kadhim screamed. "How can you do this? How would I be able to treat you if you were shot by the Americans?"

"Maybe we'd go to a different hospital," growled a voice, and Kadhim turned to see another looter, perhaps the boy's father, pointing an AK-47 at him. Helpless, the medical student put up his hands and backed away slowly. The looters continued in a craze, feverish with the sickness of stealing and destruction.

There was nothing a few unarmed doctors could do against hundreds of armed looters. The ER, still full from yesterday's patients, had now bulged to accommodate over four hundred patients, despite a maximum capacity of 200. This meant one medical professional for every hundred patients. They could not possibly fight the looters as well. Their patients were everywhere, between beds, on floors, and blocking walkways. The pool of blood that had flooded the floor slowed everyone down as they tried not to slip. Lack of food formed a thick knot of hunger in Kadhim's stomach, and he thought achingly of the feast his mother had prepared for him two weeks ago. How ironic that he had laughed it away as unnecessary.

In the midst of the madness, Kadhim noticed people shouting at something on TV. He looked up to read the news line.

Baghdad has fallen. Saddam Hussein and the Ba'ath regime have been toppled. A scene of Iraqis pulling down Saddam's statue played again and again.

This was it, the end of the regime. The end of an era. Kadhim felt too overwhelmed to take it all in. *This* was the true shock and awe. After some thirty years of silenced tongues, oppression, and torture, after the slaughter of hundreds of thousands, the dictatorship had finally been toppled. He had abhorred the regime, but it was the only life he had ever known, and Kadhim was stunned. He stopped for a moment, unable to move, and slowly, he felt an immense gratitude bubbling up from deep within.

The Americans have indeed liberated us. For the first time in my life, I will know true freedom.

He couldn't believe it. He wanted to laugh for joy, or cry. He wanted to thank Allah for the opportunity that Iraq had at last been given. *It's over. It's all over. We are free.*

April 10, 2003. Officially, there was still neither food nor anesthesia. The medical staff had been working nearly nonstop for days. When they could work no more, they passed out in empty exam rooms upstairs, or fell asleep accidentally against a window. When they had gone nearly two days without food, hunger forced the doctors and staff to turn to the patients' families for help.

It was humiliating for a doctor to beg for food, but it had to be done. Family members would not return home for food, but many shared what they had. By mid-morning on the 10th, after nearly 44 hours without eating, Kadhim gratefully received a cup of tea and some bread, disbursed by the chai-chi, who had now taken to helping out around the hospital with the foreign volunteers.

The head doctors had decided that the only way to address the lack of anesthesia was to raid closed medical facilities. They sent runners, who broke into smaller hospitals, clinics, and pharmacies and stole all the supplies they could find, but the brief surge of supplies always ran out quickly. The question, "Can you handle surgery without anesthesia?" was repeated endlessly. Bodies lay in piles around the hospital.

The waves of patients shifted from gunshot wounds, Iraqi soldiers, and looters, to patients transferred from other hospitals that had reached maximum capacity and to victims of acts of revenge.

Realizing that the regime was no longer in place to protect its minions, Iraqis with years of repressed rage at last released their fury on high-up Ba'athis who for decades had spied on them, tortured them, and ordered the deaths of their loved ones. Some of the worst finally got what was coming to them. Kadhim, however, thought of the *mukhtar* who had saved his brother's life only a few months ago, and worried what might become of him.

April 11, 2003. The Shiite sheikh, his beard graying and crows-feet around his eyes, watched the doctors as he patiently awaited their response. He was the figurehead of both a small local mosque and a small local gang, and when news of the hospital's shortages reached him, he had decided to reach out. This was the closest hospital to his neighborhood, which stood to directly benefit from its being fully equipped, but he had also felt a sense of responsibility. Once the fighting had died down and the Americans were no longer shooting in the streets, the right thing to do was to help.

It was late in the evening before the religious figure and his gang made their way to the hospital, where he met with the Head and some of the senior physicians.

"You need anesthesia, food, and beds," the sheikh stated simply. The doctors nodded in exhaustion. They had reached the end of their strength and were ready to leave the hospital, patients or not.

"I think I can help," the sheikh continued. "I have access to several large trucks for hauling goods and furniture. With your consent, my men will break into all the hospitals that shut their doors during the war and bring back needed supplies. It's not fair that they refuse their services and save their supplies while you take the brunt of the war's victims. It's time they made their contribution as well. I'm not looking for any type of compensation. You all have done so much for the community already, may Allah give you vitality and good health."

The doctors listened with gratitude. They suspected that the sheikh's gang would also be taking other items that they deemed useful, a type of tax for their Robin Hood venture. However, they needed the equipment desperately, so necessity made their decision for them.

"You have our consent and our appreciation," said the Head of the Hospital. "The doctors will write up a specific list of needs, but the main ones are those that you already mentioned: food, anesthesia, and beds. Go, but be careful."

That evening, cardiothoracic surgeon Dr. Abdulqasim decided at last that it was time to leave. Kadhim saw him as he was about to exit and was shocked by his appearance. Day after day of energy-draining surgery seemed to have added ten years to his age. His previously clean-shaven face was bearded, his eyes bloodshot and lined with deep black bags. Even his drooped posture and slow, shuffling gait betrayed his extreme fatigue.

"Are you leaving, Doctor?"

"Yes, I'm going home. I should be back in a couple days, but first I want a hot meal and a week's worth of sleep. I'm beat, uh... my son." He clearly could not remember the student's name, but Kadhim didn't mind. "I couldn't possibly do a single surgery more than I've already done."

Fumbling, he pulled on his jacket, and Kadhim wondered whether he could even drive home without falling asleep behind the wheel.

"You deserve the rest. No one will blame you for leaving."

As they spoke, two men carrying a limp and blood-soaked victim burst through the ER doors.

"Help! Help us, please! He has a bullet wound to the chest but he's still alive!"

Kadhim jumped to respond to their shouts of panic. Judging by the placement of the entry wound, if the bullet had missed the man's heart then it hadn't missed by much. It was clear, however, that the man was still fighting for his life, and to survive he would need emergency surgery.

Dr. Abdulqasim watched in a daze of exhaustion. Stubbornly, he fought the urge to reach out and help the man, wishing he could find the strength to walk around him to the hospital's exit. He was so close.

He hesitated for just a moment longer. Then, breathing out a long sigh of resignation, he pulled off his outer jacket.

"To hell with it. I'm going back to the operating room. Put him on a gurney and bring him up. Now!"

By April 12th, the perfect storm was finally coming to an end. The torrential downpour of trauma patients slowed to a light drizzle. The blood that flooded the ER gradually receded. Even the looters went home, their fever broken. The sheikh kept his word, and over the next several days large trucks brought equipment to the hospital. With taxis and buses up and running, auxiliary staff gradually returned to restock shelves with food, drink, medications, equipment, and toilet paper. A cleaning crew and plumber with lots of work to do were on their way.

After two straight weeks in the hospital, Kadhim finally picked up the phone.

"Hello?"

"Mama?"

"Praise be to Allah! My son! My Kadhim! Thank God you're okay! Where are you? What's going on? Why haven't you called?"

"I'm coming home."

On May 1, 2003, President George W. Bush declared the end of major combat operations in Iraq—the official end of the war. The words of his ultimatum speech still rang in Kadhim's ears.

"Many Iraqis can hear me tonight in a translated radio broadcast, and I have a message for them. If we must begin a military campaign, it will be directed against the lawless men who rule your country and not against you... We will tear down the apparatus of terror and we will help you to build a new Iraq that is prosperous and free. In a free Iraq, there will be no more wars of aggression against your neighbors, no more poison factories, no more executions of dissidents, no more torture chambers and rape rooms. The tyrant will soon be gone. The day of your liberation is near."

BULLET WOUND

"I need to make a quick trip to pick up some more clothes from my house. Just ten minutes, and I'll be back. Want to come?"

It had only been five days since Kadhim had left the hospital, and he was more than content to spend this time relaxing at home, but his uncle wanted company. Mama and Baba's house was still an impromptu hotel for many of their relatives, and although some had left for their own homes, others were still arriving to check on everyone and make sure they were okay. Uncle Ehab had just dropped off two of his sisters after picking up more clothing for them and wanted to make a similar trip for himself, but he hesitated to do it alone.

"All right, I'll come. Let's just make it quick." Kadhim stood and grabbed his wallet and phone.

"Half an hour max. I promise."

The streets of Baghdad had changed. With buses and taxis back up and running, those in private cars no longer felt the need to wave white flags as they drove past American tanks. Nevertheless, the atmosphere was tense. Tanks were stationed at various points throughout the city, temporary checkpoints were being established, and the Coalition Forces were still chasing down the final remnants of *fidayee* Saddam.

They had just left Kadhim's neighborhood in Uncle Ehab's car when the two suddenly heard the rapid fire of a machine gun.

Pop! Pop! Pop! Pop! Pop!

"Get down!" Kadhim shouted, and they both ducked in the car. The shooting had come too quickly for them to know its origin or target, and after a moment of silence, they sat up cautiously.

"I bet it was that American tank behind us." Kadhim looked around carefully. "I think they were shooting in that direction." He pointed ahead.

His uncle looked around, and suddenly clutched at his stomach.

"Ugh—maybe... *what is this?*"

Kadhim glanced over at him, and watched as Uncle Ehab pulled a hand away from his abdomen.

It was covered in blood.

"*Oh shit!* Uncle Ehab, you need to get into the passenger seat. You've been shot."

"What?" Ehab looked down in confusion. His shirt was quickly turning crimson. "I'm bleeding!"

"Yeah, you are! Get in the passenger seat! I'm taking you to the hospital!" Kadhim jumped out and ran around to the driver's side to help his uncle.

"I don't understand how this happened... I didn't even feel anything! Just a sharp pain!"

Within fifteen minutes, Kadhim had driven to Baghdad Medical Complex, the closest hospital. He jumped out and delivered his uncle to the ER, greeting those he'd been working with less than a week before. He tried his best to explain what had happened, but even he couldn't figure it out. There were no bullet holes in any of the car windows.

How the hell had his uncle been shot?

The doctors took one look at Uncle Ehab and rushed him to the operating room. They were back a few hours later.

"His spleen was hit, as was his diaphragm. He's lucky his bowel wasn't ruptured, or he could have suffered even more severe damage." The doctor looked at Uncle Ehab's sleeping form and shook his head in amazement. "We didn't find the bullet, but I can tell you that it passed within an inch of his heart. He's lucky to be alive."

Kadhim stayed with Uncle Ehab in the hospital for two days before other relatives arrived to take over. Uncle Ehab himself was in the hospital for a week before at last being discharged, and rather than go home, he returned to the Al Baghdadi house, where Kadhim, the family's resident medical student, took care of him and dressed his wounds for a month and a half until they healed. The rest of the family was amazed to see his bullet wounds: one in his stomach and one in his back.

"How did this happen?" Mama was incredulous.

"I honestly don't know!" Uncle Ehab rubbed his stomach proudly. "I felt nothing until it was already over!"

"I can tell you."

Everyone turned and looked at Kadhim expectantly.

"While Uncle Ehab was in surgery, I went back out and looked at his car. A single bullet entered through the trunk of the car, passed through the back seat, ripped through the front seat on the driver's side, entered his back, passed through his stomach, and exited through the front of the car near the tire. It went through the entire length of the car without stopping. I've never seen anything like it."

For a moment, they were stunned into silence.

"Wow. What are these weapons the Americans are using?" Mama breathed.

"I was lucky you were with me." Ehab reached up and patted Kadhim's arm.

"Yeah, well, I'll tell you something, Uncle Ehab. Next time you promise me that it'll just be a quick trip—'a half hour max'—I won't be so quick to take your word for it!"

REVENGE

It felt surreal to return to medical school after the outbreak of the war. Nothing was the same. The mandatory Ba'ath meetings and protests? Over. The Ba'athis who had run the school? Gone. Many doctors and professors were missing: from those who had fled, to those who were killed, to those who had been forbidden to return to their posts by the Coalition Provisional Authority (CPA), the temporary government set up and run by the Americans. In an attempt to "de-Ba'athify" Iraqi society, CPA chief executive Paul Bremer had banned anyone with the rank of "comrade" and higher from all governmental posts, effectively relieving tens of thousands — perhaps even one hundred thousand — Iraqis of their jobs.

Unemployment skyrocketed, and basic services suffered. Ministry workers, university professors, doctors, military officials, and many others were affected. There were several distinct levels of "comrade," and only those at the higher level and up had been banned, so fortunately, Baba, being a lower level comrade, was permitted to continue his work as an English teacher. Al Kindy Medical School, however, lost many of its best physicians and lecturers. Most were individuals who had not misused their political power, but had simply risen in the ranks as the only way to advance their careers, and both the university and its students suffered greatly from their absence. As the university scrambled to make up for the loss of faculty and manpower, the students suddenly found under-qualified internal medicine physicians lecturing in surgery. While they still gained knowledge from their textbooks, the exams were no longer written by the stringent surgeons who knew which questions were the toughest. As a way around the de-Ba'athification process, a few doctors who had formerly been department heads were brought back in low positions, while far less qualified individuals became their superiors. Physicians and lecturers in large numbers remained missing.

Even the students changed overnight, and suddenly, almost unbelievably, everyone could at last speak their minds openly for the first time in their lives. Gone was the worn phrase "the great leader Saddam, may Allah keep him safe and raise him high" that had flown automatically from cautious tongues. Now, Kadhim finally saw who was truly loyal to the fallen regime, and who — like he — abhorred it. Those who had been on top, through high rank and strong Ba'athi connections, were suddenly on the bottom, their status and protection lost overnight, scorned and hated by many of the students over whom they had previously lorded.

For Kadhim, the turning of tables was symbolized by the moment he ran into Ala Al-Tikriti. He had not forgotten his classmate's scornful words:

"I don't get why you're so happy, Kadhim. Work as hard as you want; be the top. You're still just going to end up in some shit hospital. Meanwhile I can sit back and relax without learning a thing and I will still be more successful, better paid, and in a higher position than you because I'm Tikriti. And you? You're just a low-life Shiite with no connections... No matter how hard you work, I will always be better than you."

Those insults still burned, and although he knew he should be the bigger person, Kadhim couldn't stop himself from saying, as he passed Ala Al-Tikriti in the hallway, "Remember what you said to me a year ago?"

The look on his classmate's face said it all. Ala remembered exactly what he had said, and his cheeks burned red with shame.

"I'm sorry, Kadhim. I'm so sorry. I was an idiot. I didn't know what I was saying. I didn't know how to talk properly. I was a pompous asshole—Please forgive me."

He continued stammering and apologizing until Kadhim had to ask him to stop. He seemed afraid; perhaps others had punished him for old remarks. Regardless, it was clear to Kadhim that his classmate had already lost everything—his high stature, his secure future, his high income-to-be—within a matter of weeks. That was enough. There was no need to make him feel worse.

Kadhim dropped the matter and walked away, although every time he saw him afterward, Ala apologized. His classmate had entered medical school based on connections, not merit, and did not have the mental stamina to keep up with the heavy workload. He had already failed twice and was now two years behind Kadhim. By the end of the year, he dropped out of medical school entirely, no longer having the high-up connections that had kept him in place. A new system was evolving.

"Did you hear?"

113

"Hear what?"

"About Abu Zaman?"

It was a rare moment alone for Kadhim and Hind, as they made their way to join the others in the clinic.

"What about him?" Come to think of it, Kadhim hadn't seen the former Head of Ba'athi Affairs since returning to school, but as all Ba'athi officials had been banned from their posts, he hadn't thought anything of it.

"He was murdered," Hind said. "I heard that within three days of the start of the war in Baghdad, someone went to his house, knocked on the door, and shot him. Can you believe it? He didn't last *three days* after the fall of the regime!"

"Wow." For a moment, he was silent. "May he rest in peace. I can't believe it. You know, I never thought he was a bad guy. I mean yes he put pressure on us to be loyal to the regime and all that, but he was always true to his word. He must have really crossed someone while Saddam was in power."

"What do you mean crossed someone?" Hind asked. "These Shiite thugs are just out killing Ba'athis for sport. I mean, is it really necessary? Is this why we have to lose some of our top professionals?"

"Why do you assume they're Shiite? You know that acts of murder for revenge don't happen lightly here, Hind. If you kill someone, your entire tribe and their entire tribe get involved, and before you know it, they've agreed that it's *your* head on the chopping block. No, I guarantee that Abu Zaman must have used his power to really ruin someone's life, maybe even take someone's life, and that's why they came after him. People here know the difference between a Ba'athi who was vindictive and evil, and one who just held rank to advance his career but didn't hurt anyone."

At least, I hope they know the difference, he thought to himself.

"Still," she insisted, "these Shiite gangs are going to ruin our country and put a rift between our people if they keep running around and killing innocent people."

"Why do you keep insisting that they're Shiite? Innocent people? Where are you getting this, Hind? How can you call them innocent? Have you forgotten so soon what Saddam and his Ba'athis did to us? All the innocent people they captured, tortured, raped, and hanged? They cut off tongues, fingers, and other things that I won't mention in front of you. They wrote false reports, *destroying* the lives of their neighbors, just to increase their rank. And you say they're innocent? Do you really think only Shiites suffered at the hands of the Ba'athis? I don't deny that there are Shiites out extracting their revenge right now, but there are a lot of others with them, Hind. Don't blame the Shiites."

She huffed, exasperated that he could contradict her so directly. Kadhim, too, found himself oddly annoyed and even slightly insulted by the conversation. But there was something else gnawing at him. As they joined the other students, he decided that tonight he would finally ask what had happened to the *mukhtar* who had saved his brother's life.

For months, Mohammed had been living out of a duffel bag, finding a new place to sleep every few nights, always worried, always watching his back. He had only returned home on the rare occasion for some of Mama's home-cooked meals and clean laundry. When the war broke out, he had watched in amazement as the regime fell, and despite the enormity of that moment and what it meant for the people and future of Iraq, a tiny part of him felt that Allah had toppled the regime just so that he could at last return home and resume his life.

The tables had turned. Now, it was the Ba'athis who were on the run. It was *fidayee* Saddam who were being hunted down and persecuted, and by the American military no less. What more could he ask for? Mohammed was one of the lucky few on their hit list whom they had not disposed of before losing power, and now, as they tried to save their own skins, their old hit list was meaningless and forgotten.

Mohammed went home.

The dinner table was full, surrounded by Mama, Baba, Ali, Mohammed, Kadhim, Salih, Firas, Uncle Ehab, and Aunt Rita, and the dining room was a loud and exciting place to be. Kadhim was talking about some Ba'athi official at his school that had been killed, but Mohammed paid little attention, deciding instead that this was a prime opportunity to mess with his little brother.

Firas loved this game. Whatever Mohammed did to him, Firas had to do back. Mohammed would rub Firas on the head, and Firas would reach out and rub him back. Mohammed would gently bump him on the ear, and Firas, grinning, would box his ear back. No war could change Firas. He was an eternally loveable, gentle, and innocent soul, and they adored him for it.

Mohammed turned to listen as he heard Kadhim ask about the local *mukhtar*. He, too, wondered what had happened to the man who had helped him.

"I just spoke to someone about that today," Baba answered. "With all these acts of killing and revenge against former Ba'athis, the neighborhood has started to worry. Our neighborhood knows that our *mukhtar* is a good man. He's done nothing to hurt us; in fact, he's often helped us. But would outsiders know that? After all, he's a Sunni in an all-Shiite neighborhood, *and* he's from Tikrit, which could be very dangerous for him now.

"Recently, a group of concerned neighbors went to speak to him. They told him that they didn't want him to come to harm, and that with him being Tikriti, they might not be able to protect him now that the regime has fallen. They told him he should take his family and go somewhere safe. They weren't trying to kick him out, mind you, but they had his best interests at heart."

"What was his response?" Mohammed asked.

"Apparently he doesn't want to leave. He said that this is his home, he's happy here, and he's going to stay put. So they wished him the best and let him be."

"May God bless him," Mama inserted. "I will never forget how he saved my son, and the people have not forgotten his kindness. While others are at last being punished for their evil acts during Saddam's regime, he'll be reaping the rewards of his compassion."

"Well, if he ever needs anything, I'll be there." Mohammed stood up, wiped his mouth, and rubbed Firas's head one last time.

"Where are you going?" Mama looked worried.

"Now that I can go back to school, I'm going to return to my university and take my final exams so that I can finally get my Bachelor's degree."

"Good idea." His father nodded approvingly.

As Mohammed stepped out the door and shut it behind him, he said under his breath, "But first, there's something I have to do."

The sun was setting when Mohammed found himself at the doorstep of Professor Qasim's house. Others had waited years, even decades, before they could extract their revenge; he had only waited a matter of months.

During those months, he had fantasized about this moment, about what he would like to do to the man who had been a close friend and had betrayed him so vastly. He had attended Professor Qasim's wedding, even helped pay for it, and that dog had turned on him, used him, caused him to hide for months from a death squad, all so that he could get a small promotion. To say that Mohammed was angry did not do justice to the feelings of hatred that had built up inside him. He remembered his mother's desperate sobs as she packed his bag, and the anxiety that had plagued him over what would happen to his family should *fidayee* Saddam appear at their door. He brought his gun with him, and he knew he wanted to hurt the man, but the truth was, he didn't know what he might do.

He knocked on the door.

When it opened, Mohammed was taken aback. It was not Professor Qasim, but his wife, red-eyed and pale-faced. Women did not answer the door to men when a male relative was home. It was a man's job to protect his family, and he was the gateway through which male guests would enter. Why was Qasim's wife greeting him?

Instead of peering through a crack in the doorway and explaining that her husband was not at home, as most Iraqi women would have done, the wife slipped outside altogether and shut the door behind her.

"Mohammed," she said, and her voice trembled, "Mohammed, please don't do this." Her voice faltered and suddenly her eyes filled with tears.

"Where is Qasim? Where is he? Let him come out here and meet me like a man." The anger that Mohammed had felt for months, hiding in various cities, fearing for his life, now boiled into a rage. Where was this coward, who sent his wife out to protect him rather than face Mohammed himself? Unconsciously, he reached for his gun.

"Mohammed, please, I'm begging you, please spare him!" The woman fell to her knees, grasping at Mohammed's hands, tears spilling over her cheeks. "Mohammed, I swear I have no one in this world except for God and Qasim."

Her words jarred him. It was true, Mohammed recalled. The woman was an orphan and had no children. Without Qasim, she had no one. Mohammed felt sick, and his heart hurt for her because of what he was about to do to her husband. He had waited for this moment for so long, and now the coward was hiding, too afraid to take responsibility for his own actions.

"Do you know what your husband did to me?"

"Mohammed, please, if you take him I'll have no one left! I'm begging you!" She could scarcely get the words out between her tears. "I won't lie to you and say he's not here. The truth is, he's hiding under the couch. But I'm begging you to have mercy on him, please, for my sake. He's all I have!" She was kissing Mohammed's hand, pleading, tears streaming down her cheeks.

"QASIM!" Mohammed shouted at the top of his lungs. He couldn't look at her anymore. The image of that spineless bastard, hiding beneath a couch, infuriated him.

The neighbors had started to take notice of the scene and quickly deduced what was happening. No one seemed surprised.

"Qasim, get out here! You dog! You coward! Come pay for what you did to me!" Mohammed was screaming at the top of his lungs now. "Come on, Qasim, you pig! You want to have me killed? Well, now it's your turn to run! Get out here! Come outside, you spineless bastard! Come pay for what you did to my family, and to me!"

The wife sobbed even harder and kept up a constant stream of pleas. Mohammed did his best to ignore her. He could have just pushed past her, opened the door, and pulled that coward from underneath the couch where he hid. It would have been so simple. Mohammed was not only taller; he was far stronger than Qasim. Even if he chose not to kill him, he could easily beat him to within an inch of his life. It was the least Qasim deserved for what he had done.

Yet despite his shouted curses and the rage that pulsed through his veins, years of cultural conditioning prevented Mohammed from pushing past Qasim's wife. He could not touch her, much less push her aside to enter the house, no matter how gently. To treat a woman in this way was such an insult, such a taboo, that he could not bring himself to do it. Furthermore, her tears of angst and her insistence that she had no one but Qasim burned at Mohammed's heart. How could he take away the only family she had? How could he make this woman an orphan for the second time in her life?

Qasim never came to the door. He would never live up to what he had done.

Heart pounding, Mohammed at last tore himself away from the wife's grip and left.

Mohammed heard many years later that Professor Qasim had eventually returned to teaching, this time in a university in Mosul.

A few of Mohammed's friends came to him. "Just tell us where he works, and we'll take care of him. We'll start by getting him fired, at the very least."

"Whatever," Mohammed replied. "Let him be. Allah will bring his punishment."

It was over. If he could not exact his revenge that day at Professor Qasim's house, then he never would. Let Qasim get away with it, the dog. If Mohammed had actually died at the hands of the *fidayeen*, his family—his tribe—would have come for Qasim and settled his debt. So in the end, it was the war that saved them both.

The *mukhtar*, on the other hand, continued to live in his neighborhood, year after year, without ever coming to harm.

PAIN IN THE POSTERIOR

It was hot. Miserable, pants-stick-to-your-legs, can't-breathe hot.

The massive air conditioning units spread liberally throughout Baghdad were of little use without electricity, and Kadhim found himself longing for the days when Saddam's regime used to redistribute electricity from southern Iraq to the capital. During the cooler months, when Baghdad's AC units were used sparingly, there were often twelve luxurious hours of electricity per day. Now, under the Coalition Provisional Authority and in the heat of summer, the enormous burden on infrastructure resulted in a mere four to six hours of electricity, which was why Kadhim found himself—as usual—studying by oil lamp, while beads of sweat ran down his forehead and textbook pages grew damp from his sweaty fingers.

He shut his textbook with a resolute thud. This break, between his fourth and fifth year, would be his last before graduating at the end of six years, and he needed to take advantage of it.

It was time for a road trip.

If the Iraqi youth had a spring break, then Kurdistan was their hot spot. Only three to four hours away, it boasted green landscapes, mountains, rivers, waterfalls, canyons, and a more open society where the 21 and 22-year old boys could revel in drunkenness and debauchery without the judgmental glares of Arab society.

Kadhim, Malik, Mahjoub, and Farouq had all squeezed into Kadhim's car, and by evening they were dropping off their duffle bags in a small grungy hotel and heading for dinner at Sarchanar Restaurant in Sulaymaniyah. Their table was soon spread with a veritable feast of lamb, beef, and chicken kabaabs, rice, a buffet of appetizers, and stacks of freshly baked round bread, which the boys used as utensils. The imported beers such as Bud Light, Amstel, and Heineken were too expensive for his student budget, so Kadhim drank a local beer from Baashiqa, which at 3,000 Iraqi dinars cost him a mere $2. The beer was absolute crap, but it was the taste of freedom from responsibility that attracted him. Mahjoub preferred a much stiffer alcohol and was sipping

dancers took a sharp knife in each hand and incorporated them into their routine. Another shook her thighs and rump with increasing and incredible speed, gradually leaning further and further backwards until she was belly-up and her long hair swept the ground. Then all three spun their necks in unison until three feet of hair whirled around each of them. Excited men jumped up and began showering the women with money, which was quickly and discreetly gathered by the women's male relative.

It was past midnight before they at last left the restaurant, still high from the excitement of the party, and they drunkenly debated their next move as they walked the darks streets of Sulaymaniyah.

"I still think we should go back to the hotel, get some sleep, and get up early tomorrow morning so that we can visit Al Askari Mosque," insisted Farouq for the hundredth time.

"Are you kidding?" Mahjoub groaned. "It's still early! We're not old and decrepit yet. Let's enjoy ourselves!"

"I'm in the mood for falafel." Malik rubbed his rotund belly. "I'm feeling a bit faint."

"How could you want falafel after mixing hookah, beer, and *araq*, Malik?"

Some lights caught Kadhim's attention from the corner of his eye, and as he examined their source, an idea came to him. "Hey, guys..." he said with a gleam in his eye, "when was the last time we crashed a wedding?"

"Let's do it!"

"I bet they have ekshellent food!"

"No. No way."

All three turned in exasperation to the fourth member of their group, the squeaky wheel. Farouq had stopped walking and had crossed his arms in front of his chest.

"There is *no* way I'm doing that again. Do you know how *boring* it is to attend the wedding of people you don't know?"

"But that's the best part!"

"Yeah! Whatsh your problem, Farouqy?" Malik stumbled a bit and sat down next to a fountain.

"You're going to have a blast, dude. Just lighten up. You'll scare off all the girls with that scowl of yours."

They convinced an unwilling Farouq to go with them and were soon met with a hearty welcome and heaping plates of food and drink, a full display of Kurdish hospitality. They made friends with guests, danced wildly, marveled at the bride's thick coat of makeup, and tried to talk to as many beautiful girls as they could. It was a stunning wedding, under open starry skies and surrounded by mountains, and the Kurds proved once again that they knew how to have a good time.

It was four o'clock in the morning when they finally left, and the wedding festivities were just starting to wind down. Tired, full, and deliciously happy, they made their way to the hotel. They could not have enjoyed themselves more.

Except for Farouq.

"Well, I'm glad *that's* finally over with."

"*What?*"

"It was dull, the girls were ugly, the dancing was slow and the food was terrible."

"You have *got* to be kidding, Farouq!" Mahjoub rolled his eyes. "If tonight didn't please you, then nothing will."

"Tomorrow we should make a trip to Al Askari Mosque."

"We already planned on hiking," Kadhim replied.

"In that case, I'm not going."

"What do you mean you're not going?"

"I mean I'm not going. I've put up with you guys all night. We went to a terrible restaurant with cold food, saw some awful dancers, and I had to watch you guys get drunk. Enough. Either we go to the hotel and get some sleep so that we can go to the shrine tomorrow, or I'm leaving."

"*You've* been putting up with *us?*" Mahjoub's voice rose several pitches. "*We're* the ones who have had to put up with your complaining all night! No one forced you to come on this trip with us, Farouq!"

"Look, all three of us want to go hiking tomorrow, and you're the only one who wants to go to the mosque," Kadhim said. "Why don't you just come with us?"

"Yeah, Farouqy, come with ush!" Malik wheedled.

"No! I'm sick of this! Either we go to the mosque tomorrow, or I'm leaving!"

"Yeah? And where are you going to go?"

"I'll go to Baghdad, if I have to."

A cab sped past, and Mahjoub and Kadhim shared a look.

"You know, that's actually a pretty good idea," Mahjoub said slyly.

"Huh?" Farouq turned around in surprise as he watched his friend hail a cab.

"Yeah. Maybe you *should* go to Baghdad," Kadhim said.

"I—"

"Come on now, Farouq. You keep saying that we either have to skip the hiking or you're going back to Baghdad. Well, it's time to go back to Baghdad, buddy!" Kadhim grabbed his protesting friend's arm and started wrestling him toward the taxi.

124

"What? Wait—no, I didn't mean—" Farouq suddenly found his friends manhandling him into the cab. His face turned red with anger. "You're not seriously sending me back to Baghdad in the middle of the night, are you?"

"Well, you won't stop complaining!"

"Yeah, we've had enough!"

"Wait a minute—you want me to take him to *Baghdad*?" The driver interrupted.

"Yup—don't stop till you get there!"

"But it's four o'clock in the morning!"

"Don't worry," Mahjoub replied. "Farouq here will tip you extra."

"You guys aren't even going to pay for it?" Farouq looked at them in shock.

"No, I think you've got it covered."

"That's it! I can't believe you're doing this to me! I'm never hanging out with you guys again!" Farouq shouted.

Unperturbed, Mahjoub turned to the driver. "The faster you get there, the less complaining you'll have to listen to."

The taxi sped away, and within an hour a text message beeped angrily on Kadhim's phone.

"He says that we're bastards, and by the way, there's not enough padding on the seat and his butt is killing him."

Mahjoub just laughed. "That's what he gets for being a pain in the ass!"

THE HEART OF A SAINT

Mohammed was at a checkpoint, not on duty, but watching incomers and hitting on female soldiers to pass the time. He had found the checkpoints—the gateways into the IZ—to be prime real estate for picking up girls who, despite their teasing, flocked to the tall Iraqi like bees to honey.

"You're such a pimp," one girl joked. "Every time I see you, you're with a new girl. Maybe *that* should be your nickname."

Mohammed laughed. All the interpreters were given nicknames to protect their real identities from insurgents. Too many interpreters had already been killed for working with the Americans, and their families threatened, tortured, or killed along with them. Precautions had to be taken. Mohammed still hadn't settled on a permanent nickname, and the Americans usually liked to choose the names themselves.

"No, not pimp," another girl interjected. "How about 'Womanizer'?"

"No, you can't have a nickname like that," said a girl with long blond hair. "How about 'Saint'? You know, because you're like a young Val Kilmer. You're tall and sexy and you're all about action and danger and excitement, except that you keep getting distracted by girls."

"Well then, wouldn't '007' be a better nickname?" the first girl retorted.

The debate continued and Mohammed was basking in the attention when he noticed a small child approaching on foot with his mother. What struck him was that the two of them came alone.

The checkpoints leading into the Green Zone had become prime locations for terrorists—Sunni and Shiite alike—to pick off, kidnap, and kill those who they suspected were dealing with the Americans. Contractors, interpreters, even newly released prisoners feared walking outside the gates, where they felt the eyes of the Red Zone watching them. The taxi driver who pulled up and offered a ride; was he planning to kidnap them and sell them to terrorists? It happened frequently. The man standing outside the clothing booth texting on his cell phone; was he taking pictures of them and sending them to a militia? Justified paranoia weighed on the steps of every Iraqi who entered and exited those fateful gates, and Checkpoint One was the first, the largest, and the most well-known gate of them all.

What could possibly have driven an unprotected woman and child to enter this dangerous territory on foot?

"Please. Please help my son." They were the only English words the young Iraqi woman knew, and anxiety creased her pretty face. She had practiced these words ad nauseum, with the hopes that somehow their utterance would form the bridge she needed in order to help her child. With that, she switched into Arabic and through an interpreter pled her case to the Americans in a torrent of desperation.

Mohammed was barely listening. From the moment he set eyes on him, Mohammed fell in love with the child. The boy was only three or four years old, and he had a sweet and beautiful innocence that instantly endeared him to everyone. He was dressed in miniature khaki pants and a sweater-vest, as if prepared for a special event, and yet there was something about him that was just... wrong.

Mohammed left the female soldiers and, much to their surprise and amusement, unabashedly dropped his bulky six-foot frame down onto the dusty ground of Checkpoint One to play with the tiny boy, who was tracing small shapes in the road.

"What's your name, habibi?"

"Amjad," the boy replied with a shy smile.

"And how old are you, Amjad?"

He held up four trembling fingers. "Thwee!"

"Wow! High five!"

With bright, inquisitive eyes, the child reached out to slap Mohammed's raised hand. His tiny hand shook. He giggled and tried tentatively to stand up, but he wavered dangerously and fell over. The child did not seem surprised in the least. He tried again to stand, and once again, he toppled. He didn't fall the way toddlers usually fall, tripping over their own feet in an excited burst of movement. He tumbled sideways, having barely taken a step, falling as though the earth had tilted beneath him. And all the while, his hands and arms trembled.

Mohammed had always loved children, and children loved him. Babies laughed in delight as he threw them up so high that their mothers shrieked at him to stop. He had no problem lying on his belly under the kitchen table in front of complete strangers in order to bang pots and pans with a toddler. Young schoolboys wrestled him and little girls sang him songs. Teenagers adored him like a wild older brother. Mohammed was like a fish in water around children.

But this boy was special. This boy was a kindred spirit to his sweet and innocent Firas. Whatever love Mohammed had for kids, it was nothing compared to the soft spot he had for ill or disabled children, who brought out a tenderness in him that had been born of his love for his

127

little brother.

Mohammed laughed and played with the child, holding his hands to help him walk around as the mother continued to speak with the soldiers. The blond soldier with whom he had been flirting only minutes before approached and was watching the two play with a warm smile on her face.

"What's wrong with him?" Mohammed asked the mother as he played with the boy. "Why does he keep falling over?"

"He has something wrong with his balance. I took him to all the doctors; none of them could help. I came to the Americans to beg them to help him." Anxiety and love for her son was written on her face and in her every action.

"Is he cold? Why does he keep shaking?"

She smiled sadly. "He has seizures."

"What did the Americans say? Can they help?"

"No. These soldiers have called the American hospital and requested their help multiple times, may God bless them for trying, but the hospital refuses to see him." Her voice trembled slightly.

"Is this true?" Mohammed turned to the soldiers.

"They say it's against protocol," one of them said apologetically. "The hospital says they can't even send a car here to pick him up. It's too dangerous."

"But they *have* to help him!"

"What are they supposed to do?"

"They should at least send the child out of Iraq so that he can get the treatment he needs! Let me talk to them." Mohammed picked up the phone and had a heated conversation with someone at the hospital, but the end result was the same. *It wasn't possible*, they said. *It was against protocol. The woman and her son were not allowed entrance into the Green Zone.*

He'd had enough. Mohammed slammed down the phone and turned to the mother. "Let me see what I can do."

He brought his car and with mother and child in tow, they left the Green Zone and, using his badge, entered through another checkpoint to the Combat Support Hospital. A colonel who worked as a lead physician at the hospital came out to talk to him.

"Mo, we can't take this child—" the colonel started.

"Look at him!" Mohammed exclaimed, unable to contain his distress. "Just *look* at him!"

How could a fully equipped hospital with world-class doctors refuse to examine a sick three-year-old? What were they afraid of?

The colonel glanced at the child, who smiled a shy smile and trembled. He looked up and saw the mother, holding her son's hand, who met his eyes with a beseeching look of hope. He looked away quickly.

"I told you, Mo. I'm sorry, but we can't help him."

"Just examine his body and *tell her* what's wrong with him, sir! No one in Iraq could help this child, and now you turn him away too? At least *pretend* that you're taking a look at him!"

The colonel regarded the stubborn Iraqi for a moment, then sighed. "Come on. We'll figure something out."

The mother and child entered the hospital with the physician, and Mohammed returned to the checkpoint where the girls met his return with enthusiasm. He had done all that he could do.

A few hours later, a medical vehicle transported the Iraqi mother and her little boy to the checkpoint, and she got out with several documents in hand.

"So what happened?"

The mother's smile grew wide as she saw Mohammed.

"They examined my little Amjad and gave us an entrance pass to the Green Zone for weekly appointments to continue his therapy and medications. They even said that they would help send him out of Iraq for further treatment if need be." She laughed from pure joy and relief. "Thank you, thank you, thank you *so* much for your help! May God protect you and keep your family safe."

Breaking social boundaries, she threw her arms around Mohammed and kissed his cheek, tears of joy streaming down her face. Mohammed picked up little Amjad, whirling him in the air until he giggled with delight. The mother laughed with them, even as the tears rolled down her cheeks. That day, after years of worry, stress, and heartache, she had at last been able to find help for her beloved child.

As the mother and child left, Mohammed turned to see the blond soldier watching him. He was surprised to see tears in her eyes.

"You know," she said softly, "I was wrong when I said that we should nickname you 'Saint' after Val Kilmer in that movie. We should nickname you 'Saint' because you really *are* a saint."

After that, the nickname stuck.

Mohammed often thought of the little boy and the mother who had risked her life to bring him to the American gates. To do so without a car, without a gun, and without the protection of a male escort in the midst of growing violence showed incredible grit. He wondered if he himself could do what she had done.

He thought of little Firas, and a swell of love overwhelmed him.

Yes, he would do it. He would lay down his life for any of his family members a million times over.

But then, he was a man in a man's world. And he had a particularly large and threatening presence at that. He radiated confidence, which people felt and subconsciously respected. How different, then, would it be for a woman? He had rarely thought of what it must be like to be a woman in Iraq. Her life was to be sheltered and protected even in the best of circumstances. These days, with kidnapping, rape, and murder on the rise, the streets were a perilous place for a woman. Yet she had chosen to walk to the enemy's doors in spite of this, and would continue to do so weekly, with her only armor an all-consuming love for her son.

They may call him Saint, he thought, but *she* was the hero.

PSYCHOSOMATIC

"My *whole* body hurts from head to toe."

The middle-aged woman sat on the examination table, looking indignant at the questions being asked of her. Years of hard labor and child rearing had added a tire-like cushion around her middle, and she wore a black hijab and abaya with dirt on the cuff, where she often wiped her nose and face.

"Can you be more specific, *hajjiyeh*? Is there one part that hurts more than another? Can you describe the type of pain?" Kadhim was stumped.

"No. Everything hurts, all over." She had a thick rural accent, and Kadhim's examination hadn't revealed anything significant. His responsibilities as a fifth-year medical student had increased, and he now took histories, conducted physical exams, and presented cases to the attending.

He had begun to notice a pattern in uneducated women from rural areas. They came from a conservative society where they were not accustomed to expressing psychological or emotional distress directly, but instead presented with a series of illogical symptoms and physical exams that revealed nothing. Such cases indicated an emotional problem more often than not: severe boredom, depression, or some family blowout or scandal that had manifested itself as physical symptoms of stress.

The attending sat in the corner of the room, smoking a cigarette as he languidly stared out the window. He looked up at last, clearly annoyed at how long the exam was taking and anxious to move on to a more interesting case. "What's going on here?"

"I'm feeling pain in my whole body," the woman wailed on cue. "I'm like a corpse!"

She continued complaining as the physician grumbled under his breath, "Damn broad wasting my time." He barked at Kadhim, "Did the exam reveal anything?"

Without bothering to wait for an answer, he turned to the patient. "Who do you live with, *hajjiyeh*?"

"My husband and my two youngest children."

"And how is your family? All doing well?"

"*Well*? My man is useless—he don't work, just sits at home all

131

day. He don't help, and he's no good in the house, no good at all."

The physician grabbed his pad and scribbled something quickly. Kadhim expected the usual for such cases: antibiotics, vitamins, anything that could act as a placebo without harming the woman. Instead, the doctor warned her as he handed her the prescription, "*Hajjiyeh*, this is for your husband, not you. Maybe if he's a bit more... helpful around the house, you won't feel so tired or be in so much pain. And next time you come in, bring him with you so I can examine him properly."

The woman nodded, a bit mystified, but satisfied to have a solution to her problems in hand. Hers was not to ask why.

Kadhim gave Hind a ride home that evening, and it was nearly dark by the time they approached her neighborhood. He went into a back alleyway for a few moments of privacy, hoping to steal a kiss before dropping her off at her parents' house. He squeezed her hand and looked at her.

She smiled back, leaned over, and kissed him. It was a longer kiss than usual, and Kadhim wondered if she was signaling that she was ready for something more. He ran a hand down her side.

"Kadhim!" Her tone was admonishing as she backed away abruptly. He chuckled.

"Sorry—couldn't help but hope..."

"Habibi, you know that before this goes any further, you really should propose to me. I don't like sneaking around like this. If we just get engaged, then we can be seen together in public. I could invite you to my family's house for dinner sometimes; we could start looking at houses and furniture..."

"God willing." Kadhim stared out at the silhouette of houses cast against the setting sun, silently willing the conversation to end.

"We've been dating for nearly two years. Isn't that long enough? It's time to start talking about marriage."

It didn't feel long enough. He felt like he barely knew her, and now he was supposed to make her his wife?

"I mean, I'd have to talk to my family about you being Shiite, but I'm sure once they meet you and see that you're from a respectable family, they won't have a problem..."

"What do you mean you have to talk to them about me being Shiite? Is that really an issue?"

"No, no, it's not an issue per se. It's just... well, Kadhim, you have to admit that Shiites are destroying our country."

"*Excuse* me?"

"Obviously, I don't mean *you*, or your family. I mean regular Shiites—the rest of them. They brought the Americans, got rid of Saddam, and look at the mess we're in now!"

"Are you serious, Hind? *We* brought the Americans?" Kadhim shook his head in disbelief. "And what's wrong with getting rid of Saddam? We're better off without him."

"At least when Saddam was in power we had order in the streets, Kadhim. Letting him be overthrown was a huge mistake. Look at us now—unemployment, disorder, car bombings... and for what?"

"That doesn't mean that Saddam should have stayed in power. Have you forgotten what he did to us? Tyranny, back-to back wars, a regime of injustice and cruelty. For God's sake, Hind! Getting rid of Saddam—getting rid of the Ba'ath party—was our *only* shot at freedom!"

"I'd rather have no freedom than have this," she retorted stubbornly.

"I understand that. But at least now we have a shot. We can build a democratic Iraq, a *free* Iraq. Don't you want that?"

She pouted. "Just take me home. I have a headache."

Kadhim pulled out of the alley and they continued to her house in silence, both annoyed with each other. He dropped her off at a safe distance from the prying windows of her parents' home and drove away feeling exasperated.

Was she excited to get engaged simply because she wanted a wedding, a house, and children? It was hard to imagine tying himself to someone he only knew superficially, particularly someone whose thoughts seemed to be marching along increasingly sectarian lines. He pushed the gas pedal harder, as if running from the very thought. A headache, huh? Kadhim began to wonder if their increasing arguments were really a sign of a larger underlying problem.

About a week later the middle-aged patient was back, this time with a plump, middle-aged man sitting placidly next to her. Kadhim was glad that he had chanced upon the case. He was still curious to know what mysterious medicine had been prescribed.

The physician read the file, took a quick look at the man, and then, instead of grabbing his stethoscope, he lit a cigarette and asked casually, "So, how are you doing today? Feeling better?"

Out of respect, he didn't address the woman directly in the presence of her husband, but it was clear for whom the question was intended.

"Much better," exclaimed the woman. "Thanks, my son, for helping a woman in her old age. May God keep you safe and bless you, and may God keep you healthy and give you a long life, *inshallah*." She kept up a stream of expressions in this vein as the couple stood, whereas the husband shook the physician's hand and muttered something unintelligible, a hint of a smile touching his craggy features.

After they'd left the exam room, Kadhim turned incredulously to the attending physician. He'd been expecting more than that, perhaps some wide-eyed account of how the mystery drug had healed the woman's pains or changed her life.

"That's it?"

"Yup, looks like it worked out alright."

"What in the world did you prescribe?"

The physician took a long draw on his cigarette, a grin cracking his features for just a moment, and said simply, "Viagra."

SHRAPNEL

Mohammed had been dating "Nina" for a couple months and was thoroughly enjoying himself. She was a local who first caught his eye at an internet café where she worked in the Green Zone. Nina was pretty and well-proportioned, with enticing brown locks that reached halfway down her back. And she was crazy about Mohammed.

In the beginning, she had made a display of modesty, but she had quickly taken to spending frequent nights with Mohammed. It was against policy to host such nocturnal guests, but this was Saint. He had been there from the start, volunteering for missions, hitting on all the girls, and generally living life to the fullest. He wasn't about to change now, and the Americans knew it. They learned to recognize Nina, and with a knowing smile, they looked the other way. As long as she wasn't a soldier, they weren't going to interfere.

It was a cool and foggy morning in mid-January, 2004, when after one of her overnight visits, Mohammed escorted Nina to Assassins' Gate. The checkpoint was named after the American unit that had originally manned it, but this moniker would later be deemed inappropriate and culturally insensitive. The first and primary checkpoint would go through a series of other names: Mother of All Checkpoints, Checkpoint One, ACP1, and Maingate.

On that particular morning, however, the entryway to the newly established International Zone still bore its original name and its original crude elements. No concrete Jersey walls protected it; Assassins' Gate consisted of no more than a few Hesco bags and some coiled barbed wire. The extreme security measures that would later be put into place had not yet occurred. A few scattered car bombs had struck since 2003: the Jordanian Embassy in Baghdad, the United Nations building, a few police stations... They seemed to be isolated incidents. It simply didn't occur to anyone that car bombs and suicide bombings would soon escalate to a magnitude that would make Iraq history's most bombed country.

Mohammed left Nina just inside the gate, where, once she crossed through, she planned on catching a taxi and running a few errands in Baghdad.

"Be careful, habibti," he warned, planting a quick kiss on her cheek. She smiled, soaking in his affection.

"*You* be careful! And call me!"

He watched for a moment as she made her way to the checkpoint, then turned and started to walk away briskly. He was supposed to interpret that morning at the conference center and was running late, having been distracted by the morning's activities, but if he hurried he could still make it on time.

He had only made it a few paces when he felt the impact. An enormous explosion of sound and heat detonated through the air, and Mohammed was pummeled by flying dirt and debris from behind him. He was so stunned by the force of the explosion that it took a few seconds for him to realize what had happened. Chaos suddenly erupted around him and Mohammed turned to see smoke billowing from a small blackened pick-up truck—driver still inside—sitting just outside the checkpoint. He ran back toward Assassins' Gate.

Nina...

It was chaos. Bodies were scattered, injured, dead, or dying. The cars that had been in line behind the exploded truck were burnt and destroyed.

Mohammed saw a black American soldier, standing in shock next to the truck. Blood ran from his ears, eyes, and nose. He had been calling for the truck's driver to slow down. The truck had continued unchecked. He had raised his gun, pointed it directly at the driver and screamed in increasing urgency, "Stop! Stop! *Stop!*"

Instead, the suicide bomber had pushed a button, and the truck had exploded. One thousand pounds of explosives caused windows to rattle as far as a mile away. Twenty-four people died, one hundred and twenty were injured. And yet somehow, the soldier next to the vehicle survived, saved perhaps by the dirt Hesco barriers before him that were destroyed in the blast.

Mohammed's eyes took in the disastrous scene in seconds, and he kept hunting.

Nina... he had just left her here! Left her to die...

Desperately, he searched. His eyes combed bodies dead and alive as the medics arrived. Iraqis, dazed by the blast, wandered aimlessly down the street, blood dripping from their ears.

Mohammed's ears rang. His head hurt. Twinges of pain afflicted his back and legs, but he didn't notice. He had to find Nina.

"*Mohammed!*"

The voice was weak, but a rush of hope swelled in his chest.

"Nina?" Mohammed followed the voice and saw his girlfriend's fragile body lying on the ground in a pool of blood and debris.

"Nina! Oh my God! Thank God! Nina, are you okay?" He saw

blood everywhere, and it scared him.

"Mohammed..." Tears flowed uncontrollably down her cheeks. She was unable to lift her head, and she looked pale and weak. Mohammed grabbed her hand and was shocked by how cold it was. The blood thudded in his ears, and his heart raced.

"Nina, stay with me! The medics are here. They're going to help you! You're going to be okay!" He jumped up, frantic. "I'll bring them right now, Nina. You'll be fine."

"Mohammed, no! Don't leave me!" She reached out for him. "I'm in so much pain!"

"What is it, Nina? Where's the pain?"

"Mohammed!" She winced, letting out a moan of anguish as yet more tears found their way to the dirt. Mohammed grabbed her hand and held it to his chest.

"What is it, habibti?"

"Mohammed, my behind!" She rolled over slightly, and as Mohammed peered behind her he saw blood on her pants where a piece of shrapnel had firmly lodged itself into one of her perfectly-shaped buttocks.

He stood and burst into laughter. "You got hit in the ass!"

"It's not funny, you asshole! I'm in pain!"

"Your poor little tush! Hold on, I'm bringing the medics. You just wait here and keep a hand on the wound." He roared with laughter. "Right in the ass!"

THE BRIDGE

The Mahdi Army would have a major and versatile role in the Iraqi civil war. At times siding with the Americans and oftentimes fighting against them, this Shiite militia arose in response to increasing Sunni terrorist attacks on vulnerable Shiite communities. Eventually, it would be composed of some fifteen thousand largely poor and impressionable youth. It was led by Muqtada al-Sadr, a minimally educated man from the bowels of the Baghdad slum of Sadr City who, through no merit of his own, had inherited the massive following of his well-respected father, the late Grand Ayatollah Mohammad Mohammad Sadeq Al-Sadr.

The Mahdi Army functioned as a protector and provider of services to its own constituents, and a kidnapper and killer of others. It would one day have channels of informants and kidnappers that ran deep into the ranks of the Iraqi interpreters and hospital staff that Mohammed and Kadhim called their colleagues. Mohammed's first encounter with the Mahdi Army during its early days as a paramilitary, however, was a meeting that neither side would ever forget.

They came marching unannounced—thousands of them—from the slums of Sadr City some fifteen kilometers away in northeast Baghdad, arriving just outside the Green Zone walls. And there they stood, a sea of ebony in black clothes and black bandanas, carrying AK-47s, Kalashnikovs, and RPGs, and chanting in Arabic on loudspeakers.

The Coalition Forces were shocked and wary.

Never before had they seen anything like this, thousands of armed men outside their walls stretching far into the distance. Saddam's forces certainly had not presented a unified front in the face of Shock and Awe. Was it a protest? An army come to do battle? Their amplified shouts did not sound welcoming, but how could one tell when they were incomprehensible?

The gates remained closed. Soldiers, armored Bradleys, and tanks were stationed behind the T-walls as a first line of defense.

Mohammed was called, and he reported his findings to the full-bird colonel in charge of investigating the scene.

"It's the Mahdi Army, sir. They're saying over their megaphones that this is a peaceful demonstration."

"Did you talk to them?"

"No, sir. Do you want me to go amongst them? Are you serious?"

The colonel turned to his Department of Defense contract interpreter, or "DOD," an Egyptian who had spent the last twenty years of his life in the United States. The DOD spoke Egyptian Arabic, and found the Iraqi dialect strange, harsh, and often difficult to understand. Even high-risk pay of over $100,000 a year did not equip him to handle a protest of thousands of upset Iraqis. He looked at the ground and shook his head nervously.

"I'm sorry, sir. I can't go. I don't understand the culture. I don't know…" His voice trailed off.

"You're the colonel's interpreter. You're supposed to be taking care of him." Mohammed suppressed a snort of derision. His own pay was $450 per month, and he took the same risks, greater risks in fact, than interpreters who had been hired in the United States and had left their families safely behind. He met the colonel's eyes. "I'll do it. I'll talk to them and see if this is going to go peacefully."

The sight of masses of armed, bandannaed men made Mohammed's heart pound, but he shook it off. If anyone knew how to handle the situation, it was he. He knew how to talk to people with respect, in a way that would soothe and mitigate a tense situation. And if they didn't respect him in return, he was confident that he could *make* them respect him. Steeling his nerves, he placed a loaded gun into his belt and climbed over the gates, still closed for security, and stood at last—all alone—before the cacophonous uproar of thousands of armed protestors.

As he approached, they hailed him with insults and waved their AK-47s. "You traitor… agent for the Americans… you *filth!*"

Mohammed laughed it off. *Who gave a damn what they thought?* But his nerves were tense and he kept his gun in hand. If they put a finger on him, he'd shoot. The Americans were behind him, protected by the wall. They had promised to cover for him, but could he really trust that they'd be willing to start a crossfire with an armed crowd of this size on behalf of a single Iraqi interpreter? He doubted it. He was alone.

"Where's your sheikh? Where's the person who's responsible for you?"

"There is no leader. We are all one. Our only leader is Imam Al Mahdi, may God speed his arrival so that justice will come." This phrase often followed the name of Imam Al Mahdi, the twelfth generation descendant of Ali. It was believed that Al Mahdi would accompany Jesus when he returned to Earth at the end of time to bring justice.

"May God speed his arrival. Look, I want to speak to someone who is responsible for you. Who organized this protest?"

There was some scuffling in the crowd and a man came forward. He had a thick beard and wore the cloak of a religious cleric, but instead of white, his turban was black. This man was a "sayyed," a descendant of the Prophet Mohammad.

"*Salaam 'alaykum.*"

The sayyed didn't take Mohammed's outstretched hand or respond to his greeting. Mohammed was dirty for working with the Americans, and shaking Mohammed's hand would have made him unclean.

Mohammed ignored the rebuff. "With your permission, sayyedi, what kind of protest is this?"

"What do you mean?"

"Is it peaceful? Or is your intent to threaten?"

"What, are you going to inform on me?"

"No." Actually, he would, but he didn't need to openly aggravate a group of thousands. "But do you see these tanks?"

"Yes."

"If a gun goes off, if *accidentally* a single bullet is fired, then all those people behind you? They're going to get killed."

The sayyed glanced at the thousands that had followed him in protest and a look of worry flitted across his face. "How would they get killed?"

"You don't see those tanks? How are the Americans supposed to know what you want, whether you're coming here to protest peacefully or to start a war? All they see is a full army. What do you expect? Just shoot at me. Or shoot at them. A single shot fired, even accidentally, and *you* will be accountable for all those who die."

The sayyed became more cooperative. "To the contrary, we're a peaceful demonstration. We came simply to present our requests."

"And what are those, exactly?"

"Firstly, we want to become an officially recognized army, part of the new Iraqi government. We want to protect Sadr City and its constituents. We want to work hand in hand with the Iraqi Army.

"Secondly, the Americans have shut down our newspaper, *Al Hawza*. We want it reestablished.

"Thirdly, we demand to know what has happened to the water, electricity and garbage disposal services in our district. Sadr City has almost two million people living within eight square miles. Do you know what it's like to live in those conditions without reliable water, electricity, or protection from attack?"

As the sayyed spoke, the men behind him grew increasingly agitated. They were all Shiite, and many of them recognized Mohammed from his numerous patrols in Sadr City with the Coalition Forces. Why was their leader speaking with this filth? Their voices grew louder and angrier, and suddenly one of the men brushed past the sayyed and shoved Mohammed.

"Filth! Dirty son of a dog!"

Within a fraction of a second, the man found his collar in the choking grip of Mohammed's fist, a gun driven into his temple.

"You didn't even have the courtesy to respect the sayyed in front of you, and you dare come and push me?" Mohammed's furious eyes were only inches from the man's own, and spit flecked the man's face as Mohammed growled, "Look at me, you son of a bitch! I'll burn your father right here in front of you if you touch me again!"

The sight of Mohammed holding a man at gunpoint spurred a sudden rush of action on the other side of the wall. The American team that Mohammed had been working with, personal security detail for the commander, jumped over the gate and came running. Saint may have been from another land and another culture, but he was their interpreter, and the Americans took care of their own. The tanks, meanwhile, moved closer to the walls and positioned their guns at the protestors.

The protestors panicked.

"Take it easy! Take it easy! Nothing's going on! We don't want any trouble!"

"See? If another person so much as bumps into me, I'll turn him to blood right here."

American soldiers arrived, a dozen armed men in front of the masses, listening to Arabic that they didn't understand.

"We're here," the commander called out. "If they harm a hair on your head, we're behind you."

They were frozen in an instant in which they had no idea what was wrong or what would happen next, their fate tied to their interpreter's ability to be a skilled negotiator.

"I'm Iraqi, from Karbala. Not so different from you." Mohammed released the struggling man and returned to the sayyed. "But I'll tell you one thing. Without me, neither you nor the Americans would be here.

"The linguistic wall that separates you from the Americans? *I'm* the one who controls it. Not you, not them. You don't speak English and they don't speak Arabic. Come, speak two words to them in Arabic and see if they don't shoot you. He'll think you're threatening him. Or maybe he'll shout something and you'll think that he's insulting you, even if all he's saying is that he doesn't understand. I'm the bridge between two neighborhoods. You want to get to that neighborhood? You go through me. The bridge of language."

The sayyed raised his hands in surrender. "May Allah bless you."

With those words, Mohammed could breathe again. He turned to the soldiers to explain what had happened, as the sayyed tried to calm his protestors. After a brief conference with his commander, Mohammed once again addressed the crowd's turbaned leader.

"Okay, let's reach a deal. Empty *all* of your weapons of their bullets. Right now, in front of us. If a single bullet is let loose, it's over for you. You think you can hit a tank with an AK-47? They're going to laugh at you."

"Just make sure your guys don't shoot at us," came the nervous retort.

"Disarm first. Like I said, not a single gun fired."

It all came down to one bullet. A single bullet could decide the fate of thousands.

The sayyed raised his microphone. "Everyone who has an RPG, remove the rocket. Everyone with Kalashnikovs and AK-47s, remove the bullets. BE CAREFUL NOT TO FIRE! I am Sayyed Hashim, and I REPEAT: I AM COMMANDING YOU, AND THIS IS AN ORDER! WHOEVER DOESN'T FOLLOW IT WILL BE PUNISHED! DO NOT FIRE A SINGLE SHOT! DISARM IMMEDIATELY!"

Through the ups and downs of shifting targets and alliances, the Mahdi Army never forgot Mohammed's unmasked face. He may have won that day in 2004, but unintentionally he continued to incite them by aiding the Western occupier in raids of Sadr City, including the homes of its sheikhs and sayyeds. Mohammed did not realize it then, and perhaps he would not have cared, but he was quickly making his way to becoming one of the terrorist militia's two most wanted men.

LOBECTOMY

"Do you remember our old classmate, Omar?"

"The Jordanian, right? The one who started to grow out his beard after the war..." Mahjoub cut Kadhim off mid-sentence.

"Yeah. He's a terrorist. He blew himself up last week in Mosul."

It was happening. The world was starting to split into two, and people were sliding off opposite sides.

Kadhim's class—the first graduating class of Al Kindy Medical School—was slowly fracturing into pieces.

They had originally been a tight-knit group, united in the common exhaustion of medical school. They had made group outings to local restaurants and had gone on day-trips together, singing popular songs on the bus en route. Soon after the war, this camaraderie started to dissipate.

Omar, the Jordanian, was one of the first to be noticed. Shortly after the fall of Saddam, the previously diligent medical student grew his beard, replaced his slacks, dress-shirt, and tie with a short dishdasha, and disappeared from university grounds.

Long beards and knee-length dishdashas were not worn by accident in the Middle East. They weren't a fashion statement; they had become a political statement.

Who had gotten to Omar? What had they said to him to alter his perception so drastically? From saving lives, to ending them.

When Saddam was in power, this radicalization would never have happened. Iraq's former leader, while harsh on his own people, had been equally brutal toward any extremist elements within his borders, and the growth of such tumors had always been quickly and violently extinguished.

Within the months preceding the 2003 invasion, however, Saddam had not only released most of his prisoners from Iraqi prisons, but had also publicly invited wahhabis and jihadis to fight the Americans

143

in Iraq. They had answered his call. They were the vermin whose car bombs and suicide vests now wreaked havoc in Shiite communities.

Kadhim was increasingly uneasy with the changes he saw happening around him, both in the streets and in his university cafeteria. Some classmates began to proclaim their support for Muqtada Al-Sadr and the Mahdi Army. Others extolled the virtues of Osama bin Laden and his great Islamic jihad. Still others longed for the days of Saddam Hussein and the Ba'ath regime. Kadhim could scarcely believe what he was hearing. Had they gone mad? Where was the voice of reason in their changing beliefs? It seemed that they were breathing in the air of sectarianism and extremism, and many were gradually becoming infected. These were classmates, his friends, and they were going crazy.

"This is Musa Al-Tunisi, age thirty-nine. Due to a growing tumor in the frontal lobe, he has recently undergone a frontal lobectomy and is here today for post-operative follow-up."

The attending, his back to the patient, was too busy explaining the procedure to Kadhim's group to notice that none of the students were listening.

"As you know, the partial or full removal of the frontal lobe can affect the patient's personality and behavior, particularly behavior related to appropriate social responses. The patient's lowered inhibitions are one of the reasons we've been called in to consult today."

Behind the attending, the patient grinned and winked ferociously at Fatma, whose face was quickly turning pink. The boys tried hard to contain their smiles.

"It's possible that some of these changes had already started to occur prior to surgery, as a result of constant seizures in the frontal lobes."

The patient, his head still wrapped in white gauze, giggled and made a lewd gesture, winking suggestively. This time, Kadhim and the boys could not stop themselves from grinning.

To openly flirt with a girl was dangerous. To make *this* gesture in a girl's presence was simply unheard of. Kadhim tried desperately to choke his laugh into a cough. The patient, meanwhile, made small kissing noises toward the girls, pointing toward his crotch as if making a gracious offer.

"Frontal lobectomies have a mediocre success rate…"

An idea suddenly occurred to the patient and he jumped off the exam table, bounded across the room, and grabbed both of Fatma's breasts, squeezing them enthusiastically while uttering sounds of pure delight.

This was too much to handle. Kadhim, Mahjoub, and the other boys began laughing so hard that they fell to the ground, tears running down their cheeks, gasping for breath amidst their mirth.

Hind was aghast. The attending, after staring for a moment in wide-eyed shock, jumped forward to pull his patient off the student. Fatma was furious. Her face a spectacular shade of crimson, she shoved the man away and ran out of the room in utter humiliation.

For the boys, although they later apologized to Fatma for not having gone to her aid, it was a moment of unmitigated glee.

This man had literally lost part of his mind. What excuse, then, did the rest of Iraq have for *its* insanity?

"I'm sick of hearing the news of these Shiite dogs murdering innocent Sunnis and leaving their bodies in the streets. We'd be better off without them. All of them."

Hind's eyes flashed with anger as she reacted to the latest killing spree by Shiite militias and gangs. The noise of the cafeteria was quieting down around them as students gradually finished their lunches.

"May the victims rest in peace," Kadhim responded in a conciliatory manner, although her words irked him. "It's terrible."

"I just don't get it! What did we ever do to the Shiites to make them hate us?"

"Well, there was a series of bombings in Sadr City and Kadhimiya two days ago, Hind. Hundreds of Shiites were killed. I'm not defending their actions, but these militia attacks aren't out of the blue. It's a retaliation."

She took a sip of juice and shook her head in disgust. "Well, Sunnis would never react like this, taking it out on innocent people. Only Shiites…"

"It wasn't Shiites in general, Hind." Kadhim glared at her. "They were specific Shiite militias. You said that regular Sunnis wouldn't take it out on innocent Shiites. Well, it's the same for us. Not all Shiites are gang or militia members, and we're not all out for innocent blood."

"Don't take it personally, Kadhim. I don't mean *you*. I mean *regular* Shiites. All those backwards barbarians who just want to kill people. They can't tell the difference between guilty and innocent, and furthermore they don't care. You're different. That's why I like you."

"*Don't take it personally?* Hind, you're talking about my family, my relatives, my community! You're lumping all of us into one group with terrorists! How do I not take that personally?"

If he had heard this from her only once or twice, he would have dismissed it as the rants of a girl upset and scared for her community. But these days, they were constantly getting into spats over the same tired topics, and he didn't like the changes he was seeing in her.

She rolled her eyes. "You're being overly sensitive, habibi. Maybe not all Shiites are terrorists, but they're supporting terrorists and raising their children like them. Shiites just don't have the same quality upbringing. The Sunnis knew how to govern properly. When Saddam was in power, we had peace and safety. And now that Shiites have taken control of the government, they're going to run our country into the ground..."

"ENOUGH! Do you even hear yourself, Hind? All of Iraq's top artists, singers, writers, and poets are Shiite! Sunnis ruled through Saddam's iron fist, not because they're any better than Shiites!"

"Wait, Kadhim—"

"No, I'm sick of listening to you group all Shiites together and acting as if Sunnis are better! How can you become a doctor when you would look down on the majority of your patients just for their religion? How can you treat your patients equally when you think some are arbitrarily better than others? How can you talk to me about marriage when you house this hatred for my sect?"

"But Kadhim, I keep trying to tell you! You're different!"

"That's not good enough, Hind. I'm NOT that different from most Shiites. You're just not bright enough to distinguish between a regular person and a criminal. You keep lumping us together, and it's insulting! We aren't even engaged yet, and already I'm sick of this. That's it, Hind. I think we'd be better off just ending this now and going our separate ways."

"Kadhim, no!" Tears started to roll down her cheeks. She pled loudly, oblivious to the stares of others in the cafeteria. "Kadhim, please! Don't end it! I respect you! I'll be better, I promise! I love you!"

He looked at the tear-filled brown eyes that had once held him captive and felt nothing. He could barely talk to her anymore without feeling disgusted or insulted.

"No, Hind. It's over.

For several months, Hind tried to win him back. She had never meant to hurt him, never meant to insult his family. She begged him to forgive her.

"You don't understand, Hind. Even if I forgave you, the underlying problem doesn't go away. I can't be with someone like you, someone who thinks along sectarian lines. You would always be ashamed of me for my sect, regardless of my virtues and morals as an individual. You would raise our children to hate Shiites, to detest a piece of who they are. Maybe we would have worked, Hind. But not like this."

It was over. Hind had inhaled the air of sectarianism, and she too was infected. The whole world was going crazy.

CROSS-LEG FLAP

"Doctor, I'm begging you. Please save my leg." The boy's eyes filled with tears as he pled with the renowned orthopedic surgeon standing next to Kadhim. He had dark olive skin and startling green eyes, and it was only the blind hope of youth that brought him to this hospital. "Doctor, *please*! I'm only twenty years old! I'm not ready to lose my leg!"

His leg was a grotesque sight. The patient had barely survived a powerful bomb that had ripped through the marketplace, taking with it dozens of lives. And while it had not taken his life, the force of the blast had managed to rip all the muscle and soft tissue from his left calf, leaving behind bare, exposed bones with a shriveling blood supply. It was painful for Kadhim to see, and just as painful for him to see the boy's desperation and the despair in the eyes of all the relatives who had come to support him.

Kadhim was in the middle of an orthopedic surgery rotation that was a standard part of the fifth year curriculum. On that particular day, as fate would have it, he was thrilled to be rounding with Dr. Abbas, one of Baghdad's top orthopedic surgeons. Thrilled, that is, until he saw the boy's leg and realized that it was hopeless.

"Doctor, you're my last chance," the boy begged. "We have gone to other hospitals. We even went to the Italian Hospital of Baghdad with all the European surgeons and they all said the same thing: the leg has to be amputated within twenty-four hours."

"Yes, and do you know why they said that?" Dr. Abbas asked him gently. The boy shook his head as a tear rolled down his cheek. He knew the answer, but he couldn't bear to respond. "Son, if we don't amputate the leg immediately, you could die of gangrene."

The surgeon sat down next to the boy. "Look, when your bones are exposed like this and have no blood supply, they die. It's like trying to live without oxygen. And once the bones die, they will start to degrade, and they will be a source of serious and life-threatening infections. The European doctors are right; the leg must come off."

The boy burst into tears. His father rubbed the young man's shoulder and murmured softly, wishing that he could console his son.

"It's okay," the orthopedic surgeon said softly. "It is better to be alive with one leg than be dead with two. You're young and strong; you could be fitted with a prosthetic."

This only made the boy sob harder. "I can't," he whispered. "I can't do it. You have to help me, doctor. Please help me save my leg. I'll do anything!"

Dr. Abbas sighed. For a long time he gazed at the useless limb in silence, deep in thought. Around him, students, relatives, and a hopeful patient held their breath. At last, he turned back to the patient, and his voice broke through the silence.

"There is one surgery that *might* save your leg. It's a risky surgery and it would require a great sacrifice from you, in addition to a long and painful recovery period. This surgery might save your leg, and you might even be able to walk again one day. But there's also a chance that you could die during the surgery, or that we'll get in there only to realize that we have to amputate the leg in order to save your life, and then that's what we would do. It's dangerous, my son, but if you want to save your leg then it's the only option."

The boy took a deep breath. "I want you to do it," he said resolutely. "You're the only surgeon who has agreed to help me. I'll take my chances."

The days flew by, and in the constant flow of patients, surgeries, and studying new techniques, Kadhim forgot about the green-eyed boy. He ran into Hind once or twice, and they exchanged awkward hellos, but the closeness between them had dissipated. The last thing on Kadhim's mind these days was girls. More than a year had passed since the outbreak of the war in 2003, and the situation only appeared to be worsening. Kadhim spent his days committed to medicine and his nights at home with his family. Although the occasional outing with his friends lightened the mood, he was growing increasingly apprehensive of the escalating violence. The possibility of a civil war seemed to be looming like a sandstorm in the distance.

Several months went by before Kadhim came across the green-eyed boy once again. He had been brought to the clinic in a wheelchair by his family for a follow-up visit, and Kadhim realized that he had no idea what had happened with the leg. He had not been able to observe the surgery, nor had he seen the patient in the post-operative recovery area. He watched in suspense as the blanket covering the boy's lower half was lifted.

It was strange... and incredible. Both of the boy's legs were still there, but during surgery, the thick muscle had been partially severed from the right calf and attached to the bare bone of the left, essentially fusing the two legs into one. Without a blood supply, the left leg would have died. In sharing the muscle and blood supply of the right leg, some of the blood vessels from the cross-leg flap would attach to the left leg and connect to newly forming blood vessels higher up the limb. Muscle and tissue would gradually be adopted and incorporated into the vascular system of the left leg as well. At that point, the legs would be ready to be separated. In the meantime, the two legs remained fused like conjoined twins.

Dr. Abbas had come himself to check on the boy's progress. It was clear that this was a case that had become near and dear to his heart, and he greeted the boy like a son.

"Everything seems to be going beautifully!" The surgeon smiled broadly as he examined the affected area. "A spectacular surgery if I do say so myself. Have you been following all my instructions, son?"

"Yes, doctor, don't worry. I'm following your instructions to the letter."

"And you'll let me know immediately if you have any fever, pus, increased pain or swelling?"

"I haven't experienced anything like that. But I'll let you know if I do."

"Excellent!" The orthopedic surgeon stood up to greet the boy's father, who shook his hand heartily.

"Thank you so much for taking such good care of him, doctor. We can't tell you how grateful we are!" The sincerity of the father's words came through in his big smile and his bright eyes.

One day, nearly a year later, when Kadhim was in his final year of medical school and was finishing up a long day at the clinic, he saw a tall, slim young man leaving one of the exam rooms. He walked with a slight limp and relied heavily on a cane.

A voice came from behind Kadhim. "Son, do you remember that young male patient on whom we performed a cross-leg flap?"

It was Dr. Abbas.

"Yes, I do."

The orthopedic surgeon clapped a hand on Kadhim's shoulder and gazed with deep satisfaction at the young man limping down the hall. "That's him."

As they watched, the young man turned around slowly and delicately on two abnormally thin legs, and with a hand on his cane he waved a goodbye to his surgeon. With a grin that stretched from ear to ear, and green eyes that twinkled with pride, he pointed at his legs. He could walk.

On his very own legs.

STOOL IMPACTION

There were some health problems so embarrassing in nature than even the medical students found them painful to watch, and this happened to be one of those cases. The patient, a short, round male in his early fifties, was lying stomach down on the examination table with his pants around his ankles, staring glumly at the wall as the physician pulled on a glove, preparing to insert a digit between the bountiful white buttocks that faced the students.

"Who wants to review the symptoms for this case?" The attending peered at Kadhim and his group expectantly.

"The patient has been diagnosed with renal failure and has been complaining of disorientation, difficulty breathing, and swelling," Fatma offered, gazing resolutely into some remote corner of the room.

"And...?" The physician pointed a gloved finger at the two looming buttocks on the table, drawing the group's attention despite themselves.

"And severe constipation." Her cheeks reddened. "For two weeks."

A faint groan from the other end of the exam table punctuated her point.

"That's right." The physician snapped the glove into place and absentmindedly rested his hand on one of the generous cheeks as he continued questioning the students. "And why is it necessary to complete a rectal examination in this instance?"

"We need to determine whether the bowel is obstructed," Mahjoub said. "The presence of stool would indicate that the obstruction is not in the bowel."

"And lack of stool likely indicates that the obstruction is higher up and could be caused by a tumor or possibly a twisted bowel," Kadhim volunteered.

"And if that's the case, what tests would you run?"

"Well, the x-ray didn't show anything so you should probably do a colonoscopy."

"And if the colonoscopy shows nothing?"

No one answered.

"Come on, you guys, we *just* went over this last week!" The physician punctuated his point with a loud slap on the patient's buttock.

"Hey!" came a muted protest from the other end of the body. The doctor started and looked down with surprise at the place where his hand rested.

"If you've finished enjoying the view, I'd rather like to get this over with," the patient grumbled.

"Yes, of course." The physician turned to the students and held up the box of gloves. "Anyone else want to have first crack at it?" Someone snickered at the back of the group. "It's not that difficult once you get the hang of it."

Surprisingly, no one volunteered.

"In that case, I'll just explain as I go." With a dab of lubricant, the physician slid a forefinger between the two white cheeks. "Now, what you want to do once you've inserted the digit is to feel around for abnormalities in the wall such as a lump—don't forget to check the prostate in males—and of course, check for the possibility of... ah yes, it's as I thought..." he twisted his hand a bit and closed his eyes slightly, concentrating, "...impacted stool."

He shifted his hand again. "Here we have a case of hard stool that won't move due to severe constipation, likely caused by renal failure, which reduces the motility of the bowel. It's possible that we may have to evacuate the rectum manually, which I won't do right now," he gently withdrew his finger and began to remove the glove, "but which can be done by—"

A terrible sound suddenly trumpeted from the hole where his finger had just been, and before there was time to move, an explosion of diarrhea erupted from between the two white mounds, spraying the students and soaking the doctor in its brown liquid. It was never-ending, a product two weeks in the making, and before it was over, the physician's face and white lab coat had become an awful, dripping mess of diarrhea. Pieces of the hard stool that had been accidentally dislodged by the finger lay on the exam room floor, and the room reeked of human feces.

The students froze. The patient, without turning around, reached back ever so slowly and delicately covered his buttocks with a clean, white drape. Then, as the others stood in stunned silence and tried to avoid breathing in the terrible smell, he said in a muffled voice, "I would apologize, but the truth is, I feel *so* much better."

Kadhim had fallen into the habit of calling his brother several times a day to check in. The streets of Baghdad had become so hazardous, and Mohammed's job in particular was so dangerous, that he never knew which phone call might be the last. He called that evening after returning home, and the phone rang longer than usual before Mohammed answered.

"Hey brother, what's up?"

"Mohammed, how's it going? I hope this isn't a bad time."

Mohammed just chuckled.

"How's Nina?"

"She's good, she says hi." Something in his brother's mumbled tone made Kadhim pause.

"Is she there with you now? Did I interrupt you guys or something?"

"No. I mean you didn't interrupt me with Nina." He laughed wickedly.

"Someone new?"

"…Maybe."

"Did you split up with Nina?" Kadhim could hear Mohammed moving into a different room and shutting a door behind him.

"Hell no. I like Nina. But listen to what she did to me the other day. I've been working a lot in the BIAP lately, and she got jealous thinking that I'm hooking up with girls there. So she comes up to me and puts a wedding ring on my finger in front of the soldiers and everyone, and tells me that I'm like a husband to her and that she wants everyone to know it! All the guys were hooting and whistling."

"Seriously? What did you do?"

"I told them to shut the hell up! I asked jokingly if I was supposed to go out and get her a ring now, and she says, 'Don't bother. I already have one,' and shows me the ring on her finger that she had already bought for herself!"

The brothers burst into laughter.

"So how are Mama and Baba?" Mohammed asked when they had regained their composure.

"They're fine. They asked about you and want to know when you're going to visit."

"Probably no time soon. You know I can't just leave the Green Zone and drive home—if someone follows me I'll end up getting you all killed. It's too risky. I'll see if I can visit later when it's safer."

"Don't worry about it, habibi. Just stay safe and keep out of trouble."

"Speaking of keeping out of shit," Mohammed laughed, "you

should hear what happened to a unit I worked with last night. We had a night mission on Haifa Street—" Kadhim let out a low whistle; it was one of the most dangerous places in Baghdad, known for the presence of terrorist snipers hiding out of sight in the tall buildings.

"We were sweeping the area for a target, wearing night-vision goggles and all that, and taking it nice and slow. It was really important that no one notice us, and we were trying to stay quiet and keep a low profile. I was walking behind this new lieutenant who was fresh off the plane and jumpy as hell, and suddenly he disappeared right in front of me!"

"What? How do you mean?"

"I mean one second he was there, and the next he wasn't! I started looking for him and then I heard this pitiful voice calling for me—*Saint! Saint!*—and I realized that he had fallen straight down a huge manhole in the middle of the street!"

Mohammed burst into laughter. "I couldn't help it—I started laughing right there in the middle of the mission. He sounded like he was about to cry, so I shouted down to him, *'What's wrong?'* As if it were the most normal thing in the world to be at the bottom of a manhole. Ha!

"'I'm covered in shit!' he screamed at me, and the unmistakable smell of human shit started wafting up out of the hole." Mohammed cackled mischievously. "Turns out it wasn't just any manhole—it was an open septic tank!"

Kadhim couldn't help chuckling. "So what happened next?"

"Well, we pulled him out of course, but we had to cancel the mission. Even if the sound of our laughter hadn't given our position away, his smell certainly would have! When he hit the pool of crap at the bottom, the impact must have caused a veritable shit shower all over him—he was soaked! I couldn't even walk next to him, he smelled so bad!

"It's like this joke I heard the other day about the growing sectarian violence," Mohammed added. "*Iraq was already a full septic tank ready to explode—America just lifted the lid.*"

Kadhim laughed. "It's true," he joked. "Iraq was a case of impacted stool, and the U.S. unintentionally conducted a manual evacuation."

"Huh?"

"Wait till you hear about the day I had."

INFECTIOUS DISEASES

The patient, tired-eyed and covered in a red rash, lay on a bed surrounded by more than twenty medical professionals. Pulmonologists, cardiologists, surgeons, residents, medical students and nurses had all discussed and examined him, and not a single one of them had a clue what was wrong. Reluctantly, the head physicians turned to one another.

"I guess it's time to call Dr. Al Qazzaz," one said, glancing at the patient one last time, as if willing him to shout out his disease and save them from the harranguement that was surely on its way. No such salvation came. A medical student went to find the renowned nephrologist, and they gloomily awaited their fate.

Within minutes, the doctor entered the exam room. Dr. Al Qazzaz loved a medical challenge, and the chance to address a diagnostically difficult case while simultaneously lecturing his peers was even more enticing. The air grew silent and static as he shut the door, washed his hands, and pulled on his gloves.

"Dr. Samarraie, present the case."

Dr. Samarraie did not dare object to being ordered around like a resident. "Patient admitted yesterday, age 36, presents with bullous lesions, enlarged lymph nodes, and skin discoloration. According to the patient, all symptoms had recent onset. He reports not having any previous infections or pneumonia that might suggest lowered immunity."

"Occupation?"

"Truck driver, delivers goods mainly between Jordan and Iraq."

"Labs?"

"We suspect that the illness might be travel-related. Tested for salmonella, brucellosis, TB, and numerous others. All came back negative." He indicated the patient's chart with a detailed list of diseases both common and rare in the region for which the patient had been tested.

Dr. Al Qazzaz continued his cross-examination of the medical staff, asking for a differential diagnosis. One claimed autoimmune disease, another connective tissue disease, and yet another bullous pemphigoid. None spoke with any confidence.

Dr. Al Qazzaz turned to the patient. "How is your throat? Are you swallowing food and drink easily?"

"No, it's difficult to swallow," replied the patient. "I feel like my

156

throat has been infected for a while now, like some kind of rash."

With the aide of a small flashlight, Dr. Al Qazzaz peered inside the patient's mouth, then turned in exasperation to the medical staff.

"Did anyone think to conduct an HIV test?"

His question was greeted with silence and shock.

"HIV?" Dr. Samarraie finally ventured, his expression incredulous. "Iraq doesn't have any HIV!"

"God help us. It doesn't take a genius to figure this one out," Dr. Al Qazzaz snapped. "Run the test."

They took a blood sample, and within days, the results were back. The patient was HIV-positive.

Doctors, residents, medical students and staff were all shocked. News of the HIV patient quickly made its way around the hospital, and in fear and awe they peered into the patient's room and read his chart. It was 2004, and this was the first HIV patient they had ever seen in Al Kindy Hospital, and for almost all of those present, it was the first HIV patient they had ever seen at all.

Dr. Samarraie's claim that Iraq didn't have any HIV cases was not entirely accurate. However, between the low prevalence rate and state propaganda, many presumed HIV and AIDS to be nonexistent in Iraq. The first cases of HIV in Iraq were discovered in the mid-eighties, afflicting mostly children who needed blood transfusions on a regular basis. At the time, Iraq had a major contract with a French company to import blood products, because while Iraq had whole blood, they did not have the technology to separate the blood into different components. In 1985, shortly after the discovery of HIV, Iraq began noticing an outbreak of cases with similar symptoms within its borders. HIV had been shipped into the country via French blood products, which did not yet have an HIV screening process in place.

It caused a huge upset in Iraqi media, and eventually a settlement was reached with the company. The patients, however, suffered greatly. Over the years, when a rare HIV case was detected in Iraq, the patient would suddenly and inexplicably disappear from society, never to be heard from again. There were rumors that Saddam's regime burned them alive, though in actuality, the patients had been quarantined in special centers. Some were not allowed visitors and were not permitted to leave, often remaining under guard until they died.

The Ba'athi government, meanwhile, continued to claim zero incidence of HIV in Iraq. Throughout medical school, Kadhim and his peers would come across chapters in their British textbooks dedicated to HIV and AIDS, as a part of virology, medicine, oncology and other topics.

"Skip it," the professor would order. "We don't have HIV in Iraq."

And so they had not studied it. Not a single word.

The truck driver was eventually transferred to another hospital. Al Kindy simply did not have adequate resources to treat such an advanced case of HIV. Although many did not realize it, the incidence of HIV in Iraq had been steadily increasing since 2003, as the method of infection shifted from blood transfusions to sexual transmission.

Meanwhile, Iraq was becoming infected, not so much by HIV, but by another disease far more dark and devastating.

During the months that followed the March 2003 invasion of Iraq, the country experienced a short period of relative peace and security. Many felt a surge of hope that they could at last live in a free and democratic society. Those days would soon become a distant memory.

Slowly, almost imperceptibly at first, the infection began to make its way across Iraq's borders.

With her government toppled, her army dissolved, and lacking any protection of her borders by the Coalition Forces, Iraq's immunity was compromised and her defenses down. Like contaminated blood arriving unscreened, foreign terrorists began to make their way by the thousands, unchecked, into the body of Iraq, prepared to turn the country into their battleground for holy war.

They hailed from throughout the region, including Jordan, Syria, Palestine, Egypt, Saudi Arabia, Libya, Tunisia, Pakistan and Chechnya. One of the earliest and deadliest vermin to cross the border was Abu Musab Al Zarqawi, a Jordanian salafi extremist with his own terrorist organization, who by 2004 would swear his allegiance to Al Qaeda and become, according to Osama bin Laden, "The Prince of Al Qaeda in Iraq." Al Zarqawi, however, was not alone in his quest to oppose the Western presence in the Islamic world and condemn Shiites along with it. Many other "Arab terrorists," as the Iraqis called them, crossed the borders, clearly distinguishable to the Iraqis as foreign by their strange Arabic dialects, or by the fact that they did not speak Arabic at all.

At first, the symptoms of their presence in Iraq were few. But after the car bomb witnessed by Mohammed at Assassins' Gate, scattered car bombings and wearers of suicide vests increased exponentially. By the end of the year, explosions were taking place all over Iraq, the vast majority of them targeting Shiites.

At times, Kadhim witnessed the effects of these bombs in his own Shiite neighborhood: shattered windows, blown-out buildings, blood-washed streets, and locals missing limbs and family members. More often, however, he saw them during his rounds in the hospital, where the bomb victims came pierced by shrapnel, with arms and legs blown away, and internal organs pulverized by the sheer impact of the blast to the atmosphere. Many bombs were so powerful that they could kill upwards of one hundred people in an instant, and injure hundreds more. They were devastating, and the unprotected Shiite neighborhoods suffered tremendous losses.

Initially, the response of anger was directed toward the foreign terrorists who attacked them. Soon, however, a seed of awareness spread throughout the general Shiite population.

Terrorists couldn't live on the streets. Who was providing them with food, shelter, and weapons within Iraq?

As the U.S. Forces and Iraqi government began to make arrests, it became clear that relatives of Saddam, former high-up Ba'athi officials, and other Sunnis who had lost everything, including status, power, money, and protection, had been aiding the foreign terrorists. They wanted this new Iraqi government, this democracy project, to fail. Many of them fled to Jordan and Syria and granted the terrorists free access to their homes in Iraq, often providing them with weapons and monetary support. Through them, Al Qaeda cells and other terrorist factions nestled themselves among Iraqi Sunnis, turning Sunni areas such as Anbar, Fallujah, Ramadi, Mosul and parts of Baghdad into terrorist strongholds.

Kadhim didn't know whether the intent of these Iraqis was to harm Shiites, or just to fight the American occupier and tear down the new Iraqi government. However, when the terrorists began targeting Iraqi Shiites even more than they targeted the Coalition Forces, the Iraqis who supported the terrorists did nothing to stop them. Perhaps they feared that the Shiite majority would now have complete control over the new government, and that they, consequently, would suffer. Regardless, this continued terrorist support from a select group of Iraqi Sunnis was, for many Shiites, the last straw and greatest betrayal.

The lifeless bodies littering Shiite streets revived in Kadhim dark memories of his ten-year-old self, jumping over dead bodies around his childhood home of Hilla in the wake of the 1991 uprising. Other Shiites, it seemed, had also not forgotten the way they had been betrayed by their Sunni brothers at that time.

To make matters worse, decades of Sunni favoritism on the part of the Ba'ath regime had pitted one sect against another, making relations brittle. Sectarian tension had grown beneath the surface during Saddam's regime, setting a hot and dry atmosphere that made the perfect kindling for war.

The Shiites' true enemy, however, had been Saddam and his regime, and their old grievances with Sunnis might have been forgotten. The two sects had, after all, lived peaceably intermixed and intermarried for decades. On their own and without instigation, it was possible that they would have settled any remaining grievances and disputes through tribal law, much as they had been doing for centuries.

It was the sickness of terrorism that drove a deep and painful wedge between Sunni and Shiite. And it was the same dark sickness that crawled like parasites in growing waves over Iraq's borders and increasingly infected the Iraqis themselves. The most catastrophic strategic mistake made by the American-led forces was that they had not protected Iraq's borders when her immunity was down, and had thereby allowed the entrance of a deadly infection whose prevention might have averted an entire civil war and saved countless Iraqi and American lives.

By the time Kadhim graduated from Al Kindy Medical School in mid-2005, Shiite militias and gangs had cropped up in response to the attacks on Shiite neighborhoods, seeking revenge on terrorists and the Sunni population at large. The Shiites' slaughter of innocent Sunnis propelled an equal and opposite response, leading to the formation of Iraqi Sunni terrorists, armed groups, and death squads.

Despite the chaos around him, Kadhim managed to graduate sixth in his class in 2005. He was thrilled to be accepted into a prestigious plastic and reconstructive surgery residency, which would start after the completion of his intern year.

However, as the new graduate excitedly prepared to start the intern year of his long-awaited residency at Baghdad Medical Center, Iraq was already descending into a full-scale civil war. Kadhim did not realize then that what he was about to face would be the scariest and most soul-wrenching year of his existence, a year that would rip him from his dreams and radically alter the course of his life.

PART III:
INTERNSHIP YEAR

WEEK ONE

The air was oddly tense in the curtained exam room, and Kadhim had a nagging feeling that all three of them—mother, daughter, and doctor—knew exactly what was wrong.

"So you've been experiencing abdominal cramping, vomiting, nausea, and fatigue…"

The patient nodded. She looked young and scared. And unmarried.

"Any fever, chills, sweating? Have you come into contact with anyone who's sick?"

"No."

The mother, in her white *hijab* and conservative black *abaya*, could not sit still. She was practically trembling with anxiety, rubbing her hands and brow, standing one moment and sitting the next.

"When, er… when was your last period?" Although he spoke as respectfully as he could, even a medical setting could not ease the discomfort that arose between male and female from breaching such a cultural taboo.

"It hasn't come lately. But that's normal, right?"

The mother jumped up and fretted to herself, wiping imaginary drops of sweat off her brow with a dirty tissue.

"Do you think it's possible you might be pregnant?"

For a moment, the words dangled dangerously in the silent room.

"Of *course* she's not pregnant!" the mother squawked. "How could she be pregnant? She's not married! How dare you even ask such a question!"

"I apologize. I understand that she's not married, but as a doctor, I have to make sure." He looked pointedly at the girl, who shook her head vehemently.

"Miss, if you are pregnant, then I shouldn't do an x-ray of your abdomen, as it could harm the fetus."

"I'm not pregnant."

"Did you hear that? She's not pregnant!"

"Alright, well let's start with some blood tests and see if they give us any answers. In the meantime, I'll conduct an exam of the abdomen." Kadhim decided to put off the x-ray as long as possible. He still had his suspicions.

It was his very first week as a surgical intern, and he had arrived at Baghdad Medical City with a duffel bag of clean clothes and wistful dreams of becoming Iraq's top reconstructive surgeon.

That was Sunday.

It was now Monday evening, and as he skimmed the results of the blood test, Kadhim's heart sank.

"Mama," he said gently to the girl's anxious mother, "can I speak with you privately for a moment?"

She followed him to an empty exam room, rubbing her hands together and whispering voiceless prayers.

"I've received the results of the blood test." He held out the paper. "Your daughter is pregnant."

The woman crumpled before his eyes.

"Soot, and it has dirtied my face! How do I escape from this shame?" She beat her face in agony, sobbing and crying out Iraqi expressions of calamity. "May Allah protect our family from such disgrace and disaster! My daughter! Are you sure? Are you absolutely sure?"

"Yes, I'm sure."

"Oh God, what are we going to do? Her father is on his way to the hospital right now!"

"No, don't let him come." Kadhim's pulse quickened. "We don't want any problems here. Not in the hospital."

She nodded fearfully. She knew exactly what he was afraid of, and she was afraid too.

"I'll go wait for him outside," she whispered.

Kadhim ran to call the Facility Protection Services—the hospital's security team. "We have a situation in the ER. Unmarried girl is pregnant and her father's on his way in. I need you down here immediately."

"We're on our way now."

"Don't let the father anywhere near his daughter," Kadhim warned before hanging up the phone. "You know as well as I do… when he finds out what's going on, he's going to kill her."

Within half an hour, shouting just outside the ER door alerted Kadhim to the father's arrival.

"I *demand* to know what's going on! You have no right! I want to see my daughter!"

It appeared that he, too, had suspicions as to the cause of his daughter's illness.

"Sir, please sit down and wait here. Sir, you're like our father—please don't make us have to lay hands on you. Please, sir. Sir, please sit down!"

Kadhim had hidden the girl in a corner station, hoping fervently that they would transfer her to the ob/gyn department before the father entered by force. He tried to tend to another patient, but the yelling continued.

"Look, I am going to see my daughter right now! You can't stop me! Who do you think you are?"

"Sir, please! Put down the gun! We're just asking you to wait, that's all. You can find a better way to settle this! Give us the gun, *hajji*. Just stay calm and give us the gun!"

Here we go. Kadhim had heard of shooting matches in the hospital over extramarital pregnancies, and now it seemed he was about to witness one. *Come on, you guys, just transfer the girl already, and get her out of my ER!*

The father was armed, angry, and on the brink of learning that his daughter was going to bring shame to the entire family. The next few hours were critical. If they could just buy some time, maybe he would calm down and consider his options.

For cases like this, the unborn child's father was often hunted down, and the two tribes would come to an agreement and force the couple to marry. For others, the father and entire family disowned the girl, a process that could actually be carried out with legal documentation in Iraq. Once the papers were signed, at any age, the girl was no longer his daughter and no longer a part of their tribe. They would never speak to her again.

Sometimes, however, the offending girl and boy were both killed. Kadhim just hoped that it wouldn't happen to his patient, in his hospital.

"I'm here for the pregnant patient?"

A young nurse interrupted Kadhim's thoughts.

"Yes, she's over there in the corner. Go quickly, and don't let the father find out where she is! Go, go, go!"

The transfer to the ob/gyn department was finally made, even as the screaming match outside continued. Kadhim would never learn the fate of the child or its mother, but he knew that she would not die that day. The rest was out of his hands.

FORBIDDEN LOVE

"Saint, you have to help us out. This girl is driving us crazy!"

Mohammed, having taken an extra job with KBR to keep himself busy, was approached by a group of angry and humiliated Iraqis.

"Our supervisor keeps yelling and insulting us. She called us all thieves! I'm telling you, she hates Iraqis and she's taking it out on us! You've got to talk to her for us, Saint. Technically, she's our boss, so we can't say anything, but you're a supervisor too. Maybe she'll listen to you."

"Don't worry." Mohammed flicked aside his cigarette and stood up. "I'll take care of it."

He found her in the laundry room, sitting on a plastic chair and reading a magazine.

"Are you Melissa?"

She looked up in surprise at the handsome, surly Iraqi who stood towering over her. "Yes. What do you need?"

"Melissa, I'm Saint. I'm a security supervisor with KBR, and I've come to address some complaints that have been raised about you by some of the Iraqis."

"You can't be serious..."

"I *am* serious." She had, knowingly or unknowingly, overstepped some serious cultural boundaries with her insults, and Mohammed was angry. "Look, who are you calling thieves? What are you doing in my country? You think it would be okay if someone went to your country and called all Americans thieves? Well? Guess how much those Iraqis get paid to work in this place! Two hundred bucks a month! That's *nothing* compared to what you get paid for sitting around all day doing nothing!"

"Do you know who I am?" she asked angrily.

"I don't care who you are! While you're in Iraq, you better respect us, or I'll make sure you're sent home!"

She started to cry as Mohammed walked out the door.

The problem appeared to be solved. The Iraqis reported that she didn't criticize them anymore; in fact, she barely spoke to them at all. Mohammed, however, felt a twinge of guilt. Perhaps he had been unnecessarily rough on her. And was it just him, or had she been rather pretty?

166

"Saint! Saint!"

Mohammed was dropping off his laundry in FOB Bulldog when he heard someone calling his name.

It was Melissa. Four or five months had passed since their encounter, and he wasn't sure how she would feel about seeing him. To his surprise, she came up and gave him an awkward hug. "How are you, Saint? How have you been?"

"I'm good. What have you been up to?"

"Well, I work here now, at the laundry facilities in FOB Bulldog." Her blue eyes seemed transformed when she smiled, and her blond hair was cut in a cute bob above her shoulders. She *was* pretty. Beautiful, even.

Mohammed's guilt grew.

"Listen," he said in embarrassment, "I'm really sorry that I was so hard on you before. I shouldn't have yelled at you like that."

"No, *I'm* sorry. I was wondering when I would see you again. I wanted to apologize to you for the way I acted. Iraqis are really nice people; I realize that now."

"Well, I still felt bad for yelling at you... especially because you're so pretty."

She blushed and her smile blossomed even further. "Thanks, Saint. You're so sweet. I knew it wasn't like you to get angry like that. The stress of living here... it can be hard."

"It can't be easy on you either, being so far from home. Someone should show you what it's like to have a *good* time in Iraq." He winked and Melissa laughed.

"And after that," Mohammed chuckled as he recounted the story of his latest girlfriend over the phone to Kadhim, "I 'read her the book,' as they say. I told her what she wanted to hear, and she slipped just like the rest of them!" Mohammed's laugh was infectious, and Kadhim couldn't help but join him.

"What about Nina? Aren't you still seeing her?"

"Yes, but Nina and I kind of have an... open relationship."

"And is *Nina* aware that the relationship is open?"

Mohammed burst into laughter. "I should hope so! There have been times when Nina has left the room so that I could hook up with Melissa!"

"Wow, brother. I don't know how you get away with this. What about Melissa? Does *she* know about Nina?"

"No, I'm pretty sure she wouldn't be too happy about that. She thinks Nina is just a friend."

"I'm not even going to say anything, Mohammed. You know how I feel about this kind of stuff."

"You don't know what it's like here, Kadhim. Life is hell. People I know personally, soldiers and interpreters, are dying every day. It's to the point where sometimes I hook up with two or three girls in the same day and don't even know their names. I'm not proud of it, but I just don't care anymore. And most of the girls don't care either."

"So how long have you been seeing this girl?"

"Quite a while now. The better part of a year, I guess. You know, I'm the first Iraqi to date an American on the base," Mohammed bragged.

"And is that allowed?"

"No, but what are they going to do? I haven't told anybody about it, so as long as she keeps quiet too, we should be fine. I really like this girl, Kadhim."

"You do? Is it getting serious?"

"She loves me. I might even love her." He paused. "We're thinking about getting married."

"Wow." For a moment, Kadhim was stunned. It wasn't like his brother to fall for a girl. How could he be serious about marriage when he wasn't even serious about monogamy? "Mohammed, you better not be thinking about marrying her just for a visa to the States. Marriage isn't a game, you know."

"No, that's not it at all, I swear." For once, Mohammed wasn't laughing. "Look, she's a great girl. I'm serious. She's beautiful, smart, kind... I think I'm going to tell Mama and Baba about her soon."

"That's great, habibi. I hope to meet her someday."

"You will, inshallah. As long as she can keep our relationship a secret."

"Saint, I know about this American girl you're dating." The commander's tone was serious as he sat down for a talk with his favorite interpreter. "Me, personally? I don't mind. You can do whatever you want, as far as I'm concerned. But you need to make sure no one else knows. She could get fired for this, as could you."

"Yes, sir."

"I'm serious, Saint. You need to talk to her. She's been telling everyone about you."

"I will, sir. Thanks for the warning."

Melissa had been bragging about her "*habib*," her handsome Iraqi boyfriend, to everyone she knew. They were in love and were going to get married, and she was excited to go to the Red Zone to meet his parents. She showed up that day wearing an abaya and with a hijab covering her fine blond hair.

"How do I look? Do I look good?" She smiled and twirled around for him to admire. She did in fact pull off the look very nicely, although it was strange to see her in Iraqi clothes.

"You look beautiful, *habibti*. But why are you wearing this?"

"I'm going to go meet your parents! I'm ready to meet my future in-laws."

"Melissa, *I* don't even go to visit my parents. The Red Zone is no joke. It's dangerous for you to go out there, even dressed like this. And if any terrorists track me back to my parents, then I'm putting them at serious risk too."

Her smile was quickly replaced with disappointment.

"You don't think they'd approve of me?"

"How did you get *that* from what I said? They said they'd be happy for me to marry you, if that was what we wanted." And it was true. They, like Kadhim, had been concerned that their son was visa-hunting, but when he'd convinced them that this wasn't the case, they had given him their blessing. From everything they'd heard, she seemed like a great girl.

"And while we're at it, babe, you need to be careful who you tell about us," Mohammed warned. "Word is getting out that we're a couple."

Her response was nonchalant. "Don't worry about it, honey. We'll be fine."

She was lying naked next to him when they heard a pounding at the door.

They had come for her.

In an attempt to catch the couple off guard, the police had arrived at five o'clock in the morning, and as the door swung open and the lights flicked on—temporarily blinding the sleepy couple—Melissa screamed and clutched the blanket to her naked breasts. *"What the hell are you doing?"*

The military police stomped in and grabbed her, pulling her out of bed and throwing a blanket over her. "You're coming with us."

"No, I'm *not!*" She pushed at them and tried to kick them away with her bare legs. They took no notice, holding her roughly as she shrieked and fought.

"Come on, Melissa. You should have known this was coming," one of the police admonished as they dragged her kicking and screaming out of the trailer. Mohammed threw on some clothes and ran after them.

"Where are you taking her?" His pulse was quick, and her sobs wrenched at his heart.

"I love him! I *love* him and I'm going to marry him! You *can't* split us apart!" Tears streamed down her cheeks and she tried to hit them as they pushed her into the humvee. "You assholes! I love him! My happiness is with him!"

"That's it, she's done here."

"You can't just take her like that! What's going to happen to her?" Shocked and incredulous, Mohammed found himself in a shouting match with the military police as they tried to arrest him too. Several of the soldiers watched wide-eyed as others ran for their commander, who arrived within minutes, looking angry.

"First of all, you may have the right to take her, but you can't take him. He's *my* employee, not yours. He's not in your jurisdiction!" The commander's eyes flashed as he entered the scene. "Second, how *dare* you enter my FOB without informing me first!"

"Well, how could *you* let them carry on an unsanctioned relationship right under your nose? Don't you know what's going on in your own FOB, that we have to come and take care of it for you?"

"I knew about the relationship, and I allowed it. I let him live his life. But you still don't have the right to arrest my interpreter."

"We're the military police."

"I don't care *who* you are. Get out of my FOB and *ask* for permission to come in this time. *Then* we'll talk about what to do about Saint."

There was nothing the police could do but begrudgingly follow his orders. With Melissa in tow, they left the FOB like reprimanded children. The commander turned to Mohammed.

"Look, I can't stop them from taking her. That's out of my control."

"What's going to happen to her? Are they really going to fire her over this?" Mohammed felt miserable as he thought of her tears. Would her love for him really cost her her job?

"I don't know. She may..." The commander was interrupted by the sound of the military police knocking at the gate.

"Permission to enter the FOB, sir."

"Don't open that door!" the commander ordered his soldiers.

The voices on the other side grew angrier. "Sir, open the door! You can't leave us out here! We *will* report this!"

"Do what you want," the commander shouted. "I'm not letting you back in!" He turned to Mohammed, speaking quickly. "Listen, I can keep you out of trouble as long as you don't leave this FOB. I'm serious—don't try to go *anywhere* in the Green Zone for a day or two. Give me some time to fix this mess."

"Yes, sir. And thank you." The sky was slowly growing lighter as Mohammed returned to his trailer. He wouldn't forget how the commander had stuck his neck out for him. *This*, he realized, was what his dedication to even the most unwanted of missions had earned him. Loyalty was something valued and given in exchange.

A few hours later, he received a tearful call from Melissa.

"Where are you, babe? What happened? Are they going to fire you?"

"I'm in Dubai."

"*What?*"

"They gave me five minutes to get dressed and they deported me. I didn't even have time to pack my bags. All my clothes, everything, is still in Iraq."

"Oh my God, Melissa, I'm so sorry."

"I love you, Mohammed."

By the next day, she was in the United States. Her personal effects were later shipped to her. Mohammed was in shock. He couldn't believe that she had lost her job over him, and that it had happened so quickly. It was his fault, he knew, but *damn it*, he had *told* her not to keep bragging about their relationship!

Melissa didn't give up on her love. She filed papers for a fiancé visa for Mohammed, hiring an attorney and sending Mohammed the documents. As time passed, Mohammed felt increasingly conflicted. His family still supported the marriage, but his feelings for her had started to wane. Was he truly in love? Or did he just love to feel alive?

After working on the visa for a year, Mohammed finally ended it. He just wasn't ready for commitment, and he certainly wasn't ready for marriage.

GLUCOSE INTOLERANCE

"You're not going to believe what happened to us the other day."

It was a rare night off from the hospital, and Kadhim was spending it with the guys. He, his brothers Ali and Salih, and Ali's two closest friends Omar and Yuhanna, were enjoying a tray of nuts, a collection of hookahs, and the relative cool of the night air. It was Omar who addressed them now, his voice low and hoarse, as if telling them his deepest secret. He was Sunni, Yuhanna was Christian, and Ali was Shiite, but it mattered not. The three had been inseparable since boyhood, and whatever dark story Omar was about to share, he felt that it was safe here.

"A few days ago, Yuhanna and I had to make a trip to Samarra to get some supplies for the Americans." Omar took a deep pull on the hookah and slowly exhaled the flavored smoke, preparing himself for the retelling of the event. "We took the main road and were about an hour outside of Baghdad when we hit a fake checkpoint."

The mere mention of the checkpoint caused goose bumps to form on the men's skin. Everyone knew that very few made it safely through these traps, established by armed terrorists in fake uniforms to kidnap and kill as many and as quickly as possible. They were becoming increasingly common in late 2005, popping up around the country like weeds, only to disappear hours later.

"*Sakkaka* or *allasa*?" Salih asked. "Trappers or Chewers?"

"That's one of the first things we wondered too," Omar answered. "To be honest, we hoped they were *sakkaka*, because we might be able to convince a Shiite militia member to let us pay a ransom and get away with our lives. They're easier to bargain with, even if we are Sunni and Christian. But then we saw the cars—Opels—and we knew we were screwed."

Sunni terrorists had begun buying German-made Opels by the hundreds or even thousands, perhaps because they were fast and well made, or perhaps for reasons that those present could not fathom. In fact, as the years passed, it became so common to find Sunni terrorists (the *allasa*) driving Opels that the Iraqi army began to stop all Opels for questioning. Civilians unlucky enough to own an Opel quickly sold it, not wishing to be associated with terrorism. The terrorists, on the other hand, did nothing to hide their identity. They drove their Opels, wore their *dishdashas* a few inches shorter, and grew unkempt beards with a fierce and ugly pride that instantly reflected their identity.

Not to be outdone, the Shiite terrorists also adopted a car, the official mascot of their own style of kidnap and murder. Theirs was the Toyota Mark II: fast, luxurious, and with an enormous trunk that eased the difficult task of stuffing people fighting and kicking down into it. Practical, really, but still a ride with style. In fact, that's how the Shiite militias' nickname had developed. *Sakkak* came from the Baghdad slang word for shutting something closed, and it was well known that a favorite pastime of a run-of-the-mill Shiite terrorist was trapping people in trunks in order to torture them and extract a ransom for their release. "*Rah asukkak*; *I'll trap you*," was their favorite threat.

In turn, the Sunni terrorists frightened people with: "*Rah a'alsak; I'll chew you up.*" At times, they made it frighteningly obvious which side they worked for, if one had the distinct displeasure of meeting them up close.

"So what did you do?" Kadhim prompted. "Did you turn tail and get out of there?"

"Trust me, there's nothing I would have liked more," Omar replied. "But as we pulled up, an Opel full of armed men came up behind us and waived at us to stop. We were trapped. So we got stuck in a line of cars creeping through the check point, and as we got closer I saw a man sitting there holding a huge, bloody sword."

He took another deep drag on the hookah, and his voice shook. "Entire families were being dragged out of their cars and pulled to the side. They were Shiite families, God rest their souls. Women and children too. I hate to think of the fear they must have experienced."

They sat in reverent silence for a while, the room filling with hookah smoke and thoughts of slaughtered families.

"We pulled closer, third in line, second in line, and I kept looking at this old, masked man holding a sword. We couldn't see more than his eyes behind the mask, but he had wrinkles and age spots on his hands. He was sitting on a plastic chair, his hands resting on the sword hilt, just waiting to cut heads. He was all I could look at, him and his blood-crusted sword."

"God help us," Ali breathed.

"Yeah, I was about ready to piss myself at this point." Omar laughed shakily. "My heart was pounding so hard I thought it was going to burst through my throat. Poor Yuhanna was sitting there in dead silence, green faced, just dripping sweat and shaking.

"You should have seen us, an unlucky pair of contractors about ready to shit ourselves with fear. I swear to God, I was positive that we were about to lose our heads like the rest of them. If they knew that we were contracting with the U.S. Army, or if they even figured out that Yuhanna was Christian, that would be it for us."

Omar shivered despite the sweat on his forehead. Yuhanna was resting his head back on the chair, staring straight up at the ceiling and chain smoking, a potent glass of 'araq nestled in his other hand.

"Our turn came." Omar continued, "We were approached by this young *allas* whose voice kept cracking and who couldn't have been more than seventeen years old. And I was still scared shitless of him. He asked for my name and I.D. I told him I was Sunni and pulled out my wallet to get my I.D. I was so fucking scared and shaky that of all the I.D.s in my wallet it was my dumb luck that I pulled out the American one."

The men gasped out loud.

"That's right," Omar laughed wryly. "I'd already handed it to him when I realized what it was, and that's when I *knew* we were fucked. The whole damn card is printed in English! It says "military contractor" and has "United States of America" written across it in bold letters! I may as well have committed suicide on the spot! So the kid looked at the card, and he looked at me sitting there trying not to vomit, and he looked at the card again and said, 'What the hell is this?'

"'It's my I.D.' I said. What do you say in a situation like that?

"'It's in English,' he said, and he looked at it kind of funny. Then he looked at me again, and I suddenly realized that he couldn't read a word of it.

"'It's the new Baghdad I.D.' I lied out of my ass. 'This is how they make them these days.'

"'That can't be right. I've never seen one of these,' he said. 'Who do you work for?'"

Omar laughed, taking a swig of 'araq. "He suspected that I worked for the Americans, but I was starting to think that he might be stupid enough to be convinced otherwise despite the American I.D., so I told him that I worked for an electrical company.

"He wanted to know where I was from and what I was doing, so I told him that I was going to visit family in Fallujah. 'Who?' he asked.

"And maybe he couldn't read English, but I guarantee he had studied names and faces and knew just about everyone there was to know in Sunni areas, and if I lied he'd see right through it, and that would be our heads. Thank God I have an abundance of Sunni relatives in Fallujah.

"I started listing names like there was no tomorrow, and eventually the kid turned to the old head cutter behind him and asked,

'What do you think, should we let them through?'

"After what felt like a year, the old guy nodded. I was so relieved that I immediately pushed the gas pedal.

"Then suddenly the kid shouted, 'Wait!' He grabbed my shoulder, and I was sure he was going to ask about poor sweaty Yuhanna in my passenger seat, just ask a name, ask for any of his I.D.'s, and the kid would know that he's Christian. Or he'd pull out that huge cross that Yuhanna always wears around his neck under his shirt and then we'd both lose our heads. Yuhanna was thinking the exact same thing—*that's it. It's over. We're about to die.*"

Yuhanna laughed wryly.

"So what happened?" Salih prodded.

"The kid shouted at us to stop, grabbed my arm through the window and peered in at us..." Omar paused. "And then he politely handed me my United States military contractor identification card and said, 'Don't forget your new Baghdad I.D.'"

The men burst out laughing. "Thank God you guys are safe," Ali said, and Kadhim and Salih echoed the sentiment. "Unbelievable."

"It doesn't quite end there." Omar turned to Kadhim. "I wanted to ask you something, doctor."

"What is it?"

"Well, a couple miles after we got away from the fake checkpoint, I couldn't hold it in anymore and I pulled over and vomited on the side of the road. My nerves were shot. Yuhanna was just as bad. The poor guy didn't utter a single word for about two hours. He just sat there, shaking. That night and the next couple of days I continued to feel pretty sick, so eventually I went to the doctor, and do you know what he told me?"

"What's that?"

"He saw that my blood sugar level had spiked, and he told me that I had diabetes! Can you believe that? I got diabetes just from the fright of running into a terrorist checkpoint!"

"Wow. They can do that?" Ali asked, eyes wide.

Kadhim laughed. "It's not that simple. Most likely, you already had a light form of diabetes, known as glucose intolerance. The symptoms typically don't appear in someone who's healthy, but when you go through a physical illness or mental shock like the one you just experienced, the corticosteroids spike, and the imbalance in hormones exaggerates the glucose intolerance, which then basically becomes a form of diabetes."

"So you're saying the problem was already there," Omar said, slowly.

"That's right."

"Even though I had never experienced any symptoms."

"Exactly."

"Then it just appeared suddenly, literally within two miles of meeting a terrorist?" His voice was dripping with skepticism.

"Well, as I said, the condition was already present, but it was exacerbated by the experience. I'm sure the vomiting didn't help either."

Omar regarded him suspiciously for a while, then shrugged. "You're the doctor," he said at last. But Kadhim knew what he and all the other guys in the smoke-filled room were thinking.

Terrorists, when they didn't chop off your head or throw you in trunks, brought on a bad case of diabetes.

SIGNS OF DEATH

"Guess who I met yesterday in the ER," Kadhim said, helping himself to an enthusiastic serving of *tabsi*. Nearly a month had gone by since he'd been able to leave the hospital for a home cooked meal, and there was something refreshing about sharing it with his extended family. Some of the relatives had been staying with them for months, having fled from dangerous neighborhoods. Others had just dropped by unannounced, which was the way most social visits occurred.

They always asked about Mohammed when they stopped by, and each time a new excuse was given.

"He's out with friends."

"He went on a trip to Kurdistan."

"He's looking into buying a car."

Mama and Baba worried about Mohammed constantly, and feared what would happen to him—and, in fact, to all of them—if word got out that Mohammed was working with the Americans. It was a closely guarded secret, even from relatives, as one slip of the tongue could spell a death sentence. And so Kadhim was always careful to introduce a new topic whenever Mohammed's name came up, as it inevitably had that day.

"Patients come to the ER with non-emergent needs all the time," Kadhim said between mouthfuls. "If we're busy, we try to direct them to the outpatient clinic, but often we just treat them in the ER.

"So yesterday, a middle-aged guy came to the ER with high blood pressure. I gave him something to lower his blood pressure gradually, because lowering it too quickly isn't good for the brain or the heart. It was a pretty quiet day in the ER, so I had time to chat with him between patients as the medicine was taking effect.

"Thing is, the entire time I was with him, I couldn't stop thinking to myself that he looked *just* like Nuri Al Said."

"Who's Nuri Al Said?" Salih asked.

"You're in your final year of high school," Ali teased. "Shouldn't you know this by now?"

"Nuri Al Said was the Prime Minister of Iraq back in the thirties, forties, and fifties when Iraq was ruled by the monarchy set up by Britain," Baba explained. "He was pretty unpopular for being pro-British. So when the monarchy was overthrown in 1958, they caught him trying to escape Iraq dressed as a woman, and they killed him and burned and mutilated his body."

"Wow." Salih's eyes went wide. "So obviously the guy in the ER was *not* Nuri Al Said."

"Right," Kadhim continued. "But eventually I said to him, 'Has anyone ever told you that you look like Nuri Al Said?'

"He laughed and said, 'I know. Lots of people tell me that.'

"We chatted for a while longer as I checked his vitals, and after a while he said, 'Can I tell you something without you laughing, doctor?'

" 'What's that?'

" 'I'm Nuri Al Said's son.'

" 'No way.'

" 'I swear to God, I'm Nuri Al Said's son!'

" 'If you're telling the truth, I can't tell. And even if you're lying, I have no way of knowing.'

"So he got out his wallet and starting showing me all these pictures of his family, and his mother and how she was dressed, like a first lady in a castle. He had tons of pictures, even pictures of Nuri Al Said himself!

"He talked to me a bit about the revolution in 1958, and then he said, 'After what happened to my father, we fled. We gathered what money and wealth we could, which wasn't much, and snuck out of the country. We changed our names and from that point forward stayed *far* away from politics.'"

"Incredible!" breathed one of Kadhim's uncles, wide-eyed.

"I don't know if he was telling the truth or not," Kadhim finished, "but he did show me all those pictures. We spent the entire afternoon talking about Iraqi history and politics, until his blood pressure went down and he could leave."

"You've met a celebrity!" Kadhim's aunt said with a laugh.

The rest of the adults laughed and started sharing memories of the Iraq of their youths. The children, meanwhile, slipped away from the table and began playing in the living room. A few hours and many cups of tea had passed when Kadhim's aunt returned from washing up with the other women.

"I'd better get going." She wiped her wet hands on a towel and pulled on her overcoat. "I'd like to pick up some items before the market closes. Fareed! Ameer! You're coming with me to the market and then we'll be right back."

Her children reluctantly left their game behind. The older boy waved a quick goodbye, but three-year-old Ameer insisted on giving a hug to each and every member of the family before he left. Laughter filled the room as he went from one person to the next.

"Let me walk you out," Kadhim offered. No one liked the idea of a young woman and her children walking the streets of Baghdad alone, even if it was just to cross the street. She accepted, and they left the house to a chorus of goodbyes.

They had just started to cross the street when gunfire ripped through the air. In a gut reaction, they all ducked as bullets from both directions sprayed the ground around them. Within seconds, it was over.

They had been caught in the crossfire between two warring militias.

The mother felt a sudden heavy weight in her hand and as her heart started to beat again and she let out the breath she'd been holding, she looked down to see what it was.

A wordless scream erupted from her lips as an unbelievable horror met her eyes. *This couldn't be happening. It couldn't be real.*

There was blood rushing from a bullet wound in her son's head.

"My son! *My son!*" The words flew from her mouth in shock, fear, and disbelief. Fareed gathered his brother up in his arms and ran him to Kadhim a few yards away. "Kadhim, help him! Please help!"

Behind him, his mother had fallen to the ground, sobs ripped from her chest, beating her head and ripping at her hair in anguish.

"Get in the car, now!" Kadhim shouted.

Tires squealed as he drove in a race against time to the hospital, but each minute was endless agony.

"My son! Oh my God, please save my son! Is he going to die? Is he dying?" The mother clutched her three year-old tightly, sobbing, screaming, as her older son cried in the back seat. Kadhim watched the child as much as he could while tearing through the rough streets of Baghdad.

Ameer's body was stiffening. His eyes, wide open, revealed one large pupil and one small. His small arms and legs shuddered in spasms, and he was silent and unresponsive. Pain crushed Kadhim's chest as he watched the signs of death form in a child who only moments before had been so full of life. Wails of grief and fear wracked the mother's body.

"My baby boy, my little Ameer! Kadhim, please help him! Kadhim please, save him! Allah, please save my son!" She looked at Kadhim through her tears and choked out the words, "Kadhim, is he going to die?"

He couldn't do it.

He had told a thousand people that their relatives, parents, children, and spouses were dead or dying. But he could not tell his aunt that her beloved child was already gone. Tears streamed down his cheeks as he lied to her.

"No, auntie. He's going to be fine. We're going to save him. We're almost there. Just hold on. It's going to be okay."

"Dr. Kadhim, why did you bring this child in?" The neurologist recognized the resident and pulled him aside to speak to him quietly. "You *know* he's already dead. You should have taken him to the morgue."

"Yes, I know." Kadhim's heart faltered. "But I couldn't bring myself to tell my aunt, his mother. Please..."

A knowing look passed softly across the neurologist's face. He sat down with the mother, pushed aside her blind hope, and quietly broke her heart.

Months passed. Ameer's father hunted down the militia member who had killed his son in the crossfire, and he and his brothers went to the man's tribe and threatened them. The other side, fearing for their lives, quickly arranged a tribal meeting. It had been an accident, they said. The boy should not have been killed, and his death would be atoned for in a system that had been used for thousands of years.

In a tribal meeting between the two sides, they came to an agreement on how much should be paid to atone for Ameer's death.

But no amount of money could make up for the loss of Ameer himself.

JUSTICE SYSTEM

Mohammed had been interpreting at the infamous Abu Ghraib prison for over a week when he first noticed the old man. The prisoner could not have been younger than seventy, and he sat motionless in his cell as silent tears rolled down his cheeks. Mohammed had seen many prisoners, and had assisted in the capture and detainment of numerous Iraqis and other Arabs, but there was something about this man that drew his attention. Was it the age spots on his hands and the curved spine of the elderly? Was it that his white hair reminded Mohammed of his grandfather?

His curiosity piqued, Mohammed turned to a soldier standing nearby.

"What's this guy's story?"

"He's a terrorist."

"So why's he crying?"

"They all cry in here."

Mohammed looked at the old man again. His clothing, age and mannerisms didn't look like those of a terrorist. At least, not the terrorists Mohammed had seen. *What could this old man possibly have done to end up in Abu Ghraib?* He walked up and rapped on the bars of the prisoner's cell. "Uncle... *hajji*... sir!"

No response.

"Mister!"

The aged man didn't even look up. He stared at the wall as unremitting tears made gentle lines down his cheeks. An uneaten tray of food sat in the corner.

"How long has he been here?" Mohammed asked the soldier.

"About two weeks now."

"He hasn't eaten."

"He never eats."

That was all it took to convince him. One way or another, Mohammed was not going to have breakfast until he had heard the old man's story.

It took an hour of Mohammed's nimble tongue to wear the American down, but at last a commander opened the gate. Mohammed entered the cell and sat directly in front of the old man. The man did not look up.

"What's your story, sir? Why are you crying?"

Silence.

"Mister, I'm not leaving until you talk to me. What happened?"

The old man's voice was distant. "What's the point? You won't be able to help me."

"But maybe I can. Maybe God put me here to help you. We'll never know unless you tell me what happened."

The old man stared at him for a long time.

"I was trying to help the Americans," he said at last.

The old man had been living in this neighborhood since he was a child. He could remember the days of the fifties and sixties when beautiful Iraqi women walked these streets in tank tops and miniskirts. Now, the streets had become unrecognizable. Here, an immense car bomb had destroyed a local grocery store where he had been a faithful customer for the past sixty years. There, an IED had devastated a tiny corner tobacco shop, taking the life of one of his oldest friends, a man he had known since boyhood. It pained him to see the extremism that gradually infiltrated his neighborhood. He missed the days when it was enough just to pray at the mosque on Fridays and live a peaceful life where you respected your neighbors and cared for your children. These days, even his fifty-year-old son went nowhere without a revolver.

One evening, he noticed some men digging a large hole at the end of his street, and knew instantly what they were doing. They were planting another bomb. They were out to destroy yet another piece of his beloved neighborhood and scatter his childhood memories with the debris of concrete and human bodies.

He was exhausted. He was too old for this torment. It was time for bed.

The next morning, the old man watched an American convoy make its way down his street. He braced himself for the impact that he knew would come the second their vehicle drove over the IED. He didn't relish the idea of watching as the children of foreigners were blown to bits. He tried to go inside, but his hand froze as he touched the doorknob.

There was no boom.

He looked again at the American convoy. They had stopped just

100 yards short of the spot where men had been digging the night before. At first he thought that perhaps they had noticed the inconsistency in the road and were sending experts to safely remove the bomb, and his heart leapt with hope. Then he realized that they were setting up a temporary checkpoint, and it was no more than dumb luck that had stopped them just short of their deaths. They would continue on their way down the road soon enough.

The old man had seen enough death and destruction.

Determined, he walked straight toward the checkpoint. No one paid him any attention as he passed, just an old, decrepit man.

When he reached the checkpoint, he stopped. *This was not going to be as easy as he'd thought.* He was nearly seventy-four years old—what could he possibly remember from his grade school English lessons? He found an American soldier who to him seemed barely past childhood, and he desperately wracked his brain for a way to convey his warning. He spread his arms wide. "Boom!"

The soldier looked at him in blank confusion. Then, tentatively, the boy said, "Bomb?"

"Bomb! Bomb!" The old man nodded vigorously. That was it! He was going to save lives! He was going to protect his neighborhood!

The soldier brought an interpreter, who listened to the old man and then said something quickly to the soldier, which the man could not understand. The old man was then escorted to Abu Ghraib, where with an arthritic hand, he painstakingly wrote down his account in Arabic, and handed it over, grateful for the presence of an interpreter to make sure his message was conveyed clearly.

Within half an hour, he was imprisoned. And slowly, the weeks ticked by.

Mohammed stared in disbelief as he heard the old man's story. It didn't matter whether the man was Sunni or Shiite; the truth of his statement and sincerity of his good intentions were apparent on his face. It made Mohammed think of his grandfather, may he rest in peace, or even one of his brothers. With poor English, they just as easily could have found themselves in the same situation. Anger and pity boiled in his blood, and he jumped up and left the cell to speak with the soldier.

"Where the hell is the interpreter?"

"Why?"

"There's nothing wrong with what this man did! He was trying to help you!" Mohammed was unable to control his anger at the wrongful imprisonment of an innocent man. The soldier, who didn't care for being scolded by Iraqi interpreters in the best of circumstances, liked it even less when it came from an angry, towering, barrel-chested Iraqi with a surprisingly large head.

"Why should we trust you?"

"Bring your interpreters," Mohammed snapped. "You'll see!"

There was no point arguing once Mohammed had set his mind upon something, and the truth was that the Americans were now intrigued as well. They brought an Iraqi interpreter who looked as though he were not much older than eighteen.

"Just write down two words in English for me," Mohammed ordered.

"I can't write," the boy replied, cowering. "The soldier writes it down. I just speak."

"Where did you learn your English?" Mohammed barked. "Did you sell ripped DVDs before you started working here?" This boy was like so many others. They learned English from Western music and pirated movies. Their schooling was long forgotten, and their English unpolished and unevaluated.

"Just wait a second, Saint," a soldier said to Mohammed, trying to calm him down. "There's another interpreter, a DOD contractor. *He's* the one who interpreted the statement."

They brought the DOD—Department of Defense contract interpreter—who had been shipped in specially from the United States and received an easy $120,000 per year in contrast to Mohammed's $450 per month.

"Are you the one who translated this?" Mohammed asked him in English.

The DOD ignored his question and responded with a question of his own, in Arabic. "Are you Iraqi?"

"Yes."

"Then why don't you speak to me in Arabic?" The DOD continued to speak in Arabic.

"I won't speak to you in Arabic," Mohammed replied heatedly. "I'm speaking in English because I want everyone to witness this conversation!"

"What, do you think you're better than me in English?" The DOD was clearly getting upset at what he considered a personal affront. He had too high a security clearance to accept the questioning of a local interpreter.

"No, I'm not saying that I'm better than you in English, but I want to prove that you're the one who translated this document!"

At last, the DOD responded in broken, heavily accented English. "Yes, I the one who translate it."

"Oh dear God," Mohammed replied in complete exasperation. This man was even worse than the Iraqi boy. He turned to his commander.

"Look, over my dead body will I leave this old man here! Bring some other translators! Ask for anybody!" The interpreters' inadequacy had only made Mohammed angrier and more stubborn. "I know tons of great interpreters! Carlos, Suzy, Tonka..." He used their American-given nicknames.

"Maybe he's just conspiring with these interpreters," somebody asserted.

"Okay, *you* pick whoever you want!" Mohammed barked, turning to face his accuser. "I don't care who you pick! Just make sure that they at least have a college degree!"

They brought two more interpreters, who sat down with Mohammed. All three translated the old man's statement separately. When they were finished, the commander reviewed the documents. All three translations reported one story, the same story that the man had relayed to Mohammed only an hour before. The translations of the DOD contractor and the local Iraqi boy were not even close.

The commander made a few phone calls; the information checked out. After the old man's detainment, a convoy had in fact been hit by an IED in the exact spot that he had indicated. Mohammed would never know whether any American soldiers had died in the explosion—it was not the type of information that was shared with interpreters—but he knew that if anyone had died, the people they left behind would have these worthless interpreters to thank.

It was only one instance of many where terrible interpretation had led to the deaths of innocent people, Americans and Iraqis alike. It reminded him of the time that the Americans had been carrying out a mission in the streets of Baghdad, when the American commander announced over the loudspeaker, "Everyone stay inside. Do NOT come outside!" The ghastly interpretation of this statement, carried out by one of their interpreters, was: "Come out! Everyone get outside!" Many innocent Iraqis were killed that day; the interpreter was later arrested.

When the commander realized that the statement had been translated incorrectly, he was furious. "Kick this local interpreter out before I lock him up myself!"

"And what about the DOD?" Mohammed asked, still fired up.

"I have clearance. What do you have?" the DOD shouted.

"To hell with you and your clearance!" It disgusted Mohammed to see a man who could scarcely do his job get paid so much and be endorsed with so much trust. He turned again to the commander. "What are you going to do about him?"

"Well, he's a DOD…"

"It doesn't matter!"

The commander hesitated. It wasn't as simple as firing a local interpreter. The truth was, he didn't have the authority to dismiss a DOD contractor. But it just so happened that there was someone who'd overheard the conversation who did.

"I have the authority," spoke up a full-bird colonel. "I'll remove his badge myself." He stepped up to the DOD contractor, removed his badge, and ordered, "Keep him in custody until we send his ass back to the States."

"And the prisoner?" Mohammed asked finally.

"We need to finish his processing," came the reply. "He should be out within seven to ten days."

"What do you mean seven to ten days? A man that you have arrested without reason takes ten days to be released?" He turned to his commander. "Put me in with him! I'm not leaving this place until he does!"

"Saint, there are rules. There is a process we have to go through," replied the commander anxiously. His unit was supposed to leave Abu Ghraib within a couple days and here was his interpreter, threatening to lock himself up with a prisoner for a week.

"When you put him in, how long did *those* procedures take? Ten minutes? Fifteen minutes? It didn't take more than half an hour. I know because I've helped you guys do it."

At Mohammed's exasperating insistence, they spoke with the commander of the prison, who agreed to release the old prisoner immediately. The honor of informing the old man of this decision fell, inevitably, to Mohammed.

He entered the prisoner's cell respectfully.

"*Hajji*, we re-translated the statement that you wrote. You're going to be released, God willing."

"Sure. I've heard that more than once." It was apparent that the old man did not believe him.

"Come on, get up." Mohammed extended a hand to gently help the old man to his feet.

"Where are you taking me?"

"I'm taking you out."

"What do you mean, you're taking me out?"

"I'm taking you outside. You've been released. You're free to go!"

The old man fell from Mohammed's outstretched hand to his knees. He grasped Mohammed's hand and kissed it in grateful relief as tears flowed freely once again.

"May God protect your honor and the women for whom you're responsible. May Allah protect your parents, and may the Lord bless you for being such a kind and honorable person. Thank you, my son, thank you!"

Embarrassed, Mohammed helped him to his feet. The white-haired man continued to cry all the way to the gate, praying that God would protect his liberator, and thanking him profusely. When they reached the road, Mohammed bought him a Pepsi from the young boys in the street, as he often did for Iraqis coming into Abu Ghraib on business, and he waved down a cab for the old man.

"Feel better now, Saint?" His commander was waiting for him when he returned, a partial smile on his face.

Mohammed looked at him squarely. "Yes, I do."

"Our official business here at Abu Ghraib is finished, so you have a few days off. We just need to wait here a couple days for a shipment to come in before heading back to the IZ."

"In that case, I think I'm going to go visit my family in the Red Zone."

"Are you sure? Wouldn't it just be safer to stay here with us and ride back with the convoy to the Green Zone?"

"No, I have nothing to do here and I haven't seen my family in months. I'm going to visit them and I'll see you in the IZ in a couple days."

He called his brother, but Ali was not available to pick him up, so it was a simple matter of taking a taxi home.

What could possibly go wrong?

THE BEHEADING

As Mohammed left the prison, there was only one thing on his mind: a home-cooked meal of mouth-watering proportions, made only the way his mother could. The air was unbearably hot, and the ground was covered with a typical layer of dust. The neighborhood children who sold Pepsi, water and other simple items were making their usual daily rounds, going from one person to the next to push their sales.

One of the boys noticed Mohammed and shouted out to him, "Boy! You seem like a nice boy!"

It made Mohammed laugh to hear a ten-year-old address him this way. "*Habibi,*" he replied affectionately.

"No, I swear! You've helped people a lot! They really praise you!" The boy grinned, squinting up at him. "Where are you going?"

"I'm going out."

"Going to your parents' house?" He looked suddenly anxious.

"That's right."

The boy paused, a serious expression of concern etched on his face. "Be careful," he said in a low voice.

Mohammed laughed. "It's alright. I'll be fine."

"No, I'm serious," the child insisted. "You should be careful."

Although it seemed to upset the boy, Mohammed could not suppress a chuckle. "Okay, I'll be careful," he said indulgently, then moved on, forgetting the incident nearly instantly.

He was careful to walk a ways down the road before looking to hail a taxi, trying to distance himself from the base as much as possible, lest anyone suspect the identity of his employer. He needn't have bothered; there were no taxis. In fact, no one would stop for him at all. It was hard to blame them, considering the circumstances. Everyone had to protect their own skins. But as the scorching sun reflected heat waves off the road, and ten minutes turned into half an hour, he wished that at least one of the cars he was waving to would stop. His visions of a home-cooked meal were quickly morphing into dry-mouthed fantasies of ice water. He thought wistfully of the warm Pepsis being sold by the base—anything wet would do—and then, at long last, a car slowed and stopped for him.

The little red Opel stopped ten yards away, and he ran with relief to catch up, fearing that they might change their minds. Inside sat two men wearing *keffiyehs*, a traditional white and red-checkered headdress, and *igals*, the black bands that circled the domes of their heads and kept the *keffiyeh* in place. The man on the passenger side rolled down his window.

"Where are you headed, brother?" he asked kindly, squinting into the sun.

"May God bless your parents," Mohammed panted gratefully. "I'm going to Baghdad."

"Where in Baghdad?"

"Mansour." He wouldn't risk giving away the actual neighborhood of his parents, but once in Mansour it would be easy enough to catch a taxi home. "Where are you two going?"

"We're also going to Mansour."

"Then it's on your way," Mohammed said, relieved. "I'd be happy to help pay for gas."

"Are you kidding?" The man laughed. "Are you really going to try to pay for something that's on our way? We just want to help. We're the sons of tribes, you know."

It was an expression meaning that they were well-raised and had principles of dignity, respect, and hospitality. Mohammed dropped the matter, not wanting to insult such thoughtful and well-meaning gentlemen. The child's warning, the proximity of Abu Ghraib, all of it flew from his mind in his gratefulness at finding a ride home in the sweet relief of air conditioning.

"God bless your parents and keep them safe," he said, climbing awkwardly into the back seat of the two-door hatchback. "I can't tell you guys how much I appreciate this!" The car pulled away and started speeding down the highway toward Baghdad.

"Don't even worry about it." The man in the passenger seat rolled up the window, and as he did a gust of wind blew his *keffiyeh* to the side. He reached behind his shoulder to replace it, but not before Mohammed caught a glimpse of what was underneath. A thick ammunition belt was draped heavily over his shoulder and disappeared ominously beneath the loose collar of his robe.

Suddenly it all clicked; the Opel, the ammo, the little boy's grave warning as he left Abu Ghraib. A sickening fear turned Mohammed's blood to ice as he realized with whom he had caught a ride.

The terrorist turned to him and confirmed his fears with a crooked smile. "So, how are our brothers the Americans?"

❖ ❖ ❖

Kadhim was just returning to the ER after yet another frustrating visit to fight with the pharmacist. After one too many unfilled prescriptions, he began starting every shift with a visit to the pharmacy to check the available meds. Where there should have been five or six types of a medication, there would be one, and it seemed to Kadhim that it was always the most expensive and the least useful. This morning, he found the pharmacist gone and the pharmacy closed. It wasn't the first time the man simply disappeared, leaving the pharmacy unattended during business hours as patients waited outside. It had forced Kadhim to return again later that day, taking precious time out of his busy schedule, which only frustrated him more. The rampant corruption and apathetic attitudes towards responsibility that pervaded the hospital were pushing him to a boiling point, and by the time he reached the pharmacy, he couldn't hold in his anger.

"Where the hell were you this morning? Do you know that there was a line of forty people waiting for their meds?"

"I had an errand to run." The pharmacist didn't seem in the least concerned.

"Oh really? Was it by any chance obtaining some amoxicillin like I asked?"

"No, we're still out of that."

"Well, then your errand could have waited until you were on break. What *do* you have today?"

The pharmacist swiveled around on his chair and read off a list of names. The list was depressingly short.

"Look, I *know* that when meds are ordered to restock the pharmacy, the list is complete." Kadhim was too exhausted to try to mask his anger. "Can you tell me what the hell happens to two-thirds of that order? Huh? Does it even make it to the pharmacy?"

The pharmacist didn't answer but gave out a short bark of laughter that displayed more anger than amusement.

"Is that where you were this morning?" Kadhim snapped. "Selling my patients' medications on the black market? Paying off some of your men and pocketing the rest? Do you know that I had a patient die yesterday because I had to give him antibiotics that work only on gram-positive bacteria when he needed gram-negative coverage? Do you know what those antibiotics did for him? Jack-shit, that's what! I may as well have given him a damn placebo! This hospital receives more than enough money to pay for all its medications and equipment, but do we save lives? No, we let our patients die so we can line our pockets! Oh you think that's funny, do you? Well, wait till it's *your* son coming into the hospital and see how *you* feel about him dying like the rest of them."

"That's enough!" The pharmacist's angry laughter ceased abruptly and he glared at Kadhim. "I wouldn't speak to me like that if I were you. You'd better watch it."

"You better believe I'll be writing an official complaint to the hospital administration," Kadhim replied angrily. Then he turned on his heels and left; it was better to leave without winning the argument than to anger someone who likely had strong ties to a militia. His only hope was that the man didn't know him by name. There were enough threats in this hospital already without getting killed by a pharmacist.

He was still fuming when he reached the ER, and no sooner had he pulled on a fresh pair of sterile gloves than he was accosted by an out of breath firefighter running in the door.

"Doctor, we need your help! There's been another beheading!"

"Look, haven't you learned by now? All these corpses need to be taken to forensics—or better yet, just drop them off at the morgue. I mean, when a man has no head the cause of death is pretty obvious. You guys keep bringing me headless bodies and bodiless heads. What do you expect me to do with them, huh? Do you think I can just sew them back up and bring them back to life like miniature frankensteins? I have so many patients coming in right now that I don't have time to look at these dead bodies, and I don't have space for them either!"

"You don't understand!" The man interrupted him urgently. "The firefighters are bringing him in right now! The beheading was botched—this guy's still alive!"

"*What?*"

Kadhim turned just as the doors to the ER opened, and what he saw stopped his heart in its tracks and made his blood curdle.

It is said that in life or death situations, the two instinctual human responses are fight or flight. Mohammed, trapped in the back seat of a two-door hatchback, warily eyeing the two *allasa* terrorists with whom he had hitched a ride, now discovered a third. Suddenly, unnaturally, and involuntarily, a cold-blooded calm came over him.

Unruffled nerves of steel produced a reply to the terrorist's question that belied the heart-pounding, nauseating fear that gripped his chest.

"Our brothers?" His tone feigned astonishment and disgust.

"Yeah, our brothers the Americans." The accent was from Fallujah, or perhaps Ramadi, both Sunni areas well-known for the presence of terrorists. "Didn't they liberate us from the tyrant, Saddam Hussein, that sadistic son of a whore?" He was trying to trick Mohammed into giving a reply that would prove that he worked or even sympathized with the Americans. *No Sunni would talk about Saddam like this*, Mohammed thought, *even if they hated him, and there were many who did*.

"Fuck the Americans," replied Mohammed's cold exterior. The U.S. Army had provided specific training to Iraqi interpreters for cases like this. *Curse Americans, call us assholes, tell them you hate us*, they had said, *say anything that will distance yourself from us. Do whatever it takes to save your own life. Just don't EVER admit that you work with us.* As if he would. He knew better than to make that fatal mistake. "They're godless occupiers, here to rape the land and strip it of its strongest leaders and resources. Dogs and cocksuckers all of them." He spewed a string of profanity against the Americans.

"Take it easy!" The guy laughed. "Don't you work with them?"

"What do you mean work with them?"

"Haven't you been here for three days, working with them?"

"What the hell are you talking about?"

"Hah, did you think that we didn't know about you?" The passenger's eyes flashed with disgust. Mohammed's thoughts went instantly back to the child's warning, each word suddenly ringing with crystal clarity.

The boy, he **knew**. *These men could be his uncles or cousins or even brothers. That kid knows what goes on here, he's not deaf and blind to their actions—nor mute, apparently. What the hell was I thinking? How could I not realize that he knows this area like the back of his hand? God damn it, how could I do this to myself?*

In his heart, he knew that he was dead already. He had been dead the instant he set foot in that vehicle. His heart was pounding so rapidly he feared that it was visible through his chest. Yet somehow, like a gift from God, a cold-blooded composure hid his terror, and produced calm, calculated responses.

"I don't work there." He spoke flatly, angrily.

"Then what are you doing, if you're not working with them?" The driver eyed Mohammed skeptically in the rearview mirror.

"My idiot little brother, dog son of sixteen dogs, got into an argument with some American assholes in our neighborhood. My father's a high up Ba'athi comrade, and my brother snuck into his drawer, stole my father's pistol, and used it to shoot at a couple of them, including a commander. It's one of the Ba'athi pistols from my father's work with the government, and they could tell from the bullets."

Immediately he produced the story, the insta-lie created in its complete and detailed perfection by his involuntary cold-blooded crust. Meanwhile, his interior quaked with fear and listened in astonishment. "So they arrested him and brought him to Abu Ghraib. I've been here for the past couple days trying to get him out or negotiate something before they send him to Buka Prison in Basra, because if they send him to Buka they'll probably end up transferring him to Guantanamo. Maybe it depends whether any of the soldiers he shot died or not, I don't know, but I have to try to get him out, the freaking idiot."

"So you don't work with the Americans?" The driver's tone dripped with skepticism, but there was trace of a look in his eyes, a slight rise in pitch at the end of the statement that Mohammed's heightened senses latched onto—*he was wavering*.

The passenger displayed no such emotion. In fact, he appeared not to give a damn about the story as a whole. He pulled a heavy revolver from his side, placed it to Mohammed's forehead, and removed the safety.

"You lying sack of shit," he spat. "We've been watching you for three damn days. You've been interpreting for people at the gate." The terrorist rubbed the revolver angrily in his forehead, but Mohammed's cold exterior did not crack.

"No, brother, I got my college degree in English. What's the sin in being able to speak English, huh? Why shouldn't I help other people who are going in? Look, if I was working with the Americans why would I help these Iraqis out? I mean who was the one buying people cold drinks and helping them catch cabs? I even helped a prisoner get out while negotiating for my brother! Fuck the Americans! I was doing this to help out my own people, and I get executed for it?"

The two men exchanged glances, and the passenger shook his head angrily, refusing to remove the hot revolver from Mohammed's face. The turnoff bridge leading to Baghdad came up on their right... and Mohammed watched with growing dread as they passed it without slowing down. His sliver of hope began to ebb; his thick crust grew brittle.

Nearly an hour went by as they drove deeper into no-man's land, where all signs of life gradually faded and then vanished entirely. Mohammed kept repeating his story to the revolver, adding supporting facts and details, anything he could to plead his case. The revolver never lowered, and the driver never looked back, though his brow creased and dripped with sweat.

Day was turning into early evening when the car finally pulled over, nothing around them but desolate acres of dust and small dry shrubs. The two men got out of the car, and the passenger pulled open the front seat.

"Get out," came the *allas*'s flat command, directing the gun at Mohammed through the door.

"No," replied Mohammed stubbornly.

"What?"

"If I get out, you're going to kill me." He crossed his arms like a petulant child. "I'm staying right here. At least if you decide to kill me here, I get to ruin the interior of your car."

"Wow, you have a long tongue," replied the passenger in angry astonishment. The driver laughed.

"No! You want to kill me and I haven't even done anything wrong! You want to take my soul? Well, I'm going to tell you something. My name is Mohammed Abdurahman Al Baghdadi. I swear to Allah, if you kill me, your hands will be stained with my blood, because I'm innocent. And I swear by all that is holy, if I see you on the other side, *wallah* I am going to kill you. Right now the gun is in your hand and there's nothing I can do, but even if I see you next to God, I'll fucking kill you. I don't care if I *am* dead. My soul will destroy yours, whatever's left of it. Because I'm from a huge tribe, and they're going to hunt you down and take care of the first part of the job for me."

The terrorist laughed. "You think they're even going to find you? Let them try to find your body first and then we'll see."

And with that, he hit Mohammed over the head with his revolver and the two men dragged Mohammed out of the car.

It was like nothing Kadhim had ever seen before, nor ever wanted to see again, and despite his high threshold for mutilated bodies, it nauseated him and brought up bile.

The victim's throat was cut more than a quarter of the way through, the trachea and jugular vein completely severed. Veins large and small spurted blood in all directions. The man had been slaughtered, his throat slit like a goat, but his terrified, blood-shot eyes, and the way his windpipe slipped in and out of his neck as he tried desperately to suck in oxygen, indicated that he was still very much alive. It was a miracle that he had even made it to the hospital in this condition, particularly as neither ambulance drivers nor firefighters in Iraq were trained in any basic life-saving procedures. An Iraqi ambulance was nothing more than a taxi to the hospital, and often a very slow one at that, because traffic would not make way.

The shock and the sickening, gut-wrenching, nightmarish horror of this sight nearly froze Kadhim in his tracks. He panicked—*he was just an intern for God's sake!*—but he was the only one around who could do anything to help. He took a deep breath, and then knew what he had to do.

He grabbed an endotracheal tube and inserted it rapidly into the severed windpipe, watching with satisfaction as the man at last took a deep, reviving breath of air. The patient's relief was tangible. He grabbed Kadhim's arm and gave it a squeeze of gratitude. *He could breathe at last.* Meanwhile, Kadhim tilted the angle of the bed so that the man's head was slightly lower than his legs, preventing the veins from sucking in air on their way to the heart and causing a fatal embolism. He grabbed a thick wad of gauze and, pressing hard, applied it to the jugular vein, trying to stop the heavy flow of blood. The gauze was soaked instantly.

"Call the cardiothoracic resident now!" Kadhim shouted, "Bring him here! Go, go, go!" He thanked Allah that the carotid arteries had not been cut, and struggled to keep his hand in place as the terrified patient grabbed voicelessly at his arms in a panic.

The cardiothoracic resident did not come. Instead, within minutes, in sprinted a third year general surgery resident, Dr. Ameer Abdulhussein.

Thousands of surgeries and countless types of trauma had molded him into a skilled surgeon, but it was his attitude that perfected the physician. He took in the situation instantly, and addressing the patient, spoke with a complete and gentle calm.

"Relax. It's okay. You're not going to die. Your injuries are not fatal. You're going to be fine. I need you to let go of my arms now. Believe me, you're going to live. Just let go of my arms. That's right. There you go. Everything is going to be fine."

The panic in the man's eyes eased and was gradually replaced with trust. His gasps of air slowed slightly, and he let go of the doctor's arms.

Working with lightning-quick fingers, Dr. Ameer applied a local anesthetic to the man's neck and began to sew up his veins with a tiny needle and silk suture while the man watched him with horror in his eyes. The anesthetic had done little to lessen the pain, as too much would have caused a spasm of the arteries and could be just as dangerous. Kadhim's job was to give blood transfusions through a vein and continuously soak up the blood with gauze, clearing the field so that Dr. Ameer could see what he was doing. The patient was taking in blood from one side and hemorrhaging it out the other. Within minutes, the veins had been closed and the cardiothoracic team had arrived, preparing to take the man into surgery.

As Dr. Ameer and Kadhim backed away from the patient, the man grabbed the surgeon's hand one more time and held it to his face with a beseeching look. He could not speak, but they knew what he meant. He wanted to kiss the doctor's hand, to thank the man who had saved his life.

Dr. Ameer gave him a gentle smile. "This is my job."

And with that, the man was whisked away. He would live. His children would get their father back, his wife would have her husband.

Kadhim realized he had forgotten to breathe. His heart was pounding so hard that it felt as though it would come through his ears. He took a shaky breath, looking down at his scrubs, and noticed that he was soaked with thick spatters of blood. He looked up and his eyes met those of Dr. Ameer, his hero, and he saw that the good doctor's lab coat had turned a deep crimson red, with not a spot of white left from his neck to his knees.

The man's brother arrived in the ER soon afterward, and he approached Kadhim and Dr. Ameer both.

"I can't thank you enough," he repeated over and over. "God have mercy on your parents and keep them safe. If you have sisters and brothers, may God watch over them and keep them safe for you. God bless your children, and if you don't have children, then may you have many." Tears ran down his face.

"Do you know how this happened?" Dr. Ameer asked when the man had collected himself.

"Yes. My brother and I are Shiite, and my brother went through a Sunni neighborhood on his way home. The firefighters told me that he was stopped and pulled from his car—probably a fake checkpoint—and they took him under a bridge to behead him.

"They were in the middle of cutting off his head when an Iraq Army unit passed by, and in their paranoia they thought that the soldiers were coming for them. So they fled the scene, leaving my brother with his throat slit under the bridge. Well, it turned out that the army had no idea they were even there. So although my brother was moving and was trying to shout for help—he could barely make a noise with his windpipe cut—the army never noticed him under the bridge, and they went on by. It was the firefighters who finally saw him, and I'm grateful to them and to you for saving his life. May Allah watch over you and protect you and your family all the days of your lives."

When Mohammed found himself on his knees in the dirt before his executioners, he knew it was time to beg. The passenger, he realized, would not budge in his desire to slaughter, so he directed his pleas to the driver.

"Look, I'm telling you I have nothing to do with the Americans. I swear to God, it's the truth. Fuck the Americans! May God burn their houses down! I was just there to get my brother out!"

The driver regarded him coldly and didn't reply. His partner was opening the hatch to get something out of the back of the car.

"What do *I* have to do with this?" Mohammed begged. "You've got the wrong person, I swear! It's not too late. You don't have to do this! It's a mistake that you'll go to the afterlife regretting! Please, don't kill me!"

"Should we shoot him or behead him?" The passenger came back from the car, in one hand his gun, in the other a huge, rectangular, stainless steel butcher knife, more than a foot long, its thick blade covered in dried blood. Deep inside Mohammed, the cold calm composure that had protected him cracked, and through the crack slipped his soul.

It was like nothing he had ever experienced. It was not a hyperbole, not an expression, not a metaphor. One instant he had been on his knees, the next he was in the space above, watching as the scene played out below him. He could still hear, talk, feel his senses and emotions, but he was no longer in his own body. Was it spiritual? Was he dead? Had his instincts activated some never-used part of his brain? He didn't know. He could only watch as his body was slaughtered beneath him. Below, his physical self was dry-eyed and brave-faced. Above, his soul cried for his body, wept for its needless death and for the pain it would endure. He wished he could protect it, but there was nothing he could do.

"Shoot him or behead him? Shoot him or behead him?" The

passenger kept chanting. It was fun for him, like a game. He put the butcher knife on the back of Mohammed's neck and from above Mohammed felt its extreme weight. *How could something that thick slice through his neck? It would never make it. It would have to swing down tens of times before it would cut all the way through. It would stop halfway and botch the job, leaving him half dead, half alive.*

The thought of this pain filled him with indescribable terror. He thought of his family, his brothers Ali, Kadhim, Salih, and Firas, whom he would never see again. He thought of his parents, who would never find his body and would never know what had happened to their Mohammed. His soul wept for the agony they would undergo—thoughts even more painful than the physical pain. He thought of his youngest brother, dear, selfless, kind-hearted Firas, who would not understand where he'd gone, and his soul wept even more.

"I am innocent," his body said, below. "And you will know this when you reach God. I meant what I said. I will find you."

The passenger ignored him. "Go get the video camera from the car. Let's make this a proper beheading."

The driver hesitated, but he went. He pulled out the video camera and pushed a couple buttons. "It's not working," he called.

"What?" The terrorist looked over, annoyed. "How is that possible? I thought they just sent it over new from Qatar."

"I'm telling you, it's not working."

"Let me see it." Exasperated, the terrorist grabbed the camera and played with it for a minute. Above, Mohammed watched and prayed. He wished that there were a way to see his family one more time, to say goodbye.

"Damned Japanese electronics," the terrorist muttered, tossing the camera back in the trunk. "I guess we'll have to do it without posting it to Youtube."

"I don't know," said the driver reluctantly. "It really seems like he doesn't have anything to do with the Americans." It was as though something inside the man had responded to Mohammed's deep, urgent prayers. All of a sudden, Mohammed's soul returned to its proper place in his body, just as involuntarily and abruptly as it had left.

"Wow, your intentions are pure," Mohammed said sarcastically. "When I asked for your help on the road back in front of Abu Ghraib, you said you would help me. What happened to being the sons of tribes, huh? What tribes treat their guests with this kind of hospitality and respect? You're a disgrace to your tribe and to Iraq."

"Those will be your last words," snarled the passenger, raising the butcher knife.

"Wait!" the second terrorist called suddenly. "It really seems like he's innocent. Let's just go."

The passenger paused for a very long time, glowering. Annoyed, angry, and disappointed at the turn of events, he waved his gun at Mohammed. "Get up."

Mohammed rose.

"Now run."

"No."

"*What?*" Exasperation and disbelief rose in the passenger's voice.

"No. If I run, you're just going to shoot me in the back." Mohammed already knew the passenger's plan. He would shoot for sport as Mohammed ran, and the end would be the painful and gradual draining of his life into the sands of this God-forsaken place.

"Damn it! Would you just do what I tell you for once?" It had to have been the first time someone had repeatedly looked down the barrel of the terrorist's revolver and refused his requests.

"No. I'm not running. Either kill me, or take me back to the main road so that I can catch a ride home. But don't leave me here."

"You're crazy. We really will kill you."

"Kill me then, just don't leave me here. Even if I can walk to the next village in the middle of the night, they'll see that my clothes and accent are different and they'll kill me anyways. Take me back. When I asked for a ride on the road, you patted your chest and took me in and made me think you were a man of your word. Is this who you are? Your word means nothing. You're a disgrace to men."

The two terrorists gazed at each other in amazement. "Are you insane? You dare to talk to us like this? I'm telling you I'm going to kill you! Go! Run if you want to stay alive!" He threw a punch that landed on Mohammed's jaw. The other *allas* joined in, and the two tried to force Mohammed to leave by kicking, punching, and throwing dirt.

"No! No, I'm not leaving you two until you take me back!" Mohammed was shouting by now, reaching the full heights of a temper tantrum. The terrorists couldn't believe their ears.

"This guy's lost his mind!"

"It's fucking ridiculous! Unbelievable!"

Mohammed saw his opportunity. Pushing past them, he ran to the car, where to their amazement he climbed into the backseat and stubbornly returned the front seat to its place. The keys were in the driver's pocket, so unfortunately there was no driving away without the *allasa*, but he could sit and wait until they were ready to go.

The terrorists were stunned.

"Can you believe that?" one of them breathed. The other shook his head in disbelief.

"Fuck it. Let's just go. We're not going to get our way with this guy anyway."

Cursing him, they climbed into the car.

"Look, I'll get you to the main road, and that's it."

"No, that won't work for me," Mohammed replied.

"Okay, as far as Abu Ghraib, but no more."

"No way, I'm not going back there. The Americans will kill me, and besides I don't want to risk getting picked up by two more jackasses like you. Take me to the busy intersection where the taxis are."

"Alright, alright," the terrorist shouted in exasperation. "I should have had a damn meter installed before picking you up!"

When they dropped him off, the passenger looked at Mohammed as one looks at a prey that has eluded him for years. "I swear to God," he snarled, "I don't care who you are. If I ever see you again, I'm going to chew you up before you can say a word."

"Then you'd better see me before I see you, because next time, I'll be prepared."

Fearing that they might be following him, Mohammed switched from one taxi to another the whole way home, a trip that took all night. By the time he made it home, the adrenalin was gone and his defenses down. He collapsed outside the house and cried.

Ali came out running. "Mohammed, what's wrong? Are you okay? What happened? Why did it take you so long to get home?"

"Where are Mama and Baba?" was all Mohammed could reply. Ali and Salih helped him inside, where he was greeted cheerfully by little Firas. When his parents returned home, Mohammed knew that he couldn't tell them the true story. He had to protect them from the fright and the shock, the pain of it all. They would forbid him from ever returning to work with the Americans. He told them that he had seen someone slaughtered in front of him. He couldn't tell them that this person was himself.

When Mohammed returned to the Green Zone, he remained unable to sleep for several weeks, plagued by fear and psychological trauma. He felt like he was being choked, stifled, and felt the constant need to cry. Hoping for the return of his equilibrium, he visited an imam at a holy Shiite shrine, where people stared at him in amazement and pity; this beast of a man, broken and weeping by the side of the shrine. He relayed his entire story as though it were someone else's, but the imam saw straight through his cover, and when he finished, the imam's cheeks were also streaked with tears. He put a gentle hand on Mohammed's shoulder, and spoke.

"My son, firstly, don't tell anyone this story. You need to be very careful; just the retelling gives away too much. Secondly, don't ever go back to working for the Americans. And thirdly, when you felt your soul come out of your body, it was because you were already dead. Allah took you out of harm's way, He was ready to receive you in heaven. Your mother's prayer is all that saved you."

Together, they read several passages from the Quran, then Mohammed thanked the imam, and left. As he drove away, he received a call from one of the sergeants. "Hey man, where the hell are you?"

"I'm in the Red Zone."

"Well get your ass back here! We've got some beer with your name on it, and a mission ready to depart tomorrow. You up for it?"

"Sure, what have you got?"

And so it was that Mohammed hitched a ride with terrorists, talked his way out of a beheading, and forced them to taxi him to his destination. Many years would pass before anyone knew the full story.

FUNGATING CANCER

The aging couple sat mutely in such shock and despair that Kadhim realized, after a moment's silence, that if he didn't repeat himself they were never going to move. He wasn't surprised. The last time he made this request, informing a father that this was what he must to do to save his son, the father had flat-out refused.

Kadhim sighed and reiterated the message.

"I'm deeply sorry, but we don't have the equipment needed to conduct your granddaughter's dialysis. You need to go to Mushajjar Street, where they sell stolen medical equipment, and buy a dialysis access catheter off the black market."

"But this is the largest hospital in Iraq." The woman's voice was nearly a whisper, her eyes disbelieving. "How can you not have the equipment?"

Kadhim felt himself flush. What could he tell her? *'I'll write another report that will never be investigated'?*

He looked her straight in the eyes.

"Much of our medicine and medical equipment is stolen and sold on the black market before it ever reaches doctors' hands. Please, try to bring us a dialysis catheter as soon as you can. I'm so sorry that you're paying the price, but at this point it's the only way."

And pay the price they would. It was a gruesome road to Mushajjar Street, filled with suicide bombers, car bombs, and fake checkpoints where terrorists were eagerly waiting to cut heads.

In other countries, medical residents complained about the long hours and heavy workloads. In Iraq, despite increased workloads and longer hours, they complained about the corruption. Kadhim and his classmates had heard stories of corruption while in medical school, but escalating violence and instability had increased the corruption several times over. There were no longer any repercussions, and this was the result.

Kadhim wondered as he left the room whether he would ever see the old couple again.

"Damn it! This is the third CPR kit in a row today that's missing a valve on the Ambu bag! Bring me some more emergency kits. Now!" Kadhim kept up rapid chest compressions as the young nurse hurried off. The nurse returned with ten CPR kits falling from his arms.

"Great, now get me an Ambu bag! No, that's not an Ambu bag, for God's sake! Yes, that's it. What the—it's missing the valve too! Quick, open the next kit. My patient needs to breathe!"

One by one, the nurse tore open each of ten CPR kits, and one by one they revealed incomplete Ambu bags.

The patient's lips and fingers were turning blue.

"Go get an Ambu bag from another patient!"

"But—"

"Go! Now!" Kadhim continued resuscitation, watching the clock desperately as valuable seconds ticked by.

The nurse returned, running at full speed with an Ambu bag that only seconds before had been in use by another patient. Kadhim was very aware of the fact that the bag wasn't sterile, that he was breaking all kinds of codes, but there was nothing he could do. He needed the equipment.

He grabbed the Ambu bag and applied it, but it was too late.

His patient was already gone.

"Shit!" Kadhim stood to ease an aching back and angrily wiped the sweat off his forehead. He glanced at the dozen useless emergency kits that lay scattered about the floor and looked back at the man whose life could have been saved. "*Shit!*"

The deficient CPR kits, Kadhim discovered, had been obtained by an employee with no more knowledge of medical supplies than a dog had of personal space. He had been hired based on "*wasta*"—personal connections—perhaps the nephew or son-in-law of some administrator. Kadhim had started to track instances where he suspected foul play, and when he found proof, he wrote official letters of complaint. This witless employee quickly earned a starring role in a long letter to hospital administration listing the patients who had died due to his oversight. Kadhim never received a response.

The nurses, too, were painfully inadequate. Their education fell far short of sufficient, for those who had actually completed it. Other "nurses" paid thousands of dollars for a forged degree, and dropped certain names when applying for employment. The next week they had jobs.

Doctors and residents had discovered that they could disappear whenever they wished. Between those who had been killed and those who had fled, the hospital had become so short-staffed and overwhelmed that when a doctor reappeared after a month of unexplained absence, he was welcomed back with open arms. More and more, Kadhim was left to tend to the floor alone, resorting to skimming the textbook when he couldn't find an attending physician for a consult.

His one or two letters quickly became dozens as the same corruption that was sweeping the country spread through the hospital like a cancer. Pharmacists who didn't distribute needed medicines, lab attendants who didn't conduct labs, missing medical equipment, doctors and staff who skipped their shifts without notice, needles like crochet hooks when he needed the finest points possible: all were dutifully reported.

Kadhim even offered to testify in instances where he suspected corruption.

Usually, his letters were met with silence. Sometimes, they were met with:

"You should be careful. You don't know who you might upset with these letters."

"You're just accusing me because I'm Sunni," or *"...because I'm Shiite."*

"Do you know what you're doing, complaining about this? You better watch out!"

They weren't idle threats. Kadhim and his friends watched as doctors and nurses began to disappear around them, their bodies later reappearing in the morgue. Names were being slipped from the inside: this doctor represented a nuisance to the Mahdi Army; that doctor was well-off and could be used to extract a generous ransom.

The Mahdi Army, lacking the big investors enjoyed by Al Qaeda, was always on the lookout for sources of ransom, both from other sects and from its own. The Diyala Secretary of Health entered the Ministry of Health one day and was never seen or heard from again. Even children on their way to and from school were kidnapped. Sometimes the person was returned alive after the ransom was paid.

But not always.

Kadhim stopped leaving the hospital. He was too angry to stop writing reports of deficiencies and corruption, but with each letter, he feared that he was writing his own death sentence, a sentence that would be enacted the minute he left hospital grounds. Increasing paranoia trapped him in the hospital and plagued his every step.

Occasionally, Kadhim and some six or seven other residents would go on strike. They made signs and picketed outside the hospital, demanding safer conditions and a better work environment. There was no media coverage of their feeble attempts, and besides, they made terrible protestors. The instant trauma victims arrived from the latest car bomb, they dropped their signs and ran in to help.

For a short while, security in the hospital improved as Baghdad Medical City bulked up their Facility Protection Services. But when the violence outside worsened, even the FPS became too scared to guard the hospital. And still, Kadhim kept writing letters.

Even Malik, it seemed, had grown corrupt.

When it became apparent that his medical skills weren't up to par, Kadhim's pudgy old friend had been put in charge of running the cafeteria. Overnight, their cafeteria fare transformed from eggs and hot rice to stale sandwiches. Malik, whose tastes were too refined to eat from the cafeteria himself, explained that the changes were due to a tight budget. However, he seemed none too happy when Mahjoub offered to help him find quality food for cheap.

Kadhim was hopeful when he ran into Mahjoub not long later. "How'd it go with connecting Malik with some better vendors?"

Mahjoub rolled his eyes. "I and some others called up our buddies in the restaurant business. We found fresher, tastier food and even came in under budget. It was perfect."

"But...?"

"But Malik wouldn't hear of it, the prick. He just kept talking nonsense about a strict budget and having contracts with certain vendors."

Kadhim gave a wry laugh. "I can tell you where our cafeteria budget went. Good old Malik has never had a penny to his name, and just last week he went out and bought himself a brand new Peugeot worth over $100,000."

Mahjoub gasped, "He's lining his pockets with my lamb and rice, that bastard!"

The stench coming from the exam room was unbearable, so strong that it wafted in sickening waves down the hallway. Kadhim recognized it instantly and knew, even without entering, both the diagnosis and prognosis. He had encountered this smell once before;

only that time it had been much worse.

The stench had been brought to the hospital by an elderly Kurdish woman who was accompanied by her young daughter-in-law. Kadhim was only a fifth year medical student at the time, but he had already been exposed to the wide range of strong odors that came with work in the hospital. Vaginal infections, foot fungi, feces, vomit, death, even bodily odors and bad breath made worse by infection and disease: all had helped harden his stomach to this nauseating odor.

The patient did not speak a word of Arabic. Her daughter-in-law, as well, spoke only Kurdish. They had traveled from the far reaches of Kurdistan with only a note, written in simple Arabic, explaining who they were and why they had come.

Kadhim knew that medical services and health awareness in parts of Kurdistan were limited, and he feared the worst, but when the aging woman lifted her gown to reveal her naked body, even the most veteran among them was shocked.

What had started as a malignant breast tumor had been allowed to grow, untreated, until her breast had multiplied several times in length and size and the tumor had burst through the skin in a large, fungating mass. No longer did any skin cover her left breast. In its place was a thick, lumpy mass of dead and dying cancerous flesh, black, oozing blood, and green where the fungi had grown.

The stench increased to dizzying waves in the small room. Kadhim quickly grew light-headed. He wondered how the family had tolerated such a smell, and why they had waited so long before seeking treatment.

The attending, grave-faced, conducted a full exam. Then he stepped outside and vomited.

With the help of a Kurdish doctor, the attending informed her of the prognosis. "Please, tell her to go home and live out the rest of her days the best she can. The cancer has spread far beyond what is treatable and is completely inoperable. Any attempt at surgery would fail, and she probably would not survive the operation. She has only a month or two to live. I am sorry."

So powerful was the stench of fungating flesh that Kadhim continued to have a headache for a week. The memory of that smell, however, stayed with him forever.

"Dr. Kadhim, that's my cousin's son you have there with you. Why didn't you order a CAT scan for him?" The President of Baghdad Medical Complex did not sound happy as his voice came over the phone.

"Sir, with all due respect, we haven't had a working machine in months."

"Yes, we do. It's in room 713. Take him there immediately."

What? After asking about it so many tims, why was this the first he was hearing of a CAT scan machine? Was Radiology secretly storing it for VIPs, or were they, too, kept in the dark? If the hospital president himself was keeping it a secret, then how could Kadhim hope for any iota of transparency, and to whom could he protest?

He thought bitterly of the letters of complaint that he, Mahjoub, and many other doctors had written regarding Malik's blatant misuse of cafeteria funds. As usual, they had been ignored.

It was that stench again. The terrible smell of corruption was making its way through the hospital, untreated, inoperable, and cancerous.

OLD SCHOOL & NEW SCHOOL

Mohammed realized, as he tried to outrace the car of armed men behind him, that visiting his family was no longer a simple matter of hopping in his car and going. It was not the first time he had been chased by insurgents, who would watch him leave the Green Zone and try to catch him. This time, however, he made it nearly all the way to his neighborhood before he noticed they were following him.

The men in the car behind him pulled up closer and waved their guns at him, motioning for Mohammed to pull over.

Yeah right. Mohammed pulled out his gun and fired a warning shot into the air through the window. Sometimes that scared them off. Not this time. A cold sweat broke out all over his body and his heart raced even harder as he glanced out the window and realized that they were not giving up. In fact, they were gaining on him, and he ducked as he heard the sound of gunfire behind him.

Fuck.

As much as he could while still driving, he reached back and began shooting at the car directly. He managed to crack their windshield, and they backed off a bit. Meanwhile, Mohammed gunned the gas. *This* was why he had purchased a BMW. No matter how fast they were, he needed to be faster. He spun through several small streets—he knew this neighborhood like the back of his hand—and tried to lose them. As for visiting his parents? Mission aborted. There was no way in hell he was going to lead his killers directly to his parents' house so they could murder his family as well.

After twenty breathless minutes of sharp turns and speeding through back streets, the car no longer appeared in Mohammed's rearview mirror. He had probably managed to lose them, but his nerves were still on fire so he drove at top speed all the way back to the base.

He thought, with an ironic smile, of the last time he had been chased. He had hit a gut-dropping 172 miles per hour going the wrong direction down the highway, while his cousin cried tears of fear and panic in the passenger seat. Mohammed laughed at the memory and lovingly patted the steering wheel. Once again, the BMW had saved his life.

Incidents like these had made it clear to Mohammed that it was becoming too dangerous for him to leave the base, particularly on his own. He was constantly out on American missions, and he was one of the few Iraqi interpreters who did not wear a mask outside of the Green Zone. Because of this, both Mohammed and his occupation were becoming increasingly well known throughout the city, and the more people saw him, the more he became targeted as a traitor and an agent for the enemy.

If it weren't for his buddy, Mohammed didn't know what he would have done. "New School," as the Americans called him, was an Iraqi interpreter of about Mohammed's age, and his father "Old School" also worked on base. They had been friends for years: Mohammed and the shy, skinny kid who looked up to him in adoration and awe the way a boy looks up to an older brother. He was harmless. Their friendship became particularly close, however, after Mohammed was banned from leaving the Green Zone unless on a mission.

"Look, Saint, we just received intel that you are now the number two guy on the Mahdi Army's most wanted list."

"Why? Who's number one?"

The commander laughed. "You *would* ask that. Number one is your buddy Mo, who runs the restaurant here in the IZ"

Figures. Mo's restaurant in the Green Zone was always full of girls, and as a result, it not only attracted Mohammed as a regular customer but also attracted suspicion that Mo was running a full-scale Iraqi brothel for American soldiers.

"Look, you need to start wearing a mask like the rest of the interpreters," the major continued.

"I don't want to. I'm not doing anything wrong. I'm serving my culture, I'm serving the U.S. Army, I'm serving Iraqis and I'm serving myself at the same time. I'm not going to hide behind some mask like I'm ashamed!"

"It's dangerous, man. You're putting yourself at risk every time you leave the base. That's it. You can't leave the Green Zone on your own anymore. It's just too dangerous, and we don't want to lose you. I don't think you should go out at all, but if you have to go out, take at least two soldiers with you—American, Iraqi—I don't care. Just have someone with you at all times."

"But I'm going crazy in here," Mohammed protested. "I need to get out, get some fresh air. I feel like I never get to leave the base. I'll be careful, I promise—"

The major cut him off. "Saint, there are 'wanted' posters with your face on them pasted in mosques throughout Baghdad. You're not going out without protection, and that's an order."

There had been no point in arguing, but Mohammed was still upset. He had grown increasingly depressed and frustrated from being stuck in the IZ, and was suffering from "Green Zone cabin fever." The major had given orders to stop Mohammed at the gate if he tried to leave alone, and soldiers had to accompany him for things as simple as grabbing a sandwich, although even their presence did not guarantee his or their safety. The last time he had gone with a couple of American soldiers to Bab Al-Sharji to buy some clothes, the locals had remembered him and had started throwing rocks as soon as they stepped out of the vehicle. Who knew what the locals might do next time. Mohammed had interpreted for missions at Bab Al-Sharji too many times; he could not go back.

He complained about this to New School one day, and the young man spoke up. "You want some new clothes, Saint?"

"Well, mostly I just want to get out of here, but yeah, some new clothes would be nice."

"I can go to Bab Al-Sharji, if you want, and pick some things up for you."

"I appreciate the offer, but it's too dangerous. I can't have you risking your life just so that I can have some new jeans."

"Don't worry about it. I'd be happy to do it for you."

Mohammed's protests fell on deaf ears. New School idolized Mohammed and everything about him—the way he carried himself, his outgoing personality, his way with girls, his courage, and even how much the Americans trusted and respected him. If Mohammed needed some clothes, then New School was happy to help him.

Since then, New School had made periodic trips to Bab Al-Sharji, about a mile away from the Green Zone, to pick up a selection of jeans and shirts for Mohammed. When he got back to the IZ, Mohammed would select the items that he wanted to keep, and New School would once again risk his life to return the unwanted items.

It wasn't easy for the kid. *Anyone* who left the Green Zone, known or unknown, was targeted. It didn't matter whether they were interpreters, patients at the hospital inside the IZ, or prisoners being released; all were suspected of and indeed treated as though they were traitors working for the Coalition Forces. Certain gates in particular were well known for the constant presence of terrorists, just waiting for someone to leave the Green Zone so they could hunt them down, torture them for information, and kill them.

Many of Mohammed's acquaintances had been killed this way, including a good friend of his who had left the base to give his fiancée a ride to her university. While on the way there, they forced him to pull over and shot him fourteen times as his fiancée screamed in hysterics. At other times, interpreters just disappeared without anyone ever seeing or hearing from them again. Mohammed had several acquaintances who were among the ranks of the missing, such as "Beyonce", who had recently disappeared, as well as "Luke" and "Buddy" before her. He worried that New School would be next. There were very few interpreters that Mohammed trusted, but after seeing the boy's devotion, New School became one of them.

From time to time, New School brought home cooked meals, compliments of his mother, and when he did he would call Mohammed to eat with him at the checkpoint. New School went home fairly frequently, as his neighborhood was not far from the base, and Mohammed always appreciated the home cooked meals. They satisfied his cravings for something other than "chow-hall" and fast food, while also whetting his appetite for a proper family meal. He and New School would spend the night at the checkpoint, eating, drinking alcohol, and shooting the breeze until New School's shift was over in the early morning hours.

New School's father, Old School, also worked at this gate periodically, but his hours had been reduced because he was constantly late, having some business that he was running outside the IZ. Mohammed had inquired once about his other work, but New School's answer had been vague.

It was shortly after one such meal that Mohammed went to visit New School where he was interpreting at Checkpoint One. It was a Saturday, and Mohammed was in a particularly foul mood.

"How's it going, man?" New School was happy to see him, as always.

"Same old shit. How are you? How's Old School?"

"He's good. My mother says hi and asks when you're going to come to the house for dinner."

"God willing." Mohammed brushed it off.

"You know," New School said as he took a drag on his cigarette, "if there's one thing the Americans love, it's you." He laughed at

Mohammed's pained expression. "No, I'm serious! They listen to you, man! I've seen it! You guys are out on a mission or something and the commander will say to go down some street or use some tactic, and then you'll tell him that this street is too dangerous and they should go down another one, or that this tactic will only insult and anger Iraqis... and they actually listen to you and follow your direction!"

"Well, I also have to protect my own skin out there! I'm not going to let some poor commander pick the most dangerous street in the neighborhood and watch the entire troop get killed, myself included! Besides, they're like brothers to me!"

"It's okay, you don't have to defend yourself!" New School laughed. "I'm just saying that you really do a lot for the Americans. *You* are the heart of their raids. I'm serious! I'm impressed that you've managed to build such a relationship of trust with them. That must've taken a while... How long have you been working with the Americans anyway?"

"Long enough," Mohammed grunted.

"What's wrong?"

"I feel like I'm imprisoned here. This place is choking me." Even nightly visits from Nina, interspersed with other girls, could not relieve Mohammed's depression. The girls, the video games, the workouts, the drinking and joking around with friends, nothing could reduce the anxiety of being a caged animal.

"Why don't you come with me sometime? I've been telling you for ages that you should come visit. Come on, Saint, you're like a brother to me! My mom will cook you a nice dinner... you got to get out of here and relax a little."

New School's numerous invitations had been particularly insistent as of late. Mohammed had already experienced enough danger outside the gates to be wary of leaving the IZ, and New School lived in the close but particularly dangerous Shiite neighborhood of Hai Al-Jihad, making his proposition even more perilous. In the end, however, Mohammed relented, and they agreed on an evening later that week when Mohammed would ride with him to his parents' house.

Mohammed ran into Major Freeman the next day and stopped to say hello. In passing, he decided to mention his upcoming trip.

"Do you remember New School, who works at Checkpoint

One?"

"Yeah, I remember him. He's your friend, right? Nice guy."

"Well, he keeps hounding me about visiting his family's house for dinner, and honestly I'm so bored and sick of being stuck on the base. I feel really bad, seriously, like I'm trapped in a prison, so I'm thinking of going with him for dinner. His mom cooks some really good food, and I can't reach my own house, but at least I can reach his."

The major's attitude suddenly shifted from friendly to cautious.

"Don't go. It's not worth the risk of leaving the base, Saint. I'll bring you food and we can hang out here and eat. Just don't go."

"It's not just the food. I want to get *out*," Mohammed insisted. "I have to go outside the wires. I really feel depressed! The only time I get to go out is either on a mission or when I take two other soldiers with me!"

"What day are you planning on going?"

"In three days—this coming Wednesday."

"Ok, well just think about what I said and be careful. I'm worried about you. You're like my little brother, and I want to make sure you're safe."

On Wednesday morning, Mohammed received a phone call from Major Freeman.

"Saint, I need you to get over here to Checkpoint One."

"What's the matter?"

"There's something going on. Just get over here."

Mohammed didn't think too much of it; he was frequently called to various gates for a particularly sensitive or dangerous interpretation. He found Major Freeman waiting for him at the checkpoint.

"What's going on, sir?"

"How are you doing, buddy?" The major's tone was oddly gentle.

"I'm fine. What's going on?"

"I have bad news."

"What is it?"

"New School…"

Immediately, Mohammed knew that his friend had been killed. His breath caught in his throat. It hurt to think of that gentle soul being murdered, and it hurt even more to keep losing his friends in this fashion.

"What's wrong with him?" Mohammed could hear the panic

213

building in his voice and dreaded the answer. He thought of the friend who had been shot fourteen times, and anger boiled up inside of him. "Who killed him?"

"Nobody killed him, nothing like that." The major put a hand on Mohammed's arm. "You know how you told me that he kept insisting that you come with him to visit his family's home? Well, we decided to do an in-depth background check. We sent some of our guys to follow him, just to watch him for a few days and see what he's up to. Saint," he looked Mohammed squarely in the eyes, "New School has kidnapped three translators before by inviting them to his house and drugging them with food. Then an armed group comes and takes them away. They torture them, cut off their fingers, and if they can't recruit them to start kidnapping other interpreters, they kill them *and* their families. New School admitted it personally. And you were meant to be the fourth."

Mohammed felt as though he'd taken a blow to the gut. It just didn't make sense. Not New School, not the guy who had risked his life for Mohammed countless times, who had sat around and laughed with him, shared meals with him, told stories with him. No, something was wrong here. It couldn't be true. Mohammed couldn't believe that the boy who idolized him and who had been one of his closest and most trusted friends on the base had all along been plotting to kidnap and murder him.

"Are you *sure*?"

"He admitted it personally," the major repeated.

"Did you torture him?" Mohammed growled. *Maybe he didn't mean it. Maybe he had just made something up to stop the torture.*

"Just calm down. Look, because I respect you and love you as a brother, I'm going to take you somewhere."

He led Mohammed to the interrogation room where New School was being held, his eyes blindfolded. Then Mohammed heard the unbelievable words coming from the boy's own lips.

"Please, don't hurt me. Have mercy on me," New School whimpered.

"How many people did you kill?" the interrogator asked.

"I didn't kill anybody, but I helped kidnap three interpreters. Two guys and a girl from the BIAP—Luke, Buddy, and Beyoncé."

Mohammed *knew them*, the interpreters who had been kidnapped and killed. He felt his world spinning around him in nauseating waves of hurt, anger, betrayal and disgust. Could this be real, the world that he lived in, where his best friends plotted his murder? He felt like he was going crazy, and the buzz of anger in his ears was so loud that he almost didn't hear what New School said next.

"I smuggle weapons onto the base too. My father and I both use our badges and our English to sneak weapons in our cars past the temporary checkpoints. The soldiers trust us and don't even check." New School's voice cracked in fear and emotion.

Mohammed had heard enough. He turned away in incredulity.

"This is my friend! *My friend!*" he repeated to Major Freeman. "He risked his life for me!" The thick wall of shock would not allow the information to compute in his mind, even after hearing the words directly from his friend's mouth. He had spent too much time, had too many laughs with New School, to forget their friendship so quickly.

"He wasn't your friend, Saint." The major's tone was grave. "He did this to everyone he kidnapped. He pretended to be their best friend, in order to lull them into a false sense of security so that they'd go with him. And he didn't risk his life for you. He gets your clothes from an area controlled by the Mahdi Army—and he's one of *them*."

New School was arrested. Mohammed never asked about him again. The betrayal was too great. He could not believe how close he had come to once again riding away with someone who planned to murder him.

After New School, he would never trust an Iraqi again. Male, female, it made no difference to Mohammed. The guys he might hang out with, the girls he might sleep with, but *none* would ever be given his trust. He trusted his immediate family members and no one else.

Never *ever* again.

THE BOXER

Every morning, Sergeant Major Harley got up, stretched his muscular legs, and stepped out onto the balcony to smoke his morning cigarette. Outside the Green Zone, the streets of Baghdad were dusty, full of potholes, and increasingly dangerous. Electricity was intermittent at best, and bloodstains and burnt out cars were a common sight. Inside, the "Emerald City" boasted a surreal world of swimming pools, nightclubs, manicured lawns, air-conditioned shuttle buses, and cafeterias serving pork chops and bacon. For those who never left the Green Zone, it took occasional mortar showers and panicked trips to bomb shelters to remind them where they were. That, and the engless boredom of living in a shiny cage.

Mohammed was always up for a mission outside the gates and often volunteered for missions that were not with his own unit. But when there were no missions to be had, he turned to other pursuits to pass the time, and one of his favorite activities was shouting up teasing insults at Sgt. Major Harley as he smoked his morning cigarette.

Sgt. Major Harley was not the kind of guy people messed with. If Mohammed was a big guy, Harley was *huge*. He was tall, broad, extremely muscular, and a frequent contender in the boxing ring in front of Saddam's old palace. Mohammed, like others, had infinite respect for the Sgt. Major's power, both physically and as a leader, but that didn't stop him from shouting up to the commander, "What the hell are you doing, moron?"

"I'll come downstairs right now and beat the hell out of you!" The American threw down his cigarette.

"Bring it!" Mohammed flashed a wicked grin and a middle finger, and as the Sgt. Major ran from the balcony, he jumped into the humvee with the other soldier.

"Lock the doors! Now! If any of you opens the door for him, I'll kill you!"

Harley ran out to the humvee and shook it, to no avail, shouting curses all the while. All in a day's fun.

It was during a boxing match that Sgt. Major Harley at last had the opportunity to teach Saint a lesson. A small crowd had formed around the ring, and Mohammed joined them to partake in the exciting atmosphere of the fight. Opposite Sgt. Major Harley was a young soldier who was short but very well built, and he was doing his best to avoid his opponent's heavy blows, while landing a few punches himself that seemed not to affect the Sgt. Major in the least. As the shouts grew louder and the atmosphere more intense, Sgt. Major Harley suddenly landed a stunning uppercut to the soldier's head that picked him up off his feet, tossed him through the air, and left him unconscious before he even hit the ground.

A roar of approval erupted from the crowd as several ran up to check on the unconscious soldier, and suddenly through all of it cut Mohammed's taunting shout, "Ooh! You weak-ass! That was just a little boy! If *I* jump in the ring, I'll kick your ass!"

Red-faced and sweating, with his veins popping and muscles bulging, Sgt. Major Harley shot him a piercing glare. Mohammed hadn't been able to resist the opportunity for a teasing jab. The Sgt. Major gave a slight nod to the soldiers on either side of Saint, and before he knew what was happening, Mohammed had been tossed into the ring.

"Have you seen the patient in room 513?"

There was something about the male nurse's excited tone that intrigued Kadhim.

"I was just about to check on him now. Why?"

"He's a famour boxer! Well, famous around *here* anyway. They say that he even competes in places like Dubai and Turkey. He's huge!"

Kadhim smiled. He didn't follow the Iraqi boxing world, but from the way the nurses kept peering with fascination into the room, it was clear that the boxer had several fans among the night staff.

Kadhim took a look at the chart as he stepped into the room. It was a severe case of Hepatitis A, a viral liver infection that was common in Iraq due to contaminated food and water. He scanned the lab results, but the truth was that he needn't have read them to know how advanced this particular case was; a single look at the patient would have sufficed.

The boxer's eyes and skin had turned bright yellow from a severe case of jaundice caused by the infection. He was suffering an uncommon complication wherein the liver had stopped functioning properly and was no longer able to remove the body's toxins and bile, which now gave the boxer his yellow hue.

However, it was not the patient's extreme jaundice that startled

Kadhim, but rather his enormous build. When the nurse had mentioned that the boxer was "huge," Kadhim had assumed that he meant it figuratively. But this man was a *giant*. Even lying down, it was obvious that he towered over most men, and his physique was almost frightening in its extremes. He reminded Kadhim of an ox, and even the weight loss had not diminished his bulging muscles, which made his hospital gown look small and ridiculous.

Kadhim examined the patient, who seemed scarcely aware of what was going on around him, and double-checked the multiple IV lines through which he received glucose. The lab tests indicated fulminant liver failure, and Kadhim was sure that this was going to be a long night for him and the patient both. For the time being, however, all was quiet.

Kadhim left the boxer's private room and was heading to check on the next patient, when he heard a roar of fury behind him.

Mohammed found himself suddenly tossed into a boxing ring surrounded by loud and excited soldiers, and across from a very fired-up Sgt. Major Harley. Somehow, the major looked even bigger from inside the ring than he had from the outside.

"Hold on! Hold on!" Mohammed shouted over the din, as he strolled over to the side of the ring. "Before I get too angry..." He chuckled, pulled out his gun, and set it aside.

"Alright, Saint, let's see what you got!" Sgt. Major Harley teased. Mohammed found that a pair of boxing gloves had been quickly and deftly strapped to his hands, and within seconds, the match had started.

Okay, he's heavier than me, Mohammed thought as they circled the ring in anticipation, *but I'm faster than him. I've been working out. I've been running every day. I can do this.*

They circled the ring for a few interminable seconds, each making jabs that didn't land, as Mohammed jumped around and did his best to look like a boxer. Harley looked huge and angry, like a bull, and Mohammed could almost see the steam rising from his nostrils. The tension was rising...

Enough of this. Time to strike.

Barreling forward, Mohammed put every ounce of energy and every fiber of his being into a shattering blow that struck the side of the Sgt. Major's head. Even as Sgt. Major Harley stumbled several steps backward from the force of the blow, Mohammed felt a pain in his knuckles through the thick gloves that radiated up the muscles in his arm. It had been a solid strike.

But Sgt. Major Harley did not fall. He seemed only slightly stunned by the heavy punch and came back even angrier.

Oh shit. Now there really *was* steam fuming from his nostrils.

With a roar of anger, Sgt. Major Harley rushed at Mohammed, and the latter didn't even have the time to raise a defensive arm before his opponent landed a spectacular right hook to his ear.

"Saint! Saint, you okay?"

When Mohammed opened his eyes he was on the ground. "What happened?"

"You were unconscious for a couple minutes." Sgt. Major Harley's voice was low and rough, but there was laughter in his eyes.

"You motherfucker!" Mohammed shook his head as they helped him up. "I'm going to kill you!"

"You better never touch me again after this!" Sgt. Major Harley pointed at his own cheekbone, which was pink and slightly puffy. They both laughed.

These were the kinds of people that Mohammed liked and respected in the military. They were powerful, dedicated, and incredible human beings. And as long as you were loyal, worked hard and weren't a jackass, they respected you too.

When healthy, ammonia is converted by the liver into urea and safely exits the body in the urine. For the boxer, the liver was rapidly failing, leading to a dangerous build-up of ammonia and other toxins in the bloodstream. As these hazardous molecules accumulated in the blood vessels supplying the brain, they quickly reached a level that the special lining known as the blood-brain barrier could no longer prevent. Suddenly, a wave of highly reactive, corrosive ammonia and other toxins flooded into the boxer's brain, leading to a state of hepatic encephalopathy. The most common signs and symptoms of such a state are sleepiness, lethargy, confusion, and circadian dysrythmia. The boxer, however, had a completely different and entirely unexpected reaction.

Hearing the roar behind him, Kadhim turned just in time to see the boxer rise unsteadily from the bed and angrily rip out his IV lines. An unfortunate male nurse who happened to be in the room was tossed against the wall like a rag doll.

Kadhim had seen enough to know that he needed to get out of the way, and fast. He sprinted to the next patient's room and slammed the door shut, peering out the glass window at the scene of destruction unfolding in the hallway.

It was as though the true Frankenstein had been awakened. The boxer, yellow from jaundice, lurched unsteadily through the hallway as he bellowed with anger, blood dripping from his arms where he had torn away the IVs. He was clearly suffering from extreme disorientation and agitation, and Kadhim knew he should step out and help. But this was no normal patient.

The boxer was even more enormous and frightening standing up than he had been lying down, and the flimsy hospital gown was suddenly little more than a mini-skirt, baring two tan and shockingly muscular buttocks from behind. Kadhim gazed wide-eyed as the monster stumbled down the hallway, throwing gut-wrenching and nose-breaking punches at the male nurses who tried to stop him and leaving a trail of bloodied staff in his wake. Patients who were able to walk jumped out of their beds and locked their doors. Nurses and hospital staff screamed and ran for safety, trying to lock themselves in with the patients. Three male nurses ran after the boxer and tried to tackle him, and Kadhim gasped as the boxer—even in his weak and sickly condition—knocked them off easily, landing a blow to one man's mouth that broke several of his teeth.

When security arrived at last, they took a single look at the lurching, roaring monster knocking over people and carts as he unsteadily roamed the hall, and their mouths dropped. They conferred with one another, and, for an agonizing moment, Kadhim thought they were going to turn and run. In the end it took five grown men to pull him down, return him to his room, and tie him to his bed.

With his heart still pounding, Kadhim rushed to the monster's bedside. If left uncontrolled, the boxer's precarious condition would progress to coma and then death. He was hesitant to give the patient anything that might further precipitate a coma, but he had no choice. If he didn't give the boxer some sedatives, they would not be able to treat him. In fact, they would barely be able to protect themselves *from* him. Kadhim administered what he hoped would be a safe dose of sedatives and reestablished the IVs. He nimbly readjusted the hospital gown that had been nearly ripped from the boxer's brawny frame in the scuffle, but not before he saw the bulging muscles that only minutes before had been wreaking Frankensteinian havoc on the Internal Medicine floor. Yes, he had expected a long night alright.

But he had not expected this.

THE PACEMAKER: MEETING GEORGIE

Every time Mohammed ran into Georgie, he went out of his way to be friendly. He would greet him, invite him to events, joke with him about girls—nothing worked. Avoiding Mohammed's eyes, Georgie would simply grunt a rigid response to Mohammed's greeting and walk away. Mohammed had thought that they were on the road to recovery when Georgie stopped screaming at him every time they crossed paths, but there had been no noticeable improvement in the months that followed. Which was a shame, as "Georgie" really was one of the nicest interpreters he had ever met.

No, it was clear that Georgie was not about to forgive him, despite the fact that it had all been nothing more than a minor misunderstanding.

The whole mishap could be blamed on a laptop. Mohammed's old one was slow and annoying, and he wanted something larger, faster, and with better graphics for video games. The problem was, the only way to get that was to go into the Red Zone, and in order to do that he needed to take someone with him. It was with this in mind that Mohammed went to the interpreters' trailer that day, hoping to find someone he trusted enough to come along.

He realized, as he gazed around the group of interpreters eating, smoking, and playing video games, that his recent close call with New School had changed his entire outlook. Now, all he could see were potential threats, as one by one he ruled them out in his mind.

Too creepy...Don't trust him...He knows me too well...

He mistrusted those he didn't know, and feared those who knew him too well, who might have valuable personal information they would sell or use against him the instant he set foot outside the Green Zone. Others simply looked suspicious. One looked up and noticed Mohammed standing there.

"Hey, what's up, Saint? You need something?"

"Oh, it's nothing. Just looking for someone to go with me into the Red Zone. I need to buy something."

Several of them offered to go along, but Mohammed thanked them politely and was about to leave when Georgie walked out of the bedroom. He brightened as soon as he saw Mohammed.

"Saint! How are you, man? Good to see you!" He clapped a hand on Mohammed's arm and kissed his cheeks. "I've been meaning to thank you for putting in a good word with Sgt. Major Harley for me!"

The interpreter nicknamed "Georgie" was a Chaldean Christian, one of the oldest Christian sects in the world. He had previously worked with Mohammed's girlfriend Nina at the Internet café until obtaining a job interpreting for Sgt. Major Harley. Georgie's English left a lot to be desired, and it was with the help of Mohammed's recommendation that he'd been hired by the American commander, a fact that Georgie hadn't forgotten.

"You've already thanked me several times," Mohammed laughed.

"Well, thanks again! God bless you and your parents! You're awesome—one of the best guys in the IZ!"

Mohammed eyed him squarely. As a Christian, it was unlikely that Georgie was involved in any kind of terrorist group or militia, because Christians were such a small minority that it was in their interest to keep their heads low and stay out of trouble. The fact that they didn't know each other much more than the occasional hello also put Mohammed's mind at ease. He had to go with the odds.

"I was going to leave the Green Zone to buy something. Want to come?"

Georgie barely wavered. "Sure, I'll come." They were in Mohammed's car and leaving Camp Prosperity before Georgie finally asked where they were going.

"I was going to stop by Industrial Avenue to pick up a laptop. It's the best place to get what I want."

"My brother actually runs a computer shop on Industrial Avenue. We can go there if you want."

Something in Mohammed's head clicked suspiciously. *How convenient.* His mind went to the two revolvers under his seat, and his nerves were tight as they made their way out of the Green Zone.

While other interpreters had offered to go with him, he knew that in reality most of them would have backed out at the last minute, as many had done before. They didn't fully trust Mohammed—or each other—and they knew that Mohammed in particular had a high price on his head. If seen with him, they would also be targeted. To make matters worse, everyone knew that Mohammed would not go down without a fight. Entering Baghdad with Saint meant potentially putting oneself directly into the line of fire. So Mohammed was stuck with Georgie, who didn't know him well enough to realize all this.

Maybe he's telling the truth about his brother's shop and maybe he isn't. Well, I'm in the driver's seat and I'm armed, so I'm willing to risk it, Mohammed thought.

Besides, he *really* wanted that laptop.

As Mohammed and Georgie left the FOB, he reached under his seat and pulled out a hefty fully-automatic MP5K, and out of the corner of his eye he saw Georgie stiffen. The MP5K was empty—weapons were not allowed to be loaded inside the FOB—but Mohammed nevertheless made a show of locking the safety before handing the gun to his companion.

"What's this?" Georgie took it, startled.

"It's a weapon."

"For what? I've never even seen one like this before! I have no clue how to use it!" His voice rose slightly in panic.

"Keep it on you for now. Just in case. If we need it, you'll have to release the safety lock. I'll show you how, if necessary." Mohammed's voice was low, brisk.

"You mean if we run into trouble, you'll let me shoot it?" Georgie asked gleefully, examining the gun in amazement.

"Don't point that thing at me," Mohammed warned. "But yes."

"Cool!" Georgie pretended to take a couple shots into the floor, making small "bang" noises like a child with a new toy.

For himself, Mohammed pulled out the Glock .45. As Georgie watched, he had the Glock fully loaded before they'd even left the Green Zone. There was no way in hell he was going to drive the streets of Baghdad unprepared, particularly with an acquaintance he didn't fully trust. Georgie, meanwhile, pulled out his cell phone.

"Who are you calling?" Mohammed was immediately on guard.

"Just my brother," Georgie responded, then put up a hand as his brother picked up. "Hey, brother! How are you? Saint and I are just now leaving Camp Prosperity. We're on our way to come pick up a laptop from your shop—he wants one of those new Toshibas. But listen..." Georgie lowered his voice and glanced at Mohammed. "Saint is *really* wanted, and there are a lot of guys out there trying to get him, so just make sure your shop is empty when we get there. There can't be anyone inside. There's not a day he's left the Green Zone without getting threatened or shot at..."

Mohammed listened in disbelief. *Why the hell was Georgie giving his brother all this information? What kind of game was he playing? Was he planning something?* Mohammed had one hand on the wheel and the other on his Glock. Georgie didn't seem to notice how tense his driver had become, and continued his phone conversation.

"Yeah... Yeah, we're just about to leave the Green Zone... We're leaving from, hold on—Saint, what checkpoint are we exiting the IZ from?"

Mohammed's jaw clenched. *Was he trying to give away their position to someone outside? What the fuck?* "Checkpoint 11," he answered curtly.

"Check point 11, the Karrada gate," Georgie said into the phone. He kept the line open as they went through the final gate and left the Green Zone behind them, then said to whoever was on the other end, "Now we're entering Abu Nuwas Street."

Mohammed was becoming increasingly agitated, listening to a steady stream of information being passed over the line. He was about to say something when he noticed an extended cab pick-up truck behind them. The cab and the truck bed were filled with men carrying AK-47s, and they were all pointed at Mohammed's car.

Instantly, Mohammed's nerves were on fire. Even his BMW could not outrace the truck in the thick traffic of Abu Nuwas Street. To his right, Georgie continued his point-by-point narration of their location into the cell phone. Behind them, a truck full of armed men shouted angrily and trained their rifles on the BMW.

"Georgie!" Mohammed barked. "Who the hell are you talking to?"

"My brother." Georgie shrank visibly in his seat.

"What do you mean, your brother? Who's your brother?" Mohammed shouted.

"He's just my older brother. What's wrong with you?"

"Georgie, who the *fuck* are you talking to?" Mohammed's voice grew louder and angrier. He didn't believe a word his passenger said. Behind them, the truck's men shouted for Mohammed to pull over and fired a warning shot. *Not a chance in hell.*

"My brother! He owns the electronics shop!" Georgie still had not ended the phone call, but instead seemed to be purposely leaving the line open. Mohammed's knuckles grew white on the steering wheel.

"Georgie, I'm not fucking playing games. *Who the hell are you talking to?*" His voice had become a roar.

"My brother! I swear! I'm just talking to my brother!" Georgie's voice rose in a high-pitched panic.

"No, you're not!" Mohammed wrenched the cell phone from Georgie's hands, ended the call, and threw it to the floor. Jaw clenched, he grabbed the Glock .45 and pressed it hard into Georgie's cheek. "Did you sell me out, Georgie?"

The Glock had no safety latch.

"Oh my God! Saint, what's *wrong* with you? *Are you crazy?*" Georgie's voice rose to a breathless squeal, and he gripped the seat as his chest rose and fell in terror.

"Damn it, Georgie! I'm not going to ask again!" Mohammed roared with anger. "*WHO WAS ON THAT PHONE?*"

"My brother! My brother! I swear by God and by the Bible and even by the Holy Quran that I was just talking to my brother!" Georgie was breathless, and his face had drained of all color. Tears began to form in his eyes as the Glock remained buried heavily into his soft cheek.

"Then *who the hell* are these guys behind us?" Mohammed jerked his head toward the pick-up truck of armed men who were still close behind them, despite Mohammed's best efforts to maneuver away from them on the busy street. They had their AK-47s ready and pointing, and they were still shouting angrily for the BMW to pull over. Beads of sweat formed on Mohammed's forehead. *Traitor. A traitor and a fucking liar. Georgie had set him up in front of a goddamn death squad.*

Anger coursed through Mohammed's veins and into his finger, which found its way to the trigger and prepared to pull.

Georgie turned and looked behind them, and noticed, as if for the first time, the pick-up truck. "*Holy shit! Who the fuck are* those *guys?*"

He screamed in panic, clutched at his chest, and began to hyperventilate as tears rolled down his cheeks.

Mohammed was not put off by the act. He kept the gun pointed at his passenger's head. He was prepared to kill and might have done so if the effects of shooting a man in his beloved BMW had not given him pause. *The window was up. Would the bullet pass through Georgie's head and break the window? Should he roll it down first? Would he get blood all over his nice new seats like in the movies? Would the smell of blood stay in his car?*

In that instant, while Mohammed focused on pointing the barrel of his gun into his companion's temple, the BMW drifted from its lane. Cars honked, and Mohammed looked quickly behind him.

He saw not one but two pick-up trucks of rifle-wielding men, a dark-tinted sedan, followed by two more fully armed pick-ups.

It was someone's security detail—a convoy for some politician or important figure.

Oh.

Mohammed pulled over instantly, allowing the convoy to pass, and lowered the Glock to his lap.

"False alarm," he remarked nonchalantly.

"You *asshole!* You *fucking piece of shit!*" Georgie's voice had reached a decibel only dogs could hear.

"Well, what was I supposed to think?" Mohammed replied casually as he pulled back into traffic. He glanced at Georgie and noticed how deathly white his companion had become. "Sorry," he added.

"Sorry? *Sorry?* You fucking bastard! You dog!" Georgie resumed his screaming between breaths.

"Take it easy and respect yourself a bit," Mohammed said calmly. "It was just a little misunderstanding. These things happen."

"Are you fucking kidding me?" Georgie could scarcely breathe, and tears continued streaming down his face. His cheek and temple had faint round indents where the Glock had left its mark. *"You want to kill me? Huh? Are you trying to kill me?"* He continued to hyperventilate. "Stop the car! *Stop the damn car!*"

"What's wrong with you?" Mohammed pulled over, and Georgie stumbled out and began vomiting on the side of the road. Mohammed stepped out and came around to the passenger side where his companion was covering the roadside with his vomit. He lit a cigarette.

"Georgie, come on. Calm down. Have you finished? Get back into the car; you're making us look bad."

"What? Get back in there with *you?* You want to kill me? Huh, Saint? *You want to kill me?*" Between dry-heaves, he continued to scream at Mohammed in front of all the passersby, and Mohammed started to get embarrassed.

"Just get in the car," he said, exasperated. Georgie refused and kept screaming. "Damn it!" Mohammed pulled out his Glock again and pointed it at Georgie. "If you don't get in the car, I *will* kill you!"

Frightened, Georgie clambered back in the car. "Take me back to the Green Zone," he said stubbornly as they continued down the road. "I know what I'm going to do. I'm going to go back there and submit a complaint that you tried to kill me!"

"Georgie, we're almost to Industrial Avenue. I'm going to go get my laptop, and you're coming in with me, and *then* we'll go back and you can do whatever the hell you want."

"All this and you're *still* going to make me go with you?" Georgie grumbled as the car made its way to Industrial Ave. "What, are you going to put a gun to my head and make me help you buy a laptop by force? From my brother? Are you going to kill my brother too, Saint?"

Mohammed rolled his eyes and parked the car. They had arrived.

As the two men got out of the car, Mohammed gripped Georgie's arm and spoke in a low voice.

"Do you see these?" He lifted his shirt slightly and Georgie's eyes grew wide. Around his belt, Mohammed had stashed two hand grenades. They were the fastest and most successful way to escape an attack, and he liked to take them with him whenever he left the IZ, just in case he felt the need to blow up the car behind him.

"*Holy fuck*," Georgie breathed. "Now I *know* you're crazy."

"Look, I swear to God, if I suspect *anything* from you or your brother, if you so much as *hint* to him about what happened on the way here," Mohammed tapped one of the grenades, "I'll kill you both."

Georgie was stunned speechless, and Mohammed saw in his eyes something stronger than hatred. In that moment, Mohammed was certain that if he could, Georgie would have killed him. It didn't matter. Georgie was new to this life; he didn't understand. If there was anything Mohammed had learned after numerous attempts on his life, it was that self-preservation came first. If Georgie's brother suspected that Mohammed was trying to kill one of them, he would instigate a fight, perhaps call others over to help, and Mohammed would be instantly outnumbered. The only way Mohammed could protect himself was by making sure that no one in Georgie's family knew what had happened.

They went upstairs to the electronics shop on the second floor, where Georgie's brother was eagerly awaiting them.

"Welcome, come on in!" He smiled and kissed Georgie on both cheeks, then greeted Mohammed warmly. "I already have your laptop ready—Toshiba, right? Would you like to drink something? Water? Tea?"

"No thanks."

A couple strange-looking men entered the shop and Mohammed looked pointedly at Georgie and gave the gun in his hand a warning shake. Immediately, Georgie said a few soft words into his brother's ear, and the brother spoke up.

"I'm sorry, gentlemen, but we were just closing up. You're going to have to come back another time." He ushered the two men out the door and locked it.

Mohammed examined the new laptop, happy to discover that it had all the features he'd been looking for, and paid. He was turning to leave when the brother stopped him.

"I just wanted to say thank you." The brother grasped Mohammed's hand and kissed him on both cheeks. "Thanks for taking such good care of my brother. I pray that you make it safely back to the IZ. God be with you both."

A twinge of guilt plucked at Mohammed's heart. He thanked the genuine young man and left with Georgie. Throughout the ten minutes that he'd spent in the shop, he'd been checking out the window to make sure no one had planted a bomb near his car. Now, before they got in, he checked again, around and underneath the BMW and even under the hood, just to be certain. Then he ignited the engine, and they took off at top speed. He needed to get out of the Red Zone as quickly as possible.

As they approached the first entry gate into the Green Zone, Mohammed broke the silence and began to apologize.

"Georgie, I'm sorry."

Silence.

"Seriously, I'm sorry. It was just a mistake. It could have happened to anyone."

Silence.

"Georgie, would you please just talk to me?"

"Just get me inside the Green Zone and leave me alone."

"Georgie, for God's sake, you have to understand! There you were chatting on your phone giving away minute-by-minute GPS coordinates, and behind us we were being trailed by a pick-up truck full of AK-47s! What was I supposed to think?"

They passed slowly through a series of gates and checkpoints. No more did they rely on the coiled barbed wire of the early days. Now, in addition to other security measures, there were car-cracking speed bumps and thick concrete walls constructed in a maze that forced a car to slow to nearly a stop. Georgie sat tight-lipped, glaring straight ahead. It seemed he had set up as many barriers to Mohammed's profuse apologies as the Green Zone had to terrorists. As they at last passed the final checkpoint and entered the Green Zone, Georgie jumped out of the car.

"Georgie, what are you doing? Camp Prosperity is too far from here to walk! Let me just drive you there!"

"Hell no! I'd rather walk fifteen kilometers in 125° heat than ride with the asshole who tried to kill me! You want to kidnap and kill me? Is that what you want, Saint? You pulled a gun on me! You threatened me! Well, now I'm going to tell the Americans!"

Mohammed watched as Georgie stormed away angrily. He drove back to his room and began messing around on his laptop, delighted with his new toy. He had forgotten all about the incident and was playing a video game when he received a phone call from Sgt. Major Harley a half an hour later.

"Hi, Sir, what's up?"

"Saint, get your ass over to the battalion immediately!"

"What the fuck, man!" Sgt. Major Harley's face was angry and he was standing at full, impressive height as Mohammed walked in. Georgie was sitting in the corner, arms crossed stubbornly across his chest, and even Colonel Peters had shown up to listen to the account. "Are you killing people now?"

"I didn't kill him!" Mohammed laughed. "Look at him! He's not dead, is he? I didn't even hurt him!"

"Then why did you threaten him?"

"Let me explain." Mohammed launched into a fully detailed account of the incident and as Sgt. Major Harley and the colonel came to understand what had happened, they began to chuckle. Soon they were roaring with laughter.

"He try to kill me!" Georgie shouted indignantly, frustrated at the mirth surrounding him. His life had been *threatened*, for God's sake.

"And who told you to leave the IZ with Saint?" Sgt. Major Harley replied.

"I did to help him!"

"No one leaves the Green Zone with Saint without getting threatened! Half of Baghdad wants to kill him, and you decide to get in the car with him and go? Of course he's going to be on guard while he's out there!"

Georgie shook his head, angry, frustrated, and hurt, and stormed out of the room.

A few months passed, and Georgie continued to ignore Mohammed's apologies. Mohammed did feel bad for him; Georgie was a good guy, after all. Mohammed caught up with Georgie one day in a dining facility and tried again.

"Hey Georgie, how are you doing?"

"Fuck you."

The other interpreters instantly moved several seats away. No one talked to Saint like that and got away with it.

"Look, Georgie, how many times do I have to tell you how sorry I am? I swear by the holy Quran, I feel terrible! I just didn't understand why you kept talking to your brother like that!"

For once, Georgie actually replied. "I was scared, Saint! For God's sake, I thought if I died or if you kidnapped me, then my brother would at least know where to start looking! But you! You goddamn nearly killed me right there!"

"No, I didn't nearly kill you. I mean yes, I put a gun to your head, and I'm sorry for that. But I didn't pull the trigger. And you're fine! You went a little white and got a bit sick, but I didn't do any lasting damage! It's not like I can kill you simply by putting a gun to your head!"

Georgie stood up and unbuttoned his shirt to reveal a scar on his chest. "See this scar? It's for my pacemaker. I have a heart arrhythmia, you asshole."

As Georgie stormed away, Mohammed breathed a sigh of disappointment. It had been nothing more than a slight misunderstanding, but it was clear that Georgie was not about to forgive him.

And how the hell could he have known about the heart arrhythmia?

BURNING

It was a relief to get back to the IZ after the day he'd had. Mohammed had spent all morning and afternoon on a mission, searching houses and questioning locals. They'd been too afraid, most of them, to be seen associating with the American troops. People had been killed for lesser infractions.

It was evening by the time Mohammed returned to the IZ, and as he pulled through the checkpoint, he noticed some of his friends on the civilian side waiting to be checked through. He waved at them eagerly, his friend Ammar, Ammar's wife, and their two beautiful young children with whom Mohammed often played. All four of them waved back with enormous smiles, and Mohammed motioned to them that he would wait to talk to them on the other side of the checkpoint.

It had been at least several weeks—perhaps a month or two—since he'd last seen them, Mohammed reflected. Well, they'd picked the perfect day to show up. He was feeling worn out and depressed, and they were the kind of people who knew how to make him laugh. He wondered if they might consider having a third child, since Maya was at least—

BOOM

Mohammed was stunned momentarily by the impact of the bomb. Perhaps it was only fractions of seconds, but it felt like ages before he figured out what was happening. Around him, there were shouts and screams and people running. The car bomb had happened behind him, outside the checkpoint...

...just in front of Ammar's car...

Oh fuck.

Panic struck Mohammed's chest and he ran back, through the chaos of the checkpoint, to the scene of the car bomb.

Please God let them be okay. Please Allah, save their lives.

Oh God.

Immediately behind the car bomb was Ammar's car. Or what had been Ammar's car. The front half of his small Honda was now engulfed in flames. Ammar and his wife were no more than blackened, lifeless forms.

Panic. Fear. Pain. Heat.

Maya and Layla! They were still in the back seat!

Mohammed didn't hear the shouts of those around him as he ran up to the car, still alight. The two little girls were in the back, screaming from the pain of their inferno.

He reached out to open their door, to pull them out, to save the girls who only moments before had been laughing and giggling and playing games. The handle had melted. The glass of the windows was melting. Pain seared his hand as he touched the car. The mere heat of the blaze was unbearable.

"Maya, Layla! I'm coming! Hold on!" Mohammed shouted. "Somebody help me! *SOMEBODY HELP! Oh God, oh God, please help them!*"

He was crying, sobbing, without realizing it. The girls' screams and their wide-eyed looks of terror and pain seared his soul. He watched in horror as the flames overtook them. He could hear the crackling of the children's flesh as it burned, and still the girls screamed to him.

"Help us! Help! Get us out!"

Every second felt like an hour as he tried to pull open a melting door. He vaguely heard people shouting at him. Hands pulled him away from the car even as he fought them and struggled to help the girls. He felt himself being pulled roughly away from the burning car and tossed to the ground, then covered by a heavy weight.

An instant later, the small Honda exploded.

It was over.

Mohammed pushed the weight off of him. It was an Iraqi soldier who had pulled him away and saved his life. But Mohammed could feel nothing but pain and shock. He leapt up and shoved the man who had saved him.

"What have you done? *What the hell have you done?*" Tears streamed unbidden down his cheeks. "There were two *children* in that car!"

He punched the soldier. He swung at him again, and the soldier dodged the blow. He was saying something, but Mohammed couldn't hear him over the pounding in his ears. Words had lost all meaning.

An unbearable pain struck his chest, a deep, physical, searing pain.

I'm sorry, Ammar, Um Layla. I'm sorry I couldn't save your children. I'm sorry. It should have been me.

It should have been me, not innocent children.

The image of the parents' blackened corpses, the sight of children engulfed in flames, the screams of pain and fear, the sound of burning flesh, the heat, the smell... The pain was too intense... the vision too raw, vivid, horrific...

...Relief would never come. It would be burned into his memory forever.

OVERNIGHTERS

"So, this Nina girl—is she your wife?" The major waved a document inquiringly as Mohammed passed. He had just picked up one of numerous girls he kept in rotation, and she was waiting for him in the car.

"Um, why do you ask?"

"She keeps asking to move in with you from the interpreters' quarters. She said she's your wife and you both wear wedding rings..." He glanced at Mohammed's conspicuously bare hands. "Is she at least your fiancée?"

"No." He laughed. "She's just a girlfriend."

"Well, do you want her over here with you or not?"

"Uhhh..." Mohammed grinned uncomfortably. *Perhaps his promiscuity was spiraling out of control, but the truth was, he just needed something—anything—to lessen the monotony of living in the caged paradise that was the Green Zone, to tune out memories that haunted him and to ease the starkness of his insomnia.*

The major raised an eyebrow and his mouth twisted into a small smirk.

"You know what? Don't worry about it. I feel ya."

"Thanks." Mohammed laughed as he left. So Nina wanted to move in with him, did she? This was one of the reasons he made her and any other girls who spent the night leave his room within a day, tops. He didn't want them getting too comfortable. He was the only interpreter he knew who had his own suite, and he wasn't about to give up that privilege anytime soon.

It was late in the evening several weeks later when Mohammed chanced upon Georgie, who was standing glumly outside the interpreters' quarters, scowling and smoking a cigarette.

"What's wrong, man?"

Georgie looked up to see the man who only four or five months ago had nearly killed him.

"Screw you. I don't want to talk to you."

Clearly, his feelings had not thawed.

"I really am sorry, Georgie. Come on, just tell me what's wrong. Is someone bothering you?"

For several minutes nothing was said, as Georgie stared off into the distance. Then, without meeting Mohammed's gaze, he grumbled, "I can't get any sleep in this place. I share a room with five other guys, all on different shifts, and every time I'm about to fall asleep, somebody new comes in and starts making a racket. Marwan keeps trying to play that godawful guitar, I haven't slept in weeks, and I'm exhausted."

"Did you try to get a trailer?"

"It's a no-go. They don't give trailers to interpreters. They stick all of us here together. You're the only one living by yourself."

"Of course. I'm different."

"Yeah, you're different. You're fucking special, you are!" Georgie snapped. "To make matters worse, I can hear all the commotion from the other dorms too, because they only have us separated by those flimsy pieces of wood. It's killing me."

This, Mohammed realized, was his chance to finally make up for what he'd done and reconcile with Georgie. He took it. "Why don't you live with me?"

"Yeah right. Like you'd let someone live with you."

"Just try it out."

"Are you serious?"

"I'm serious. I have a two bedroom two bathroom suite in a guard tower in the corner of FOB Prosperity. It even has a balcony. It's nice and quiet, away from all the action, and I can do whatever I want."

Georgie hesitated, but the thought of months of sleepless nights convinced him to grab his duffel bag and once again get into the car with Mohammed.

"I should warn you," Georgie said as they entered the suite, "I snore."

"How bad is it?"

"It's pretty bad, I'm not going to lie. But if it's really bothering you, just wake me up so I can roll over and that usually helps."

"Fine. But I should warn *you*, I like things quiet."

That night, a ghastly noise of unbelievable volume filled the room, like a freight train rumbling into the station, or the trumpeting of a sick elephant. Georgie wasn't kidding. He didn't just snore. He had the snore to end all snores.

Mohammed's agony grew as one sleepless hour followed the next, marked only by the cacophonous snorts of his new roommate. No wonder none of the interpreters could sleep—it was *Georgie* keeping them up. Rolling him over didn't seem to help, so—at his wits' end—Mohammed decided to try a different tactic.

Georgie awoke with the strange, dreamy sensation that someone was standing next to him. He cautiously opened his eyes to see Mohammed standing directly over his head, holding over his face a twelve-inch army knife that caught the eerie green glow of the Xbox. Georgie jumped up with a squeal.

"*Mohammed! What the hell is wrong with you?*"

"Georgie, I swear to God!" Mohammed's voice climbed up several pitches, on the verge of hysteria. "Your snoring is KILLING me!"

After that first night, Mohammed and Georgie grew accustomed to sharing the trailer, and quickly became close friends. Georgie's outgoing and friendly personality endeared him to all, but he was a joker and a troublemaker in his own right, and one of his favorite games was thwarting Mohammed's efforts with the ladies. There were two rooms in the suite, but as Georgie had neither TV nor Xbox, and the two liked to play video games late into the night, he frequently dragged his mattress into Mohammed's room and slept there. The only downside to getting used to Georgie's snoring was that if Mohammed could sleep through *that*, he could sleep through anything. Even an alarm clock set at fire alarm decibels could no longer wake him.

Georgie, for his part, quickly learned to move to the adjoining room whenever Mohammed had "company," and often this company was not Nina. So Georgie took it in stride when Mohammed met someone new, the latest being a short and fiery young woman named Zara.

The fact that it was one of Mohammed's own girlfriends who introduced him to Zara didn't appear to bother Mohammed in the least. He was always happy to help girls find jobs in the Green Zone, and so when his female friend asked him to help Zara, he obliged, despite her weak English. He had an escort badge, meaning that he could go wherever he wished within the IZ without being accompanied by a soldier, so he took her to PSYOP.

"I need a favor from you."

"Whatever you need, Saint."

"She's looking for a job."

The commander took a critical look at Zara. "Do you speak English?"

"Yes, Sir." Her accent was thick, and she stumbled over those two simple words.

The commander and Mohammed shared a look.

"Keep her under training for a while," Mohammed chuckled. "And just in case she screws up, I don't know her."

Zara lasted only two and a half weeks at PSYOP before Mohammed had to find her a job that didn't require so much English. She moved in with female interpreters, and on the first night she called Mohammed, crying.

"What's wrong, *habibti*?"

"It's impossible to sleep here, Saint! People keep shouting and talking and someone's trying to play an electric guitar! I can't do it! I can't stay here!"

It was nearly ten o'clock at night. Mohammed looked at the girl lying next to him and weighed his options. He wasn't in his own bed, so he would probably leave soon anyway, and the prospect of potentially being with someone new was one that he could never resist. Much to the girl's annoyance, he got up and excused himself.

"Alright, I'm coming to pick you up and I'll try to find you someplace to sleep," he told Zara. And wonder of wonders, the place he found for her to sleep was in his own suite. He didn't sleep with her but rather put her in the adjoining room, waking up his roommate and warning him not to go in there.

"Why? Who is it?" Georgie asked sleepily.

"It's a girl. But if you hear something in the night, just be prepared."

He wasn't talking about a hook-up, although that was a possibility that he never ruled out. He meant simply that he didn't trust her. New School and numerous other experiences had taught him to be wary. As with every girl, he had visions of her attacking him with a knife while he slept, or perhaps gathering his personal data and selling it to terrorists. Mohammed slept with a gun under his pillow that night, and even Georgie groggily reached out and pulled a wooden bat close to him.

She called him the next day and asked him to join her for lunch.

"I don't know, Zara. I'm really busy and pretty soon I have an interpretation appointment..."

"But it's a home cooked meal! My mother just brought it to me fresh!"

Zara had scarcely finished her sentence before Mohammed was out the door. "I'm on my way."

He learned over lunch that she was married but had been separated from her husband for some time.

"So you're separated and you came to look for a job in the IZ," Mohammed commented between bites. "How strange that you wear the hijab."

"What do you mean, strange? It's *better* for me to wear the hijab, don't you think?"

"You probably just wear it because your hair is starting to fall out." A wicked grin adorned Mohammed's face.

"Hey! I have great hair!"

"I don't believe it."

"I'm serious! My hair is beautiful!" He was obnoxious, but something about this man made Zara desperate to impress him.

"Then show me."

"No, I can't do that."

"Falling out hair it is, then."

Defensively, she removed her hijab to reveal long, flowing locks of auburn hair and he grinned the grin of a child who had just gotten his way.

Georgie had stayed out late. He slipped into the suite quietly, and found Mohammed and Zara fast asleep together. He was just about to go to the next room when he saw Mohammed turn in his sleep, unintentionally slamming a sharp and heavy elbow deep into Zara's throat. She opened her mouth to complain, but her protest was drowned out by Mohammed's own sleepy garbles,

"*Yumyumyumyumyum.*"

Georgie burst into giggles.

"How's Yum Yum?" he asked Mohammed the next morning after she left.

"Who?"

It wasn't long before the nickname was adopted, and it spread to the point that soon no one could even remember Yum Yum's original name.

"Hello?" Mohammed's phone had been ringing all morning

before he finally answered. A female voice greeted him with a sexy and familiar tone.

"Good morning, Mohammed."

"Hi, sweetie, how are you?"

"I'm good. I missed you last night..." Her voice took on a suggestive lilt.

"Me too, *habibti*."

"I was thinking, Saint, maybe we should meet up soon..."

"Sure, babe. When were you thinking?"

"Maybe tonight? At Mo's place?"

"Sounds good, hon. I'll see you there." He hung up the phone and rolled over to go back to sleep.

"Who was that?" Georgie asked from the other side of the room.

"No fucking clue."

He turned over to see Georgie giving him a Look.

"'Saint,' my ass. You better watch out, Mohammed. You're going to get yourself into trouble with all these women."

BLOOD LOSS

His ears were still ringing with the sound of gunfire when Kadhim at last went to sleep the next morning, though whether the shots were real or just mental echoes he could not tell. His world had shifted once again, just as radically as it had the day the Americans set foot in Iraq in 2003. As he fell into an exhausted sleep, his mind drifted gradually backward to the moment when his country had descended from sporadic acts of violence, to a full-scale civil war.

2:18 A.M. February 23, 2006. Outside, the streets rang with the terrible sound of non-stop gunfire. Hour upon hour of shooting. The ER was packed with gunshot victims, most of them dead, some still fighting to survive, all of them Sunni.

Kadhim couldn't believe how many victims there were. Never— *never*—had he seen hour after hour of mass casualties like this, brought into the ER twenty-five or thirty at a time. His legs shook with exhaustion and low blood sugar. The previous morning when he had started his work in the ER seemed like eons ago.

"Tea?"

He looked up to see one of the nurses, a kind, elderly woman with a mustache, offering him a cup of tea. Such was his surprise and fatigue that he couldn't stop himself from blurting out, "In the midst of all this blood and death, you're making tea?"

The mustache smiled. "We have to have tea."

"But it's so unsanitary!"

"It's fine, really. I was careful. Would you like some?"

He took the tea gratefully. It would still be many hours before he got any sleep.

12:01 A.M. February 23, 2006. The TV was reporting that nearly one hundred Sunni mosques had been burned already, and that indiscriminate slaughter of Sunnis young and old, man, woman, and child, was continuing to take place throughout Iraq. It was all a brutal response to the act that had taken place, to the shock and sorrow of an entire nation, only hours earlier.

9:05 P.M. February 22, 2006.

"It's not a surprise, you know, that this happened." Covered in sweat and blood, Mahjoub took another bite of his cold sandwich and remarked knowingly to Kadhim, "Al Qaeda's been threatening to do this for over a month now."

Kadhim knew this, but he let his friend speak.

"The Iraqi government warned the people of Samarra that if they allowed this to happen, the fallout would be catastrophic."

"To be fair," Kadhim said, "the people of Samarra did try to prevent this, despite the fact that they're Sunni and it's a Shiite shrine. They have respected and guarded this shrine for hundreds of years. In fact, I heard that more than one Sunni lost his life trying to protect it. The government was just too weak to do anything."

"Nothing will be the same after this, regardless," Mahjoub replied. And they both knew it to be true.

3:48 P.M. February 22, 2006. Kadhim was working with a young nurse, trying to stabilize a patient who'd suffered multiple gunshots to the back so that he could be taken into surgery, when they heard a heavy thump and the crash of falling metal instruments behind them.

"What was *that*?" The nurse, new to the ER, jumped with a start.

Kadhim glanced quickly behind them to see a male physician slumped unconscious on the floor.

"*That*," he said as he returned calmly to his work, "is Dr. Khalid."

"Oh my God!"

"Calm down. I need you to focus on this patient."

"Shouldn't we go help him?"

241

"Right now, you need to hand me a tourniquet and stay focused. Leave Dr. Khalid be. He'll be fine."

"Are you sure?" The nurse looked doubtful. He kept glancing back at the white-coated figure lying in a heap on the floor.

"Dr. Khalid faints every time he sees something gruesome. Don't worry; he'll wake up and take care of himself in a couple minutes. He just needs to find a place where he can be helpful without passing out, poor guy. *Our* patient, on the other hand, will *not* wake up and take care of himself. Now grab this gurney and wheel him to the O.R."

Poor Khalid. Doctors like him didn't last very long under these circumstances, and he would soon join the many others who had fled the country to practice medicine in peace. There were a few doctors who tried to avoid the worst of ER duty by protesting that they couldn't stomach the more gruesome sights, but Dr. Khalid hadn't needed to protest at all. It took little more than a particularly grotesque wound for the young doctor to drop unconscious to the floor.

8:13 A.M. February 22, 2006. Without plan and without organization, Shiite thugs and militia members began to swarm the streets of Iraq like cockroaches, killing indiscriminately in every city where Sunnis could be found. An epidemic of gunshots had now replaced the heavy booms and thick smoke of Al Qaeda's bombs. That was it. Sunnis had gone too far and now it was time for revenge, on any and all.

The death toll that Americans would hear of on the other side of the ocean was skewed. Three to four hundred? That was ridiculous. Before the week was over, *thousands* would be dead.

7:21 A.M. February 22, 2006. An emergency meeting had been called by the hospital, and for the moment TVs and radios were silenced. In the tightly-packed room, there were scuffles and murmurs, and the sound of a few female nurses crying.

"I don't need to tell you how serious the situation is. I need everyone, *everyone*, in the ER today." The chief looked at each of them gravely. "Tonight, we will not sleep."

◇ ◇ ◇

6:44 A.M. February 22, 2006. In the city of Samarra, members of Iraq's Facility Protection Service, who guarded one of the holiest shrines in Shiite Islam, sat sweating with fear, captured and bound since the previous day. Al Qaeda terrorists, dressed as members of Iraq's special forces, had rigged the dome of the mosque with explosives. The scene was set. The shrines of the 10th and 11th imams and other important Islamic figures, who had rested there peacefully for more than a thousand years, lay silent, unable to protect themselves.

In that moment, a single button held the power to enrage a world and spark the civil war that would kill and displace millions.

The button was pushed.

TO SAVE A LIFE

Mohammed woke up in a cold sweat, panting and frightened. Minutes passed as the cobwebs of his nightmare finally faded, and he found himself in the darkness. *It was just a nightmare... this time.*

Sleep didn't come. Sleep was so far away in fact that all he could do was stare into the darkness and fight the weight that bore down on his chest after each of these episodes. It was a thick knot of emotions, wound so tight that he couldn't unravel them enough to find and address each one.

He thought about playing Xbox to stifle the memories, but he couldn't get himself to move from his bed. Instead, he picked up his phone.

Kadhim awoke to the ring of his cell phone. He stared groggily at the clock—it was nearly 5:30 in the morning—and glanced at the caller ID. It wasn't like his brother to call this early, and it worried him.

"Kadhim? I'm sorry for calling you so early. Did I wake you?"

"Don't worry about it. I was about to get up anyway. Is everything okay, Mohammed? Are you alright?"

"Yeah, yeah, I'm fine. I just had to... I don't know, I just wanted to check on you."

"I'm fine. You sure you're okay?"

There was a silence on the other end.

"Mohammed? Mohammed, what's going on?"

"I had a shit day the other day, that's all."

"What happened?"

"Look, I don't want to make you worried. It's nothing, habibi. Go back to sleep. Everything's fine."

"Mohammed, talk to me. If you prefer I not tell Mama and Baba then that's fine, but at least tell me. What happened? Are you alright?"

There was a long pause.

"They're gone, Kadhim."

"Who's gone? What are you talking about?"

"A few days ago, I was out on a mission with one of the units.

We were sitting in the back of the Bradley on those benches, three of us on each side. I was sitting in the middle of one, with a soldier on either side..."

Mohammed's breathing grew heavy, irregular.

"What happened?" Kadhim's voice was barely above a whisper. He wasn't sure he wanted to know.

His brother's reply came in a short staccato between shaky breaths, "We drove over an IED... One minute we were all there, all six of us... Then half of the Bradley was gone... The guy sitting on my right, and the guy across from me... gone." His voice shook with emotion. "There was nothing left of them, Kadhim. Their bodies were disintegrated, blown to smithereens..."

"May they rest in peace. And you? Are you okay, Mohammed?" Kadhim's heart was pounding. He prayed that his brother hadn't been hurt.

"I'm here. I'm whole."

"Thank God."

"It's fucked up."

"I know."

"I don't know what the hell to do."

"There's nothing you could have done, brother. No way you could have known. Only Allah knows when it's someone's time to die." Kadhim felt like he could breathe again. "I guess it wasn't your time."

"I don't know what to do with *myself*. How the hell do I...?" Mohammed's voice trailed off. He couldn't find the words to express the anguish.

"Mohammed, I'll support you whatever you decide to do. You want to quit and go back to our parents' place? It's fine. I'll understand."

"No. I can't do that."

"You're in the right place, Mohammed. You're doing the right thing. You're saving people's lives."

"How the hell am I saving people's lives, Kadhim? I kill people. And I see people die everyday. *Innocent* people. Children, even. Those soldiers who died, they were just kids. They had just graduated from high school, and here they are, far from their parents... And this? This shouldn't have happened to them..."

"It's not your fault, Mohammed. Do the right thing in front of God, and you'll have no regrets."

There was a pause.

"Don't you get tired, though, sometimes?"

It hurt Kadhim to hear the pain in his brother's voice, a pain he knew so well.

"Exhausted."

"At least as a doctor, you *know* that you're saving lives, that you're doing the right thing…"

"Not always, habibi. Not always."

Daylight brought with it another mission, this one in the Sunni Triangle, an area renowned for the presence of Al Qaeda. Mohammed was there with his unit as well as Iraqi soldiers, making their rounds of the houses, and asking locals for information. *Had they seen anything strange? Anyone digging to place IEDs? Did they know of any terrorists in the area?*

Most were too afraid of the consequences to give an answer, even when Mohammed told them that it was for their own safety and that of their children. No, they had not seen or heard anything suspicious. Everything was quiet here.

The soldiers passed out cards with a hotline number, so that people could call from the safety and privacy of their own homes to report suspicious activity, without being seen aiding "the enemy."

Some were willing to point out homes or lodgings of suspected terrorists. Still others helped only when the Americans promised to relocate them and their families to the States, far from Iraq, where they would be safe. They gave valuable information, and then they were killed while they waited for their paperwork to make its way through an interminable maze of bureaucracy.

"Saint!" An Iraqi soldier approached the interpreter. "One of the neighbors reports that there's a moaning coming from that abandoned shop."

"Are you sure?"

"Yes. They say it sounds like a girl."

Mohammed quickly spoke with the American unit. They often investigated kidnapping cases, although the victim was usually dead by the time they arrived. A moaning from an empty shop? It could be a trap.

They put on heat vision goggles and tried to see through the door, but the heat of day made it nearly impossible. Such goggles worked best at night, when the blazing Iraq sun had set and the surroundings had cooled.

They couldn't see past the heavy shop door, but decided to take the risk and break it down nonetheless. Within minutes, they had busted through the door and were staring into the darkness inside.

Kadhim was still thinking of his early morning phone call with Mohammed when the call came in to the ER.

"There's been a suicide bombing in Shurja. Shiites were targeted as usual. We're bringing them in now."

"Any idea how many?"

"Not really. We're towing in the bus as we speak."

"The bus?"

The Iraqi soldier had already hung up.

Within fifteen minutes, Kadhim saw what the soldier was talking about. The suicide bomber had boarded one of the tightly-crowded mini-buses that looped the Shiite neighborhoods, and rather than pull out the victims, the Iraqi soldiers had towed the entire bus, blackened and charred, back to the ER. There were no survivors.

"This is an ER. We take *live* patients. Why didn't you take this bus to the morgue?" Kadhim pulled on gloves and a mask as he addressed the commanding officer.

"The morgue's full."

Kadhim heaved a sigh, and together with some other doctors and nurses they entered the charred bus and began the process of extracting the bodies.

There were about twenty-five passengers in all, most of them children, all of them burned to the bone. Their corpses stuck to the remains of their seats and to the thin metal walls of the bus. As gently as he tried to remove their small bodies, they were too fragile, too melded to their surroundings. Fingers fell from hands. Hands tore from wrists. Kadhim thought with dread of the rush of parents and relatives that would soon crowd the ER, grief-stricken, searching for children and family members who were no longer recognizable.

The Iraqi soldiers initially tried to help, but they quickly became overwhelmed with the sight. Kadhim watched with increasing alarm as each and every one of them were sickened from the sight, the smell, and the shock. Soon, it was the soldiers who were their patients, most of them vomiting, some passing out, others needing oxygen. They had signed up to protect their country. They had not signed up for this.

One of them, dizzy, vomiting, and gasping for air, tried to

247

apologize as Kadhim put him into a bed and set up an IV.

"It's okay, don't be sorry. You were trying to help," Kadhim soothed as he started him on fluids. "You're young—early twenties, right? You shouldn't have to see things like this."

"And how old are you?"

"I'm twenty-four."

The soldier shook his head in sorrow. "This war has aged you." He lay back in the bed as he grew calm, and said after a pause, "It doesn't make you feel bad, seeing shit like this?"

"Of course," Kadhim replied without skipping a beat. *But it was a lie. He felt bad because this had become normal. He felt bad because he didn't feel anything anymore.*

As he was treating the soldiers, another flood of victims arrived. A second suicide bomb had occurred on the heels of the first.

Kadhim called for back-up and began triage. He found a thirteen-year-old boy with shrapnel in his hand and an arm that had broken so badly that it flopped in the opposite direction. His pulse was gone and there was no heartbeat. Kadhim almost left him to run to the next, but something made him pause. He had found over the course of hundreds of bombings that children, more than anyone else, had an amazing ability to survive. Maybe the boy's heart had stopped simply from the shock. Perhaps he could be saved...

With the help of a nurse, Kadhim began CPR. Minutes passed. Then several more. He had nearly given up when suddenly the heart came back to life. Many children had died that day, but this boy would walk away with nothing more than a cast on his arm.

Kadhim turned to hurry to the next patient and was met with a sight that shocked him out of the thick haze of numbness that usually enveloped him.

It was the second suicide bomber. With his own victims dead and dying around him, he had somehow survived his very own suicide.

It took several seconds for Mohammed's eyes to adjust to the darkness of the abandoned shop, but he heard the moaning instantly. It was coming from deep in the shadows of a far corner.

And then he saw her.

She was huddled up on the floor, naked, shaking and bruised. Her mouth was taped shut, and her arms and legs were tied tightly behind her.

Mohammed ran to the woman and removed the tape from her mouth. She began to cry and gasp breaths of relief.

"Who are you?"

"My name is Hanan Al Abdali." Her voice was shaky as she replied in Arabic. "I'm an interpreter."

She had been kidnapped, tortured and raped by Al Qaeda for her work with the U.S. Forces, and then left to die in the abandoned shop. She didn't know how long she'd been there. It felt like years. She had thought that it was over, that this was how her life would end. To think that Allah had not forgotten her, that He had sent someone to save her life... it was a miracle.

He was not the one who overheard her moans, nor did he break down the door, but to her, Mohammed became the one who had saved her. She returned to her work as an interpreter with the Americans, who felt guilty for what had happened to her on their account. They kept her in the Green Zone for the rest of her employment, to keep her safe as she struggled with flashbacks and PTSD.

She saw Mohammed often as the years passed, and whenever he made his way through the checkpoint where she worked she ran up to him, hugged him, and exclaimed to all that he had saved her life.

He protested in embarrassment that it was not he who deserved the credit.

But it was a joy to see her there, alive and animated. And it was wonderful to feel her gratitude for the small role he had played in saving her life.

There was very little left of the suicide bomber after his explosion, but what was left of him was still very much alive. So strong were these blasts that it was rare to find the original bomber or discern which body pieces may have belonged to him, if anything was left at all. This, however, was a strange and unique case of a suicide bombing that had not gone off quite as the terrorist had planned.

He'd been wearing a thick belt of explosives around his waist, and upon entering the busy Shiite market, he had triggered it, or perhaps it had been triggered for him from afar. The belt blasted outward, killing or maiming all those in a hundred foot radius, and taking with it the suicide bomber's arms and legs. What was left at the center, like the eye of a storm, were the bomber's head and torso, shocked, bleeding, but still alive.

It didn't occur to Kadhim to question whether or not he should save the terrorist's life. In all likelihood, he was treating thieves and murderers all the time without realizing it. But this man had now shifted into a different category.

He was now a patient.

And it was Kadhim's job to treat patients, to save lives, withholding any and all judgment of who deserved to live and who deserved to die. That was what it meant to him to be a doctor. Choosing who lived and died was the terrorist's way. It would not be his own.

It was mind-blowing, nevertheless, to frantically work on an armless, legless terrorist who had survived his own suicide bombing. *Stop the bleeding. Stabilize the heart and lungs.*

The man was floating in and out of consciousness. Surely he could feel the agonizing pain that he'd brought upon himself.

No more than fifteen minutes had gone by when the U.S. Armed Forces appeared and whisked him away. The Americans had learned that he was still alive and wanted him for questioning. No one knew what happened to him after that.

But what would it have meant to have saved a terrorist's life?

ERECTILE DYSFUNCTION

"How is it that you're *always* sleeping? That's three days in a row you've done nothing but sleep! Wake up! Get up! *Do* something!" Mohammed nudged Georgie's inert body, which was snoring loudly.

There was a muffled, "mmhhg," and a stubborn hand shot out from nowhere and pulled the blanket over a sleep-ruffled head.

"I'm going to rename you Polar Bear, you're so lazy! You're like a big, hibernating teddy bear!" Mohammed yanked the blanket away with a laugh and began shaking Georgie's bed. "Wake up! Don't you have work to do?"

"No, no work," Georgie groaned, squinting his eyes resolutely shut and reaching blindly for the blanket. He gave up and pulled a pillow over his head.

"Are you kidding? *Wake up!*" Mohammed grabbed a baseball bat and whacked his friend's thigh until the increasingly loud groans erupted into a small roar and at last Georgie blinked open dark, sleep-filled eyes. He did indeed look rather polar bear-like.

"Nothing like waking up to a baseball bat," he grumbled.

"Dude, why are you always sleeping? When do you work?"

"I never leave the base."

"Okay, so he doesn't take you on outside missions. Don't you have something to do here?" Georgie was still working as an interpreter for Sgt. Major Harley.

"No." Georgie sat up and rubbed his eyes. "He just has me walk him to the checkpoints from time to time."

Mohammed burst into laughter. "That's it? You go for occasional walks with him? I guess he's keeping his little polar bear out of trouble then! Well, it's only three o'clock in the afternoon, Georgie. No reason to wake up now!" He punched him teasingly and Georgie punched him back.

"Where are you going?"

"I'm off to the internet café to visit Nina. Want to come?"

"Yeah, I'm coming. Just give me a second to wake up."

"You guys, I think I have a problem." Musa's voice was low and he looked worried as he took Mohammed and Georgie into his confidence. They had known him for years as an employee of the internet café, but it was rare for them to see their friend in such an agitated state. He had waited anxiously for Nina to leave in order to talk to them privately.

"What's up, man?"

"To put it bluntly: my girlfriend is coming over in an hour when I get off work, and I really want to have sex with her."

"So what's the issue?" Georgie asked. "She doesn't want to?"

"No, she's willing alright..." Musa's voice trailed off.

"Having a problem with the hardware?" Mohammed inquired with a grin.

"It's not funny!" Musa hissed. "And keep your voice down! It's just that I'm so damn stressed out. I just turned twenty-six and I look forty! My hair is graying, I've lost weight, I'm having nightmares and panic attacks..."

Mohammed laughed. "And here you just want a way to relieve all this stress through a fun night with your girlfriend."

Smoking, drinking, girls... they were a form of self-medication in a society that didn't believe in shrinks and anti-depressants.

"Exactly! Thing is, I've been so wound up lately that I haven't been able to... I mean things aren't exactly... I just don't think I'll be able to have sex with her!"

Musa took another gulp of his energy drink and went to help a customer who had just walked through the door. Mohammed eyed the half-empty energy drink for a second, then turned to Georgie with a wicked grin on his face.

"I have an idea..."

Musa was home with his girlfriend several hours later when he began to feel a bit off. He was excited that he'd finally been able to perform, but throughout dinner afterwards he'd had a growing headache. By the end of the evening, he felt dizzy and lightheaded, and his skin was clammy.

"Sweetie, what's wrong?" She looked disappointed.

"I don't feel so well, babe. I'm feeling a bit... nauseous."

"Ah, *habibi*, I'm so sorry!" She sat down in his lap and jumped up with a start. "If you're not feeling well, then what the hell is *that?*"

That was the other thing. He still had a throbbing erection. The thought crossed his mind that as long as *it* was there, and *she* was there, they may as well take advantage of the situation. *Perhaps his penis had finally come to life after a long and brutal hiatus.*

But as his vision started to blur, Musa realized that something just wasn't right. He picked up his cell and made an embarrassed phone call to two of the guys he trusted most.

"Saint! I'm in the hospital with Musa!" It was Georgie on the phone, and he sounded desperate.

"What's going on?" Mohammed was just coming back from a night mission and hadn't been able to answer Musa's calls.

"Dude, he's in bad shape. *Bad.* I don't know what to do."

"You took him to the Troop Medical Clinic, right?"

"Yes, but they keep asking what he was doing when the symptoms started."

"And what did you tell them?"

"Musa just keeps telling them he doesn't know!"

"Well, of course he doesn't know! For God's sake, Georgie! You have to tell them!"

Georgie turned to the American doctors and muttered, "We crush three or four Viagra pills and put them in his energy drink."

"*What?*" Musa screamed. "You *assholes*! You *drugged* me?"

"Oh boy!" The doctors looked at each other in amazement. "Get him to the emergency room! STAT!"

In an Iraqi hospital on the other side of Baghdad, it was the commotion outside the hospital doors that first alerted Kadhim to the patient's arrival. They were experiencing an uncharacteristically quiet day in the ER, and so the young man and his entourage made a grand entrance, exacerbating the splitting headache that had been hounding Kadhim all day. The patient, a man in his early twenties, was unconscious, and was being carried haphazardly by a group of shouting boys. He wore a long white dishdasha, but it was what was underneath the dishdasha that caught Kadhim's attention.

A small towel had been placed over his mid-section to hide the sharp protrusion that grew below, but Kadhim had a good idea what it was before removing the cover.

It was an erection. The kind of erection that made its bearer lose consciousness.

"Doctor, doctor, hurry! Help him! He's had complications!"

"What happened?" Kadhim examined the man as he questioned the companions. The boys looked at each other nervously.

"I don't know... he got a bad headache and uh, passed out. I guess he took one of those blue pills."

"What blue pills?" Kadhim inserted an IV to raise the patient's blood pressure, which was extremely low.

"You know..." the boy kept his eyes averted as the others snickered. "Viagra."

"And why did he take that?"

"I don't know." But it was clear that the boys *did* know. From what Kadhim could surmise, the group of guys had hired hookers for a *tibyata*, an "overnighter," and his patient had taken the pill, or perhaps several, in order to get his money's worth.

He and the male nurses started to chuckle.

"Well? Help him!"

"There's not much I can do. I raised his blood pressure, which will ease the headache when he wakes up, but basically the drug just needs to pass out of his system. He must have taken a bad pill—maybe it was a cheap knock-off. In the meantime, worst-case scenario, we need to prevent penile necrosis."

The term hung in the air like a death sentence until one of the boys whispered, "What is that?"

"If he has an erection for too long, his penis could go black and die."

Their eyes widened and jaws dropped as the horror of this fate ran rampant in their minds. More than a few thought anxiously of the pills that they themselves had consumed. *May Allah forbid that any of our penises should shrivel up and die.*

"Don't worry, I won't let that happen," Kadhim smiled indulgently. "I just need a way to induce vasoconstriction." He called one of the senior residents for advice, and when the resident had finished laughing, he gave Kadhim a tip.

The boys stared in amazement as Kadhim returned with a pack of cigarettes, some Tylenol, and a bowl of ice.

"Is this how you will save him?" one of the boys whispered in awe. The rest waited with bated breath to see the magical concoction that would save their friend's penis from a cruel and certain death.

Kadhim laughed.

"Calm down. The cigarettes are for you guys. The Tylenol is for me. And the bowl of ice," he set the bowl down with an air of finality, "is what we are going to put his penis in."

Sure enough, five minutes later the young man's penis had

shrunk to the size of a small carrot. Kadhim was sure, however, that neither the patient nor any of his companions would ever try Viagra again.

OB/GYN

Kadhim had been waiting all day for the other shoe to drop. It had been unusually calm and uneventful for the wartime hospital, and he had barely spent any time in the emergency department at all, for once completing the daily duties for his current rotation in the obstetrics and gynecology ward. In fact, it was with a sense of surprise and relief that he finished an uneventful evening round of the female patients in record time, partially due to the fact that several rooms were empty. By ten o'clock he was in bed, thanking his lucky stars for an early bedtime and a peaceful day. Perhaps he should not have expected something to go wrong every day in Baghdad Teaching Hospital.

The harsh knock at his door came about an hour later, startling Kadhim from his sleep. For a moment, he wondered if it was morning and if he had somehow overslept. A groggy glance at the clock told him otherwise. Throwing on his scrubs, he opened the door to find a male nurse, one whom he knew to be in cahoots with the Mahdi Army, eying him sourly.

"Yes?" Kadhim sent up a prayer that whatever the issue, it would not require his immediate attention and he would be able to go back to sleep. This had never yet been the case, but he hadn't given up hope.

"Doctor, you didn't check the patients in rooms 111 and 112."

"That's because there's no one in there." Kadhim struggled not to show his irritation. He had been woken up for *this*?

"Yes, there are. Look, here are their charts." The nurse handed over several files, and Kadhim perused them in growing astonishment and anger. The patients were males. With bullet wounds. In the ob/gyn ward.

"Who admitted these patients?"

"I don't know. Some doctor admitted them and left." The nurse's tone was shifty and sarcastic, and it was clear that he knew more than he was letting on.

Kadhim felt suddenly awake, and his brain ran through several quick calculations. He hadn't been called down to the ER, which meant that there was no mass trauma event with an overflow of patients that would warrant the use of the ob/gyn ward for housing males. They had been put there on purpose, in exactly the wrong place, the most *unlikely* place. Were they hiding from whoever had shot them? If this particular nurse was going out of his way to help the men, then chances were good that the patients had ties to the Mahdi Army. Who was coming after them? What would happen if they found out that these men were in the ob/gyn ward?

The possible ramifications made Kadhim dizzy.

Not in his ward. Not tonight.

"Who admitted them?" Kadhim repeated, angrily this time. "Aren't I the one who's supposed to admit them on my floor?"

"Look, I don't know. Just come see them."

Cursing, Kadhim marched to the ward. The other shoe had finally dropped.

A quick look in the rooms confirmed his fears. There was a patient with a chest tube to drain blood and air from internal injuries, and another with a bullet wound in his thigh. Most strikingly, each patient was accompanied by two armed guards in government security uniforms. Kadhim could tell by the patients' clothing that they were affiliates of the Mahdi Army, and one of the patients took the liberty of explaining that they had gotten into a crossfire with Al Qaeda.

Perfect. So ob/gyn can expect a visit from Al Qaeda anytime now.

Kadhim shut the door with a bang, determined not to examine either patient. He had taken a brief look at each one, checked their breathing, and made sure that they were stable, but that was as far as he would go. It had nothing to do with their ties to the terrorist militia. He simply would not examine them, mark their charts, and sign his name, thus becoming the responsible party that had officially admitted them to an all-female ward. Later, any questions regarding them and their presence in that particular ward would be addressed to him. They should not be here. They represented a threat to the lives of all the rest of the patients, for whom he *was* responsible. They were a ticking time bomb.

Kadhim returned to the nurse.

"Who are these guys? What are they doing here?"

"I don't know. I just received orders that they be placed in this ward."

"Yeah? Orders from where? Who admitted them? Just *tell* me."

"It was the Head of the Residents. Who else?" The nurse's tone was insolent. Kadhim ignored him and lifted the phone from its cradle. Time for a talk with the Head.

"What's going on, Hayder? Who admitted these guys onto my

floor and why?" Kadhim didn't take the time for niceties. The grim voice on the other end seemed not to care.

"It has nothing to do with you. Just take care of them."

"What do you mean take care of them? They need to be transferred to an appropriate floor."

"That's none of your business, Kadhim. Just do your job."

"No, I won't. I didn't admit them and they're not my responsibility. I don't want the ob/gyn ward to be attacked by Al Qaeda because I welcomed the damn Mahdi Army! You know full well that terrorists could come if they find out! I *cannot* have fighting break out in the middle of the floor amongst our female patients! God only knows who will die. They'd kill me for sure!" Kadhim took a breath and growled into the receiver, "Hayder, I want these guys out of here. Now."

"It's not up to you, Kadhim."

"This floor is MY floor as long as I'm in charge of it and I'm sure as hell not going to round on them. *You* admitted them! You want someone to round on them, come do it yourself!" Kadhim slammed down the phone, his heart pounding.

He knew he should not anger anyone with ties to the Mahdi Army. His fierce resolve to remain unaffiliated and uncorrupted by the militia's chokehold over the hospital was one of the main reasons why his existence here grew more dangerous every day. But a possible visit from an Al Qaeda-related group and the carnage it would wreak on his ward scared him even more. There would be no sleeping now. All he could do was wait.

Within twenty minutes, the ward's phone rang.

"Hello, Kadhim. This is Adil Muhsin, General Inspector of Corruption with the Ministry of Health."

Kadhim froze, barely knowing how to respond. Here was one of the highest officials in the entire Iraqi healthcare system, addressing him personally. The General Inspector continued in a diplomatic fashion.

"I just received a call from your superior, Hayder Al Mayahi. He mentioned that there are a few patients that you refuse to treat."

"Yes, sir," Kadhim replied. What was going on? Was it possible that the General Inspector had seen this for what it was—a case of severe corruption within the hospital—and was following up on it? Would his many letters of complaint regarding corrupt doctors, nurses, and staff finally begin to be addressed?

"Son, tell me why you're upset. Just take a minute to calm down and tell me why won't you round on these guys. Isn't that your legal and moral duty as a doctor?"

"I understand and respect your opinion," Kadhim replied with as much respect as he could muster. *He should have known that the General Inspector of Corruption would not actually be addressing corruption. This was Iraq, after all.* "If these patients had come to me directly, and if I had seen them first and admitted them myself, then yes, I would assume responsibility for them. But I don't know what's wrong with them or what brought them to this floor. It's clear that they're hiding here from a fight with Al Qaeda, and they're putting my entire ward at risk!"

"Son, you understand the current security situation," the General Inspector said. "I will send a complete set of guards right now to protect your ward. Don't worry."

"I don't *want* a complete set of guards! You're not getting it! This is an all-female ob/gyn ward with pregnant patients! I don't want any weapons on my floor!" Kadhim's voice rose in frustration, and he suddenly felt a pressure at his elbow.

"Kadhim, let it be!" A voice hissed in his ear. It was his friend Fadi, who was also stationed at ob/gyn with him that night. "Kadhim, don't go against the General Inspector. Just admit them and *I'll* round on them."

"No!" Kadhim shouted, turning on Fadi.

"Please, Kadhim. Let's just admit them!" Fadi urged, eyes wide. In the receiver, Kadhim heard Adil Muhsin also insisting. He returned to his phone call.

"General Inspector, with all due respect, I am not going to admit these patients and that's final!"

"Well, I'm coming over then." The inspector's tone was no longer diplomatic.

"You want to come, come. It makes no difference to me. Come and have them transferred to a different ward. Transfer them to surgery. I have nothing to do with them and I don't want them hiding here!" Kadhim slammed the phone into the receiver and turned to see Fadi sitting with his head in his hands.

"Oh God, Kadhim, what have you done? Do you want to get us killed? These guys are Mahdi Army! You don't just refuse to see them!"

"Screw them!" Kadhim was too angry to care. "What the hell do they think they're doing putting an entire ward of pregnant women at risk?"

"For God's sake, they have to hide somewhere! The Mahdi Army is the only thing protecting Shiites from getting slaughtered by *salafis*! Don't we owe it to them to help them hide and treat them if they get injured while trying to protect us?"

"Don't even get me started, Fadi! You call these guys protection? Their idiot tactics that don't discriminate between guilty and innocent are half the reason we're *in* this war! They'd just as soon turn around and kidnap, torture, and kill *me* if they saw some gain from it. Is that what you call protection? Getting attacked by others *and* by your own?"

"They're all we have!" Fadi protested.

"No, as Iraqi citizens we could have invested more in our army, and with the help of the Americans..." Kadhim stopped. "Enough. I don't want to get into another argument with you about the same old topic. You want to admit these guys, *you* sign your name to the papers. I'm going to bed!"

"You know I can't admit them without your permission. Kadhim, this isn't up to us. The order is coming from the top! We have no choice! Please, they're suffering here! We have to at least check on them and give them some pain meds. We can't, as doctors, just let them bleed to death on our watch!"

"They're stable. They'll be fine if someone just transfers them to the correct ward."

Fadi, however, was not giving up. After nearly an hour of listening to Fadi's pleading, Kadhim at last relented. It was clear that no one was coming to transfer the patients despite multiple requests on his part, and they would have to be seen eventually. Kadhim just wanted to get it over with and go to sleep.

Shouts and scuffling from the hall woke Kadhim not much later from an exhausted sleep. Cautiously, he looked out the door, afraid of the sight that might greet him. The obstetrics and gynecology ward was filled with armed guards wearing Iraqi Army fatigues and carrying AK-47s. The General Inspector had arrived, personal security detail in tow.

Kadhim marched to the room and threw open the door. Inside lay the bloodied Mahdi Army patient, and next to him sat Adil Muhsin, General Inspector of Corruption, murmuring over his prayer beads. He looked up as Kadhim entered.

"Salaam alaykum," Kadhim greeted him briefly.

"Alaykum as-salaam, my son. I wanted to thank you. I see from the charts that you allowed the patients to be admitted, and I'm grateful to you for that. Thank you, son."

"Don't thank me," Kadhim replied. "I attended to them only because it was the humane thing to do, in front of Allah. But they *must* go to the surgery ward. I do not have the necessary supplies to treat their wounds in this ward, nor am I close to the operating rooms if they needed an emergency operation. I honestly don't even know the extent of their injuries. They're completely wrapped and covered! That guy with his leg all wrapped up? I have no idea if he's still bleeding or not. This guy with the chest tube? It could collapse at any moment and I wouldn't have the tools here to save him. You need to arrange their transfer."

"My son, you know our current security situation," the General Inspector replied gravely.

"Look, if you're worried about what would happen to them if they were found in the surgical ward, then what about here? If Al Qaeda came to obstetrics and gynecology, then what protection do we have? Take your security detail and go with them!"

"It's okay, it's okay. I'll bring even more security for your ward."

"No, that's not what we need! Bringing all this security into ob/gyn is only going to focus more suspicion on this ward! It's too dangerous! Sir, I'm begging you. If you don't get these men out of here, I will make a huge fuss over this tomorrow with an official complaint to the Ministry of Health!"

"Son, I'm going to ask for a brotherly favor. I'm like your big brother. Please, do *not* leak their names. These files here, make it as if they don't even exist in this hospital. Just do what you have to do, and I *promise* you, they'll be gone within two days."

"Look, sir," Kadhim gazed straight into the inspector's eyes, "the only thing that's protecting your men right now is the fact that it's three o'clock in the morning. Tomorrow, when my patients start opening their doors, and when visitors, doctors, and other staff arrive, your 'security detail' will become the biggest threat here. People will start talking, phone calls will be made, and before you know it, Al Qaeda will be here to collect your men. Then it'll become an all-out battle in the ob/gyn ward, and I cannot let that happen. You need more than just keeping their names secret. You need to get your guards off this floor."

"I can't do that. I can't leave them unprotected."

"Then I can't protect your men, my patients, or myself from what's coming."

"Well, what if I just reduce the presence of my guards?"

Kadhim sighed. So it had come to this. Bargaining with the most senior inspector of corruption in the entire Iraqi healthcare system over how to best hide his extremist allies in the gynecology ward despite risking the lives of all involved. He felt exhausted, overwhelmed, and disgusted. *This* was not medicine. This was not the way a hospital was supposed to function. In that moment, he wanted nothing more than to leave Baghdad Teaching Hospital, separate himself from all the corruption and killing, and never return.

Instead, he bargained.

"Remove all guards from the hallway—I don't even want someone standing outside their doors—and you can keep two guards *inside* each room. No more. And have these patients out by early morning of the second day before anyone wakes up—that's five A.M. You do that, and I promise I will treat them and keep their names and charts completely confidential."

They struck a deal, and it was over.

If there had been any doubt in Kadhim's mind before, it was there no longer. Aided by a predominantly Shiite and increasingly polarized staff, and by the hospital's proximity to Sadr City, the Shiite militia known as the Mahdi Army was escalating its chokehold over the operation of Baghdad Medical Complex. At other hospitals around the city, extremist Sunni groups were also staking their claim. Entire hospitals had now become the territory of terrorists.

He wondered, as he at last sank into bed that night, how much longer he could remain uninvolved and true to his principles before giving in or being killed.

It was only a matter of time.

THE NIGHT SHIFT

"Are you married, doctor?" Um Haroun, a full-bodied woman in her late forties, batted heavily-mascaraed eyelashes at Kadhim, who was seated in front of her and holding her wrist as he took a pulse.

"No, ma'am, not yet. Life is too busy for a wife right now." He kept his eyes trained on her wrist, trying to look anywhere but at the heavy bosom that was leaning inappropriately close.

"That's too bad." She seemed delighted. He was acutely aware of a thick calf rubbing against his, and her fingertips tickled his arm. He gazed resolutely at his watch, wishing it would speed up.

"You look a lot like my husband in his younger years, God rest his soul." She looked at him wistfully. "I used to be quite a beauty myself, but my body has gone to bits since then. No man will even look at me anymore." She waited expectantly.

Kadhim paused, hoping the moment would pass, then said reluctantly, "No, ma'am, you still look quite healthy for your age. I'm sure it wouldn't be difficult to remarry."

"Why, I'm old enough to be your mother!" She giggled, pleased. She may even have blushed, but it was difficult to tell under the heavily powdered face.

Kadhim counted a few more seconds, and then released her wrist at last. He made a few notes on the chart as he headed toward the door.

"Well, everything looks good. If you don't have any questions, you can pick up your medicine at the pharmacy on the way out—"

"Actually, doctor, there is something else." She grasped Kadhim's arm as he turned to leave the exam room, and to his alarm started to unbutton her blouse. "Would you mind completing a breast exam while I'm here?"

"But you came in for high blood pressure," he said, groaning inwardly.

"Yes, but I've had a lump in my breast that has been concerning me for some time now. You don't mind, do you?"

He caught a glimpse of heavy cleavage, then turned away quickly. "We'd be happy to take a look for you. Let me just call for a female nurse."

"Oh no, no need to bring a nurse. I'm sure you're very busy, and this will only take a second."

"It's not a problem, and besides, this is standard policy. For your comfort, let me bring a nurse to chaperone the exam."

"That's okay, doctor, perhaps another time. I'm really busy actually. I... let me make a separate appointment. Perhaps it's better that way."

He was out the door before she had even finished buttoning up her blouse.

Kadhim had noticed over time that there were women who came to the hospital with needs that were more than medical. For some of them, the attention of a male, and particularly a doctor, was intoxicating, and there were those who would do anything to get the type of attention they were seeking. Women needing "special attention" who had overnight stays in the hospital were known to knock on the on-call doctor's door, requesting a private late-night exam. Being a slim, handsome young doctor without a ring on his finger, Kadhim had been forced to diplomatically side-step such advances on many occasions. Young, old, fat, skinny, beautiful, ugly, women of all types came knocking on the doctors' doors. Those who truly had a medical need did not fight the doctor's request that he conduct the exam in the patients' shared ward, but those with something else in mind would insist on the doctor's private quarters. Not all doctors were opposed to providing such services either, and at times it was difficult to determine who was taking advantage of whom. Kadhim had at first been shocked that some would stoop so low as to violate the doctor-patient boundaries by sleeping with their patients, but it was known to happen, and the sad truth was that things far worse than this occurred all the time in the war-torn hospital.

Kadhim had just finished up in the next exam room when he was called to the emergency ward to respond to the victims of crossfire between two militias. He grabbed his equipment and several boxes of gauze and ran down to the ER, but not before seeing Mahjoub leave the neighboring exam room, a small smirk on his face. Inside, Um Haroun was buttoning up her blouse, unattended.

"Well, how did it go yesterday?"

"How did what go?" Mahjoub looked up innocently from his lunch tray as Kadhim joined him and Malik in the cafeteria.

"How did it go with Um Haroun?" Kadhim laughed and gave him a small wink.

Mahjoub looked alarmed. "What? I didn't—How did you know?" Mahjoub met Kadhim's eyes for a second, then gave up the pretense and started laughing with him. "So I see you've met her."

"Who's Um Haroun?" Malik looked up from his meal in interest, little bits of sandwich spraying from his mouth. "Or, more importantly, what does she look like?"

"She's a widower in her forties, with a mask of makeup for a face," Kadhim inserted before Mahjoub could speak.

"Hey! She's thirty-nine!" he protested.

"No she's not!" Kadhim laughed. "Did you even look at her chart before you started feeling her breasts?" The men chortled and Mahjoub grew red.

"Well, what was she like? Did you do it right there in the exam room?" Malik's round cheeks grew pink with interest.

"Of course not. I had her admitted for an overnight stay, and she came to my room last night." Mahjoub gave a low whistle and his eyes grew wide, "Boy did she know what she wanted! Wow! An *experienced* woman! I'll be honest, boys, she was almost more than I knew how to handle. She was like a wild woman—she had to have it!"

The men burst into laughter. "Well, at least you had fun," Kadhim said, still laughing. "I can't believe you though. I mean, you shouldn't be doing this with *any* patient, but a forty-eight year old widow? Really? She's twice your age!"

"Hey, she's better than nothing!" His friend was defensive. "I think *I* even learned a thing or two from her last night! Besides, Kadhim, can you seriously tell me that with all the hell you go through on a daily basis, that you would say 'no' to a beautiful little package of 'stress relief'?"

"I would and I have, many a time."

"I wouldn't!" Malik inserted, between bites of falafel. "If you've got some extras, would you send them my way?"

"Take it easy on that falafel and I'll consider it," Mahjoub laughed. "As it is, you'd hurt my reputation!" He turned to Kadhim. "Seriously though, Kadhim, I know girls come knocking on your door all the time. You've never even considered it...?"

"I have a system," Kadhim replied. "If she's unattractive, I send her back. If she's too attractive, I send her back, because I don't trust myself and I don't want to get in trouble. But if there's someone else with me, and if the girl is cute, then I let her hang out with us for a while for some good conversation and some laughs. But eventually, they all get sent away."

"You really never do anything with *any* of them?" Mahjoub looked unconvinced.

"Never. I always send them away. It's a matter of principle. Look, when you cross that boundary with a patient, not only are you doing something immoral, but you're also potentially jeopardizing her healthcare and your own future as a doctor! It's a violation of the Hippocratic oath. I never have and never will cross that line."

Life in the hospital went on; every day agonizing and exhausting. Kadhim was growing numb to the blood, suffering, and death that filled his days. The joys of hospital life were few. The cafeteria food had continued to decrease in quantity and quality since Malik had taken over, and there were no more trips home for Mama's home cooked meals. If he had time and energy at night after his evening rounds, Kadhim would play a video game or watch a TV show in his bedroom, which converted into a patient exam room during the day. He spent most of his time in the emergency ward, as the hospital staff was still decreasing daily and his presence was needed there most. When he wasn't called to the emergency ward, he would focus his attention on the assigned rotation, and it was during a month-long rotation in Hematology and Oncology that he met Layal.

"Layal Al-Batal, nineteen year-old female, in remission from leukemia for eighteen months. Repeat visits from Jordan every four months to take follow-up doses of chemotherapy. Has been admitted for a week for the current round of chemo..." Kadhim paused in his case presentation for a moment to glance at the patient, and stumbled a bit— she was pretty. Very pretty. "Has um... has been admitted for a week for current round of chemo. Needs exams prior to and after chemo treatment."

"What types of exams, and what will you be checking for?" the presiding oncologist quizzed him.

"Prior to chemotherapy, we should complete full general exams, make sure there are no residual cancerous cells. After chemo, we should check for any side effects from the drug. Check electrolytes and blood vessels, do another chest x-ray to screen for pneumonitis, check for fever and keep an eye out for possible infections, as chemo weakens the immune system."

"Excellent. Dr. Kadhim, you will be the presiding intern for this case. Please let me know if anything of interest comes up in your exams."

Layal lived in Jordan, but—prices being what they were in

Amman—had been receiving treatment in Baghdad for several years. Her leukemia had been in remission for long enough that her dark brown hair had grown in shiny waves to her shoulders. She was young, but frequent travel, a harsh disease, and a touch of eyeliner and lip gloss made her appear more like a young woman than a teenager. An elderly aunt accompanied the girl and sat in on all of her exams, but she left the hospital at night while the girl slept in a dormitory-style room with other female patients. Kadhim checked in on her twice a day during morning and evening rounds, and Layal seemed to look forward to his visits and enjoy his company.

"Do you have any brothers or sisters, Dr. Kadhim?" Layal asked him one morning as he checked her IV drip. Her elderly aunt was sitting in the corner, her head at an awkward upward tilt, snoring loudly.

"I have four brothers. No sisters." He made sure the chemo drip was slow and unrushed, so as not to hurt the patient's veins or make her sick. He turned to her to double-check for reactions to the drug.

"Four brothers—wow! I bet they're all handsome, like you." She giggled a little. Kadhim laughed. She liked to flirt, but she was a harmless little thing. "Are they all doctors too?"

"No, I'm the only one."

"Ooh—then I'm lucky. I met the good one!"

"What about you, Layal? Any siblings?" He checked her pulse. It was fine.

"I have a little sister. She and I have lived with my mother in Amman ever since my parents divorced several years ago."

"I see. Layal, I'm going to call a nurse in briefly while I check your heart and lungs."

"There's really no need," Layal started, but Kadhim had already managed to pull one of the nurses into the room.

"I'm afraid I can't get an accurate read over the gown," he said, pulling out his stethoscope. "Would you mind opening the back a little so I can insert the stethoscope?"

She obliged and continued talking as he attempted to auscultate the lungs through her upper back. "As I was saying, it's just the three of us women living together in Amman."

"Take a deep breath in and out, please."

"It's really difficult to live there without any men. Everything's different now that Baba's not around."

"Deep breath, please." He tried a different position.

"It would just be so nice to have a man in the house. Your mother's lucky to have so many."

Kadhim paused before answering, listening to the heart and lungs. "We try to help her, yes. My father does a lot to provide for the family. But to her credit, my mother also works as a teacher, and having five boys means she works a lot more at home as well." He moved to the front to listen to her heart. "Would you mind opening the gown a little here as well?"

"Sure," Layal said, and before Kadhim could say more she removed the top portion of her gown entirely, exposing two full and naked breasts. A faint gasp came from the corner, and Kadhim shot a nervous glance to the side—it was just the nurse. The aged aunt had not moved other than to tilt her head even more impossibly backward and release a staccato of snorts. He refocused and placed the stethoscope below the left breast, lifting the breast slightly with his hand for the best angle.

"Ooh, that's cold," Layal started, placing an awkward hand on his arm and giving it a little squeeze. He ignored it.

"Deep breath, please. You can close your gown a bit more if you'd like."

For once, she did take a long, slow breath, gazing at him intently as he inadvertently watched her breasts rise and fall while listening to her heartbeat.

"Well, I wouldn't want to prevent you from doing a good job, would I, doctor?" she said coyly, making no attempt to cover herself further. He averted his eyes quickly, embarrassed, and moved the stethoscope to a different position.

"It's not a breast exam, Layal," he chided. The nurse in the corner said nothing, but she watched with the faintest hint of a smile and a knowing look in her eyes. Kadhim felt his cheeks redden.

Layal laughed and responded cheekily, "And how would I know what it is that you want to check?" She took another deep breath, but while Kadhim kept his eyes focused on a dirt streak on the wall, the vision of her round breasts and hardened nipples still played itself in his mind.

"Doctor, would you mind checking in on one of your patients when you get a chance?" The nurse rushed up to him. "It's your girlfriend."

"What?"

She winked at him and laughed, and he recognized her from

Layal's exam.

"Is it urgent?" he asked resignedly.

"She doesn't seem to be doing so well... She asked for you anyway."

"Okay, I'll check in on her when I have the time."

"What's going on between you two?" The nurse raised a conspiratorial eyebrow.

"What do you mean, 'what's going on'? She's my patient."

"Are you sure about that?"

"She's an outgoing girl, and she likes to be social, but that's all there is to it!"

"You'll invite me to the wedding now, won't you?"

"There'll be no wedding," Kadhim grumbled, moving past her.

"Not if the social butterfly has it her way," the nurse teased, laughing as she walked away.

"Everything okay, Layal?" Kadhim entered the patient ward a bit later and drew the curtain to give her some privacy from the other patients. A few days had gone by since the chemotherapy and she had done pretty well, but there were still tests to run and results to read.

"I'm not sure, doctor. I just feel tired and hot. I think I might have a fever."

He quickly found a thermometer to check her temperature, annoyed that the nurse hadn't done this herself.

"Well, your temperature is 37.5° Celsius—that's a little high, but still within normal range. I'll keep an eye on it just in case. Anything else bothering you?"

"How are things going out there? Are you really busy? Are a lot of people dying?" She was worriedly eyeing a bloodstain on his scrubs, and she looked scared and lonely. It occurred to Kadhim that it could not have been easy to have lost the presence of a father, battled leukemia, and to continue to make trips into a war-torn country for treatment more or less on her own as a woman not yet twenty years of age.

"It's not so bad," he said gently. "Don't worry, you're not alone. You have many people here to take care of you." The phone in the corner started to ring, and Kadhim had a sinking feeling that he knew what it was for.

"Everything's going to be fine," he said hurriedly. "I'll come back and check on you during my evening rounds, and in the meantime if you need anything, or if you get any worse, just let one of the nurses know."

He rushed to pick up the phone. It was the emergency room:

three back-to-back car bombings, dozens of bodies on their way in. All hands on deck.

It was nearly midnight before Kadhim made it back to his bedroom. The emergency ward had been a mess, packed with people, shouting, and confusion. Everywhere there were bodies in various stages of death, missing limbs, riddled with shrapnel or choking up blood. He triaged, stabilized those whom he could, and sent them off to surgery. He wrote death certificates for shouting, sobbing, and grief-stricken relatives until his fingers cramped and developed blisters. When things finally quieted down he made a quick round of the oncology ward, and at last fell exhausted into his bed.

A knock on the door woke Kadhim from his sleep. He glanced at his clock in a sleepy haze. It was 12:32am. He had only slept twenty-eight minutes, damn it. He pulled on his scrubs, patted down his sleep-mussed hair, and opened the door to find Layal standing there in her nightgown.

"I have a stomachache." She rubbed her stomach as if to remind the doctor where it was.

"Okay, let's go back to the ward and I'll check it for you," Kadhim replied sleepily, grabbing his stethoscope. He started toward the door but Layal stopped him with a hand on his arm.

"Why don't you just do the exam here, in your room? This is the same exam room where you check me every morning." It was indeed, and Kadhim glanced with slight embarrassment at his makeshift bed in the corner as the on-call intern, where rumpled covers, a small television, and some empty wrappers on the floor betrayed more of his private life than he cared to reveal.

"It wouldn't be appropriate. I don't want my reputation as a doctor, or yours, to be tarnished by a private midnight exam that could just as easily be done in the dormitory."

"No, it's fine, really. It's not a problem. What's the big deal? A quick exam here and I'll go back."

"That's not up to you. It's just not appropriate." Kadhim pushed past her to start walking her back to the oncology ward. "Look, Layal, you seem like a good girl from a reputable family. I wouldn't want you to face problems because of something like this. It's not worth it."

"I don't understand what you're afraid of," Layal protested. "It's just a little exam. No one's even awake!"

"It's not a matter of fear," he replied as they entered the quiet dormitory. "It's a matter of principle. This is my reputation as a physician!"

She stopped suddenly and grabbed his arm.

"I don't understand, Kadhim. You don't like me? You're not attracted to me?" She looked up at him with beautiful brown eyes and took a step closer.

"Wow, that's pretty brazen of you. You shouldn't talk to me like this, Layal! I'm your doctor!" Kadhim laughed out of sheer incredulity that she could say and do such things in front of two nurses and a dormitory full of patients, dead to the world though they may be.

"I know you're my doctor, but how old are you, Kadhim?"

"I'm twenty-four."

"I'm almost as old as you are then. So what's the big deal if I talk to you like this?" She was standing dangerously close to him now.

"Age has nothing to do with it. This is a conservative society! You can't talk to your doctor like this!" He kept his voice low, so as not to wake the others, but while he meant what he said, he couldn't help but be amused.

He did not want to go down this road with a patient, but he wasn't upset with her. After all, it was hard to be angry when a young and beautiful woman expressed her interest so openly. She was standing so close to him that he could smell her perfume, and his thoughts flashed back to Mahjoub's expression "a beautiful little package of 'stress relief'." There they were, in the dark, just the two of them, and although he desperately wanted to, Kadhim couldn't seem to step away from her.

Layal looked up at him, her face dangerously close to his, and said with a wicked little smile, "I might get a stomachache tomorrow night as well."

The next day, Kadhim worked in a half-distracted state, plagued by his thoughts. *What would he do if she came again? If he kicked her out directly she might be hurt and upset and might cause a scene—it would be a mess. On the other hand, he could let her in just to hang out for a while as he had done with others before her. But she was very pretty, and she was coming on very strong. He was a young man with needs; he hadn't asked for this. She was the one who wanted it... How wrong could it be if so many doctors were doing it? It had been a long time since he'd had any "stress relief" as Mahjoub had put it, and he didn't trust that he could keep pushing her away. Did he not deserve a bit of fun after all he'd been through? And didn't she need it too?—No, no, of course he could not do this. What the hell was he thinking? It was*

wrong, and what's more, it could seriously harm his reputation—and hers—and cause him problems in the hospital. No, it was out of the question. Absolutely not. There just needed to be some way to avoid her, to stop her advances. It was becoming too much at this point. Her long hair, her dark eyes, her slim waist, those breasts... No! Stop fantasizing! Stop thinking about her, period!

He tried to push her from his thoughts, but instead she stubbornly sat there in the back of his mind as he worked, smiling her wicked smile and twisting his thoughts around her fingers.

His morning round with her in his bedroom-turned-clinic was awkward and filled with tension. They spoke little, and when she gave him another of her conspiratorial smiles and lightly brushed his hand with hers, it was as though an electric shock had run through him. He instantly thought with equal parts dread and anticipation of their inevitable upcoming encounter. It had been so long since he had anticipated anything at all that the sensation felt foreign to him. He told himself firmly that nothing was going to happen, but deep down he was not sure whether he had that much self-control.

It was 12:02PM when the knock came at the door. It was Layal, her wavy dark hair falling around her shoulders, wearing a little pink nightgown tied around the waist that showed off a curvy figure and two slim legs.

"I had another stomachache, doctor." She grinned. "I had to come see you."

"Layal." His heart jumped in excitement upon seeing her, despite the warning sirens going off in his mind. "Are you crazy, coming here?" He stood in the doorway, trying not to let her in.

"I'm crazy about you." She pushed the door open a bit wider.

"Look, you can't do this. You know very well that if you come in here, there's no telling what I might do." Kadhim was straightforward. The time for playing games was over.

"That's exactly what I want," she replied, slipping inside and shutting the door behind her.

Then it was just the two of them, alone in the room. His pulse quickened despite himself, and he started to feel his defenses slipping. He made another effort.

"Layal, stop it. You need to go back to your room. Now."

"You can't tell me that you don't want this as much as I do."

"I can assure you that I don't."

"And now?" She untied her robe and slipped it off, and stood before him in a lacy black bra and matching underwear. "Can you still tell me that you don't want me?"

The sudden revealing of her nubile body stunned Kadhim into silence. He could do nothing but stare at her slim figure as she took a step forward, leaned in, and kissed him.

She pulled away and looked at him. "I've been wanting to do that since I got here."

"This is wrong, Layal. Please, go back to your room." He was practically begging her at this point.

"Not until I get what I want." She kissed him again, harder this time, and pulled him closer to her while she ran her other hand along his chest. That was it; his defenses were gone. He gave in and kissed her back, putting his hands on the small of her back, feeling her smooth, warm skin and small waist. He ran his fingers through her hair and along her small stomach until he reached her full breasts, where he stopped, still not ready to cross that boundary.

"Don't stop," Layal breathed. She slowly undid her bra, dropped it to the ground, then grabbed his hand and placed it on her breast. He cupped the breast and touched her nipple—and as if on cue, the phone rang, and he jumped, jerking his hands away from her.

"Don't answer that," she whispered.

"It's not optional." He already knew what it was as he picked up the phone, and he cursed his luck and thanked God in the same breath.

"Kadhim, we need you down here now!" The voice on the line was urgent. "The ER is overflowing, it's chaos. Get down here, help us triage, and prepare any space you have on your floor for patient overflow." The line went dead.

"I have to go." Kadhim grabbed the top of his scrubs and pulled it on over his t-shirt. A wave of relief washed over him, mixed with heavy disappointment. She had been a small ray of light in what seemed an unending darkness. In the whirlwind of constant violence, chaos, and fear for one's life that surrounded them, maybe God would have forgiven them this one transgression, this shared moment of tenderness... although he doubted his mother would. He allowed himself to steal one more glance.

Layal watched him from where she stood leaning against the exam table, still wearing nothing but her panties. She looked incredible.

"I'll wait for you here."

"I don't think you will." Kadhim laughed.

"And why's that?"

"Because pretty soon this exam room and the entire ward are going to be filled with an overflow of trauma patients, including males."

Her face sank, and he paused for a moment and looked at her. "It was never meant to be, Layal. I'll see you tomorrow when I do your discharge papers."

And with that he was out the door.

THE MORGUE

"Kadhim, your cousin has been beheaded." His father's words seemed oddly unfathomable as they came over the phone line, and it took several moments for the meaning to sink in.

"Which one?" Kadhim asked at last, trying to ignore the sounds of the hospital around him.

"Abu Mahmood."

Kadhim remembered him, although he had not known him very well. He was a second cousin some fifteen years older than Kadhim and was married with three children.

"May God have mercy on his soul. How did this happen?"

"Apparently he was on his way home and had to pass through a dangerous Sunni neighborhood. They stopped him and cut off his head for being Shiite."

Dogs. All of them. Kadhim's mind swirled in anger and sorrow. *Why did he have to pass through that neighborhood? He should have* known *how dangerous it was! He shouldn't have risked his life.*

Iraq was worse now, in the hellish days of 2006, than it had ever been. Car bombs and suicide bombers were no longer measured by the day, but by the hour. Those who did not die by explosions were dying by the hands of terrorists, in uncountable numbers every day. It was beyond dangerous, beyond lawless. It was the hell of complete and utter chaos.

"Kadhim? Are you listening to me?" Baba's voice was urgent. "We've just heard that Abu Mahmood's body was delivered to the morgue at Baghdad Medical City three days ago. We're on our way now, all of us, but we need your help. You need to go to the morgue and get his body."

"I'll head over there now." Kadhim hung up the phone, steeling himself for the terrible experience that was to come.

The morgue, although in a separate building, was only some two hundred meters away from the emergency department. On days when the wind came from that direction, Kadhim would often catch the faint but nauseating smell of death. He had no desire to go any closer, but this time he had no choice. Donning his white lab coat, he braced himself and stepped outside.

It was hot, the type of unbearable sauna heat that made his

clothes stick to his body and made it difficult to breathe. As he approached the morgue, he saw the mass of people who waited outside by the hundreds hoping to collect their dead. Anyone who was not medical staff was forbidden from entering the morgue, which was why Baba had requested Kadhim's help. Even before reaching the morgue the smell was sickeningly strong, but he was unprepared for what awaited him when he bypassed the long lines and stepped inside.

The stench of decomposing human flesh was unbearable, revolting, nauseating. It was so strong that it was no longer simply a smell; it had become an overwhelming and toxic gas that caused Kadhim's eyes to water and burned his throat, despite the fact that he was holding his nose and breathing through his mouth. He felt dizzy and lightheaded. If he had not had so much exposure to dead bodies and decomposing parts in the hospital, he would have become instantly ill. As it was, he was having difficulty keeping his lunch down.

"Kadhim, you made it!" It was Sulaiman, a senior resident of forensic medicine and a longtime friend of his. Kadhim had given him a quick phone call to let him know that he was on his way and hoped for Sulaiman's help in finding his cousin's body. "Listen, I'm in the middle of an autopsy right now, but I've asked Fareed here to help you out. I'll try to catch up with you later."

"Thanks." Kadhim choked on the word as he tried to breathe through the noxious gases. He was amazed that Sulaiman could breathe normally and even smile in this atmosphere. Fareed, who was not a physician but part of the morgue's staff, stepped forward, his stature short and compact, his scrunched face set in a permanent scowl.

"When was the cadaver delivered?" he asked dourly.

"Three days ago."

"All bodies that were delivered in the past two weeks are in the last room on the right." He turned to leave.

"Wait!" Kadhim called out. "Aren't you going to help me find him? I can't sift through all these bodies!"

"I don't help locate cadavers unless I've been paid."

"Are you serious?" All this, and the man was looking for a bribe. "Isn't locating cadavers your job?"

The man scowled and turned to walk away.

"Fine, fine! Come back. Just help me and I'll pay you whatever you want."

"I only take payments up front."

"How much?"

"One hundred thousand dinars."

"Are you kidding? That's like a hundred bucks!" Kadhim

couldn't believe what he was hearing, but as the man stomped away, he gave in. "Here, take it." He fished the bribe from his wallet and followed the man to the last room on the right. What he saw shocked and revolted him.

A refrigerator that should have held twenty bodies held one hundred. The drawers had been removed, and in the place of one corpse they had stuffed four or five. Once all the refrigerators were full, the corpses were left on the floor, one on top of the other, in chaotic piles that reached the ceiling. When all the rooms were full with piles, the bodies were stacked in the hallways. Everywhere he looked, all Kadhim could see and smell was decomposing flesh. In the heat of the Iraqi sun, they were decaying very quickly and were barely recognizable as human. Blackened skin, bloated torsos, and flesh, muscle, and tissue literally sliding off the bones... it was a living nightmare. In a daze of repulsion, Kadhim barely heard as the stocky assistant turned to ask him a question.

"I'm sorry. What?"

"In what shape was the cadaver delivered?"

"What do you mean?"

The man scowled impatiently. "We have rooms for whole bodies, a room for beheaded bodies, a room for unclaimed heads and various body parts, a room for burned bodies, a room for bodies that have been tampered, altered, or mutilated..."

"He was beheaded," Kadhim inserted quickly, trying to cut off the horrible list of options.

"It's in a different room then. Come with me. Watch your step," the gnome grunted, and walked away.

Kadhim hurried to keep up with him and realized quickly, as he nearly slipped, that he needed to heed the man's advice. The floor was covered in a slimy liquid that made walking perilous. It was not blood. The corpses at this stage no longer had flowing blood. It was melted fat and body oils that were secreted from the cadavers as they decomposed, casting grease over the entire floor. Kadhim watched as before his very eyes, an enormous bubble expanded in the skin of a hallway corpse, then burst, and from it oozed more of the putrid fat. The last of the blackened meat fell away, exposing a rib cage.

Kadhim swallowed hard, trying to settle the nausea that threatened to heave his stomach, and tore his eyes from the corpse. He followed Fareed into the room with the headless cadavers and hoped for the best.

One by one, Fareed brought out countless bodies for Kadhim to examine. It was pointless. They were all so disintegrated that it was impossible to see any identifying characteristics. Kadhim called his father in frustration.

"Baba, I can't tell which one's him! I haven't seen him in years, for God's sake! How am I supposed to pick one?"

"He had a tattoo on his hand. A tattoo of his name. You'll know him by that."

"No Baba, no I won't. Most hands don't have any skin left on them, and for those that do, the skin has blackened and decayed. I can't see any tattoos, on *any* of them!" Kadhim felt desperate, sickened, and an exhausting sadness. Had his cousin tattooed his own name on his hand in the off chance that this fate might befall him one day? If so, even that had not helped him.

"Okay, Kadhim, calm down. We're almost there. When we get there, we'll send in someone to help you find him."

Kadhim hung up the phone and looked at Fareed. The scowling face had turned green and sickly. It was clear that neither of them could sift through the bodies a minute longer.

As he stepped outside, Kadhim was joined by Sulaiman, who offered him a sympathetic cigarette. For once, Kadhim accepted gratefully, trying not to think about where his friend's hands had been.

"How do you handle it, man? This sight, this *smell*, day in and day out?" They stared unseeing at the crowd of grieving people as they tried in vain to calm their nerves with nicotine.

"You get used to it, I guess." Sulaiman shrugged.

Kadhim glanced at him, then looked away. He didn't have the heart to say it, but he knew without a shadow of a doubt that every last person who worked in the morgue under these conditions would eventually become sick. This type of exposure on a daily basis was deadly.

"All those people, waiting..." he mused quietly, trying to change the subject.

"I feel bad for them," Sulaiman said. "Most of them wait for days, pay a few hundred dollars, and still don't find who they're looking for. Usually they don't even know where their relatives *are*. They just go from one morgue to the next, searching for them. And by the time they find them, *if* they find them, the corpse isn't recognizable. That's what happens when you can't properly refrigerate them."

He took another deep drag on the cigarette and waved a casual finger behind the morgue. "When we ran out of room in the fridges, we rented some of those huge refrigerated semis that are used to transport perishable foods, and now they're full too. Nothing is enough to keep up with all the bodies we're receiving."

"What do you do with all those bodies? You can't store them forever. Do they all get claimed eventually?"

"I wish they would, but most don't. We have to keep the unclaimed cadavers for a certain period of time, not just for legal reasons but also because that's what is required by Islamic law." Kadhim nodded understandingly as his friend continued. "We have to give the relatives a fair amount of time to search, if for no other reason than to be able to hold our heads high when we meet Allah. But at the end of that period of time, after some three weeks to a month, the bodies are completely decomposed and it's time for the mass graves. There are some kind-hearted volunteers from the mosques who come to pick them up periodically. They read the *fatiha* over the body, and they bury it with as much dignity and respect as they can. '*Unknown number one, unknown number two, unknown number three...*'" Sulaiman's voice trailed off.

"Thank God for people like them." Kadhim scanned the crowd for his family.

"For me, the worst part isn't the bodies anymore. It's the staff." Sulaiman took a deep drag on his cigarette and flashed an ironic smile through stained teeth.

"What do you mean?"

"The doctors who used to work here left. There was nothing left for them anymore. There's no such thing as an autopsy and 'cause of death' in this climate. You see a burnt cadaver, a body torn apart by a bomb, or a headless corpse, and you know what killed them. You don't need to be a doctor for that. There's no art form anymore. The only medical professionals remaining are mostly residents. We can't afford to leave. How would I provide for my family?"

"Sounds awful."

"The main problem though is that most of the staff—those *without* medical degrees—aren't here just for the bribes. They're here because they're affiliated with militias and gangs and terrorist groups, and they use their position to suck grieving relatives dry."

"What?"

"A family will come looking for their son, and the employee will hide the body and tell them that he can't find it. Then he'll call them afterward and inform them that their son's body has been located in the possession of some armed group or another, and that they have to pay a huge ransom in order to get it back. The truth is, it was there in the morgue all along. The family knows this, but what can they do? Sometimes they pay exorbitant sums just to be able to obtain their son's body. Sometimes, they don't come at all. They're too afraid. They could be kidnapped or killed when they try to collect the corpse. I've seen it happen. So they have to live with the knowledge that they left their loved one's body in the hands of terrorists."

"That's awful..." Kadhim's heart sank as he listened. He didn't know why he was shocked. He had seen evidence of the same sick corruption in the hospital. This time, however, they were kidnapping the dead. It was unthinkable.

"I'm terrified of my own staff." Sulaiman turned and met Kadhim's gaze head-on. His face was serious. "I'm their superior, and I'm terrified of them. All the doctors are. They say, *'Let's put the corpse here,'* and I say, 'Fine.' Let them put it wherever they wish. Let them hold it for ransom. They could kidnap and kill me at any moment."

He took a deep, desperate drag on the dying end of his cigarette and closed his eyes as he exhaled. "I do whatever they want, so that I can stay alive."

He threw the butt down and crushed it with a grim sense of finality.

"I don't blame you," Kadhim replied. "We're facing similar pressure in the hospital. Sulaiman, I see my family over there. I'm going to greet them and see if we can go back in and get Fareed to help us find my cousin's body."

"Sounds good. My break is over anyways." Sulaiman turned to head back indoors, then paused and looked at Kadhim. "Word to the wise..."

"Yes?"

"Just don't piss Fareed off."

"You guys, I can't tell which one is him." Kadhim was facing his father, several cousins, and Mahmood, the eldest son of the deceased, who was no more than a boy of fifteen.

"Did you look for the tattoo on his hand?"

"Yes, I looked, but you can't see anything anymore. The bodies are too decayed.

"But it's only been a few days!"

"That doesn't matter. The heat speeds up decomposition. I need someone to come with me if we want to have a shot at identifying Abu Mahmood's body."

The boy stepped forward, his face pale, anxious and very young. "I will go."

Kadhim looked at his father worriedly. "Do you think he can handle it?"

Baba put a gentle hand on Mahmood's shoulder and said firmly, "Let him try."

Kadhim took a last breath outside, and he and Mahmood entered the morgue. The fifteen-year-old took one look at the decomposing flesh that surrounded them, inhaled the burning stench, and vomited. Tears welled up in his eyes at the task of identifying his father as one of these decayed bodies, and he began to cry. He took a few more steps forward, nearly slipped on the melted fat that covered the floor in a bright sheen, and vomited again. He cried harder.

With one hand plugging his nose and the other on the boy's shoulder, Kadhim found Fareed and asked that they look again. The one hundred thousand Iraqi dinars that the man had received only twenty minutes prior had apparently expired, and another sixty dollars was required to continue the job.

Kadhim walked with Mahmood through the hallway of the dead, pausing here and there as the boy stopped to vomit through his tears. They reached the room designated for headless corpses, and Kadhim prayed silently that this time they would find the body quickly and the ordeal would be over.

Once again, they started the exhausting and stomach-turning process of examining the headless bodies that were bloated, skinless, bare-boned or covered with boils that grew and popped like boiling water, secreting toxic gas and fat. The boy's thin shoulders were racked with sobs as he slowly shook his head at corpse after corpse. He continued to vomit periodically, but no amount of vomit could make the morgue smell worse or be dirtier than it already was.

At last, when Kadhim thought he could not handle anymore, a small voice found its way through the tears.

"This one."

To Kadhim, the cadaver looked just as black and decayed as all the rest. No tattoo appeared on either hand.

"How do you know, Mahmood?"

"The arch of my father's foot was mildly deformed. This is my father." His tear-streaked face was oddly calm for a moment, whether in shock or relief Kadhim could not tell.

"Are you sure?"

"No, I'm not sure. There's no head, the tattoo doesn't show, the skin isn't the same color, the body isn't the same shape, and the skin and muscle are falling off... but I think this is my father." A tear rolled down his young cheek.

Kadhim's heart went out to him. No fifteen-year-old should ever have to live through this. He put an arm around the boy's shoulder and gave it a gentle squeeze.

"That's it then. We'll take this one, and we'll consider it your father. And if it isn't, God forbid, then we'll consider it your father nevertheless, and the respect with which we bury him will be in your father's honor."

"That's it then," the boy consented quietly, and he leaned over and was sick. Crying, Mahmood went back outside to inform the family that his father's remains had been found.

Kadhim stayed inside for several hours as he finished the paperwork, and as the cadaver was wrapped and placed into a casket. Without his special privileges as a doctor, his family would have waited at the morgue for two or three days, and they still might have been turned away. To retrieve a body this quickly was considered record time.

It was a long time before the stench of death was finally washed from Kadhim's clothes, but the memory of it never faded. Even years later, he could remember the putrid smell vividly, and it still had the power to nauseate him. That day in the morgue, he was sure that he had seen the worst that death had to offer. Surely, *surely*, there could be no end more horrifying than this.

"What the hell *is* that?" Kadhim and a few colleagues were staring at a dead patient that had been brought to the hospital. Kadhim had by now seen death in many forms and was no longer shocked by the various conditions in which corpses arrived. But this was... odd. The deceased was a male in his forties that had not yet started the process of decay. There were a few bullet wounds—possible causes of death—but it was the strangely distended stomach that caught Kadhim's eye. It was not distended in a soft and even way, as it would have been with post-mortem bloating. Rather, the stomach was lumpy, uneven, and hard. Something was off.

Kadhim lifted the sheet that covered the patient, and saw a crude row of stitches running the length of the torso from the man's sternum to his pubic area. Whoever had killed him had also cut him open, whether before or after death Kadhim could not tell, and they had placed something inside.

Immediately, instinctively, Kadhim jumped away from the corpse. "Fuck! Get back! Get away everyone!" No one needed to be told twice. Within seconds, the area surrounding the body was deserted. One of them ran for the phone, and a bomb squad arrived within minutes.

Kadhim left them to their job and tried to attend to some other patients, but his mind remained on the strangely distended abdomen. His heart would not stop pounding, and unconsciously, he braced himself for impact.

None came.

"Dr. Kadhim?" A member of the bomb squad approached him.

"Yes?"

"We don't know what's in there—we didn't open him up—but whatever it is, it's not a bomb. We've tested and scanned everything we can, but everything in there is organic, to the best of our knowledge. No metals or explosive liquids or substances. Feel free to continue your work." The team departed, and Kadhim was left with the corpse.

He stared at it for a moment and ran a tentative, gloved hand over the swollen abdomen. His hand was met by something hard, something that for the life of him he could not discern. Blood gradually stopped oozing from the uneven incision that had been inexpertly hacked through the stomach. Although curious, Kadhim would not waste precious time and resources conducting an x-ray. Live patients were waiting. This was a job for the morgue.

Kadhim arranged for the corpse to be transferred and made a call to Sulaiman in the process.

"Hey, I'm sending over a body that has had something planted in the abdomen. I just wanted to let you know that the bomb squad came and checked it out, and according to them there's nothing in there. No bombs anyway. But we still haven't figured out what it is. Would you mind giving me a call when you open him up, just to ease my curiosity?"

"Sure, no problem." Sulaiman seemed unperturbed. Whatever Kadhim had seen in dead bodies, he had seen tenfold. Nothing fazed him.

The call came the next day.

"Hey, Sulaiman, how goes it?"

Sulaiman did not respond with his usual jovial greeting. His voice shook, and he seemed unable to breathe. "Kadhim, you know that cadaver you sent over with the distended abdomen?"

Kadhim had a sudden sense of foreboding. A part of him no longer wanted to know what was inside.

"We opened him up." Sulaiman took a deep breath. He seemed

to be on the verge of losing control. "Whoever did this, they pulled out his insides—heart, lungs, kidneys, intestines—all of it gone." There was a long pause, and in the static silence Kadhim could hear his friend's unsteady breathing. "Then they put in the severed heads of three children—*his* children presumably—and sewed him back up."

Something deep inside Kadhim screamed, and he felt his spirit crumple to the floor. No words could describe the horror that overwhelmed him in that moment. He seemed to be incapacitated for an interminable period of time trying to process the words, before coming to his senses.

In reality, he was still standing by the receiver, the phone frozen in his hand in a limbo somewhere between his ear and the wall. Distantly, he could hear his friend's voice coming through.

"Kadhim? Kadhim, are you still there?"

He hung up the phone slowly. *What kind of drug, what kind of sickness does it take to produce something so evil?* He had heard horror stories of forced cannibalism and other abominations too awful to repeat, but this confirmed it for him. These men, they were no longer human. They weren't even animals. They were monsters. The infection had spread past their minds, past their bodies, to their souls, sucking them dry of any final human thought and leaving them irreparably dark, twisted and evil. Iraq had become a black hell on earth that God no longer saw.

Kadhim tried to console himself that at least the man was dead, hopefully before but at least sometime during his "operation." Death would have been a merciful release from the unbearable pain of witnessing the beheading of his three children. Now he would be with them, somewhere far from Iraq.

Around Kadhim, the ER continued its normal buzz of activity. The fluorescent lighting washed the room in a bath of bright white light. He was a doctor, and he needed to get back to work. Nothing appeared to have changed.

But everything was different. This was no longer his home. This was no longer Iraq. *This* was hell. He was trapped in a dark cage filled with demons, and eventually, one day, they would come to eat him. His heart pounded, and a thought inside him screamed louder and louder.

He needed to escape. He *needed* to escape. *He needed to escape.*

Oh God, if You're out there, please help us...

OCCUPATIONAL HAZARDS

Eating in the hospital cafeteria had become a harrowing ordeal. It was not just the poor quality and shortages in food caused, Kadhim was sure, by the diligent lining of Malik's pockets. No, it was the increasing polarization of the doctors themselves. The quickly escalating war outside had infected the hospital with hatred and division. Doctors, nurses, and staff were rapidly dividing themselves along sectarian lines, and after several violent arguments erupted between colleagues, they had taken to sitting apart from each other in the cafeterias, schoolyard style.

For Kadhim and others like him, finding a place to eat lunch meant a decision between sitting with those who revered Osama Bin Laden, versus those who threatened anyone who dared to speak against Muqtada Al Sadr, obtuse leader of the Shiite militia. It would have made sense just to sit with the other Shiites, but the truth was that the extremism of both sides sickened him. The dangerous and tensely polarized atmosphere in the hospital was the primary reason why many of his like-minded friends quit the practice of medicine entirely and fled to other countries.

Kadhim was certain that many of the instances of doctors and staff being murdered as they exited the hospital were directly related to a disgruntled colleague with ties to a militia or extremist gang. If there was one thing that the dwindling staff taught him, it was that he could not commit the same mistake himself. Fear and mistrust of *everyone*— doctors, nurses, pharmacists, staff, patients, even security guards— silenced the words that Kadhim had once spoken freely. When he had to eat in the cafeteria, he did so in silence.

So it was back to this—a life of repression and lies. *Might as well have stuck with Saddam... perhaps fewer would have died*. He debated whether the best solution was risking the car bombs to get street food, or stocking up on nuts and crackers in his hospital bedroom. None of the options were appealing.

Kadhim was about to leave the hospital to buy lunch when he noticed Mahjoub heading toward the cafeteria.

"Mahjoub!"

Mahjoub turned, and his face broke into a smile.

"Hey, brother, long time no see!" They embraced and exchanged a kiss on each cheek, as was custom, and Kadhim held him at arm's length and grinned at him. "Where've you been, man? I haven't seen you in ages!"

"You know how work is. It's been hard to step away even for lunch."

"You weren't actually considering the cafeteria, were you? I was about to go grab some falafel and get some juice from *Hajj Izbala*. You should come."

"I was only going to have a quick bite, but you say Izbala and I just can't resist. I'm in!" They both laughed.

Poor Izbala had been born to a mother who feared that giving her son a strong name (such as "Sword" or "War") would jinx him, causing others to be jealous of his success and more or less leading to a life of hardship and failure. Hoping to protect her son from such a fate, she gave him a name that she knew would not invite envy. *Izbala* was the common word for garbage, and while it must have made his youth difficult, as an old man he now enjoyed a great deal of success as a simple juice hut owner in the middle of the capital. He had named the restaurant after himself, and as it turned out, *Garbage* became one of the most popular joints in Baghdad. It churned out fresh raisin juice that on hot summer days had a sweet and sour tang that couldn't be beat. It wasn't much more than a hut, and there was never sitting room inside, but people lined up around the block and swarmed at its entrance every day, while fancy restaurants across the street lay idle. His mother's prophecy had come true: Hajj Izbala and his *Garbage* on Mutanabbi Street were a booming success.

"So, how are things?" Kadhim asked as they got into his Espero and started toward *Hajj Izbala*.

"You know the hospital. Same old hellhole. Do you remember Fatma, who graduated with us and started an internal medicine residency?"

"Of course. How is she?"

"She dropped out. I hear she's trying to finish her training in Jordan or the Emirates."

"Ghaith and Fadi are gone too."

"From the surgery program?"

"Yeah. We started out at thirty and now we're down to ten. It's getting ridiculous. Actually, Ghaith was killed, from what I heard, as were four or five others, so you can't really blame them."

"That's too bad. I liked that guy. Scary to see people we went to school with getting killed like that." The two sat in silence for a moment, taking in the scenes of dust, trash, and bomb debris on the side of the road.

"Most of them just left without a word," Kadhim said. "Like Fadi. He just took off one day and that was it. Now if he does answer his phone I can barely get him to tell me how he is or what he's doing, poor guy."

"Fadi who?"

"He and I volunteered together at the start of the war, as med students. He's from another medical school, Baghdad Medical School, I think. You don't know him?"

"I'm sure I've seen him around."

"I can't blame him for leaving. He left pretty soon after the Mahdi Army came into the hospital and broke his hand."

"How'd *that* happen?"

"He was working in the ER when the Mahdi Army brought in one of their own with some basic injury. Long story short, they felt that Fadi wasn't getting to their guy fast enough, and Fadi kind of went off the deep end at them, so they broke his hand. He's lucky he isn't dead. The Mahdi Army may be made up of a bunch of uneducated, witless jackasses, but you have to keep your cool with them or you can get yourself killed."

"Hey, they do what they've got to do."

"Who? You mean the Mahdi Army? You're kidding, right?"

"No. I mean they're playing an important role in this war and they deserve some respect for that, educated or not."

"So we should just let them come to our hospital and wave their guns in our faces?" Kadhim looked at his friend in astonishment. "The only role they're playing is to escalate this mess into a civil war."

"They didn't start this war. They're here to protect us from getting slaughtered by these damn Sunni terrorists. Without them, Shiites would just be the dismembered victims of beheadings and car bombs."

"Look, I'm all for protecting ourselves, but that's not what the Mahdi Army is doing! Look at the Christians—*they're* trying to protect themselves. They've got militias, but they only hurt you if you try to hurt them. They don't actively hunt you down and slaughter you without provocation."

"That's because they're such a small minority. They don't have militias; they have gangs. If they tried to go up against a Sunni or Shiite militia they'd get destroyed. It's called self-preservation."

"Well, I still prefer the way they do it. The Mahdi Army and other Shiite gangs aren't protecting Shiites. Hell, almost half the people they kill *are* Shiites! All they do is kidnap and kill innocent civilians from all sides, and their provocation is half of the reason that this civil war is escalating the way it is!"

It felt good after months of holding back to finally let his tongue loose and argue politics with a friend.

"Kadhim, don't even get me started. There *is* no such thing as an innocent Sunni. Civilian or not, if they're not out there killing Shiites themselves, then they're providing food, shelter, and weapons to those who are. And maybe the Mahdi Army wouldn't have to kill their women and children if those fucking terrorists didn't keep killing ours. *They* don't distinguish between guilty and innocent; why should we? They deserved to lose every person they lost. We've lost our own, you know."

Mahjoub's face was reddening with anger. "As for kidnapping or killing Shiites, the Mahdi Army only targets those who sympathize with the occupier, the people who grovel at the feet of a foreigner when they should be supporting our own countrymen. And lots of times they don't even kill them, they just hold them for ransom. Shiites *should* have to support the Mahdi Army—it's the only thing providing us with any protection!"

"See, that's one of the things I don't get," Kadhim retorted. "When did Muqtada Al Sadr and the whole Mahdi Army decide that they needed to fight the Americans too? I grant that the Americans came in with an agenda of their own; they want cheap oil, and they probably want to set up a puppet regime in the Middle East. But did they or did they not rid us of a tyrant who systematically discriminated against, repressed, and slaughtered his own people for the past thirty to forty years? Saddam was one of the worst things to ever happen to Shiites, Kurds, and the Iraqi economy, and we were never able to get rid of him ourselves!"

"True, but—"

"And the Americans are *also* fighting against the Salafi terrorists who have invaded Iraq and are blowing themselves up in our market places as we speak. It would be a lot easier to extinguish this type of terrorism if the Mahdi Army would join forces with the Americans to fight terrorism, but it's a little hard to do that when the Mahdi Army keeps fighting the Americans too."

"I know where you're going with this, but—"

"One last thing. As I recall, Sadr City was ecstatic the day Saddam was overthrown. Muqtada Al Sadr's father Ayatollah Mohammed Mohammed Sadiq Al Sadr was one of the greatest Shiite religious leaders and one of Saddam's most aggressive opponents. He fought Saddam for governmental reform at a time when no one else dared to speak up. As a well-educated man, he did so peacefully, and he died for his beliefs. This is a man who demands our respect. The problem is that his uneducated, idiot son Muqtada inherited his followers, and has decided to run wild with them. At the start of the war, Muqtada had a truce with the Americans because they had overthrown his father's killer. Whatever happened to that truce?"

"ENOUGH!" Mahjoub roared.

Startled, Kadhim stopped his tirade instantly. "I didn't mean to upset you." In seven years, he had never known his friend to react so strongly.

"I'm starting to think that maybe your priorities are in the wrong place, Kadhim." There was a strange menace in Mahjoub's tone. "How naïve of you to think that you can remain neutral. Iraq is at war. You *have* to take a side. Just wait till you lose someone... you'll see..."

"We've all lost people, Mahjoub," Kadhim replied quietly. "Recently my relative was beheaded, and not too long ago I witnessed the murder of my three-year-old cousin."

"I'm sorry to hear that." Mahjoub seemed instantly remorseful of his previously harsh tone. "May God have mercy on them." He paused for a moment and added in a heavy voice, "My father and brother were murdered at a fake checkpoint a few months ago. We never even got their bodies back to have a proper burial. He was my only brother... just sixteen years old..."

"May God have mercy on them, and may their spirits live on with you." Kadhim felt a cloud of guilt and sorrow come over him. "If there's anything I can do, Mahjoub, just say the word."

His friend didn't speak but nodded slightly, and the tension gradually dissipated as it was replaced with grief.

Lunch from a street vendor and juice from *Hajj Izbala*'s was cathartic for them both. There was something about eating greasy, sizzling shawarma and washing it down with ice cold, freshly squeezed juice that brought back a feeling of normalcy. Old Hajj Izbala himself was there, although he didn't do much juicing these days, having passed that off to his younger employees. People greeted him with the reverence and affection reserved for someone who was both an icon and an old friend. It felt like the old Baghdad, the days when you could pick up some items from the market, stop to chat with vendors and friends, and grab a bite to eat on the way home without fearing for your life.

Even Mahjoub's spirits lifted, making Kadhim laugh heartily as he spoke with gusto of his exploits with women. *This* was the friend he knew, the one who had sat at the back of the Ba'athi meeting halls with him and made fun of the regime, the one who plotted with him in med school on how to attract the attention of their female classmates. That other Mahjoub had surely been a temporary reaction to the deaths of his family members.

As they returned to Kadhim's car, Mahjoub said with a mischievous tone, "You know what I think your problem is?"

"What's that?"

"You're not getting any."

Kadhim laughed heartily. "It could well be," he said as he ignited the engine and they started back toward the hospital. "Dr. Malik, head of nutrition and cafeteria affairs, keeps ignoring all my advances. I'm starting to think maybe I should give up on him entirely."

Mahjoub loosed a donkey-like bray of laughter. "He's a coy one, Malik, always ready to slip through your fingers." They chuckled at the thought of their round-faced friend.

"I think he's about to get engaged anyway," Mahjoub continued.

"No way! Malik? To whom?" Malik was about the most luckless person he knew when it came to girls.

"He's got some distant cousin in Najaf, I guess. It's a family arranged thing."

"In that case, let's wait till she sees him," Kadhim replied with a laugh. "Maybe I still have a shot."

Mahjoub honked with laughter. "That's probably true. I'll be rooting for you! But just in case it doesn't work out, I actually had someone else in mind. I know how you feel about messing around with the patients, so instead I've got a little lady friend I'd like you to meet, who might be able to take your mind off things and calm you down for a while."

It was just like Mahjoub to try to arrange such an escapade.

"Do you know I haven't had a day off from the hospital in over two months? And if I ever do get a day off, I'm going to go home and enjoy some of my mother's grilled lamb and homemade baklava! I don't have time for flings!"

"We'll work something out," Mahjoub said with a twinkle in his eye. "You have your own room at the hospital, right?"

The two were still in the midst of their friendly banter when they pulled into the enormous Baghdad Medical Complex parking lot and parked the car next to the banks of the Tigris River.

"You're relentless, you know that?" Kadhim said as they got out of the car and locked the doors. "I'm lucky I don't have any sisters, or you would—"

BOOM

Instantly, the two ducked down, a heavy shower of debris pelting them and the car. Hearts pounding, they waited.

"Mahjoub, are you okay?" Kadhim called out.

Nothing.

Then a shaky voice came from the other side of the car. "Yeah, I'm okay. Are you all right, man?"

Kadhim stood up slowly, his ears still ringing, and brushed dirt and bits of concrete off his jacket. "I'm fine. What the hell was that?"

"Not a clue. Suicide bomber, you think?"

"It had to have been close. That's strange. The car's fine, and you and I are fine. The rest of the parking lot seems normal..." Kadhim surveyed the area, then glanced over at the Tigris River, where the government had long ago built slanted concrete walls to check the flow of water through the city. "Holy shit... Mahjoub, you've got to come see this."

There, no more than three yards away from Kadhim's little Espero, was an enormous crater in the banks of the Tigris where the mortar had landed. Had the area been flat, the flying chunks of concrete would have killed them. Instead, because of the angle of the bank, the explosion and its debris had been directed harmlessly toward the river. Mahjoub took this all in instantly and let out a shaky laugh. "Just a yard shorter and we would have been goners, my friend."

"That's how you know it's close," Kadhim replied. "If you hear a mortar's whistle, that means it's already flown past you. But when it lands right on you, you hear nothing but the boom. There's no way to protect yourself from something like that." He turned and started toward the hospital. "Just another day in Baghdad."

About a month had gone by when his cell phone rang and he saw Mahjoub's name on the screen. They made small talk for a bit before Mahjoub reached the point of his call.

"There's a male nurse that I've been working with for a little while over here in ortho and I just heard that he's about to do a rotation in post-op care. Isn't that where you're headed next?"

"It is."

"His name's Arshed. He's a good guy—he'll take care of you. Say hi to him for me when you see him. And give me a call next time you're in the mood for *Garbage*."

"Will do."

Kadhim watched in astonishment as yet another handcuffed senior physician was escorted from the hospital by the Iraqi Army.

"They say he was using his position to kill patients," a nurse murmured.

"God help us," Kadhim breathed.

"That's the third or fourth doctor they've arrested for killing patients or leaking names. Sometimes the Iraqi Army comes, sometimes the Americans, but they keep finding more of them."

Kadhim was shocked. He had watched as Iraq's humanity and morals vanished into the darkness of war, but *this* was a new low. When a physician who had sworn an oath to do no harm began to leak patients' names to gangs so that they would be dead within a day, or even took it upon himself to carry out the job with a lethal overdose...then there was nothing left. When patients were killed by their doctors and teachers were killed by their students, there was no hope, no good left in this world.

Who were these people? Anger and disgust brought on a fierce headache as Kadhim returned to work. *Were these his colleagues? Was this where he was meant to be trained in the noble art of medicine?*

Of the doctors left, there were some whose morals were still intact. Most, however, had long ago taken their families and fled to Europe or other parts of the world. Still others, in heartbreaking numbers, had been slaughtered or had simply vanished. The hospital system was hemorrhaging staff by the hundreds. It seemed that only those who latched onto a violent and corrupt system of protecting their interests had found a relatively safe way to stay. It occurred to Kadhim for the hundredth time that his days in the hospital were numbered. He had spoken his mind too freely and had written too many outspoken letters to hospital administrators criticizing the corrupt and evil acts of his colleagues. He was gaining enemies on all sides, and it was only a matter of time before they came to take his life.

Fear, anger, and exhaustion blackened his days.

From the moment Kadhim met Arshed, the male nurse whom Mahjoub had called about, he knew that he didn't like him. There was something about this guy, an air of being untouchable, that pervaded his actions. Despite having almost no medical training, he treated doctors and other high ranking staff with a tone of disrespect and inferiority, as though he were above them. He grated on Kadhim's nerves, and his instincts told him this man was not to be trusted.

A few days had gone by since the start of Kadhim's rotation in Post-Operative Care when he met "Abu Aisha," who spoke at such length and so lovingly of his young daughter Aisha that Kadhim took to calling him by the traditional nickname.

"My daughter's fifth birthday is coming up," the man said as Kadhim checked his test results the day after surgery.

"Is that so?"

"She's so excited." Abu Aisha broke into an enormous smile. "You should see her, doctor. She's a beauty, and when she smiles she gets these adorable dimples..."

Kadhim glanced at the huge dimples that adorned Abu Aisha's smiling face and said with a chuckle, "I can imagine."

"She has her heart set on this one toy." He looked anxious. "I know I probably shouldn't spoil her, but I feel awful that she's growing up in the middle of a war and I just want to see her happy. She had been looking forward to starting school, but we can't send her in the midst of this chaos, what with children being kidnapped and held for ransom. My wife's trying to home-school her. Maybe I'll have enough time when I get out of here to track something down for her. Do you know when I might be out of the hospital?"

"Well, you're recovering from an appendectomy, so I suspect it'll be at least a couple more days."

Abu Aisha tried to sit up and winced in pain. "I think you're right, doc. You can't rush these things."

Kadhim smiled as he stood to leave. "I'll be back tonight for evening rounds to check on you. If you feel any discomfort, please have the nurse call me."

"Will do, doc." Abu Aisha broke into an ear-splitting grin, dimples and all.

The post-op ward was full that night when Kadhim returned for a final round of check-ups. It had been another long day in the ER, and he hadn't made it back to the post-op ward until midnight. He recognized several of those in recovery as trauma patients that he had received and stabilized in the ER before sending them off for surgery. Most were asleep as he conducted his evening rounds, checking vitals, adjusting meds, and generally making sure that each patient was stable and not in too much pain. He himself was exhausted, and around one o'clock in the morning, after pointing out a few critical patients to Arshed, who was on duty as the night nurse, he finally left the ward and fell into bed, sinking into a dreamless sleep.

At six o'clock the next morning, when Kadhim return to the post-op ward for morning rounds, he knew immediately that something was wrong.

"Arshed!" The night nurse was sitting by the window and smoking a cigarette. "Arshed, where are my patients?"

"What do you mean, where are your patients? They're right here." He languidly blew out a puff of smoke.

"You know *exactly* what I mean, Arshed. Three of my patients are missing. Where are they?"

"Oh yeah? Which ones?"

His insolence was infuriating. Kadhim scanned the service list for the post-op ward and matched the empty beds to the names.

"Yazeed Al Dulaimi, Bakir Al Juboury, and Oday Al Dury." His breath caught in his throat as he pronounced the third name. All three were Sunni, and one of them was Abu Aisha.

"Oh, them." The nurse took a ridiculously slow drag on his cigarette and after a maddening pause said, "They left."

"What do you mean they left? This isn't a hotel! You can't just check yourself out! I saw them at one o'clock in the morning. They were dead asleep. Are you trying to tell me that within the past five hours, despite still being in delicate condition, they just got up and walked out of here?"

"That's what I'm telling you." His incomplete answers were beyond exasperating.

"This is *my* ward, and I didn't discharge them! If I didn't do their discharge papers, then who did?"

"They did it themselves. Look." He sauntered over to a counter and held out some documents. "Here are their discharge papers."

Kadhim scanned the documents quickly. There were the signatures, merely hurried scribbles on paper. Was he to believe that the patients had left of their own accord? Or was he to trust his instincts, that these patients had been kidnapped, as had others, directly from their hospital beds? He looked up suspiciously at the nurse, who met his gaze with a confident glare. The man's insolence and his attitude of being untouchable and above the law suddenly clicked into place. This man was an active member of the Mahdi Army, and he personally was arranging the nocturnal kidnappings of Kadhim's Sunni patients.

For all Kadhim's rage and disgust against this man, and for all that he wanted to see him immediately arrested and put on trial for his heinous acts, it was fear that stayed Kadhim's tongue in that moment. Arshed could arrange Kadhim's death with a click of his fingers. Kadhim had no more than to step out of the hospital for a bite to eat than for his slaughter to occur. This had been the case for many of his colleagues.

Kadhim dropped the papers and went about his morning rounds in a furious haze of thought. It was not the first time some of his patients had mysteriously vanished in the middle of the night, nor would it be the last. Every so often, a patient or two would be gone when he returned the next morning. He thought of trying to spend the night in the ward, but his exhaustion was already pushed to the limit. He desperately needed the few precious hours of sleep that he did get just to make it through the following day. That evening, he would write an official letter of complaint to the hospital's dean as he had before, and he would call the hotline as well. But he knew that the most that would happen was a slight decrease in the nurse's pay, if that. And the hotline was always busy.

The involvement of the Shiite Mahdi Army ran deep in this hospital. In fact, anyone who opposed the militia's corruption of the medical profession was subject to punishment, including Shiites. Other hospitals had begun to function in a similar vein—this one Shiite, that one Sunni.

But there was something else nagging at Kadhim, something that made this particular instance stand out among patient kidnappings.

Mahjoub. Had Mahjoub not called him only a few weeks ago? Had he not specifically recommended this nurse as "*a good guy*"?

'*He'll take care of you,*' Mahjoub had said.

What had he meant by that?

Could it be possible that he didn't know? Was it possible that Arshed had not arranged any kidnappings during months of working with Mahjoub? Had he somehow managed to convince Mahjoub that patients had actually chosen to discharge themselves at three o'clock in the morning, when no one in their right mind would drive the perilous streets of Baghdad?

No. Mahjoub may be a tall, over-the-top joker, but he wasn't gullible. And he certainly wasn't stupid. If this nurse was involved with the Mahdi Army, then Mahjoub knew it.

Kadhim's heart began to beat faster. *Did you place him here, Mahjoub? Did you tell him to keep an eye on me?*

His recent tirade against the Mahdi Army came rushing back to him, with a sudden stab of regret and fear.

Is that what this is about, Mahjoub? You don't have the heart to report me to the Mahdi Army, so you send this jackass? He's just waiting for me to slip up, waiting for me to throw around accusations about patients being kidnapped from their beds so he can give the word that will lead to my death.

How could you do this to me? Is that how little our friendship means to you? For seven years, you've been one of my closest friends and confidants. Hell, just last month we escaped death together! And now this?

He felt suddenly nauseous. His heart hurt, a raw, physical pain. The betrayal of this man, who had been like a brother to him, shocked him in a way that he couldn't explain. He would never again look at his friend in the same way, would never speak with him openly, *ever* again. But the betrayal ran deeper than a single person. If he could not trust this man, then he would trust no one.

Inexplicably, his father's warning came back to him from that fateful day in 2003 at the start of the war. *'You do not know yet the ugliness that war can bring, but I fear you will see it now. Just remember to hold tight to your faith, and never forget the values and morals on which you were raised. I hope you are ready.'*

You were right, Baba. People change. They become ugly. He didn't know this person who Mahjoub had become, this man who hated all Sunnis without exception, who backed an innocent-slaughtering militia, a man who would betray his best friend.

Kadhim wanted to give up. He wanted to stop caring, if only to protect his own skin. His constant reports and letters of complaint to the hospital had done nothing but create more enemies. He felt sick, felt a type of fatigue that no amount of sleep would ever ease. Something *had* to change. He couldn't go on like this.

Thoughts of quitting began to glimmer in Kadhim's mind, but he pushed them aside. He thought of the way he had been raised and the values bequeathed to him by his parents. There *had* to be a way to protect patients from the epidemic of hatred that was spreading through the hospital, and he would have to find it. Alone.

GIRLS, TERRORISTS & DEATH THREATS

"*What* are you doing?"

Mohammed looked up from his project to see Georgie staring at him in bewilderment.

"I'm switching the sim card in my phone."

"I can see that. What I meant was, why in the world do you have three different sim cards?"

"It's a necessity," Mohammed explained. "Keeping Nina and Yum Yum in the dark about each other is more difficult than I thought, so just in case, I have a separate sim card for each of my 'regulars'."

"And the third?"

"*That* I use with the 'randoms'."

"I see. So two girlfriends aren't enough?"

"Hey, don't hate me just because you can't keep up, polar bear."

"Right."

"And while I'm at it, I'd appreciate it if you would stop telling the new girls that I'm a player and a cheater. It makes the whole process take twice as long."

Georgie just laughed. "I make no promises."

"Get down! Get down! Get down!"

Mohammed ducked with the rest of the American unit as bullets sprayed the ground and walls around them. They had been chasing a pack of Al Qaeda terrorists through the houses and alleyways of Ghazaliyah for nearly six hours, and their faces were plastered with dirt, sweat, and fury.

They had been fueled by anger ever since their discovery of two children, a boy and a girl, whose severed heads lay several feet from their bodies. *Monsters. They were chasing goddamn monsters.*

Hours of heavy gunfire had passed, and they had succeeded in killing several of the terrorists, but not before losing one of their own, which only added fuel to the flame. This wasn't Mohammed's regular unit—he had volunteered for the mission—but every time a soldier died, he felt the same raw ache. The soldiers themselves now fought with a venom he rarely saw. It was a hard day on everyone.

When at last the terrorists lay down their weapons and surrendered, there were only three left, and as per protocol, the unit was tasked with transporting the insurgents to the Iraqi military base to face the Iraqi Criminal Justice system. The unit commander's face was grim as he approached Mohammed.

"Saint, the insurgents are going to have to ride with you. Alone. If I put them in the Bradley with my guys after the loss we suffered today..." He shook his head and his jaw clenched in pain, "my guys will kill 'em."

"That's fine, sir. Do what you have to do." But the images of two headless children kept replaying themselves in Mohammed's mind.

As the unit filled out the report and the helicopter came for the fallen soldier, Mohammed sat facing the terrorists on the hard benches in the back of the Bradley. They were handcuffed and blindfolded, their long beards rough and ungroomed. Their faces were thinner than Mohammed's, and a few shades darker, and they wore short dishdashas that revealed dirty, thin ankles. They sat in silence for a moment, before Mohammed spoke.

"Why do you do it? Why kill people like this?"

"You are a traitor, a godless infidel," one of them snarled. He had a heavy Yemeni accent, and spoke the Standard Arabic used in books and newsrooms, which sounded stiff and odd.

"Call me what you want," Mohammed replied. "It means nothing to me. But we found two children today—"

"Yes. A twelve year-old boy and a sixteen year-old girl."

"So it was *you* guys who killed them."

"Yes."

"*Why?* Why slaughter innocent children? What could they *possibly* have done to deserve that?" Mohammed felt his blood start to boil at the terrorists' smugness.

"The boy is an infidel."

"How could a twelve-year-old be an infidel? What has he seen of life to make him an infidel?"

"His father is in the Iraqi Army."

The poor soldiers of the Iraqi Army were targeted for collaborating with the U.S.-led forces in vanquishing terrorism from their country.

"And the girl?" Mohammed pressed.

"The girl was wearing sandals with a strap between the toes."

"So what? There's nothing wrong with that."

"No. She must not do this. It incites lust."

"You guys are fucking insane," Mohammed growled. "First you behead two innocent children, then you make us chase you for six hours, then you kill one of our soldiers... and now you taunt me with bullshit reasons like *this*?"

He felt a fire alight in his chest that burned its way through his arms and legs until every muscle was tense with rage. "What I want to know is, how can you use cars and cell phones, but you kill a boy for selling ice? You kill a barber for giving Western haircuts! In the time of the Prophet Mohammad, peace be upon him, there weren't any cars or cell phones. So why do you guys use them? Hypocrites! Why don't you travel on a fucking donkey like they did back then?"

"Those of whom you speak are infidels and sinners," came the chilly response. "We use cell phones to trigger our bombs. We use demonic Western technology for another purpose."

"And what purpose would that be?"

"We fight the devil with his own instruments."

The fire that coursed through Mohammed's veins suddenly overtook his mind until all he could see was red. He jumped across the Bradley and landed a shattering blow to the terrorist's face. The man's head banged brutally against a metal bar behind it, and for several moments he was breathless. Then at last the terrorist spoke, his tone haughty and full of hatred.

"Did you really think that we do not know who you are? That we won't find your parents and slaughter them as well? We will kill your father and disgrace your mother right in front of you." He spat in Mohammed's direction. "Even if we did not know who you were, we have those who bring us the information of dogs like you."

After that, all Mohammed could see was red.

The unit commander's face went white as he observed the inside of the Bradley upon reaching the Iraqi military base.

"Saint! What the hell did you do?"

The three terrorists, barely conscious, were black and blue with bruises, and their faces ran with blood.

"I didn't do anything." But a glance at Mohammed's bruised and bloodied knuckles said otherwise.

"What do you mean you didn't do anything? This is against the agenda!"

"Screw the agenda! I didn't *do* anything! What do you want to do? Do you want to fire me?" Mohammed took off his badge and threw it on the ground. "Do whatever you want!"

These terrorists were destroying his own country, threatening his family, coming from afar to kill his nation's children. How could the commander expect him to have less anger than an American unit? How could he be so blind as to how personal this was?

The American commander wasn't used to Mohammed's fits of rage, and his anger was growing when the Iraqi commander suddenly spoke up.

"Hold on, hold on. Let me speak to him." He had seen the escalating situation and realized that Mohammed, whom he'd come to know and care for after the capture of many terrorists, was quickly on his way to getting himself in trouble. He pulled Mohammed aside.

"Tell me, son, what happened?"

"Well, what do they *expect* me to do?" And with that, Mohammed broke down. Tears streamed down his face as he relayed the events of the day, the fallen soldier, the headless children, and the threats on his own life and the lives of his family members. The Iraqi commander rubbed his shoulder, pain reflected in his eyes. Despite being Sunni, he had lost his brothers, wife, and children to Al Qaeda terrorists for his work in eradicating them from Iraq. He, more than anyone, understood the anger and pain that Mohammed felt.

"Don't worry about it, son. It has nothing to do with you anymore."

"What do you mean nothing to do with me? How can I not worry about this?"

"Look at me. Do you trust me? I'll take care of it. Your blood will be cooled today."

"What are you going to do?"

"Don't worry about it, Mohammed. Just go back to your unit."

"I need to call my own unit commander. Maybe he can help."

"Fine, call him if you want. Just let me take care of this."

Mohammed called his own unit commander, and Major Matthews' warning was serious but sympathetic on the other end.

"Saint, don't say anything. Don't get yourself in trouble for those losers."

And so they returned to the American commander, who asked impatiently, "Well? What happened in there? How the hell do you explain their condition?"

"It was the potholes," the Iraqi commander said. "The insurgents had a very bumpy ride back to the base."

When Mohammed got back to his room, Yum Yum was there waiting for him, and she looked angry. "We need to talk."

"Look, Yum Yum, I've had a long day. Now is not the time..."

"No, I want to talk *now*." She had gradually stopped wearing her headscarf in public, and her thick auburn hair was messier than usual. From the other end of the room, Georgie flashed Mohammed a sympathetic grimace.

"Talk then."

"I've been hearing rumors that you're going out with other girls."

"Oh yeah? Is that something you can prove?"

She faltered for a moment. "No, but..." Then she steeled herself and her voice was confident once again. "I swear to God, Mohammed, if I find out that you've been cheating on me, I'm going to kill you!"

Get in line, he thought.

"I'm not joking, Mohammed. Have you been seeing other women? Have you been *sleeping* with other women?" Her eyes flashed and she looked surprisingly scary for a petite woman of only 4'11''. It was a side of her that Mohammed hadn't seen before, and it shocked him a little. But Nina had confronted him with similar accusations several times before, and he dealt with it the same way.

"Look, you hear all kinds of things on the base. There are a million Mohammeds out there—"

"There aren't a million Saints!"

"Regardless, if it's not something that you can prove, then why bother me with it? Yum Yum, I'm tired, I'm hungry, and I've had a shitty day. You don't have to be with me if things like this upset you. If you're not secure enough to put up with a few rumors, then leave."

Yum Yum looked taken aback. She had hoped, even expected, that he would fall to his knees in an effort to prove his love and loyalty to her. She hadn't wanted to believe the rumors, couldn't bring herself to believe them in fact. But she certainly was not prepared for this type of ultimatum. The idea of leaving her dear Saint was, frankly, inconceivable. Suddenly, she found herself apologizing.

"No, no, please don't be upset, Mohammed. I *do* want to be with you. It's just... well some of my girlfriends were saying things... It doesn't matter. The important thing is, I want to be with you always. I'm sorry I upset you. *Of course* I know that you haven't been cheating on me."

Mohammed stepped outside and lit a cigarette, and for the first time she noticed the dried blood on his knuckles.

"Saint! What happened? Why are your hands bloody?"

"Like I said, it was a rough day. Want to get something to eat? I'm starving."

"Of course. Poor thing, you probably haven't eaten since this morning, and here I am making you wait!"

And just like that, the subject was dropped.

Mohammed's phone rang not long after Yum Yum left. It was the Iraqi commander.

"How are you, son?"

"Hi, sir."

"How are your nerves?"

"Not well, sir, to be honest."

"Cheer up."

"Why's that?"

"Cheer up!" The commander paused to draw out the suspense. "We took them up to the roof with three of my soldiers, armed each of them with a gun so nobody could say that they didn't have the ability to defend themselves, and we let them fight it out on the roof. One of my soldiers was injured, but I wanted you to know first, Mohammed. They're dead. All three of them."

"Really?"

"Really."

"You don't know what a relief it is to hear that, sir. Like I was on fire and you've put me on ice." Mohammed called Major Matthews with the news.

"They tried to run away and were killed."

"Are you sure?"

"Yes."

"They tried to run away?"

"That's right. The Iraqi commander just called and told me."

"So you're not involved in this?"

"Not at all, sir. Not at all."

Major Matthews laughed. "I wish I could believe you, Saint."

MEDICAL RECORDS

To the respected Head of the Hospital,
And the respected Chief Resident,

Subject: Complaint

I am Doctor Kadhim Al Baghdadi, resident intern, and I was on call on Saturday October 28, 2006. I politely request a review of the events of that Saturday, wherein:

- *The on-call chief resident for Saturday attended only from 9:30am – 12:30pm and from 2:30pm – 3:00pm and from 5:00pm – 6:30pm. That means that he only attended for 5 hours despite the fact that ER regulations require the presence of a chief resident 24 hours.*
- *The on-call chief resident for the evening outpatient clinic was in attendance for only one hour, such that the ER then filled with patients needing outpatient clinic services; their needs had to be addressed by the ER, in addition to the ER patients.*
- *The reluctance of the residency programs' presidency committee in monitoring and addressing current and pressing issues in the hospital, despite the fact that I have contacted them repeatedly without any response worth mentioning. Furthermore, I have found that the committee's hotline is busy for hours on end when I am trying to address an urgent need.*
- *The failure of the evening lab to complete urgent analyses, and their absences from time to time with ridiculous excuses.*
- *The pharmacist assistant-on-call's reluctance to dispense medicines, and his frequent claim that certain critical medications such as Ampicillin were not there, whereas I would later discover that they had in fact been available.*
- *The unavailability of critical drugs necessary for treating patients and saving lives, such as Valium, Luminol, Adrenalin, and even Insulin, all missing from the ER gear kit.*

I would like to inform you that I continued working for 25 straight hours without a break and at the expense of both breakfast and lunch because I could not leave the emergency room without a doctor. I politely request that you do what you must to address these issues.

With appreciation and thanks,

Kadhim Al Baghdadi
Surgical Intern
October 29, 2006·

It had been one of those days.

The nurses were incompetent, the evening laboratory practically useless, and every time he turned around there was another incomplete emergency gear kit, leaving him empty-handed at a time when he needed it most. Exhaustion did not begin to cover how Kadhim felt after a twenty-five hour shift.

However, there was one small detail that had gone right that day. There were several patients whom he had saved from a certain gruesome fate, as he had done for many others before them. What he had done to save them, though, was illegal. And he could speak of it to no one.

The idea had come to Kadhim several months prior, during a busy day in the ER when he was approached by a graying, middle-aged man.

"Doctor? I'm sorry to bother you."

Kadhim was in a hurry to pick up some lab results, lost in a train of thought that almost blocked out the man's apologetic interruption entirely.

"Yes? How can I help you?"

"It's about my son. I need to move him to another hospital."

Kadhim looked at the man for a moment, and although he'd never met him before, he recognized him. The patient was the spitting image of his father.

"Did we receive your son last night with gunshot wounds to the chest and abdomen? Does he have a small tattoo on his arm?"

---

* *This letter is an exact translation of the original document. The name has been changed to protect Kadhim's identity.*

"Yes, that's him. That's my son."

"Why do you want to move him to another hospital?"

"I heard that Nu'man Hospital has better facilities..." the man hedged. He wouldn't meet Kadhim's eyes.

"Your son just had surgery last night. He's still in critical condition. Chances are good that he wouldn't survive a trip to Nu'man."

"But you don't understand! I... I just think... better doctors..." The father's voice faded, but he wasn't giving up. "I need to transfer him."

It didn't make sense. For all its faults, Baghdad Medical Complex was the largest and most advanced medical center in the country. Perhaps this man had found a doctor who was on par with some of the doctors here, but he certainly hadn't found someone who was *better*. Even if the doctor was better, why risk his son's life? His son needed to heal...

Then it dawned on Kadhim.

This man wasn't looking for a better hospital. This man feared that leaving his son in Baghdad Medical Complex would kill him. When the Iraqi soldiers found his son, shot, bleeding, and on the edge of death, they had transferred him to the closest hospital.

A largely Shiite hospital.

In a Shiite neighborhood.

Taken over by a vicious Shiite militia.

The man feared that his Sunni son would be kidnapped from his hospital bed or given a lethal drug by some extremist doctor, and by Kadhim's count his fears were not unfounded. Unfortunately, his son would not survive a transfer.

Suddenly, Kadhim knew what he must do.

"What's your son's name?" He interrupted the father and walked him to the patient files.

"His name?" The man hesitated for a long time. He seemed to be searching desperately for an alternative answer. At last, he looked around furtively, and whispered, "Omar."

There it was, in the name. All the proof that anyone loyal to the Mahdi Army would need to determine that this young man was Sunni. Kadhim and his brothers had all been given neutral names, a fact that had saved them on more than one occasion. But for Omar, his parents had lovingly chosen a name that now, some two decades later, would be the name that killed him.

In a swift motion, Kadhim pulled out the young man's medical chart. He glanced around to make sure that no one was looking, pulled out a pen, and quickly added one simple letter—in Arabic—to the patient's first name.

Ammar. A Shiite name if there ever was one.

The father read the adjusted chart and his eyes grew wide as he understood its implications. His features were suddenly flooded with relief; Kadhim had understood and allayed his fears.

"Thank you," he said in a low voice, reaching out to shake Kadhim's hand as tears suddenly formed in his eyes. "It's a relief to know that there's at least one Sunni in this—"

"Who said I was Sunni?" It felt awful to have to explain why he was doing this, and even more awful that he had to do it at all. It was a sad world when a patient's name could determine their course of treatment.

"But why…?"

"I'm doing this as a human, and as a doctor. Now go home and get some rest. Believe me when I say that there are still good people left in this hospital. Your son will be taken care of. He'll be fine. You can count on me."

How many names had he changed since then? How many lives had he saved?

GRIEF COUNSELING

"You should watch out, Kadhim."

"What do you mean?" Kadhim had run into Malik in the hallway, and his old friend's comment caught him off guard.

"I heard about that letter you wrote. You should be careful where you start pointing fingers. You don't want to upset the wrong person…"

Malik spoke with the usual smile on his face, but was this a helpful warning from a friend, or was there a menacing undertone to his words?

"There are others who agree with me that we can't let these kinds of things happen in our hospital, Malik. I'm not the only one writing letters."

To be fair, most of those who agreed with Kadhim had already fled the country. They couldn't stomach the sectarianism that had corrupted the hospital, and Kadhim didn't blame them.

Malik's eyebrow rose just a bit, and he smiled.

"Well, I just hope you know what you're doing."

The afternoon exploded into action with a suicide bombing. With the morgue full, the remains of six dead soldiers were brought to the ER, their bodies blown to so many pieces that they were unrecognizable. Kadhim knew them to be from the Iraqi Army only by the shreds of uniform that clung to various parts. As he prepared to transfer them to the large refrigerated trucks that held the morgue's overflow, family members started to arrive.

This was the hard part: the writing of the death certificates. After helping a year's worth of grieving relatives, Kadhim had largely grown numb to their pain. But today, as occasionally happened, there was one whose grief was so intense that it pierced through the numbness to his soul.

She arrived at the hospital with her face as white as a sheet, silently clinging to her last shred of hope. She was a young woman, just past adolescence, and she and her husband were newlyweds of only two months. They had been eking out a happy life on a simple soldier's salary, and she loved him more than she ever thought possible.

When she learned that her love would never return home, the young woman crumpled before Kadhim's eyes. A scream of agony erupted from her lips, and he caught her mutely as she fell to the floor. She beat at her chest, ripped off her hijab, and tore at her hair between sobs. Her eyes looked unseeingly past Kadhim and the others, seeing not the hospital's walls but rather only the unending darkness of her loss. Her anguish was tangible.

Kadhim and the other doctors exchanged glances. This woman was too young, too fragile, to sift through the body parts to try to find what was left of her husband.

"Does your husband have family?" Kadhim asked her, wishing desperately to be helpful. She nodded tearfully.

"Close by?"

"Very close," she gasped between sobs. "They're a... a ten minute walk... from the hospital."

A fatherly senior official from hospital security kindly offered to accompany the young woman to the home of her in-laws, in hopes of returning with the soldier's father to identify his remains. When they left, the cries of her grief still echoed in Kadhim's heart.

Less than half an hour later, a second explosion rocked the streets just outside Baghdad Medical Center. Flooded with another rush of dead bodies and trauma victims, Kadhim momentarily forgot about the young woman and was immersed in trauma. After intubating a patient and sending him to surgery, Kadhim came across a victim with two bleeding stumps where there had once been legs. Working fast, he applied tourniquets to the stumps and was setting up rapid IV lines when he saw the patient's face.

He did a double take and looked again in disbelief.

It was her, he was sure of it, the very same woman who had lost her husband in a bomb earlier that day. Desperate, Kadhim completed the IV lines and called for an immediate blood transfusion. He could not let her die.

Her story surfaced once she made it through surgery. The young woman had not even made it to her in-laws' home when they walked right past the explosion. The security official who was with her was killed instantly. The young woman returned to the hospital, but this time she returned without her legs.

Kadhim's heart broke for her, as he witnessed the shock and the indescribable pain that she was suffering. This was too much. Too much to lose a husband and both legs in one day. Where was God's mercy? How could He let this happen?

Her pain reverberated through his soul even as he left the ER that night. Deep in the pit of his stomach, where exhaustion, anguish, fear and paranoia had been growing for months, a painful ulcer was festering. He knew that he needed to seek treatment. The stress of the war, corruption, sleeplessness, and thinly veiled threats was getting to him. But he couldn't find the will to take care of himself in the midst of the pain that surrounded him.

A single thought echoed through his mind as he fell into an exhausted asleep.

I can't go on like this. I can't take it anymore.

BLOOD PRESSURE RISING

Kadhim could gauge how bad a day was by the number of blisters on his fingers from writing death certificates. Today was one of the worst. He had been filling out forms for hours as a result of the latest mass bombing in Shurja, with fingers cramped and back aching. After over seventy death certificates from a single bombing, he had at last come to the end of a long line of wailing and grief-stricken relatives when he was approached by an old man.

The instant he saw the man, Kadhim knew that something was wrong. The man's eyes were glazed and unseeing, his face as white as death. He looked as though he might fall over of a heart attack at any moment. On intuition, Kadhim decided to check the man's blood pressure.

"Please, sir, sit down and rest. What's wrong? Do you know someone who was martyred in the explosion?"

Kadhim's words did not appear to register with the man. He made no move and no response as Kadhim gently led him to a chair.

"Tell me, Baba, what's wrong?"

The man's blood pressure was soaring at 210/110. Left untreated, he could quickly succumb to a stroke or heart attack.

Wordlessly, as if on autopilot, the stricken man handed over two worn and crumpled pieces of paper. Kadhim's heart sank as he read them. They were the identification cards of the man's two children. Then, in a voice so small and distant that Kadhim could barely hear him, the man added, "My wife is bringing the I.D. of our third son."

Kadhim's eyes met those of the old man, and for a second, Kadhim comprehended the depth of his loss.

A single bomb had taken the lives of all three of his children. His pride, love, and joy, taken from him in a single instant.

The realization of this pain struck straight to Kadhim's soul. Deep inside, the thick wall of numbness cracked apart and overwhelming emotion built up inside the overworked doctor until he felt a tear roll down his cheek. And then another, and another, until he found himself weeping tears of grief as he treated the man with medications to calm him and bring down his blood pressure. He cried as he worked, without shame and without the ability to stop himself. He cried for his country, cried for the pain that surrounded him, and cried for himself because he had taken more than he could endure.

That evening, Kadhim called his father.

"Baba... Baba."

"Kadhim, is that you? What's wrong? Are you alright?"

"Baba, I can't do this anymore."

"What do you mean?"

"I can't stay in the hospital. I can't work here. I just can't handle it anymore."

"Kadhim, my son..." His father's voice ached with empathy. "You just finished your intern year and will finally start the core of your plastic and reconstructive surgery residency, which you worked so hard for. It's so much to give up at a moment's notice."

"At a moment's notice? I've been struggling with this thought, this decision, for *months*. There are a million reasons why I should have left long ago."

"Why?"

"Well, for one, the best surgeons have all fled the country, or they're dead. What kind of surgeon will I be without anyone left to learn from?"

"Surely there's still someone..."

"They're gone, Baba. And even if there was someone, the hospital has become so corrupt that it is unlivable. This is *not* the way that medicine is meant to be practiced. We *have* money, but where is it going? In whose pockets? The meds aren't there, the equipment isn't there, and the staff has become so polarized that I fear for my life! And they're afraid of me too! That's how bad it is. There's no trust left."

Baba was silent.

"But most of all, Baba, I just can't do it anymore. I constantly feel that I'm on the verge of a breakdown. I feel sick."

"Kadhim, my son. You know I will support you no matter what you do, but please, you've worked so hard for such a coveted position. How many times have you told me how excited you are to do reconstructive surgery for those maimed by war? Just promise me that you'll think through every possible avenue first."

Rami's eyes sparkled and his grin stretched from ear to ear as he pulled a jacket over his nurse's uniform the next day.

"Well, it's time! The missus has started having contractions. It's a little early yet, but I'm going to go get her now and bring her to the hospital. We don't want to run into trouble..."

Kadhim nodded with understanding. If roads were blocked by fake checkpoints, it could delay Rami for hours—perhaps all day—trying to find a safe way there and back. The nurse lived in Kifah, not far from the hospital, but between his home and Baghdad Medical Center stood the dangerous neighborhood of Al Kasra, where sectarian fighting was made all the more intense by its mixed demographic.

"May you come back safely, both of you." Kadhim gave his friend a brief embrace and wished him well.

Of all the nurses, Rami was his favorite. Ten years Kadhim's senior, Rami had started out with the same insufficient training as the rest of Iraq's nurses. The difference was that he was a hard worker, a quick learner, and had been at the hospital for a long time. Everything he needed to learn, he had learned on the job, and he never shied away from even the most exhausting or gruesome of tasks. He was quick, efficient, and responsible, and whenever possible, Kadhim preferred to have Rami working by his side.

Over the past year, the two had become good friends. Rami was one of the few in the hospital whom Kadhim trusted enough to share sparse details of his life, which was saying a lot. Doctors, nurses, pharmacists, and lab technicians had all become sources of fear and apprehension for Kadhim. He had even come to fear the Facility Protection Services who secured the hospital, after being asked one too many times whether he was Sunni or Shiite, a question that he always side-stepped.

There was no one left whom Kadhim trusted, not even his closest friends. All that was left was mistrust, fear, and paranoia. And his growing ulcer.

But Rami was a hard worker, a good man, and a constant source of humor. Kadhim had known for some time now that his friend's wife was pregnant, and he looked forward to the child's birth as an exciting change of pace in the gloom of daily life.

Several hours had gone by when the phone rang.

"Baghdad Medical ER."

On the other end, Kadhim heard only shrieks, sobbing, and the sound of a woman hyperventilating.

"What happened? What's wrong?"

The woman shrieked something, but she was gasping for breath and her words were incomprehensible.

"Ma'am, please try to calm down. Tell me what happened."

"*They killed him!*" she screamed, and she broke into a fresh wave of sobs. Apprehension grew in the pit of Kadhim's stomach. Normally, he would direct a relative to bring the body to the ER or the morgue. But this time, he needed to know more.

"Killed who?"

The woman couldn't answer; her body rocked with hysterics.

"Ma'am, please, I want to help. Who did they kill?"

"My husband," she gasped, "My Rami."

A scream of pain erupted from her lips, and she broke into a fresh wave of sobs. "We stopped... checkpoint... they pulled him out of the car... shot him... did nothing... innocent... my Rami... my dear Rami..."

It was impossible. He'd been here, bright and brimming with life, only a few hours ago. How could he be gone?

"We're sending an ambulance now to bring you both. Just tell me where you are." Kadhim stumbled, trying to refocus on the grieving widow as the pain crashed over him and panic overtook his thoughts.

He asked before he could stop himself, "*Allasa* or *sakkaka*?"

"*Allasa.*"

Sunni terrorists. Al Qaeda. Sure to pull Rami aside and torture him for information before killing him. *Killing him in front of his laboring wife.*

A deep, black fear started to build up inside Kadhim. Questions bit at the back of his mind, and he pushed them away. He should be thinking of Rami's stricken widow, who had lost her husband just as she was about to bring his child into the world.

She arrived shortly thereafter and was transferred to Obstetrics, where Kadhim went to give his condolences.

"It's a terrible tragedy, Um Jasim. Rami was the best of men."

Her eyes were dark with pain and streaked mascara. She stared straight ahead, unseeing, unhearing, and uncomprehending.

"May he live on in you."

There was no response. Shock had stopped her contractions. It had stopped her whole world.

Rami's death traumatized Kadhim in a way few deaths ever had. Even as Rami's wife gave birth to a healthy baby several days later,

Kadhim felt himself crumbling inside. This war was bigger than he, too big to fight. But deep beneath the pain, Kadhim felt something worse, something repulsive, and gradually it grew until it reared its ugly head.

What have you done, Rami?

Fear, mistrust, and paranoia swirled around Kadhim's mind like flies.

What did you tell them, Rami, before they killed you? Did you give them my name? Did you tell them that I'm Shiite?

It was selfish to think like this. The man had *just* died. How could Kadhim be thinking of his own safety? But who knew what a man would say to protect his wife and unborn child when a gun was held to his head. And who could blame him?

Kadhim had seen enough headless children and slaughtered women to know the soullessness of Al Qaeda. The fact that Rami's wife was pregnant would not have stayed their hand in the least. *So why was she unharmed? Had Rami given names, information, in exchange for her life? What had he told them?*

Month after month of increasing fear had finally reached their climax. The ulcer in Kadhim's stomach burned with a fury that ate away at his last reserves of strength.

Did you sell me to the allasa, *my old friend?*

He felt mentally and emotionally sick.

Am I next, Rami?

As if in a dream, Kadhim sat down in front of his computer and prepared to write his fiftieth and final letter.

"In the name of God, the Beneficent, the Merciful..."

BREAKING POINT

"What the hell is this, Dr. Kadhim?" The Head of the Hospital held up the letter angrily, and then, adjusting his glasses, read it aloud to the other staff sitting around the table.

In the name of God, the Beneficent, the Merciful

To the respected Head of the Hospital,
And the respected Chief Resident,

Subject: Request for Leave of Absence

I am Doctor Kadhim Al Baghdadi, surgical resident intern. I politely request that you consider granting me leave for ten days from 11/5/2006 to 11/15/2006, due to the devastating security situation and death threats that have forced my family and me to flee the Hurriyah area of Baghdad to the district of Babel.

This is, of course, with the knowledge that I promise to return to my work even before the end of my leave of absence if security situations allow, just as I promise to make up for any deficiencies that have been caused by my absence.

With appreciation and thanks,

Kadhim Al Baghdadi
Surgical Intern
November 5, 2006·

There was a moment of silence as he finished reading the letter. It seemed the entire committee was holding its breath, although perhaps it was only Kadhim.
"Well?" prompted the chief.

---

* *This is an exact translation of the original letter, only the name has been changed.*

"Sir, I am respectfully requesting ten days leave. I have been working for fourteen months without time off—"

"Dr. Kadhim, while your family has my sympathies, you know that I cannot permit you any leave at this time."

"I will come back sooner if at all possible. I just need a few days—"

"I'm afraid not." The Head of the Hospital shook his head, and Kadhim's heart sank. "As you are well aware, and as you have pointed out in previous complaints, the hospital is desperately understaffed. We cannot afford to lose another physician, even temporarily. At the beginning of this year, there were thirty-five residents. And now, yourself included, there are only seven. Even if I wanted to, how could I grant you a leave of absence?"

He shook his head, looking older than Kadhim had ever seen him, and fixed Kadhim with a meaningful stare. "And while we appreciate your hard work, I advise that you be more careful in the future."

There was a short pause as the Head let his words sink in. He then continued briskly. "In the meantime, your request for leave of absence has been denied. I'm sorry."

"So that's it? You won't give me leave?"

"No, I won't permit you leave."

"Thank you, sir," Kadhim replied quietly. He stood slowly and walked out of the room. He was trying desperately to hold onto his dreams, his future, but he felt as though he were on the edge of a cliff and his fingers were slowly slipping.

After the morning meeting was over, he returned in a haze of numbness to the ER. His mind registered in passing that there had been another gunfight and another bomb, and the emergency room was full.

Al Qaeda had taken to carrying out back-to-back suicide bombings, where the second targeted those responding to the first. A favorite tactic was to send the second bomber disguised as an ambulance, so that just when they thought help was arriving, it blew up in their faces. The response of the Iraqi Army, once they grew wise to this trick, was to shoot any ambulances that arrived too quickly to the scene. In Baghdad traffic, where cars did not make way for ambulances, a *real* ambulance, they figured, should take at least ten to fifteen minutes to arrive. Better safe than sorry.

Kadhim went about his work on autopilot, and as he worked, the words echoed in his head.

No, I won't permit you leave.

I advise that you be more careful in the future.
Your request for leave of absence has been denied.

"Hey! HEY! DOCTOR!"

Shouts from the other end of the ER interrupted Kadhim's train of thought, and he looked up from the chest tube he was inserting to see three armed men in the black garb and green bandanas of the Mahdi Army glaring at him.

In the midst of triage, he had already checked on them. Only one was a patient, a young man with a gunshot to the hand. He was in pain, sure, but there was very little blood and the risk to the man's life was minimal. Kadhim's experienced eye had passed over him in seconds, favoring the patients who had come in with gunshot wounds to their chest and abdomen. There were only four medical staff in the ER that day, two nurses, a doctor, and Kadhim. They would get to the militia member when they got to him.

"DOCTOR! Get over here! NOW!"

Kadhim ignored him and kept working. If he worked as fast as he could, inserting a chest tube here, applying a tourniquet there, he might be able to save a few lives in the next ten minutes.

"Doctor, I swear to *Allah*, if you don't help me now...!" The gang member waved a Kalashnikov with his remaining hand.

"Hold on." Kadhim's voice was calm but firm. "I'm getting to you as quickly as I can."

"What kind of doctor are you? You slow-ass piece of trash!" Furious, the black-adorned militia member pointed his gun directly at Kadhim.

Stay calm. Kadhim had worked at gunpoint numerous times throughout the past year, and he knew what to do. A friend of his had exploded in this situation, and had ended up with a shattered hand. Other doctors had been shot in the middle of the hospital. *Stay calm. Don't lose control.*

He kept working on his patient.

"Don't you hear me, you dog? I'm in pain here!" The man was screaming now, flecks of spit flying from his mouth. His two armed companions began to chime in.

Kadhim couldn't leave his patient. If he didn't finished applying this tourniquet and put him on several IV lines, the patient would die. He ignored the flying insults and the gun, and kept working.

"You piece of shit! You son of a bitch!"

Kadhim felt his temperature rise. A mother, in Iraqi culture, demanded the pinnacle of respect and honor. *No one*, armed or not, was permitted to disrespect Mama. His fingers flew as he worked faster.

"Fuck your mother, she's a cunt and a whore!"

That's it.

"She can't even tell you who your real father is, you bast—!"

Before the man could finish his sentence, Kadhim had ripped off his white coat and lost control. Forgetting about the three Kalashnikovs pointed in his direction, he grabbed the man's collar and began to punch him in the face, one satisfying blow after another, until he felt himself being pulled away by the man's companions.

"Doctor, doctor, calm down!" one of the companions urged. "Look, he doesn't mean anything he's saying right now. He's just in pain. We're sorry. Just calm down!"

"Son of a bitch!" The man cursed through his bloody nose.

"*You* calm him down," Kadhim shouted. "I am working as fast as I can! He's not dying! He can wait until I've finished with the more serious patients!"

"We understand. We'll calm him down, we promise."

The militia patient glared at him and cursed, muttering, "I won't forget this."

Kadhim ignored him and turned around to finish triaging the other patients. He was met with the stunned stares of the entire ER.

I've gone and done it now, he realized, as his fear returned and multiplied. Now, more than before, he would be targeted by both sides: terrorists both Sunni and Shiite, Al Qaeda and the Mahdi Army. *The Mahdi Army will be back for me, and when they come, I'm dead.*

Late that afternoon, Kadhim approached the Dean of Al Kindy Medical School and laid his heart bare. He had taken all he could take of the daily heartbreak and risks to his life.

"Doctor, I only ask for a month off. A month to lie low and clear my head. I feel physically and mentally broken. I fear for my life."

"I can't grant you any leave, Kadhim. It's not in my hands." The dean shook his head gravely. "The medical school may be the administrator of your residency, but you are an official employee of the hospital. It's the hospital who would have to grant you leave."

Never had Kadhim heard more crushing words than these. This had been his only hope, a last ditch effort to hold onto his dream of becoming a surgeon. He found himself staring down an unending path of exhaustion... and darkness.

"So there's no way to get some time off," he said in quiet desperation.

"I'm afraid not. No."

"Then I quit." Kadhim said it slowly, almost to himself, tasting the bitterness and hopelessness of every word.

"How can you quit? What about your career? What about how hard you worked, top in orthopedic surgery for five years, among the top of your class? How can you throw all that away? What about your spot as a plastic and reconstructive surgery resident?"

"I don't want it."

"Are you serious?"

"Yes, I'm serious. I don't want it anymore. I don't want Iraq, I don't want medicine, and I don't want this life."

"Dr. Kadhim, I'm warning you, if you go absent for more than a week, they'll fire you."

"I'm telling you now, I'm not coming back. I'm done. I quit." Kadhim stood up in a daze and extended his hand. "Goodbye, sir."

The dean shook his hand in shock. "Goodbye, Kadhim."

Suddenly, he was alone in a dark world. It was all over. He couldn't do this anymore. His dream of becoming a surgeon was done. Finished. Deep inside, he felt himself crack in two. Medicine was the only love he had ever known, and he was leaving her. He had failed.

That evening, Kadhim left the hospital the way more than thirty residents and hundreds of staff had left before him. Without a word to his peers and without saying goodbye, he vanished.

PART IV
STD'S: THE ARMY YEARS

EVERYBODY LIES

"What happened to Kadhim? I haven't seen him around the hospital in weeks!"

"Didn't you hear? He left."

"Really?"

"I called to check on him, and he said he's gone to Jordan to try to continue his medical training there."

"Oh yeah? I heard several others from our class went there as well."

"He sent me an email saying that he's in Amman, and that he's having a rough time. He says he can't find work, and the Jordanians treat Iraqis like shit."

"I heard the Jordanians make them work full-time in the hospital for a year without pay before they'll even consider them."

"That's what he says. He says it's humiliating. And to live there legally and obtain a Jordanian visa, apparently he'd have to keep a minimum of $75,000 in a Jordanian bank at all times."

"That's ridiculous!"

"God help him. Hopefully he finds success in Jordan, because I don't know where else he would go."

She drew the eyes of all around her every time she passed through the checkpoint. Slender, with stunning dark eyes and black hair that fell in waves down her back, the young Iraqi woman was a complete knock-out. She seemed impervious to the stares of those around her, and the advances of hopeful soldiers and interpreters, Iraqi and American alike, merely bounced unanswered off her thick shell of modesty.

When Mohammed first noticed her, he fell into the habit of visiting that checkpoint in the early morning hours when he knew she would be making her way through. He quickly learned that she wasn't an interpreter, but worked as an employee of the Ministry of Integrity inside the Green Zone. He'd heard rumors of her sweet but impervious demeanor, but his confidence was such that he felt none to be out of his reach. And was it just him, or did she smile in his direction every time she passed?

She would be his, whenever he was ready to make his move. But not just yet. First, there was someone far more important who needed his help. Mohammed knew something that almost no one else in the world knew: that his brother Kadhim was *not* struggling to find work in the medical field. And he certainly wasn't in Amman, Jordan.

After leaving the hospital, Kadhim went home, struggling with the aftermath of the hardest decision he had ever made.

The dream of becoming a doctor had been his passion since high school, a dream he had cultivated and sacrificed for, and suddenly it was gone. Where his future had been filled with images of many fulfilling years as a surgeon, there was now nothing. A blank. A futureless void. He felt lost and purposeless, and ached over the loss of his dream the way he would have mourned the loss of a loved one. Guilt at leaving a short-staffed hospital when his patients needed him most trailed his every step.

A year of death and destruction in a corrupt hospital had ravaged medicine like a sickness, to the point where it had become twisted and ugly and no longer recognizable. Memories of how much he had loved medicine, how badly he had wanted this future, and the twisted way in which life had betrayed him, forced Kadhim to push medicine from his mind and prepare to start a new life without it.

He wanted to mourn the death of his dream, but he didn't know how. So he buried medicine far away in the recesses of his mind, where it could no longer reach him. His worn textbooks became covered with dust. He shut his mind to memories from the hospital, and pushed away the need to wake up early, make rounds, and triage patients, until eventually these desires faded away completely. The question that plagued him now was: *What next?*

His family was supportive, but no one stood by his side more than Mohammed. The daily phone calls between the two brothers became longer and more frequent, as Mohammed spoke with Kadhim about becoming an interpreter with the U.S. Army. Kadhim had originally thought of continuing his medical education in Jordan, but after speaking with Iraqi friends there, he realized that it was a dead end.

He heard horror stories of Iraqi doctors sleeping in the streets, unable to find work. All he wanted was a way out of this godforsaken land, a way to practice medicine in an English-speaking country, whether Britain, Australia, Canada, or the States. There was no special visa program for the U.S., but Kadhim hoped that maybe, just *maybe*, if he became an interpreter, it might be easier to get a visa out of Iraq.

Despite living in the same city, it had been more than a year since the brothers had seen each other. So when Kadhim met with Mohammed early one morning in the Green Zone, it was a long-awaited reunion. After all the nights Kadhim had spent worrying about his brother, and all the days Mohammed had spent missing his home and family, there was nothing more reviving to the brothers than to be reunited. In a large family of boys, there was something special about Mohammed and Kadhim's relationship. They were more than brothers; they were best friends. And more than best friends, they were brothers.

"Look, I'm not going to let you work on combat missions like me," Mohammed said after embracing his younger brother. "Every day I come home and we've lost a soldier, or an interpreter or two. Either interpret somewhere safe, or don't do it at all."

"That's fine; I'll take anything."

"Great. Let me introduce you to some guys then." Mohammed, as he had done for so many before him, took Kadhim to Titan, which subcontracted with the Army. "Did you study for the exam?"

"No. What exam? Was I supposed to study?"

"They have two English exams, written and oral. Sign your name here, and we'll wait until they call you."

One by one, all the other applicants were called in, until Kadhim was the only one left. He was starting to think that he wouldn't be called at all, when they finally called him in for the oral exams. He interpreted a few scenarios, as a DOD interpreter confirmed the accuracy of his work, and the men looked pleased.

"I think you'll do fine here. We'll contact you with the official results soon."

"But sir, I never completed the written exam."

"You don't need to. You came in with Saint. He's been with us for years, since the beginning. Besides, we overheard you speaking in English with one of the soldiers. You'll be fine. How is your written English, by the way?"

Between an English teacher for a father, and six years of medical school in English, Kadhim was confident. "It's even better than my spoken English."

"Great."

Kadhim stayed with Mohammed in the Green Zone for the next couple nights, during which he met several of the ladies from his brother's repertoire, and it was not long before he received the phone call.

"Mr. Al Baghdadi? You've been accepted for hire as a contract interpreter with Titan. Please report for duty at the following date and time..."

And that was when he created The Lie.

Immediately after he had escorted Kadhim to his first assignment, Mohammed hurried to the checkpoint. It was time.

The young woman was about to pass through the gate as Mohammed arrived and joined a group of soldiers, all of whose eyes were trained on her.

"Who is that?" he asked one of the soldiers.

The boy whistled. "That's Jumana." He glanced and recognized the gleam in Mohammed's eye. "Give up now, man. It's impossible. We've all tried."

"I'm going to go talk to her."

The soldier laughed. "Like hell you will, Saint! I'm telling you, she doesn't have the time of day for anyone!"

"She will for me. Watch me go talk to her."

The young men crowded around her as she came through the checkpoint, smiling and saying hello. Wordlessly, she handed them her ID. As she took it back, her eyes met Mohammed's, and she smiled.

"Did you see that? She always smiles at me," Mohammed remarked in a low voice as she walked away.

"She smiles at everyone. But she doesn't talk to anyone."

"What if I got her phone number right now?"

One of the soldiers burst into laughter. "I'll give you one hundred bucks if you get her number. Better yet, I'll give you a hundred bucks if you even get her to *talk* to you!"

"You're on. Watch this." Mohammed darted after the girl, quickly catching up with her as the group of grinning soldiers watched, excited to see their cocky young interpreter finally face rejection.

"Excuse me, miss?"

She turned in surprise, "Yes?"

"My name is Mohammed."

"Nice to meet you. I'm Jumana."

Immediately, Mohammed pulled out his cell phone. "What's your phone number?"

She looked shocked to be asked for her information so abruptly, but she wasn't displeased. Somehow, she found the digits of her phone number rolling off her tongue. "But may I ask why you need it?" she asked once she had given her number to the tall, brash stranger.

"I asked because I think you are the most beautiful woman who has ever walked through these gates."

She blushed a deep red but couldn't stop a smile from gracing her lips.

"And, to be honest, we have a bet running about you."

She glanced back and saw the soldiers staring at them. Mohammed flashed her a disarming smile.

"If you don't give me your phone number, you'll make me look like a failure in front of everyone."

She laughed, "I already gave it to you."

"Thank you. I'll call you soon." And with that, he returned to the group of soldiers, a defiant grin on his face and the phone raised in his hand.

"Mother fucker! How the *hell...*?" The instigator of the bet suddenly paused. "Wait, how do you know it's her real number? Maybe she gave you a fake number just to get you off her back."

"Watch this." Mohammed called the number and in the distance, Jumana raised her phone to her ear. "They don't believe me," Mohammed said to her. "Do you mind turning around and waving?"

Incredulous, the group watched in suspense as the gorgeous young woman turned around, smiled, and waved at Mohammed.

The soldier shook his head in disbelief.

"Saint, how the hell do you *do* that?"

The Lie was born of fear. Civil war did terrible things to a people. It turned a Shiite Mahdi Army against a Sunni Al Qaeda, and it turned both of them against the occupier, the Iraqi government, and the Iraqi people as a whole. No one trusted anyone; each person became polarized as a perceived necessity of self-preservation. When Kadhim became an interpreter, he knew how many would see it. He had joined the other side, betrayed his country, and was working with the occupier, the infidels. And for that, he should be killed, along with the rest of his family.

The Lie was born of necessity. No one could know the truth of what he was doing. And so he built and maintained his Lie in excruciating detail. He was in Jordan, living a life of monotonous unemployment, searching for a way back to medicine. He knew which neighborhood he lived in, on which street, next to which shops. He knew exactly when he had arrived in Amman, and how long he had been there. He complained about his treatment at the hands of those awful Jordanians, in their awful hospitals.

He spread his Lie to old colleagues, older friends, and even to his closest relatives. *No one*, with the exception of his immediate family, knew what he was actually doing.

Most importantly, he lied to the other Iraqi interpreters, and they to him. They fabricated names, origins, where they lived, where they had worked, what car they drove, how much money they had, and whether or not they were married or had children. They lied to each other constantly, about even the most minute details, to the point that sometimes Kadhim would laugh and ask, "Is *anything* you just told me true?"

And his colleague would grin and shake his head.

After many months of working with the Americans, Kadhim saw a friend, a fellow doctor who had told everyone that he was working in Jordan. He was working on the base as an interpreter. Kadhim did not greet him; he would not expose him.

Everybody lied.

The Lie continued not for weeks, not for months, but for two whole years. Two years of lying to everyone he knew. Out of necessity and self-preservation, the Lie became so perfected that it evolved into something real. Somehow, the Lie even managed to convince Kadhim himself. He *had* gone to Jordan after leaving the hospital. He *had* been rejected by their hospitals. He had complained of it so many times that a true hatred of Jordanians and their inhumane treatment grew in his heart. The Lie became a truth that spilled from his lips even as he recounted his story many years later, and he had to be reminded... *oh yes, that part was only a lie.*

But it was the Lie that kept him and his family alive for the next two years of their lives.

PRISONER EXCHANGE

Kadhim spoke his warning in the most urgent tone he could muster. "Take my advice, man, do *not* go in there!"

The crowds of orange jumpsuit-wearing prisoners looked decidedly formidable, leaving Kadhim more than happy to interpret from the safe side of the fence. Camp Cropper was not a place for petty thieves and tax evaders; it was a detention facility for insurgents and suspected terrorists, nearly all of whom regarded the new interpreter as a traitor and infidel deserving of death. Why "Bear" wanted to enter the open yard among them to interpret was beyond him.

"I'll be fine." His colleague stretched bulging muscles and cracked his knuckles. "I'm not afraid of them."

Long hours at the gym had earned Bear his nickname, and even the way the interpreter walked showed confidence in his physical prowess. He appeared to consider himself more soldier than interpreter, and relished frisking the detainees.

"Suit yourself," Kadhim said. "But don't say I didn't warn you. These guys are happy to blow themselves up just to kill you; muscles mean nothing to them."

"Take it easy. I've done this before." And with that, Bear walked through the gate with the soldiers.

No sooner had he seen his brother than Kadhim said goodbye again, assigned to the detention facility near Baghdad airport, far removed from the Green Zone. Here, new detainees arrived in droves, kept in various camps as they awaited trial or release.

The interpreters were given the choice of wearing masks to protect their identities, and most of them did, including Kadhim. They were all given nicknames as well, and Kadhim became "Doc." He had told them that he was a physician and immediately regretted it, fearing that someone might be able to draw the link to his true identity. But once the information was out there, it was too late to take it back.

Kadhim started to earn the American commander's trust from

the moment he entered the office with a pistol and a full magazine, held away from his body like a dirty diaper. The commander's eyes flew open.

"I found these in a port-a-pot." Kadhim set them on the desk.

"Holy shit!" The commander's jaw dropped and he started laughing in sheer astonishment. "What kind of idiot leaves his weapon in the john? Fuck! Whatever moron officer did this *will* be punished. How did you even bring these to me? Everyone knows interpreters aren't allowed to carry weapons. Didn't anyone stop you?"

"No. I just walked across the base. No one said anything."

"Unbelievable." The commander shook his head. "And Camp Cropper is supposed to be one of the highest security bases in Iraq. Thanks for bringing them to me, Doc. I appreciate it."

This incident, combined with the fact that Kadhim never left the base, quickly earned the commander's trust. Within a week or two of starting his employment, the commander started to request that Kadhim do written translations as well and even—much to the ire of the other interpreters—granted Kadhim a cell phone, a privilege not permitted to "local assets."

Kadhim felt safer at Camp Cropper than he had at the hospital, and interpreting for the detainees was interesting work. He worried, though, that he might get stuck in this new life and never return to the practice of medicine. And as it turned out, he wasn't the only one at Camp Cropper who feared being trapped in the wrong place.

"Doc, what's going on with this guy?"

"I don't know, sir. He says it's nothing."

The detainee was acting strangely—quiet, reserved, and isolated from the others. He insisted that nothing was wrong, but the soldiers had their suspicions.

"Let's take this guy aside to solitary confinement and ask him what's up. I'm wondering if he has information for us, or if he's a high value detainee. He's just acting a little... off."

They pulled him aside, and once again, Kadhim asked, "Is everything alright? Is there a reason why you've been so quiet since you arrived?"

The man hesitated. "Can I speak freely here?"

"Certainly."

"Do you not have a single Shiite detainee?"

"Of course we have Shiites."

The detainee regarded the soldier and Kadhim nervously. "Then why did you put me here?"

"Well, when they asked you whether you were Sunni or Shiite, why didn't you just tell them you're Shiite?"

Detainees were screened and divided into camps according to sect. The vast majority of detainees were Sunnis, but one small camp was reserved for Shiites. The system was not without its flaws, but it had been set in place after several Shiites had lost their lives at the hands of Sunni detainees.

"I didn't think you had any Shiites! I've only seen Sunnis since I arrived, so I thought... Listen, I've been pretending to pray like them for more than a week now! Do you know that they have a leader in my camp who makes sure that anyone who doesn't follow them in prayer five times a day is beaten?"

"We've heard." Kadhim thought gravely of the Iraqi Sunni detainee who was attacked and badly beaten by a group of Wahabis for missing a single prayer. Some, in fact, were so frightened by the death threats of their peers that they purposely picked fights with the American soldiers in order to be put into solitary confinement, and when their time was up, they begged for it to be extended. This detainee looked on the verge of making such a request.

"You've got to transfer me to the Shiite camp!"

"Just hold tight and don't talk to anyone until we get this sorted out," the soldier responded. "We have to get the commander's approval first."

They had to confirm that the detainee was telling the truth, and that he wasn't plotting against Shiites, but eventually, the detainee was transferred.

◇ ◈ ◇

Kadhim was interpreting for some of the soldiers when he heard screams, shouts, and yelps of pain coming from inside the fenced yard.

"What's going on?"

"It's Bear!" an armed soldier shouted as he dashed for the gate. "They're trying to kill him!"

The interpreter had somehow been separated from the soldiers inside the yard, and the detainees had seized the opportunity. It wasn't uncommon for them to try to hit or throw rocks at the soldiers, but the Americans carried weapons and kept them ready and pointed every time they entered, discouraging attacks.

Bear, on the other hand, was unarmed. They had been waiting for an opportunity to get at this traitor for a long time, and as soon as they got their chance, the detainees had jumped him. Bear swung and hit and fought back, but as big as he was, he was no match for a group of men. The tables had turned, and now *he* was the prisoner.

The soldiers came running, and even with their guns, it was difficult to control the situation. When they finally wrestled Bear out of the gates, he was bruised, dirty, and shocked. His nose was crooked and bleeding, and his breath came in quick pants. He noticed Kadhim as they took him away to be treated, and grabbed his arm.

"Take my advice," he said urgently, eyes bulging. "Do *not* go in there!"

PAYCHECK

Jumana, or "Juju," was different than the rest of Mohammed's girlfriends. She was sweet, conservative, and most notably, a virgin. And Mohammed, like many Iraqi men, did not like to take a girl's virginity. He didn't want to be the reason that she would become "ruined" in a potential future husband's eyes. Not that Juju's virginity was up for grabs—she drew a hard line, and the amount of physical contact between them was minimal. In fact, between her beauty, her gentle nature, and her modesty, Mohammed began to think that perhaps *this* could be the girl he would marry.

There was just one problem. She became way too attached, way too quickly.

It wasn't the old lady's first time begging at the checkpoint, but it was the first time Mohammed noticed her. There was something that distinguished her from other beggars, perhaps a certain pride in her posture, or clothes that—although worn—were clean and respectable. In fact, she looked like a member of the educated class, and there was an odd inconsistency in seeing this seventy-year-old woman begging from strangers.

"I'm a widow, and my children were killed in the war," she explained when Mohammed approached her. For the elderly in Iraq, life insurance and retirement funds consisted only of one's sellable belongings and working children or relatives who did their best to support them. As she explained more, the picture began to fall into place.

"My children left behind three orphaned grandchildren, and there are several other orphaned children I found on the streets whom I took in as well. I just couldn't leave them out there to fend for themselves."

She had unintentionally put her finger on Mohammed's weak spot.

"So what do you need?" He usually preferred not to give to beggars, as he didn't trust that they were telling the truth, but he was intrigued.

"One of the children is sick, and another was badly burned in an

333

accident. I took them both to the doctor, but I can't afford their medicine, particularly the burn medicine." Tears spilled over her cheeks. "It's terrible. A child shouldn't have to suffer like this. They've witnessed war and the death of their parents, and I'm all they have left."

The woman seemed to sense Mohammed's hesitation.

"I swear by Allah, by the Holy Quran, and by the graves of my poor deceased children that I'm telling the truth. Look, here are the prescriptions."

He looked them over, remembering how expensive Ali's medications had been when he had suffered from severe burns several years prior. Perhaps she was telling the truth, but the easiest way to find out how much she truly needed was simply to walk across the street and consult the pharmacy.

As the oddly-matched pair watched, the pharmacist calculated the prescriptions one by one, his eyes growing slightly wider with each slip of paper. At last, he looked up apologetically.

"The total comes to $550."

That was Mohammed's entire paycheck for the month.

And as it happened, this woman had come on payday.

In fact, Mohammed's monthly pay, which he always received in cash, was burning a hole through his pocket at that very moment. To him, "money management" meant buying whatever he wanted whenever he wanted it, an expensive car, booze, cigarettes, electronics... He was lucky to be alive considering the dangers of his job, and spending his money however he wished was his reward. When every day could be his last, why *not* buy whatever he wanted? Five hundred and fifty dollars a month wasn't a huge paycheck, but it was decent for Iraq. He had also just gone in on a laundry business with his brother Ali, which provided supplemental income.

Mohammed was conflicted as they returned to the gate. Did he *really* need this money more than she did? An image of his youngest brother's innocent smile appeared in his mind. What if it had been Firas who needed this help?

As a rule, he didn't trust beggars and their stories, having seen too many of them swindle the community at large. But this woman, with her tears and her many prescriptions, made it difficult for him *not* to believe. Surely, at her age and with the burden she carried, apparently alone, she needed it more than he. After all, he mused, charity was not something to be done just for people. It was an act done out of kindness in front of Allah. Whether she was telling the truth or not would not diminish from the good deed itself.

Still, his entire paycheck? That was a *lot* to ask. It wasn't earned sitting behind a desk. He had risked his life for those five hundred and fifty dollars.

Even if she was telling the truth, he couldn't be expected to pay for *everything*, could he? It was too much.

By the time they reached the gate, Mohammed had made up his mind. Reaching into his pocket, he pulled out a wad of cash.

"See this? This is $550." He put it into her hand. "That's my entire paycheck, which I just received today. From their hands, to yours."

She broke into tears, grabbing his hand and kissing it until Mohammed went red with embarrassment and stopped her. The soldiers stared at him in disbelief.

"Are you nuts?" one of them asked as the woman walked away. "How much did you give her?"

"I gave her my paycheck."

"Hey, we want money too! You won't give us any?"

"This was for orphans." Mohammed smiled, but he didn't laugh. It had not been easy to sacrifice a month's worth of sweat, blood, and dangerous combat missions, but deep inside, it felt good.

Nina rolled her eyes and pushed Mohammed away as his phone rang for the twentieth time.

"Right, and you're not seeing any other girls," she snorted. Mohammed protested as she began to pull her shirt on.

"Can I help it if people call me?" He could've killed Juju. A month of this nonstop calling was getting ridiculous. Beautiful or not, there was only so much he could stand from a girl, and check-up calls every few hours that became nonstop when unanswered were enough to constitute grounds for break-up. "Look, Nina, you're my girlfriend, I care for you, and we've been together too long for you not to trust me. If you can't believe me, then just leave me."

She'd heard the speech before and could never be sure whether he was telling the truth, but it was Mohammed's conciliatory tone that gave her pause.

"Well, can you at least tell them not to call you so much? I mean, you're telling girls that we're basically engaged, right?"

"Of course, *habibti*. Anything."

He made a mental note to get a separate sim card for Juju. No sooner had Nina been appeased than the phone rang again. She huffed, smacked his hand away, and stormed off. He was ready to throw the damn phone in the street when he checked the caller ID. This time, it wasn't Juju.

"Hello?"

One of the soldiers addressed him briefly. "Saint, there's someone at the checkpoint asking to see you."

"Who?"

"Just get over here."

Was it Juju, desperate to get his attention? Or maybe another one of his hookups?

It was the old lady. And once again, she had arrived on payday.

"Look, you seem like a respectable lady. Why do you humiliate yourself with begging?" The children were sick again, and she didn't have enough money for food, but it bothered Mohammed to see this well-educated woman out begging in the streets, particularly in streets such as these.

"I'm not young enough to work anymore, and I have health issues as well. Arthritis, high blood pressure, heart problems..." She began reciting a litany of complaints.

"Enough. Stop begging, and I'll give you what you need. But don't come to this checkpoint anymore. It's too dangerous. What would all your children do if you suddenly died in a bomb blast, God forbid? If you need money, contact me, and I'll send you some. It won't always be my whole paycheck; it might just be what I can afford, but I'll help you if I can."

Reaching into his wallet, he pulled out his wad of cash and handed it over. The woman stared in disbelief. She didn't know how to begin to thank him, so she cried speechless tears and hugged him.

For the second month in a row, he had given her his entire paycheck.

A few months went by before the old lady returned, looking worn out.

"I'm so ashamed to keep coming back to you, but I swear, my son, I don't have anyone besides you and Allah. All the burn medications have run out, and the other children need new clothing and books for school." She looked at him imploringly. "Please, just look at these."

She handed him a new stack of prescriptions, and the trip to the pharmacy was repeated. Once again, the total came to the amount of Mohammed's paycheck.

What could he do? She had put him in an uncomfortable

position, where he would feel bad if he gave and worse if he didn't. He shook his head as he pulled out his wallet to once again hand over his paycheck to the beggar.

"I don't know… I just hope I'm doing the right thing." He gave her a sharp look. "I hope you know that this money is for the children."

"I don't want your money. Not like this." Her face grew red and tears of anger spilled over wizened cheeks. "Do you think it's *easy* for me to come here, without dignity, without self-respect, to humiliate myself and beg?" She shook her head. "If you don't believe me, if you think I'm making this up, then I don't *want* your money."

Mohammed felt like he had been hit by a truck. In a lifetime of drinking, girls, and misdeeds, never had he felt so ashamed as when he implied that this woman was lying.

"I'm sorry, I really am. Please, accept the money."

"No, I can't. Not like this."

"Please, just take it. I want to help the children. I really do."

She put her face into her aged hands and cried tears of humiliation. Without raising her eyes, she shook her head, and Mohammed felt himself crumble. He felt terrible for his underhanded accusation and for the way he had shamed her, an old woman caring for five orphans on her own.

"It's not your fault. You *have* to take it, for the children." He turned and handed his pay to a stunned pharmacist, who silently handed over the medications.

She returned for help a month later, and once again Mohammed gave her his paycheck. After that, he never saw her again. He asked around at the checkpoint, but no one had seen her. He worried about the children, wondering if they had once again been orphaned. Was it possible she had found another source of income?

In total, he had given her approximately $2,000.

But if there were sick and injured children left orphaned, then how could he feel like he had done enough?

HIGH VALUE TARGET

"So is that it? You're done searching me?" The commander directed his question to the Iraqi correctional officer-in-training as Kadhim interpreted. The officer nodded.

"Yes, finished."

"And you've checked every part and made sure that I'm not carrying any contraband?"

The officer nodded again, this time with a bit less confidence. There were certain sensitive areas that he had skimmed over a bit. He, like many others, found it difficult to cross those cultural and personal barriers and run his hand over another man's crotch. He'd gone over it quickly, hoping that his blushing cheeks weren't obvious to the other ninety or so officers-in-training who sat in the lecture hall.

"Alright then, you can sit down." The American commander dismissed him and then turned his back to his Iraqi students. They stared in curiosity and confusion as he lowered his pants slightly, dug his hand deep into his underwear, and began pulling out various objects. They heard clicks as he assembled the pieces, then he zipped up his pants and turned around.

In his hand was a fully assembled and loaded gun.

A ripple of amazed commentary flowed throughout the lecture hall.

"I know you don't like to strip search certain parts of the body, but *this* is what could happen if you're not thorough." The commander looked at them gravely, and there were nods and murmurs of agreement as Kadhim translated. It was no joke, training to work in a prison.

In addition to interpreting for detainees, managing a group of Iraqi interpreters, and helping to establish the first Correctional Officers First Aid Station, Kadhim had been interpreting for the Iraqi Correctional Officer Academy at Camp Cropper for five months, during which he had witnessed the graduation of four classes of Iraqi officers. The American commanders took both the training and officer selection very seriously, and it wasn't uncommon for the commander to ask Kadhim's opinion of the new group of cadets upon their arrival.

"Just go mingle with them, get to know them a bit, and let me know what you think." He trusted Kadhim's judgment as a secular doctor.

"Most of them are fine," Kadhim would report back at the end of the day. "But there are a couple guys... that one, over there, and this one next to the door... I wouldn't keep them."

"Why's that?"

"It's just a feeling I was getting from them, based on questions they asked me about myself, and the way they talked about politics... I think one of them is in the Mahdi Army, and the other an Al Qaeda sympathizer."

Polygraphs often confirmed Kadhim's hunch, and the candidates were dismissed.

There were other times, however, when Kadhim's warnings fell on deaf ears.

"Are you really releasing that detainee, sir?"

"Yes. He's due to leave today. Why?"

"You can't release that guy! He's a terrorist!"

"Do you have proof?"

"Yes! For the past several days I've overheard him bragging to the other detainees. He's planning to go blow himself up! He's a suicide bomber!"

"I'm sorry, Doc. That's not enough to keep him here."

"Are you serious? He *just* said it, just now! He said, '*You'll hear of my martyrdom in a few days time.*' That's not proof?"

"I'm afraid that's not proof. We need solid evidence to keep him here, and we just don't have it."

"But he's announcing to the world that he's going to go kill people!" Kadhim couldn't believe it. He knew the other end of this story: the dead husbands, wives, and children, the amputees, the shrapnel victims. How could the Americans not listen to the detainee and take him seriously?

"I'm sorry, Doc, but that's the way the system works. We need evidence."

There was nothing Kadhim could do but watch in apprehension and anger as the detainee and others like him were released.

Two simultaneous systems of justice had developed and were in play side by side. Upon capturing an insurgent, the Americans would detain him for a trial that, for lack of evidence, often never came. Then the detainee would be released. The Iraqi Army, on the other hand, killed suspected terrorists on the spot. Better to be safe than sorry.

Kadhim's mind was still on the most recent professed terrorist to walk free as he interpreted for the newest batch of hopeful officers, a group of Shiite men from the slums of Sadr City, almost all of whom were followers of Muqtada Al Sadr. They were listening intently to a lecture on the definition and treatment of high value targets.

"High value targets," the commander explained, indicating various bullets on his power point as Kadhim interpreted, "cannot be treated like regular detainees. With high value targets, it is of particular importance that they be treated in accordance with the laws of the Geneva Convention.

"For example, Saddam Hussein is a high value target. When he was captured, they had to follow a special protocol. Not because he was better than the rest, but because it was possible he could be released, could be killed, or could escape with the help of those loyal to him. For this and other reasons, there are special precautions that have to be taken."

The commander clicked a button on his laptop and the picture on the power point switched from Saddam Hussein to a photograph of Muqtada Al-Sadr.

"I'll give you another example of a high value target who hasn't been captured yet..."

"Just a second, sir," Kadhim said quickly under his breath, without translating the commander's message. "We need to talk."

Kadhim turned to the group of Iraqis, who were glaring suspiciously at the picture of their leader on the screen, and said in Arabic, "Please take a short break. The lecture will continue momentarily."

He turned to the American commander. "What are you doing? All of those guys are his followers!"

"Seriously?" The commander's eyes became dinner plates.

"Yes! And on top of that, sir, did you know that recently a deal was reached between Muqtada Al Sadr and the Coalition Forces? Officially, at this point anyway, he's no longer considered a target. He's cooperating with the government."

"Oh my gosh." The commander let out a poof of air as the ramifications of his slideshow hit him. "What should I do?"

"You could just skip this picture and move on to the next slide."

"No, I can't do that. I already showed them this picture in the context of high value targets. They're not stupid."

"Do what you like then. Apologize, maybe."

The commander looked at Kadhim for a minute, then nodded and turned to face his students.

"Men, I apologize. It seems there has been a mistake." He moved on to the next slide. "This looks as though it was an old power point that has not yet been updated to reflect the deal that was reached between the government and Muqtada Al Sadr. I realize there are people who support him, and that's your democratic right. My apologies once again."

He continued a diplomatic apology until some of the men who had been glaring started to laugh. "Okay, okay. We get it."

They didn't let the commander forget his mistake easily, however. Afterwards, as the group sat around with the Americans drinking tea, eating Iraqi dishes, and socializing, the men ribbed their American commander.

"How could you talk about our leader like that?"

His eyes widened in earnest. "I'm so sorry! I didn't mean to—!"

"We're kidding!" The men laughed. Nothing should stand in the way of a good joke. "It's nothing. We support Muqtada, but we're not one hundred percent with him. There are things we like about him, and other things we don't."

"That's democracy," the commander replied. "Muqtada Al Sadr has made a truce with the government, and I respect that. We just want peace and democracy for Iraq. But I do have a word of advice: when you guys take over this detention facility, be professional. Don't treat anyone differently just because they're Sunni or Shiite."

They nodded seriously. They liked and respected this commander, and they wanted to prove their proficiency as officers. But he still deserved some teasing.

"We'll keep an eye out for Muqtada for you, sir. Just in case."

THE HATCH

As often as it happened to them, and as much as Mohammed tried to prepare himself physically and mentally, there was no way to be ready when the humvee ran over an IED. The violent jerking of his body, the sudden rocking of the vehicle as it leapt in the air, his hearing blown away by an explosive noise... it came as a shock every time.

For the first few fractions of a second, he wondered, *Am I okay? Am I still alive? Do I still have all my limbs?*

Then: *Where is my team? Are they okay? Are they alive?*

It had happened again. Noise. Confusion. People yelling. Someone shouted in his ear, "Saint! Saint, are you alright?"

On instinct, "Yes!"

The voice was coming through his CBC headset.

"Saint, drag Matthews down! Get him in the Bradley!"

Mohammed looked up at the hatch that opened through the roof of the humvee, allowing Major Matthews to simultaneously direct the vehicle and operate heavy machinery in the open air of the roof. The major was limp and motionless.

After the 2003 invasion of Iraq, soldiers had quickly discovered that their standard vehicles were not protection enough from landmines, IEDs, snipers and other threats. They began adding scrap metal, Kevlar vests, and other materials as improvised armor to their vehicles, which they nicknamed "hillbilly armor," or "hajji armor" when done with the help of Iraqis. They would later be supplied with government-issued up-armor kits to fortify insufficient humvees and other vehicles.

By this time, in 2007, Mohammed was riding in a double-armored Bradley, with enormously weighty doors and glass so thick that they could barely see through it—which was one of the reasons why the soldier who manned the hatch helped by calling out directions to the driver. It was this doubled armor that protected them when an IED caused a vehicle weighing more than a ton to jump beneath them.

But today, even that heavy armor had not been able to protect Major Matthews.

Mohammed pulled the major down from the hatch into the Bradley, seeing as he did so that the cause of Matthews' injuries was not the IED but rather the hatch itself, which had slammed down on the major upon impact.

The major was a mess of blood and bruises, his eyes swollen shut in two black and blue puffs of flesh. Desperately, Mohammed tried to hear if he was breathing, but the rumbling of the engine blocked all noise.

"Kill the engine. *Kill the engine, damn it!* I can't hear anything!"

Abruptly, the Bradley was turned off as the others waited to hear news of their commander.

If only Kadhim were here; he could do this so much better, so much faster. Mohammed couldn't find any signs that his commander, brother-in-arms and close friend, was breathing.

"Major! Major, are you okay?" He was shouting at the top of his lungs as he worked, but there was no response. Hands fumbling, he tried to find a pulse, but the thick armor that both he and his commander wore made it difficult. *Kadhim, how the hell do you do this? Matthews, be alive. Please, please be alive.*

Finally, Mohammed did the only thing he could think of. He grabbed his friend's vest to steady him, and bracing himself, he slapped the man as hard as he possibly could across the cheek.

A red handprint quickly appeared on Major Matthews' face, and Mohammed's palm burned from the impact. It was the kind of blow that would bring a man out of a coma.

Mohammed watched, waited, and his heart sank.

There was no response. No movement whatsoever.

Damn it, brother, stay with me.

He couldn't give up. There was no way in *hell* he was going to let this man die. With his left hand gripping Matthews' vest, Mohammed raised his right hand for a second, stinging try.

"Do that again and I'll fucking kill you."

The raspy warning stopped Mohammed in his tracks. Major Matthews' lips bled and his eyes were swollen shut, but never had a death threat been so beautiful. Mohammed burst into a laugh of relief, and shouted to the driver, "He's okay! Let's take him back!"

As he tied the major to the bench to avoid him being jolted from side to side during the return journey, Matthews spoke. "Saint, get your ass up in that commander."

Mohammed had been trained to man the hatch, and despite the fact that it was the most exposed seat in the house, he was happy to do it. Making sure that his commander was secure, he appeared through the roof of the vehicle, shouting down directions as they went.

"Left, *left*, LEFT! There's a vehicle in front of you!"

They returned to the base as people stared. *Who was that Iraqi commanding the Bradley?* Matthews was carried to the Troop Medical

Clinic (TMC), where Mohammed and others waited with him as they cut slits under his eyes to relieve the swelling. The medical team stared, heads cocked, at the red handprint, but could not calculate its meaning. Matthews, meanwhile, grabbed Mohammed's arm.

"First of all," he said with a grimace, "don't you dare think I forgot about that slap. I'll get you back for that. Second of all, I want you to take the soldiers and finish the mission."

"*What?*" The commanders, soldiers, and Mohammed himself all stared at Matthews in shock.

"Take the soldiers and finish the mission!"

"Major Matthews," a commander protested, "you can't possibly mean—!"

"You heard me!" Matthews turned to Mohammed. "Saint, I always thought that you slapped like a bitch, but today you proved me wrong. That hurt like hell. Now get out there and finish the mission."

The Iraqi interpreter turned to the stunned soldiers, a mischievous grin dancing on his face.

"Well, guys, I guess you have to follow *my* orders now!"

INFIDELITY

As yet another soldier-ladden plane spiraled steeply upward until reaching an altitude safe from attack, Kadhim could only watch from below and wish desperately that he was on it. He had worked as an interpreter at Camp Cropper for six months now, living in the ring of camps strategically surrounding Baghdad airport known as Camp Liberty, and each aircraft that escaped Iraq was another reminder of just how stuck he truly was.

Time had not healed the loss of medicine. Being forced to leave something he loved while knowing he might never go back to it had left Kadhim not so much traumatized as angry. His goal of becoming a surgeon, once nearly complete, was suddenly so far away. Now, if he ever returned to the practice of medicine, it would not be in Iraq. Never again.

He thought often of the last good doctors he had left behind, who now faced vast numbers of patients alone, and was plagued with guilt and deep sadness. His entire career had been gambled on the distant possibility of restarting elsewhere. *Had he made the right decision? If he wasn't a doctor, then who was he?*

Oh God, what had he done?

Kadhim had inquired on multiple occasions as to whether it would be possible to assist in medical care or even interpret in the clinics, to no avail. His commander relied on him heavily, and had once fended off another commander's request that Kadhim interpret for their unit. "No, we need Doc here; he's too valuable."

But when Kadhim approached him directly and asked for assistance, the commander saw him for what he was—not just a local asset, but a doctor struggling to return to his field in whatever way possible—and so he put aside his own needs and helped the young man.

At long last, Kadhim landed a new job, not in the hospital perhaps, but interpreting in combat clinics throughout Camp Liberty. It had been just over six months since he'd left Baghdad Medical Complex, but amongst the doctors, nurses, patients, and medical equipment, the clinic felt like home, a tiny step in the right direction.

The American staff was intrigued by the opportunity to work with an Iraqi doctor, and one colonel in particular enjoyed quizzing him on patient care. "How would you treat this soldier with a bullet in his hand? Do you need to remove the bullet?"

"Not necessarily. If it's next to a nerve or compressing something, you should extract the bullet. Otherwise it can stay, although it's preferable to take it out, because it could cause fibrosis or issues with movement in the future."

"Tell me about antibiotic coverage, if necessary."

"The bullet should be sterile, but I would still give prophylactic treatment to be safe. There are three types of antibiotics that work on soft tissue and gram positive bacteria that I recommend..."

The nurses and doctor listened, impressed, as the young Iraqi detailed treatment.

"Wow, you really have strong medical knowledge!"

Kadhim laughed. "What did you expect?"

"No offense, but we weren't expecting Iraqi doctors to know that much."

This only made Kadhim laugh more. "I was only a resident, but I know emergency medicine. That's all Iraq is. Quiz us on trauma and we may know more than you!"

They laughed with him, pleased that he had not taken offense. The colonel, a family physician from Ohio, was excited to work with an Iraqi doctor, and he liked to have Kadhim accompany him even on cases that did not require interpretation, quizzing him and sharing his knowledge with his young Iraqi protégé. Kadhim loved it. It felt wonderful to be back in the medical field, and while it wasn't the same as actually continuing his medical training, it did help to keep some of the knowledge fresh. When they weren't talking medicine, he and the colonel discussed Iraqi culture and politics, and Kadhim admitted that he hoped one day to emigrate to the United States to practice there.

"What about staying here?" the colonel asked. "It seems like Iraq could use more people like you."

Kadhim regarded him gravely. "I'm not much good to them dead, sir."

"I really like Iraqis. Arabic is a beautiful language, and it's been fascinating to learn more about Iraqi culture." The soldier's hazel eyes sparkled earnestly as he addressed Kadhim. Geoffrey was young, blonde, and good-looking, and his innocence made Kadhim wonder how long it had been since he hopped off one of the spiraling airplanes. He had an exuberant air about him that few soldiers had, and he seemed excited to speak with the Iraqi interpreter.

"Thanks. Unfortunately, there are some Iraqis out there who are giving us a bad name. And our culture isn't helping us very much at the moment," Kadhim joked.

"Still, I've met a lot of great Iraqis. Actually," Geoffrey lowered his voice a bit and gave Kadhim a conspiratorial smile, "between you and me, I've met an Iraqi girl who I really like, and I plan on proposing to her. But no one can know, so I hope you don't mention this to anyone."

"Congratulations! That's wonderful!"

"Really? That's how you feel?"

"Why would I feel any other way?"

"That's great." The soldier looked relieved. "It's just that I heard that Iraqis don't like the idea of a foreigner, or at least an American, marrying an Iraqi girl."

"That's just close-mindedness. If I loved an American, I would marry her. Why not? We're all people."

Geoffrey relaxed visibly, and his smile grew wider as his eyes gained a wistful look. "I'm telling you, Doc, I've never met a girl like her. She's an interpreter, so I have to be extra careful, but she's worth it. Here, let me show you."

He pulled a small photograph out of his wallet and handed it to Kadhim, who took it politely. He had grown accustomed to Americans showing off pictures of their wives and girlfriends, but it was interesting to see an Iraqi woman become the subject of this cultural exchange.

"Isn't she gorgeous?" Geoffrey pressed.

"Yes, she..." Kadhim paused. The photograph was distant and a bit blurry, but the girl looked familiar.

It couldn't be.

"What's her name?"

"Why do you ask?"

"I just think I've seen her before. Does she work in FOB Prosperity?"

"Yeah, she worked there."

"What's her name?"

The soldier looked around and quickly murmured her name.

Oh boy.

"And you're dating this girl?" Kadhim couldn't believe it. No way, no way it could be the same girl.

"Yeah. We've been dating for a long time." Geoffrey started to look worried.

"I think I know her."

"Really? What do you think of her?"

"She's a great girl." But Kadhim couldn't bring any conviction to his words. The young soldier cocked his head and looked at him strangely, and Kadhim could tell that he himself had an odd look on his face. What could he say to this boy? It *had* to be her.

He didn't know what to say, and the awkwardness grew as the silence between them lingered.

"Would you excuse me for a minute?" Kadhim said abruptly, and much to the Geoffrey's confusion he was gone almost before the soldier had replied.

Kadhim stepped outside the clinic and pulled out his cell phone. "Mohammed? I have to talk to you."

"What's up?"

"It's Nina. I just met a soldier who said that he's dating her, has been dating her for a while, and that he's planning on getting engaged to her."

"Are you serious?" Mohammed was shocked. "She just spent the night with me two days ago! Are you sure it was her?"

"He said her name was Nina. He showed me her picture."

Mohammed's tone changed, somehow angry and nonchalant simultaneously. "Fuck her. I wasn't serious with her anyway. Who cares what she does. *She* was the one coming to me to hook up."

"You mean you're okay with this?"

"I don't care about her." But his tone was angry. "What the hell does she think she's doing, sleeping with me and another guy at the same time?"

Mohammed had been okay with having an open relationship with her when the openness was on *his* end. But now to find out that she was playing a similar game sickened him. What self-respecting Iraqi woman would do this? Was he not enough for her? The thought of another man touching her angered him.

"I'm going to tell him that she's still dating you."

"Go ahead, tell him."

"And if he wants to check…?"

"Give him my phone number. I'll kick his ass."

"It's not his fault, brother. How could he know? I'll talk to him and call you back."

"Fine."

Kadhim walked back into the clinic, where the young soldier

was still waiting, looking worried and perplexed.

"Geoffrey, I need to tell you something that you might not like."

"What is it?" His brow furrowed and he looked like a frightened puppy. Kadhim actually felt bad for him.

"Come here, man. Not in front of everyone in the clinic."

They stepped outside, and Kadhim broke the news.

"My brother is dating Nina. He's dated her for years and they're still in a relationship. She was with him two days ago."

"Impossible."

"If you don't believe me I can give you my brother's number and the two of you can figure it out."

Geoffrey's eyes became the size of dinner plates. He looked desperate. "No way! It's not possible! She's my fiancée!"

"What?"

"Dude, I'm telling you! I proposed to her already! She's my fiancée, for God's sake! I even applied for a fiancée visa to the United States for her! Impossible! I can't believe that she's cheating on me! It's not her!"

He started walking in circles and rubbing his hands through his hair. "I've been trying to bring her to the U.S.! I've risked my entire *career* for her, man! I could get kicked out of the army for this! I love her!" Geoffrey's face reddened and his eyes welled with tears.

"Take it easy, man, take it easy." The poor kid was falling apart in front of him. "I didn't mean to upset you. But I just called my brother, and he's angry too. You guys are both in the same boat. It looks like there's been a big misunderstanding. Here, take his number and talk to him."

The call came shortly thereafter.

"Are you Saint?"

"Yes. Who's this?"

"How about you leave Nina alone! I talked to her about you. She said that you've been harassing her."

"Are you kidding?" Mohammed laughed angrily. "She's the one who calls *me* asking to come over."

"I'm a sergeant in the U.S. Forces. If she tells me that you call her even one more time, I'll fucking kill you. I'll make sure that you lose your job and that your life is ruined."

"You think you can threaten me like that? You just messed up."

Mohammed couldn't stand being threatened, least of all by the guy who was sleeping with his girlfriend. He hung up the phone and went straight to his commander, who listened with increasing shock.

"Are you serious?"

"I swear to God."

"Let's go to Titan."

Nina was fired the same day. Unable to go home, she went to stay with a sibling who lived in the IZ, where she and Geoffrey drove her brother crazy by staying up late into the night talking through their problems. When it came to light that he was engaged to a "local asset," Geoffrey himself faced serious punishment, including a pay reduction, a lowering of rank, and a speedy return to the United States.

When Kadhim ran into her some time later, Nina was still upset.

"How could you tell Mohammed about me?"

"Really? What did you expect me to do, Nina?"

"You could have called me first and let me work it out."

"I don't think so. Neither of them deserved to be treated like that, not my brother, and not the American. He was your fiancé and you decided not to mention it to anyone."

Tears filled her eyes. "But it's so *unfair!* You know how Mohammed treated me!"

"I had to tell him, Nina. I know he's not perfect, but he's my brother."

She approached Mohammed in tears not long afterward.

"Mohammed, I'm sorry. I shouldn't have done that to you."

"Whatever."

"Mohammed, please! Just listen to me! You were my first love, and it drove me crazy that you just *didn't care.* You didn't care when I was with other men. You didn't care to be faithful to me. You drove me away!"

"Look, Nina, I'm sorry if I hurt you. But don't blame your cheating on me."

"But I miss you." She broke into tears, reaching out to touch the arm of the man she once loved. Still loved. Hated. It was so confusing.

"What is it you want from me, Nina? I made it clear from the beginning that I wasn't looking for a serious relationship. But you? You didn't even bother to tell me that you were engaged! Do you love this man?"

"I think so," she said through sobs.

"Then what are you doing here?"

"I loved you first."

In the end, Geoffrey returned to the Middle East for her, and Nina at last set foot in the United States as the wife of an American.

THE PRICE OF BOOKS

"Sergeant Major, I thought I better let you know. I'm about to get in trouble." A ubiquitous layer of dust covered the car and its surroundings, and the hot Iraq sun cast a shine on Mohammed's forehead that was quickly turning to sweat.

"Where are you?" The major's voice crackled over the radio.

"I'm at the head of Haifa Street."

"Damn it, Saint, what the hell are you doing by yourself in the most dangerous part of—"

"I'm about to kill some Iraqi policemen, sir, if they don't kill me first."

She was beautiful in a fresh, innocent kind of way. Golden hair, pale olive skin, and striking blue eyes made her a rare gem of only thirteen or fourteen years old. She and her two younger brothers of five and seven were among the many children who begged in Baghdad's streets, and her name was Farah, meaning joy.

Mohammed always saw Farah at the same intersection at the head of Haifa Street, where she and her brother sold miniature prayer books to passersby. Mohammed was accustomed to being accosted by beggars at each stop and intersection, but the blue-eyed girl with her shyness and polite mannerisms stood out. He felt protective of her, of all three children in fact, like an older brother, and it wasn't long before he began buying miniature books every time he saw them.

He'd pull up with the American convoy and Farah and her brothers would come running, with eager smiles and arms full of tiny books.

"Where are your books today?" Mohammed leaned out the window. "Let me see them."

She proudly held up a stack of books and squinted her smile into the sun. "Here they are!"

"How much?"

"Fifty cents apiece. Ten dollars for the stack. Or you can pay in dinars."

"I'll take all of them." He reached out and handed her a fifty-dollar bill. "Now take care of yourself and your brothers! I'll see you next time!"

"Bye!" She giggled shyly and waved as he pulled away.

It was the same every time, about once a month, for several years. Mohammed was constantly finding himself loaded with stacks of miniature prayer books and tiny Qurans. Some of them he distributed to people around him; some he returned to Farah so she could sell them twice.

Then one day, she wasn't there. It struck Mohammed as odd that she wasn't in her usual place, but he decided to let it go. When the next round through the neighborhood came and went and there was still no sign of Farah, he started to worry. She was like his little sister; if something was wrong, who did she have to look out for her? Mohammed grabbed his gun, got in his car, and headed out by himself to the most dangerous neighborhood in Baghdad, trying to still a disquieting feeling that something was wrong.

He wondered about the stepfather, who had made the children beg after their father had died. Perhaps there had been a conflict there. He hoped against hope that he would find her and that all would be well.

He found her at last, in a corner, and he stopped the car at the side of the intersection and got out.

"Farah!"

She turned and smiled wanly. Mohammed's relief faded as he saw the bruises that covered her face.

"Farah, what happened? Who did this to you?"

She shook her head and said nothing.

"What's going on, Farah? Tell me!"

"Nothing. Nothing's wrong, Saint. You should leave."

"I'm not leaving until you tell me who did this to you."

She remained stubbornly silent, but her seven-year-old brother appeared like a ghost by her side.

"Those policemen beat her up." He was so small, so determined.

"What police? Where?" Anger was building in Mohammed's chest.

"It's nothing!" Farah cried out, "You need to go!" She tried to softly push him away and shield him from what she knew was coming. She looked up to Mohammed, loved him like an older brother, and she couldn't bear the thought of what she feared they would do to him.

"They're over there," her little brother pointed to several Iraqi policemen sitting in a nearby vehicle. "Every time you give her money, they come and take it."

"*What?*" Mohammed was desperately bottling his fury, trying to keep his voice calm as he addressed the children. "How long has this been going on?"

"For ages. Almost since you started giving her money."

"And why is her face bruised today?"

The boy looked down. The girl's blue eyes filled with tears and she hugged her clothes tighter around herself despite the heat. She mumbled something that Mohammed could scarcely hear.

They had tried to rape her.

The fury that he'd been trying to keep down exploded from his chest and he stormed back to his car to grab his gun. He shouted a semi-coherent message to the commander of his unit through the radio and leapt out of the car.

The three policemen, sitting languidly in their SUV, recognized Mohammed and got out of their car to face him before he'd even reached them. The first put a hand on his gun meaningfully and sauntered smugly up to Mohammed. "What do *you* want?"

Without replying, Mohammed felt two hundred pounds of rage uncoil into his gun as he slammed it into the side of the police officer's head. The policeman dropped to the ground as Mohammed turned and pointed his gun at the second.

"Today, I am going to burn you alive."

The two remaining men suddenly looked startled... and afraid. Whatever they had expected, it was not this. They pulled out their guns and the three soon formed a stand-off in the middle of the street.

"How the *fuck* could you do this? She's just a little girl!"

"And *you're* the dirty son-of-a-bitch who betrayed his country!"

"Fuck you! You're supposed to be *protecting* these streets! You will never, *ever*, touch her again! If you even get *close* to her, I'll kill you!" He felt no fear. He felt nothing but anger and disgust.

They continued their shouting match, each side holding its ground. He, outnumbered but furious, and they, armed but uneasy in front of this enraged giant. There was so much adrenaline pumping through Mohammed's veins that he barely noticed when his unit arrived.

"Saint! SAINT!" It was Sergeant Major Johnson. "What the hell is going on?"

"Sir, do you see that little girl over there with the bruises on her face?" As Mohammed explained the situation, the American went from shock to fury. The Sergeant Major was a father and a grandfather. He had also met these children on many occasions, and he, too, loved them.

His face hardened.

"Give 'em hell, Saint."

With an entire armed unit standing behind their Iraqi translator, the policemen no longer had numbers or conviction on their side, and Mohammed unleashed his rage upon them until they were covered with bruises and their faces ran with blood.

"How the *fuck* could you even think about it?" He grabbed one policeman by the collar. "She's just a child! *A little girl!* How old is *your* daughter?"

"It wasn't me!" the man gasped, "It was him! *He* tried to rape her!"

One by one, each man indicated the other. And so he beat them all.

From then on, Mohammed pushed his convoy to drive through that intersection constantly, whether they were in the neighborhood or not. Even the Americans became concerned about the young Iraqi girl, and they began to check on her of their own accord.

She cried every time she saw Mohammed, "They tell me they'll kill me if I don't give them the money, Saint!" But she could not sell him books anymore, and he could not give her money, knowing where it was going.

He wished he could place her and her brothers at his parents' house where he knew they would be safe and taken care of. But what could he do? He gave her only a few dollars at a time, and hoped that she would spend it quickly.

Then one day, Farah disappeared entirely. Mohammed went out by himself many times to look for her, but she was gone. He spotted her younger brothers once and called out to them, but as soon as they recognized him, they ran away.

And so there was nothing he could do but pray, that a young girl had found safety in a dangerous world.

STDs

It was a busy evening in Whitmore Clinic, and Kadhim—called in to interpret—took one look at at the chubby, middle-aged Iraqi patient and immediately suspected an STD. It wasn't a difficult diagnosis. The man was grabbing his crotch and scratching ferociously.

"Good evening. I'm 'Doc'—the interpreter. What brings you to the clinic tonight?"

The man released himself and pulled out his badge. "I was wondering if I could get treated here today. I work with the Americans."

Kadhim glanced at the badge. Each individual's badge had codes indicating certain privileges. Kadhim's, for example, held a code indicating that he had the right to be treated in any American clinic. Mohammed's badge had even more privileges. The patient, a contract driver who transported goods for the U.S. Forces, had very few privileges at all.

"I'll ask them for you," Kadhim replied doubtfully, "but it doesn't look like they will treat you here."

"Well, do what you can."

"I'll do my best, but ultimately it's up to the floor manager. She's the one who makes the final decision on who can be seen in the clinic, and she's on break right now. I'll ask her as soon as she gets back."

"Thanks." The man grimaced slightly and grabbed his crotch again.

The gate to Camp Liberty closed every evening at six o'clock. Kadhim was certain that the driver's badge didn't include authorization to stay overnight on base. He needed to be out of the camp by six, or he could face fatal consequences.

Kadhim glanced at the clock.

It was 5:02.

And the floor manager was nowhere to be found.

Officially, sexual relations between single soldiers were prohibited in the military, as were relationships between soldiers and "local nationals." But this did not prevent the clinics from seeing more than their fair share of STDs. There were some soldiers who returned to the clinic nearly on a weekly basis for one test or another—just to be safe—and this was when the medical staff practiced *their* version of "Don't Ask, Don't Tell." Testing and treatment for STDs was provided without ever inquiring as to the complaint's origin, and free condoms were readily available. The military could prohibit sex all it wanted, but its leaders knew that nothing could check the hormones of thousands of twenty-somethings thrown together in a foreign country.

Kadhim's first experience with American girls on the base had been a bit of a culture shock. He was shocked when they farted shamelessly in front of him, flirted openly with him, and brought up personal topics that women he knew would never have *dreamed* of discussing in front of a man. Life on the base was fairly promiscuous, with both men and women seeking out ways to relieve boredom, stress, and anxiety. Even Kadhim had once indulged in a wild night with a female soldier in the sand dunes of a particularly dull mission. He wondered if all American girls were like this—he had heard they weren't—or if it was just the effects of war, Iraq, or military life. But the openness and promiscuity of the American girls did not shock him nearly as much as Iraqi girl type number two.

The Iraqi patient was well aware of the clock slowly ticking down the minutes until the gate's closing, and every few minutes he checked back with Kadhim.

"Has she come yet? Please, check with her as soon as you can!"

"I'm sorry, I think she went to get dinner. She's not back yet."

Several more minutes passed.

"Please, I'm begging you. Ask her now. The gate's are about to close!"

"I'm doing what I can, but she's not here!"

It was 5:21. The only people who left Camp Liberty after the gates were closed were Americans or those who worked with them. Surrounded by desert and with a long drive back to Baghdad, unarmed stragglers would be at the mercy of anyone who waited outside the gate. And the *allasa* terrorists would be waiting and ready for them when they came.

Nearly twenty minutes had gone by when the floor manager finally returned to the clinic, but she immediately took off to get coffee and run other errands. Kadhim kept checking her office, only to find it empty. He explained the predicament to a commander, who paged the young woman.

She was busy, she said. She'd come as soon as she could.

At last she appeared at the exam room and entered, only to exit a few minutes later. The time was 5:43.

She looked annoyed as she approached Kadhim.

"Doc, what's up with that guy? He keeps harassing me!"

"What do you mean?"

"He keeps grabbing himself!"

Kadhim laughed. "I think it's a medical condition."

She looked unconvinced. She was a young woman, appearing no more than nineteen or twenty years old. She was not part of the medical staff and had never worked in a clinic before. She shook her head. "No, we won't treat him here. His badge doesn't include clinic privileges, and it's against policy. Go tell him that he'll have to seek treatment elsewhere."

Kadhim had seen her approve the treatment of many Iraqis without clinic privileges, and he wasn't ready to give up that easily just because she had mistaken his symptoms for harassment.

"Even if he does seek treatment elsewhere, he'll have to go to Baghdad, and the gate closes in ten minutes!"

"That's not our problem. You know the rules."

"Fine. Then where is he going to stay if he spends the night on base?"

"Why would he spend the night on base?"

"Because the gate is closing in ten minutes!"

"Well, why didn't you tell him that earlier?"

"He *knows* what time the gate closes. He stayed because he was hoping for treatment. If we put him out after the gate closes, he could die!"

The girl sighed. "Look, it's not my problem, but I'll go with you to talk to the captain."

The time was 5:51.

Amongst the Iraqi community at large, Iraqi women who

358

contracted or became interpreters with the Coalition Forces instantly earned a bad reputation for presumed shameless behavior and promiscuity. The truth was, however, that Kadhim had found that there were two types of Iraqi girls on the base.

The first were those who continued to live out the values on which they'd been raised, the type of girls who typified Iraq. They were modest, conservative, and insistent upon being married before starting any type of sexual relationship. In order to protect their reputations, they conducted themselves respectfully, and most importantly, they stayed far away from Iraqi girl type number two.

Iraqi girl type two was like a caged animal who had suddenly been released into the wild. With her newly given freedom from the restrictions of home and the watchful eyes of her family members, she slept her way to the extreme end of the spectrum and then went beyond it. The Americans girls had known a measure of freedom from societal pressures, and though some went wild, they set their own boundaries. But for some of the Iraqi girls who lived and interpreted on the base, it was as if they had grown drunk on the freedom and couldn't hold their liquor. They did and said as they pleased, without shame and without regard for the social mores on which they'd been raised. As far as they were concerned, they weren't in Iraq anymore.

Kadhim felt the seconds ticking down to a man's death as he ran to speak to the captain. He knew what would happen after the clock struck six.

"Sir, it is well-known that anyone who leaves the gate after six o'clock works with the Americans. There are terrorists, insurgents, *waiting* out there for him to walk out. They'll kidnap, torture, and kill him if we put him out there now!"

"Doc, you know we appreciate your opinion and your cultural knowledge," the captain replied with a Texas drawl, "but you know the rules. He has to go."

"It's not about appreciating my opinion, sir. What I'm trying to tell you is that if you send him out there, you're sending him to his death!"

"That's not our problem. Rules are rules."

Kadhim was growing increasingly frustrated. The floor manager and captain were barely out of high school. How could they truly appreciate the value of a human life?

"How is this not your problem? That man over there works with you guys to bring supplies for you and your team! He's risking his *life* to bring you those supplies! He stayed late today hoping for a medical exam. He didn't get examined or treated, *and* he gets killed in the same night?"

"Hold on," the captain sighed. "Let me talk to the sergeant."

The sergeant was nowhere to be found. They looked everywhere, and finally discovered that he was in a meeting and wouldn't be out for at least half an hour. The time was 5:59.

Kadhim had awoken that morning before six o'clock and thrown on pajama pants, a t-shirt, and a ball cap to catch the bus to the dining facilities for breakfast. It was early enough that when he awoke, nature was still making its inconvenient visit to his groin, and he didn't have time to wait for the erection to fade before catching the bus. Whatever. It was a natural part of life and would be gone by the time he got on the bus. Besides, once he'd pulled on his pants he was convinced that it was barely visible.

He stepped outside and immediately ran into "Rosa," who was an Iraqi interpreter and one of Mohammed's previous hookups.

"Hey, Doc!"

"Morning, Rosa. How is everything?"

"I'm fine. How's your brother?"

"He's good." It was always best not to go into too much detail where Mohammed was concerned.

Rosa eyed Kadhim for a moment, then said with a naughty grin, "What's this?" She reached down and grabbed him right between the legs, cupping him tightly in her hand. Kadhim was too shocked to be angry, and had no idea how to respond. He burst into laughter and quickly stepped away.

"Are you serious, Rosa? Aren't you ashamed to do something like that?"

"No," she smirked. "Why should I be?"

That was a prime example of Iraqi girl type number two.

The captain returned to Kadhim, looking frightened.

"Doc, I'm sorry, but I can't let him stay. You know the rules. We're going to have to put him out." He was a by-the-book kind of kid, and sticking his neck out—even to save a man's life—was not something he was willing to do. Kadhim was given the thankless task of informing the Iraqi driver.

"Brother," he said apologetically, "we're going to have to escort you to the gate."

In his shock, the driver let go of his penis. *"What?"*

"You have to leave the base."

"Are you serious?"

"Unfortunately, they won't let you stay here."

"Do you want to kill me?" The driver's voice was gradually rising in pitch.

"What does this have to do with me? I've been pleading with them on your behalf for the past hour!"

"You're an *allas*!"

"I swear on the Quran, I'm not an *allas!*"

"You're an *allas* and you're going to chew me up out there! You've set it up with your people on the outside!" The man's eyes were wide with fright, he was starting to pant, and his voice was barely more than a squeak. "Please, *please* don't kill me!"

"Look, I swear to God I'm not an *allas*! Would you stop?"

It was as if the man couldn't hear him. His eyes grew watery and his face red. "I'm begging you, let me go. Don't kill me. I'll give you whatever money I have."

"Stop! I'm not—!"

"Don't chew me up! Please don't chew me up!"

"I'm not even Sunni! How could I be a chewer? I'm Shiite."

"Then you're a trapper, a *sakkak*, and you're going to trap me! *Please*, may God keep your family safe, don't kill me."

"Look, the officer can come right now and tell you that this was *their* decision, not mine! I didn't want you thrown out. I tried to get them to treat you and keep you here overnight, and they refused!"

It looked as though the man was about to cry, so Kadhim tried a different tactic. "Look, my brother and I both work with the Americans. If I didn't fear for their lives, I'd have my own parents come pick you up and give you a ride safely to Baghdad."

The driver shook his head vehemently. In his mind, he saw the interpreter's parents coming to pick him up in an Opel with machetes and machine guns.

"Well, I'm sorry to tell you this, but one way or another, you're going to have to leave the base."

"No. I won't go. I'm staying right here." The man crossed his arms and tried to root himself more firmly in his chair. "I don't want to die."

It was 6:11. The driver's death bells had already tolled.

Kadhim returned to the captain. "He's refusing to leave."

"Doc, we have to take him out!"

"Please, go tell him directly. He thinks that I'm trying to get him to the gate to kill him! He won't listen to me."

"I'll go with you and talk to him."

The driver's desperation only intensified as he spoke with the captain. Every few seconds he stopped the captain, begging for his life.

"Please let me stay... I'll sleep on the floor... Over there in the corner... I'll be so quiet, you won't even notice me... I'll leave as soon as the gates open in the morning... Please, I'm happy to sleep on the floor, I just don't want to die..."

The captain could have approved it. There were others in his position with stronger leadership skills who had made such decisions before and had saved lives. But this captain didn't have the confidence to be responsible for such an act, and so all the boy could do was repeat himself over and over to the pleading, middle-aged man.

"I'm sorry, but we have to escort you to the gate."

Kadhim's heart broke for the man, who wanted nothing more than treatment for a burning penis, and would now be escorted to a certain death. He turned to him.

"Listen, there's only one solution. You need to call your family and ask them to come pick you up from the gate, or you know and I know that you're going to be killed out there."

"No, no. It's better that I die by myself than have my family die to save me."

"It's the only way. I promise we won't put you out there until your family calls and they are ready to pick you up."

The man shook his head stubbornly, "I don't have any family."

He didn't want to give Kadhim any indication that he had any relatives, fearing that Kadhim would sell their information to the *allasa* as well.

"There's no need to lie to me. Call your brothers or your relatives and have them come pick you up! And to show you my sincerity, here—" Kadhim handed the man his cell phone "—use my phone. My information is still saved with the telephone company. If you run into a problem tonight, your family can go to Asiacell and do an investigation starting with my information."

At last, the man reached out timidly for Kadhim's phone and called his family.

The captain looked at Kadhim in astonishment. "What's he doing? He can't make a phone call!"

"He's calling his family."

"How could you let him speak? *You* have to speak to them. He's not allowed to make calls from the base!"

"I can interpret everything he says for you."

"It doesn't matter. You need to talk."

Kadhim took the phone and put it to his ear. "*Allo?*"

"Who is this?" The voice was suspicious.

"I'm Doc. I'm a medical interpreter for the U.S. Forces. Your brother Yasir is here with us at Camp Liberty near the airport."

"I don't know him." The voice was flat.

Kadhim knew that the brother was trying to protect himself, and he couldn't blame him.

"Here, say hi to him." As the captain glared, he held the phone up to the patient for him to greet his brother, proof that he was still alive. Then Kadhim returned the phone to his own ear.

"Have you kidnapped him?" The brother's voice was full of fear.

"No, we didn't kidnap him! Did you hear anything I said? Your brother is here with the U.S. Forces, and he was seeking treatment in one of the clinics. The gates are closed and he has to leave. We could kick him out, but I didn't want him to be killed. But if you don't want to come…"

"No, wait! I'm coming! Give me a couple hours to gather some men, cars, and weapons, and we'll meet him at the gate. We'll call you when we're outside and ready to pick him up!"

Kadhim hung up the phone. "*Now* do you believe that I'm not an *allas?*"

The man grabbed his hand and shook it. "I apologize, but you know how it is. These days, under these conditions…"

His voice trailed off as they both thought of the explosion of kidnappings, murders, beheadings, and deadly bombings that had rocked the country since the bombing of Al Askari mosque, making Iraq the number one most dangerous place in the world.

Then his face went screwy and he grabbed at his crotch and rubbed vigorously.

It was past eleven o'clock that night when the Iraqi driver was at last escorted to the gates of Camp Liberty. He was met by a convoy of two cars and six heavily armed relatives, enough to discourage even the most tenacious of *allasa*.

The tenacious STD, however, remained undefeated.

50 MORTARS & A CLOUD OF WHITE PHOSPHORUS

It was hot in the back of the Bradley, especially with all of their gear on, and they had been patrolling the area for hours. They were a group of six soldiers and Mohammed, strapped into uncomfortable, no-nonsense seats in the belly of the armored tank. In the hull, their driver navigated the vehicle through four periscopes, a gunner manned the turret, and Major Matthews sat up top, commanding the vehicle from the hatch.

They, in conjunction with several other combat units, had been called upon to patrol some of the most dangerous Sunni areas in Iraq, strongholds of Al Qaeda such as Al Ghazaliya, Abu Ghraib, and Hai Al Jihad. It was what they called a deadly mission, sweeping the area for IEDs and mines until they exploded so they could report on insurgent activity.

They always took the Bradley for such missions, an enormous 25-ton armored tank, which cost on average over three million dollars, because the humvees were easily burned and destroyed. The Bradley was not immune to IEDs and RPG attacks, which would eventually lead to the transition to the bigger and better MRAP, but it nevertheless saved many lives on many occasions, and it would save their lives today.

The crews of three Bradleys were cruising the marketplace of Aamriyya when they reached a pile of trash on the ground and hesitated. As a rule, the Bradleys were driven only on clean streets, because it was too easy to hide explosives beneath the garbage. But on that particular day, a car appeared on the other side of the pile, fired shots at them, and took off.

Mohammed's unit was in the first Bradley, and although it couldn't go faster than 40 mph, they decided to chase the car that had shot at them from only thirty meters away. Plastic and glass crunched beneath them as the Bradley climbed over the pile of trash, and suddenly there was a loud explosion.

Beneath their feet, a deep crack suddenly divided their armored vehicle into two sides and within seconds, a stifling gas began to waft up through it. Mohammed and the soldiers felt their eyes water and lungs burn as they began to suffocate inside the belly of the beast.

Kadhim had met all kinds of people on the base. He met soldiers who were barely more than kids, doctors with years of experience, brave commanders and strong leaders whom he greatly respected. And he met others who seemed to understand nothing of the world, who were callous to their surroundings and the people and culture of Iraq, who viewed even the interpreters with whom they worked as little better than animals.

Despite the variations, Kadhim sometimes wondered: Could these men and women from so far away really understand Iraq in all its complexities and nuances? For as much as they trained and as self-assured as they were, was there any way they could truly be prepared for all that Iraq could do to them? For the ways in which this country would change their lives forever?

Kadhim was playing Xbox in his room when the mortar siren sounded...

Eyes burning and gasping for breath, Mohammed grabbed his black and white checkered *keffiyeh*, soaked it in water, and wrapped it around his face to filter the toxic gas from his lungs.

Above him, Major Matthews was shouting, "We just got hit! Everybody stay calm!"

The soldiers had no filter. They turned red, then blue as they choked on the gas. Their eyes streamed with tears. They had run over a mortar designed to split the armored vehicle, and inside the mortar had been packed deadly white phosphorus. Highly flammable, particularly when exposed to air, flecks of white phosphorus could burn through metal, and could be fatal if it landed on the skin, where it would continue to burn deep into the body until absorbed in the blood stream. Even inhaled, white phosphorus could cause illness or death.

One of the soldiers began to cry, "Open the gate! We're choking! We need air!"

With a crack running the length of her belly, the Bradley could no longer move, but they also couldn't exit the vehicle until they had assessed and nullified the dangers around them. Opening the hatch to a powerful gust of air might ignite the white phosphorus, but in the heat of the moment and with the soldiers choking and gasping around him, Mohammed did the only thing he could think of.

He opened the emergency door and took a step out.

"What the hell are you doing?" Matthews screamed.

"We're dying inside! We need out!" Mohammed shouted back. Then, one foot outside the Bradley and one foot in, he took a look beneath him. The sight took his breath away.

Oh fuck.

Behind him, the soldiers crowded and pushed. "Let us out! Let us out!"

"No! Get back! Major Matthews, look outside!"

Matthews opened the hatch and took a look around.

*"Shit! **SHIT!** Everybody stay inside!"*

Fifty or more undetonated mortars covered the ground around them. And one of them was right beneath Mohammed's foot.

Mortar sirens were a part of everyday life on the base. For every mortar shower, despite the anti-ballistic missile systems that shot down mortars while in the air, there were always a few mortars that landed. When the sirens sounded, everyone made a mad dash to the closest bunker.

Sometimes, Kadhim went with them. When he grew tired of that, he just turned up the sound on his Xbox and stayed in his trailer.

But on that particular day, he was sick of it. To hell with it all. He had already lost everything he'd ever worked for the day he left the hospital. His memories from his intern year were stored safely away where they could not reach him and his medical books were covered with a thick layer of dust. What was the point of studying when he could die any day? The chances of a mortar making it past the anti-ballistic missile systems and landing on him were one in a million. So if he was going to be the unlucky bastard who got hit by lightning, let it happen. Kadhim stepped outside, and amidst the sound of the sirens, he lit a cigarette and watched this skies as if for rain.

"Doc! Doc, get in the bunker! What are you doing?"

The shout came from a bunker next to him, where the soldiers were looking up at him in astonishment.

"It's too crowded. I'm staying out here." The bunker was packed with anxious soldiers, and Kadhim didn't relish the idea of giving up his cigarette and joining them. He recognized one of the soldiers as a young man who had only recently arrived in Iraq on his first tour. He spent all his time in the gym, and although this was a common pastime for many soldiers and interpreters in their empty hours, this soldier in particular seemed to think a lot of himself.

He walked with a tall swagger and spoke with a cocky confidence that suggested that he would be going into hand-to-hand combat with the terrorists, and that he would kick their asses when he did. He wasn't afraid of those insurgents; he was an American bad-ass, God damn it.

It made Kadhim laugh. This kid had no idea what he was in for. How many had arrived in Iraq with mistaken ideas of grandeur and immortality, only to find that war didn't work that way? The Iraqis had experienced one war after another for decades. After everything Kadhim had witnessed, starting at the age of ten, life on the base was a vacation. These kids knew nothing.

The American bad-ass had been one of the first to arrive in the bunker when the siren sounded, and he stood with them now, packed like sardines.

They heard and felt the impact as several of the mortars landed inside the base, and Kadhim glanced in the bunker.

The American bad-ass had fallen to his knees.

The siren continued, an ear splitting noise that permeated the air. "BEEP! BEEP! BEEP! INCOMING. INCOMING."

They heard the whistles of a new round of mortar showers flying overhead.

Inside the bunker, the American bad-ass had now wrapped his arms around his knees and nestled his head in between them, shaking visibly.

"Doc, what the hell are you doing out there? Get in here. We'll make room!"

Kadhim shook his head and continued to enjoy his cigarette. They felt the scattered impact of several more mortars landing around them.

"BEEP! INCOMING!"

The American bad-ass was now curled up on his side in the fetal position, tears running down his cheeks, "I don't want to die! I don't want to die!"

Then, as abruptly as it had begun, the siren stopped. The American bad-ass was still curled in a prone ball on the floor while a commander tried to calm him. "Look, it's over. It's all over. You're fine."

"I want to go home! I don't want to die!"

Welcome to Iraq, Kadhim thought. He finished his cigarette, threw it to the ground, and returned to his Xbox.

What the hell was he supposed to do? Mohammed shut the emergency door as quickly as he could, trying to protect the soldiers inside. But him? He was stuck outside, his foot on a mortar waiting to explode.

He was living a nightmare. Nowhere to go, no way to escape. He was a cat with nine lives and he had used them all up.

Inside the Bradley, Major Matthews was calling the Explosive Ordnance Disposal (EOD) team, urging them to come immediately to deactivate the mortars. The other two Bradleys repositioned themselves in an attempt to provide protection to their disabled compatriot. But Mohammed couldn't wait that long, and meanwhile, the soldiers were suffocating on the noxious gas inside.

Fuck it.

Mohammed steadied his grip on his weapons, put his eye on the market wall some twenty yards away, and made a mad dash for it, feeling the mortars roll under his feet as he ran on top of them.

He couldn't believe it when he reached the wall still alive. Somehow, by dumb luck or the grace of God, he had made it. Matthews' voice came over the radio. "Saint, stay over there."

"Trust me, I'm not moving."

The EOD team arrived, and with the help of a special robot they disabled the mortars and extracted the soldiers. Mohammed and the rest of the unit returned to the BIAPby helicopter, where they received emergency treatment at the hospital.

Many of the soldiers had suffered badly, requiring breathing support and further treatment for burnt lungs and blood poisoning. But Mohammed, despite his mad dash across a field of mortars, was unharmed.

The cat with nine lives had survived to live another day.

YUM YUM & THE CLUSTERFUCK

"Whoa! What happened to your *face*?" An enormous black puff adorned each of Yum Yum's eyes and her nose looked swollen.

"I got a nose job. Don't you like it?"

"*What?*" Mohammed burst into laughter. "Why did you do that?"

"I did it for you! You always make fun of my nose!"

"Well that doesn't mean you should go and change it!" Her look of disappointment did nothing to quell his amusement. "You look terrible!"

"Well, of course I look bad *now*," she huffed. "I'm still recovering!"

"You could have achieved the same effect by closing your eyes and walking into a pole."

"Very funny."

It *was* funny. She just couldn't see that with her eyes so swollen.

◇ ◇ ◇

"Ali called me in a frenzy the other day." Kadhim was playing a video game with Mohammed and Georgie during one of his visits to the IZ when he decided to bring up the topic.

"Oh yeah? What's wrong?"

"He was freaking out. He said that you were planning to marry an interpreter named Yummy or something like that."

Mohammed let out a squeal of laughter. "Yum Yum?"

"Ali's completely against it; *you* know the reputation of the female interpreters. The whole family's against it actually." Kadhim chuckled. "He said Mama's been saying extra prayers that you don't marry her. You're not really considering it, are you?"

"Well, she is one hell of a cook." Mohammed grinned. "But no, that's pretty unlikely now."

"What do you mean?"

Georgie raised his eyebrows and smirked as he gazed at the screen. He knew what was coming.

"Yum Yum's been hearing rumors lately about me with other girls, and she knows that I go to the pool sometimes to pick up chicks, so she started accusing me of cheating on her. One evening she started going through my stuff and came across five or six of my SIM cards."

"Do you really need so many?"

"It's Juju, man! I gave her the phone number to one card, and if I don't answer that, she tracks down my other numbers. I have to keep buying new ones!"

Georgie and Kadhim hooted with laughter.

"Anyway, Yum Yum found the SIM cards and put one in, and you'll never believe who happened to call."

"Nina?"

"Worse. Nina's *sister*."

"You're kidding."

"I swear to God."

"Why would her sister be calling you?"

Mohammed just laughed in response. Kadhim raised his eyebrows.

"You're hooking up with Nina's *sister*?"

"Both of her sisters, actually. So Yum Yum answered, and the sister was like, 'Who is this?' And Yum Yum said, 'I'm Saint's wife. Who is *this*?' So the sister says, 'What do you mean, Saint's wife? He was just with me last night, that prick!'

"Ever since then, Yum Yum and I have been fighting constantly. So no, I don't think you have to worry about us getting married."

"I *told* you that you needed to watch out, being with all these women," Georgie inserted. "Now you're finally paying your dues."

"If I know anything about Mohammed," Kadhim replied, "it'll get a whole lot worse before it gets better."

◇ ◇ ◇

The first clue that something had gone wrong was the series of sobbing, screaming messages from Yum Yum and Juju that bombarded Mohammed as he returned to the base one morning after a night mission. The second was the smell that greeted him upon opening the door to his suite.

Holy shit.

There was only one person crazy enough to pull off a stunt like this.

371

"What the fuck happened in here?" The soldiers' jaws dropped as they surveyed the damage, having answered Mohammed's urgent call for help.

Yum Yum had happened. She had set his room on fire, destroying everything from his bed, Xbox, and clothes, to his laptop and important documents.

"Do you want her fired?"

"No, leave her be." *It was partially his fault anyway.*

The soldiers helped clean, but there was little they could do. Just as they left, another friend popped his head in. "The Hulk," a fellow interpreter, was a massive body builder whose reliance on steroids had caused most of his neck to disappear into his shoulders. "Dude, that chick is *crazy!* You wouldn't believe what she did!"

"I know, I'm looking at it right now."

"No, I meant your car!"

"My *car?*" Mohammed ran outside, and his breath caught in his throat. For a moment, he actually considered crying. The tires and body of his baby, his precious BMW, were speckled with holes like Swiss cheese.

"Dude! She *climbed over* the fence and actually *stole* a drill from the engineering department, then climbed back and started taking it out on your car!"

"Why didn't you stop her?"

"I *tried!* She put the drill through my hand!" The Hulk held up his bandaged palm. "I'm telling you, she's fucking *crazy!*"

"*MOHAMMED!*"

The two looked up to see Yum Yum approaching, her face red, her eyes ringed with dripping black circles, the drill still in her hand. All five feet of her looked positively terrifying.

The Hulk's eyes grew enormous, "Dude! I'm out of here!" The man named after an angry green giant turned and fled, and Mohammed was left to face his adversary alone.

"Yum Yum, you need to calm down!"

Instead, she raised her hand and slammed the drill with surprising force into the side of his face.

"YOU'VE BEEN *CHEATING* ON ME?" Her scream was so high that he could almost feel the terrorists who waited outside the gates perk up their ears.

"I met a girl at the checkpoint yesterday who says she's your girlfriend! Jumana or something like that. I *know* she's not the only one, you asshole!" She pushed open the door to his suite and stomped inside.

"You're *never* bringing girls back here again."

"I couldn't even if I wanted to."

"It's what you deserve." A smirk suddenly graced her lips. "And *you're* not going anywhere either. I have your passport."

"Keep it. I can get a new one in a day for a hundred bucks."

She looked suddenly defeated and broke into a fresh wave of sobs. "Mohammed, how could you *do* this to me? *I love you.* I wanted to marry you!"

"Yum Yum, I *told* you I wasn't ready for commitment. I'm sorry that I've hurt you, but... hey! What the hell are you *doing? Stop that!*"

She had walked over to his mirror and shattered it with a swing of her fist. Then, pressing hard, she drew a shard of glass across her belly, leaving a line that slowly started to trickle with blood.

"ENOUGH! Yum Yum, stop it! You're leaving NOW!" He grabbed her wrist and pulled the shard of glass from her hand, then marched her out of his trailer, kicking and screaming, until he found her captain.

"Sir, you need to get this woman away from me! She's hysterical! She's crazy! I don't care what you do with her, but keep her away!"

Yum Yum was fired the same day, but she didn't give up. She had already obtained a Special Immigrant Visa to the U.S. due to her work as an interpreter, and so she started to form a new plan. *If she couldn't have her Saint on this side of the ocean, then she would have him on the other.*

Mohammed, meanwhile, returned to his trailer and was accosted by the overwhelming smell of smoke. As he stared around at the rubble of his life, he finally had to face the fact that there was a slight chance he had brought this upon himself.

HONOR

Mohammed's first thought, when he saw the young woman wave at him, was that she was flirting. She stood at her doorstep, beckoning furtively from the semi-privacy of her half-shut door, wearing a long gown and a *hijab* over her hair. In fact, he would never have noticed her if it weren't for the fact that the patrol had been stalled by a flat tire.

Flat tires were not uncommon; their humvees had become increasingly weighed down by armor in response to insurgents' advancing technology. When the original humvees had proven weak in the face of terrorist explosives, the military began to send double-armored humvees. In response, terrorists had devised a bomb that blew straight upward with such force that it completely disintegrated one or two people in the back, while leaving the rest of the vehicle relatively untouched. America's latest answer was a vehicle with a V-shaped bottom that directed this fatal blast sideways. It was ugly, it was heavy, and its tires had to be replaced every two months, but it was necessary.

Mohammed had volunteered for this mission with a unit that was not his own, and as it was a patrol, he had chosen to wear civilian clothing rather than military fatigues and a bullet-proof vest. As he waited for the unit to fix their flat tire, the young Iraqi woman beckoned him with increasing urgency. She definitely wasn't flirting, he decided. Something was up.

After a quick word with the captain, Mohammed made his way to the modest home and greeted the woman politely.

"*Salaam alaykum.*"

"*Alaykum as-salaam.*" She spoke softly and was clearly very nervous. "I thought maybe if I talked to you, *they* wouldn't know that you were... you know... But please, *please* don't let the soldiers come over here. I'm just afraid... if they see me talking to the Americans..."

"Don't worry. I won't let them come over." A few of the soldiers looked questioningly at Mohammed from the humvee, and he waved them away.

"I just had to warn you..." She looked around quickly and her voice dropped even lower. "There were some people digging in that road just yesterday."

"Where?" They both knew what this meant.

An IED had been planted.

"Just in front of where your vehicle is stopped... no more than twenty yards away. Somehow, you got a flat tire right before you hit it. Please, warn the Americans. Don't let them continue down that road."

"I will warn them. Thank you."

He spoke with the captain, and the EOD team was called in to investigate. Sure enough, only meters away from the humvee, an active IED was found. *This* was why Iraqis were wary of freshly-paved roads. God only knew what evils lurked beneath. It felt safer to drive on roads full of potholes and blown-out portions, where the IEDs had already detonated.

As the EOD team safely removed the explosives, the captain and a few of the soldiers approached Mohammed.

"We're going to go over and thank the woman who warned us about the IED."

"No, no. Please don't do that. She specifically requested that none of you speak to her."

"But how could we not thank her, Saint? She saved our lives! The least we can do is go over there and express our gratitude!"

"Guys, don't do this. I understand that you want to thank her, but she already risked her life just to warn us. If you go over there, she could..." Two of the men were already walking to her house.

"Be killed," Mohammed finished.

It was too late. He watched as the soldiers approached her house, thanking her and handing her one of the simple gifts that they often carried with them. From behind the door, she gestured desperately at Mohammed to get them to go away, but what could he do? The damage had been done.

Within moments the soldiers returned to the humvee, and as the patrol continued, the young woman remained on Mohammed's mind. He had heard too many stories not to be frightened for her. He had even heard of children who accepted toys from an American patrol, only to have a group of armed thugs break into their house on a shooting spree the next day.

Millions of Iraqis had fled the country at a moment's notice for incidents like these, bringing only what they could stuff into bags and suitcases within a matter of hours. Depending on the neighborhood, their empty houses became terrorist dens and hide-outs for insurgent snipers. Sometimes even the soldiers would squat in an abandoned home when on a several-day mission.

And this woman had risked it all to save the lives of the strangers in her country.

The unit repeated the patrol the next day, and Mohammed went with them. Mohammed looked closely as they passed her house, hoping to catch a glimpse of the woman.

Instead, a black banner hung on the house, which read in Arabic, *"To Allah we belong, and to Him is our return (sura al-Baqara 155). Maya has returned to the mercy of God. A fatiha for this forgiven soul will be held on Thursday,"* followed by the place of her funeral.

Mohammed's heart sank. The young woman had not lasted twenty-four hours. She had sacrificed her life for this final act of honor.

Where there had once been a pit of darkness, a sliver of hope emerged. It was small, distant perhaps, but it was there. Kadhim's dream was alive again.

Like his brother, Kadhim had applied for the Special Immigrant Visa as soon as he became aware of the program in 2007. What had started as the expedited resettlement of only four Iraqis at the end of 2006 was gradually developing into a full-scale resettlement program for Iraqi nationals, although it would not be officially enacted until January of 2008. As more interpreters and contractors were killed for their association with the Americans, it became obvious that their immigration to the United States was the only thing that could ultimately save their lives and the lives of their immediate family members. But the process was slow, requiring letters of reference from American commanders, background checks, an interview, health screening, and other paperwork.

Kadhim saw it as a shot at the life he'd been dreaming of since medical school, a path to practicing medicine the way it should be: in peace, uncorrupted, and with the latest technology and advancements. The Ohio colonel, his friend from the clinic, had agreed to write a reference letter for him. But as the end of 2007 grew near, he began to wonder how long he would have to wait for the fruition of his dream.

"AT-*TEN*-TION!"

There was a scuffling of chairs as everyone in the Camp Liberty dining facility stood to the call to attention that announced the arrival of important persons. High-up colonels and even generals often dined in the DFAC across from Whitmore Clinic where Kadhim worked, due to its proximity to one of Saddam's old palaces, which had been repurposed for their use.

Seconds later, Kadhim and his friends returned to their lunch, not having caught a glimpse of whoever had just entered, and they were in the middle of conversation when the table suddenly fell silent.

"Is it okay if I sit here?"

They all jumped to their feet in respect.

They had been joined for lunch by the Commanding General of the Multi-National Force in Iraq, the four-star General David Petraeus.

He was polite, friendly, and down-to-earth, asking each of the soldiers in turn about themselves. When he turned to Kadhim, the young interpreter could barely believe it.

"What's your name?"

"Kadhim Al Baghdadi, sir."

"So you're of Iraqi descent?"

"Yes, sir."

"That's fascinating. I actually have some questions for you about local customs and practices, if you don't mind."

"Sure, ask me anything."

Impressed with Kadhim's in-depth knowledge of Iraqi politics and culture, Gen. Petraeus was soon asking him how he would recommend making a deal with the Iraqi Army, as they were having problems with loyalty from some of the Iraqi Army's constituents. When they had finished their discussion, Gen. Petraeus added, "So where are you from?"

"I'm from Iraq."

"No, I mean which state are you from?"

"I'm from Baghdad, sir."

"Wait, you mean you're a local national?" The general's eyes opened wide and he smiled in amazement. "With your English, I thought you were from the States!"

"No, sir. I'm a local asset. I've been interpreting at Whitmore clinic, and I am currently assisting this unit with a program for training Iraqi medics."

Gen. Petraeus turned and whispered something to the major next to him, and the major produced something that he in turn handed to Kadhim.

"I really appreciate your hard work and sacrifice, and everything that you're doing to help us out here."

Kadhim took the coin and stared at it for a moment in amazement. It was a bronze medal, which stated "For Excellence in Combat" and below an outline of Iraq it said "COMMANDING GENERAL" followed by four stars.

He felt his face go red in wonder and embarrassment. Surely *he* was not the one who deserved this. There was someone else who deserved this more than he, someone who risked his life everyday, who had worked with the American forces since the beginning and had saved the lives of American soldiers. As desperately as Kadhim wanted to leave Iraq, he would give up his ticket if it meant that he could save his brother. Maybe, *just maybe*, this coin would help speed up a visa application.

This would be the only chance he ever got, and he couldn't let it pass him by. With a laugh of embarrassment, he turned to the Commanding General of the Multi-National Force in Iraq.

"Thank you, sir. But is it okay to be greedy and ask for one for my brother?"

"What is your brother doing?"

"He's been working as an interpreter since 2003, sir. He goes on all the combat missions, volunteers for them actually. He goes by the nickname Saint, if you want to look him up. *He's* the one who truly deserves this."

Gen. Petraeus smiled and said to the major behind him, "Hand me another one."

After the general left, one of the soldiers, a friend of Kadhim's, jumped up and slapped Kadhim on the back with a hoot of laughter.

"I haven't even received a coin from a major, and here you are with *two* coins from General Petraeus himself?"

The table roared with laughter.

"What is the significance of this coin, exactly?" Kadhim asked.

"Well, it's not an official medal, but it's like playing cards for drinks at a bar," a soldier explained. "If I bring in a coin, someone has to buy me a beer. If they have a coin from a higher commanding officer, then I buy *them* a beer. And *you*, buddy, *you* have the Ace of Spades!"

JUJU & THE IMPROVISED ESCAPING DEVICE

Mohammed knew that things had gone too far when Juju appeared at his doorstep with a new nose.

"What have you *done?*"

"I got a nose job. I did it for you, *habibi!*" She looked at him pleadingly. "Don't you like it?"

"Are you serious?" *This is the second girl to get a nose job for me. How do I always end up with the crazy ones?* "First of all, Juju, you were beautiful before. I have no idea why you felt the need to change your nose. Secondly, we're not even together! I *broke up* with you, remember? Why would you have surgery for me?"

"Mohammed, sweetie, how can you say that we're broken up? It was just a little argument. If we were broken up, why do we keep hanging out together? Why do you still kiss me? Why do we still talk on the phone all the time? I *know* you love me, Mohammed."

And so it had gone. He had attempted to end the relationship on numerous occasions, and every time, Juju had refused to accept it. And as Kadhim pointed out, it didn't help that every time Mohammed drank too much, he would get out his cell phone and make some regrettable choices. In the soberness of morning, however, he had made it perfectly clear. They were *not* together, and she needed to accept that.

But Juju was a first class "clinger," and it would take drastic measures to get rid of her.

It was past eleven o'clock at night, and Mohammed's cell phone would not stop ringing. He had turned up the sound on his Xbox to drown it out, but annoyance was creeping up his spine and working its way into his jaw. *How the hell did she keep getting all his new numbers?*

He had leapt at the opportunity to move with a new unit to the BIAP, which was near the airport and out of the Green Zone. As with every new move, Mohammed liked to start fresh, cutting ties to old hook-ups to free himself up for a new wave of girls. Juju had somehow wheedled every phone number of his from friends and soldiers, and so with his move to the BIAP, Mohammed had once again scrapped his old

SIM cards and started clean. It was clear, however, that his freedom from her constant calling had been short-lived.

He knew that she would be angry that he had moved from the IZ without telling her, but he had a new strategy: if she wouldn't believe him when he told her outright that they were over, then perhaps she would give up if he simply stopped answering her calls.

For the past couple hours, however, the new strategy had proven unsuccessful. Call after unanswered call only led to a flurry of hurt and angry text messages, also ignored.

Mohammed was in the middle of a warring video game—Call of Duty—when the latest text message appeared.

"If you don't answer your phone, I'm going to kill myself right now."

He rolled his eyes. *For God's sake, Juju, get a hold of yourself!* With this girl, possessiveness and jealousy were like a sickness. Ironically, if it were up to her, death was probably the only thing that would separate them.

Still, with the last text message there was nothing he could do but answer the next call, and as he did, an idea formed. On a whim, he turned the volume to max, paused the game, and answered the phone in a whisper. "Hello?"

"SAINT! WHAT THE HELL! WHY HAVEN'T YOU BEEN ANSWERING MY PHONE CALLS? I SWEAR TO GOD—"

"Juju, I'm out in the middle of a night mission!" His voice dropped below a whisper. "I can't talk right now. I shouldn't have even picked up. If they see the light on my phone, it could give away our position. We're supposed to... oh **shit! Oh my God! GUYS! GUYS! WATCH OUT!"**

He pushed resume on the video game and the sound of gunfire exploded throughout the trailer. Ignoring the frantic shrieks emitted from its speaker, Mohammed threw his cell phone and began kicking it around the room, shouting anything that came to mind.

When he'd had enough, he shut off the phone, pulled out the SIM card, and threw it in the trash.

The next day, with a new SIM card and phone number, he called everyone he knew with a special set of instructions, starting with Georgie. Georgie was a frequent victim of Juju's incessant phone calls whenever Mohammed refused to answer, and it was a testament to how well he knew Mohammed that he fielded his friend's request without blinking.

"Listen, man, if you hear from Juju," Mohammed told him, "I'm dead."

A year passed.

Being dead was such a glorious relief that Mohammed wished he'd died sooner. When Juju approached them frantically, each of his friends sorrowfully informed her that her dear "Saint" had been killed in action. None played it up more than Georgie, who told her with tears in his eyes, "Poor Mohammed, taken from us so young. God rest his soul."

Life was blissfully Juju-free in the BIAP, far from the checkpoints of the IZ where she had tracked him down so often. If it weren't for one particular assignment, he could have remained happily deceased forever.

Mohammed was escorting several individuals through the Green Zone when he saw her from afar. He kept his head down and tried to move past without catching her attention, but it was too late.

Juju's eyes locked on him instantly, and she did a double take.

"*Mohammed?*"

Shit. Mohammed, as usual, was unmasked, but he did his best to look away and stroll nonchalantly through the checkpoint.

"*Mohammed!*"

"Excuse me?" He looked at her in confusion as though he had no idea who she was.

Her face grew red and before Mohammed had time to think of a better response, her palm met his cheek with the loudest and most painful slap he had ever felt.

"I THOUGHT YOU WERE *DEAD*! Do you even *know* how long I cried over you? I thought I had killed you!"

Her eyes welled up and tears began to spill over her cheeks, and for the first time in a year, Mohammed felt a twinge of guilt.

"How could you *do* this to me?"

"I'm sorry, Juju! But we really *were* caught in an ambush! I spent a long time recovering in the hospital after that, and by the time I got out, I figured a beautiful girl like you had moved on!"

"Oh my God, *habibi*," her voice choked through the sobs, "I'm so sorry! Are you *okay*? I just... I can't believe it... After all this time! Thank God, I have my Mohammed back!"

And just like that, his year of reprieve over. His one small consolation was that Juju never found out about his nearly successful Improvised Escaping Device. Before he could excuse himself, she was pronouncing the very words that he dreaded with every fiber of his being.

"You have to give me your number!"

THE FUNERAL

"I don't know what to do! Half of my face just *stopped working!*" Kadhim's uncle sounded panicked as he searched for a free consultation from his nephew. "I'm not in pain, but I look... *weird*. One half of my face is normal, but the other half sags. I can't even close my eye all the way, or scrunch up my nose on that side. They say I've been hit with Eastern wind."

"That's old Iraqi folklore," Kadhim laughed. "There's no strange wind coming from Iran that can paralyze half of the face. It's called Bells Palsy, and it's caused by temporary damage to a facial nerve. It's nothing to worry about."

"Well, how do I get rid of it? It's not *permanent*, is it?"

"No, it's not permanent. And if your eye really won't shut at night, you can tape it shut."

"You're kidding."

"Just give it time."

"A friend of mine told me that I should go to a sheikh to be cured."

Kadhim laughed, suddenly brought back to his days in the hospital where he was constantly trying to convince his patients not to resort to useless folk remedies. "And do you know how the sheikh 'heals' the paralysis?"

There was a pause, then hesitantly, "Something with a shoe...?"

"The sheikh takes a shoe and hits you in the face with it until you're 'cured.' "

"Allah works in mysterious ways."

"Listen to me, Uncle. The sheikh hits the *unaffected* side of the face until it too becomes paralyzed. That way at least both sides are symmetrical and can heal together. That's *if* he manages to paralyze it, which is not all the time. For God's sake, don't go to a sheikh. The nerve will heal on its own within a matter of weeks."

"Are you sure?"

"Yes, I'm sure. If necessary, go to a doctor and get some steroids. That *might* speed up the healing process. I'm sorry to cut this short, but I have a funeral to get to. Just promise me you won't go to a sheikh."

"Fine, fine, I won't go. But you be careful. The *allasa* are

382

targeting weddings, funerals, marches and everything in between these days."

"The deceased is Sunni, so hopefully they won't target this one, but I'll be careful."

Navigating Baghdad safely meant waiting for his brother Ali to round up a group of armed men so that he could drive Kadhim to the funeral with some measure of protection. They stopped at home briefly for Kadhim to enjoy a rare and valuable visit with his family, then Ali and the others dropped Kadhim off at the funeral, promising to return in two to three hours.

The Islamic funeral, or *fatiha* as it was called in Iraq, took place in a large open tent with chairs scattered around for the male guests, who talked, sipped coffee, smoked, and read the opening verse (or *fatiha*) of the Quran for the deceased. After a ritual cleansing and shrouding, the deceased himself had been buried a few days earlier, his body lowered into the ground without a casket, and his head facing Mecca. Cremation of the body was forbidden in Islam.

The deceased was the brother of one of Kadhim's old friends from medical school, so Kadhim was not surprised when he ran into another medical school friend.

"Kadhim! How are you?" Farouq greeted him with a smile and a kiss on each cheek.

"I'm good! How have you been? What have you been up to?"

"I'm working at Nu'man Hospital these days."

"Yeah? How is it?"

"It's awful, man. I've seen people get killed in the hospital, right in front of me. I heard that you're not at Baghdad Medical Complex anymore. What have you been up to?"

"Not much, just sitting at home, mostly. Sometimes I visit relatives in Hilla. I'm thinking about moving to Jordan to look for work there."

"Good luck, brother. I heard it's rough over there. By the way, strangest thing... I could have sworn I saw your brother Mohammed interpreting for the Americans the other day."

"Mohammed? No, it definitely wasn't him." Kadhim emitted a snort of nervous laughter.

"I swear to God, looked just like him."

"You must have been mistaken."

"I don't think so..."

"No, not my brother. Mohammed's not even around. He works with my uncle in Hilla. There's *no way* that the man you saw was him."

"If you say so." Farouq glanced around and lowered his voice. "You heard how this guy died, right?"

"No, I just came here to support Rasheed. Why?"

Farouq pulled Kadhim to the side, his eyes warily scanning the other guests, and whispered, "Rasheed's brother was an imam in one of the local Sunni mosques, and not the kind of mosque that you or I would ever visit."

Farouq, like Kadhim, was Shiite, and it was this knowledge that—even more than their long-standing friendship—helped the two to share a small bond of trust in that moment.

"Every day he'd get up there and rant that the Americans and Shiites are infidels and should be killed. He instigated so much violence that the Americans warned him to either shut up or risk detainment.

"Well, apparently he didn't give a damn. One day, the American and Iraqi forces were in the area and were attacked with IEDs and snipers and God knows what else. Turns out, Rasheed's brother and his gang were responsible. In the midst of it all, he and his guys hid in the mosque, and the Americans hunted them down. Gunfire broke out between the two sides and Rasheed's brother and his men were killed. Meanwhile, they searched the mosque and found all kinds of weapons: guns, IEDs, explosives, RPGs.... you name it, they found it. A true terrorist den."

Farouq's eyes narrowed as he looked suspiciously around the tent. "You hear the people here calling him a martyr? It's because he was a terrorist in the truest sense of the word."

"*Shit.*" Kadhim also spoke in a whisper now. *Screw Rasheed and his whole tribe. I need to get out of here **now.***

"I just came to support Rasheed," Farouq added.

"Me too, but to hell with it. Rasheed used to be a good friend, but ever since we got into that fight, we haven't been close."

"I remember."

"I did just get here five minutes ago, though. It would be bad form if I took off so soon. I'll say hi to Rasheed, read the *fatiha* a couple times and drink some coffee to be polite. It was good seeing you, Farouq."

"You too. Take care." The two shared a look of apprehension and went their separate ways.

Kadhim was stunned as he took a seat to read the *fatiha* for the deceased. What the hell was he even doing here? He still hadn't forgotten the day that he and Rasheed had gotten into a blowout argument in the medical school cafeteria. It was after the fall of the regime, in 2005, when Al Qaeda had infiltrated Iraq and begun to dismantle what remained of peace. One of their political conversations in the cafeteria had gotten out of hand when Kadhim had flown into a rage.

"*Fuck* Al Qaeda, *fuck* Osama bin Laden, and *fuck* the terrorists and anyone who supports them!"

Rasheed had stood up angrily. "Why are you talking about Sheikh Osama?"

"*Who?*"

"Sheikh Osama bin Laden! That's our leader, a fighter for our cause! He's leading the jihad against Zionism and American terrorism and occupation!"

"I don't give a damn for Osama bin Laden!"

"How can you not care? I'm a Sunni, and I still respect your ayatollahs, like Sistani and the others. You should respect the leaders that *we* follow!"

"And you follow *this* guy?"

"And what if I do?"

"Osama bin Laden is a vile, sick son of a bitch. Every *day* terrorists are blowing themselves up in Shiite neighborhoods because of him! You *support* this?"

"I don't support that part necessarily, but I'm telling you that I respect the man!"

"Then to hell with you and to hell with him!"

It had been a long time before they spoke to one another after that, and although they did eventually reconcile, the friendship was never the same. No more hanging out after class, no more visiting one another's homes. Their relationship was no more than an exchange of "hello's".

There was something off-putting in the murmur of conversation around him that jerked Kadhim out of his reverie. He looked around and felt a growing sense of horror as the pieces of the puzzle started to fall into place.

To his left sat a bearded man in plain clothes who spoke with the distinct accent of the Shiite slums of Sadr City, breeding grounds for the Mahdi Army. He was conversing with the man sitting across from Kadhim, who sported an even longer beard, a short dishdasha, and the thick accent of someone from the Sunni region of Anbar, a stronghold of Al Qaeda. This, in and of itself, was a rare enough occurrence that it instantly put Kadhim on guard. But it was the conversation between the two that caused every hair on his body to stand on end.

As he listened to them praise the deceased and his martyrdom for the jihad, then move on to the topic of acquiring weapons and explosives, it became clear to Kadhim just who these men were.

The man on his left was a member of the Mahdi Army.

And the man across from him was an Al Qaeda-affiliated terrorist.

And poor Kadhim, sitting between the two, was their only mutual sworn enemy, the infidel spawn of infidels, who had betrayed his people to become an agent for the Zionist enemy, the American invader.

A trickle of fear rushed down his throat, and immediately Kadhim's heart began pounding so loudly that he worried they might hear it.

*Don't jump up. Don't make any sudden actions. And **don't** draw attention to yourself. If they knew who you were, they'd be fighting over who got to torture and kill you first.*

He kept his head down, stared unseeingly into a copy of the Quran, and willed himself into invisibility. *What were these two even doing talking to one another? Didn't they know that they were on opposite sides?*

Their words rang, amplified, in his ears.

"Just tell me what you need," the Mahdi Army member was saying. "RPGs? Explosives?"

"RPGs and mortars, mostly." The terrorist batted a fly away from his face.

"How many? Twenty RPGs? More? And how many mortars? Fifty? One hundred? Let me know and I can arrange it for you."

Was he kidding? How much of an idiot could this guy be? For every attack that Al Qaeda launched on the Americans, there had to be at least five attacks on Shiite neighborhoods, Sadr City first among them. Did this moron really think that the weapons he sold Al Qaeda wouldn't be used against his own people?

"How much is an RPG?"

"I can get you top of the line RPGs for about 250,000 dinars each."

That was about $250. Kadhim *knew* that they had to be more expensive than that. The Mahdi militia didn't have the financial resources that Al Qaeda did. A lot of their weapons were stolen, and their funding was extracted as ransom from kidnap victims.

Something that I will be soon if I don't get out of here.

"Pay a little extra, and I can include mortar shells with the mortars," the Mahdi Army member added.

Where had he stolen these weapons? Had they been stolen from Al Qaeda and now he was selling them back? Only to be used against him?

Kadhim's mind was reeling.

I need to get the fuck out of here. **Now.**

Sweat trickled down his neck. His blood pressure rose. Images of being thrown into a trunk and tortured raced through his mind. Every so often, he read the fatiha out loud, and when he could stand it no longer, he got up and sauntered out of the tent.

Walk slowly, try to act casual. Don't draw attention to yourself. Don't look back.

"Ali, you need to come get me."

"You've only been there for an hour."

"Just come get me. Now."

Kadhim tried not to look behind him. He felt eyes burning into his back. It was with vast relief that he at last saw Ali's car pull up.

That night, Kadhim relayed the story to Mohammed. Before hanging up he warned him, "Brother, this is the *third* time one of my friends has recognized you while you interpret for the Americans. You need to stop messing around and start wearing a mask!"

"Why? I'm not ashamed of what I'm doing. Just tell them it's not me."

"I do, but for God's sake, it makes me look like an idiot. They *know* it's you, Mohammed. And if you're not going to wear a mask for your good, then wear it for the sake of the family. You're putting everyone at risk. You've done this way too openly for way too long— everybody knows who you are now, and it's only a matter of time before they trace you back to Mama and Baba. Wear the damn mask!"

"*You're* the one who needs to be more careful," Mohammed retorted. "Hell, it sounds like the start of a bad joke: *An interpreter, a Mahdi army thug, and an Al Qaeda terrorist walk into a funeral...*"

EXERCISE

"Look what we brought you, Saint." Grinning, one of the Special Forces men tossed a packet of ammunition on the table. "A little gift for ya. Now what do you say you come with us on our next mission?"

Mohammed would have volunteered for the mission anyway, but bribery had almost become a game with them. Mohammed was often approached by Navy Seals, Special Forces and others with requests to work on dangerous missions, and when it came to bribes, they knew Saint's weak spot. Weapons, ammo, and lots of it, often offered in the middle of the DFAC, in front of Mohammed's own commander.

Major Matthews just chuckled, "That's all you have? Some ammo? Saint, I think you should hold out for something better!"

Mohammed, being one of the first interpreters to be hired locally, had special privileges enjoyed by very few interpreters. He could carry weapons and ammo, but—just like the soldiers—weapons could not be locked and loaded while on base. He laughed as the Special Forces guy replied quickly, "What are they paying you? We'll double it. We'll take care of you."

The Delta Force in particular loved Mohammed, and they bargained with him in fluent Arabic. "*Tureed sayyara?* You want a car? What kind do you like? A Mercedes? We'll go get one from a terrorist right now and give it to you."

"And how do you know they're terrorists?"

"Don't you worry about that. We'll get you the car, and you come with us."

Back in the DFAC, the guys laughed as Mohammed picked up the packet of ammo.

"I'm in." He'd gone on missions with just about everyone over the past six years, from raids and hostage rescues to sniper missions where they slept on rooftops for a night or two until the target was neutralized, at which point Mohammed would run into the street wearing civilian clothes and join the crowd of people in mock surprise.

"*Allahu akbar! Allahu akbar!* Curse the Americans! What happened? Is he martyred?" He joined the crowd and checked the target to confirm that he was deceased. And if he wasn't? Mohammed had a pistol in his belt with a silencer, just in case. Fortunately, the snipers were accurate and their weapons deadly, and thus far he hadn't needed to take that final shot and run for his life.

It came as a surprise to none, then, that when they approached the interpreters with the deadly mission of hunting down one of Zarqawi's top men, Mohammed was the first to volunteer.

"Are you sure?" The commander eyed him gravely. "Saint, we appreciate your enthusiasm, but this is one mission that you might not come back from."

"Are you kidding? We've been trying to get this guy for ages!" Mohammed grinned. "I'm not going to miss this!"

That was three days ago, and Mohammed and three other men had been hiding and sleeping in people's homes, abandoned houses, and under the bridges of Haifa Street ever since. All they needed was for the damn terrorist to turn on his cell phone. Just turn it on, and the CIA spook could track him down.

On the third day, the terrorist switched on his cell phone. They could finally track him, and they wanted him alive.

Immediately, a convoy was dispatched to Haifa Street, and Mohammed sat with the others in the back of one of the humvees. Helicopters whirred overhead and a PSYOP team warned civilians not to leave their homes.

They were making their way down Haifa street when, without warning, the humvee in front of Mohammed blew apart in an enormous explosion. The blast was so strong that Mohammed's humvee jumped in the air and its heavily locked doors blew open.

Mohammed himself was stunned. It was loud and confusing, and in the aftermath of the explosion, he couldn't think straight. He was dizzy, his ears felt plugged, and his head rang from the shock wave that had rippled through the atmosphere. His eyesight blurred, and he felt something warm running from his nose and ears.

"SAINT!"

He stared in a daze at the soldier, confused as to why he could barely hear the man shout. "A R E... Y O U... O K A Y?"

Why was he talking so slowly?

Mohammed felt himself being dragged to the side of the road.

With soldiers injured, the mission was canceled and the convoy sped back to the Green Zone. The radio was barraged with messages, and one in particular found its way to Major Matthews, causing him to freeze in his tracks.

"Saint is down! Saint is down!"

Mohammed hadn't returned. He hadn't survived the mission.

The relationship between Mohammed and Major Matthews had evolved to one of deep respect and friendship. Mohammed had always admired the fight in Major Matthews. In fact, in Mohammed's opinion, no one was a fiercer warrior, a bigger jokester, a better leader, or a more loyal friend. When Mohammed had developed a delirious fever of nearly 105°, Major Matthews had come to the clinic, ordered the medic away, and fed him by hand.

And Major Matthews, for his part, never forgot the day when Mohammed saved his life. They had been caught outside their humvee in the middle of an ambush, and Matthews had turned to see Mohammed pointing a gun in his direction. The gun went off before he had time to react, and it was then that Matthews realized that Mohammed had shot the insurgent right behind him, the man who had been about to take the major's life. He had hugged the burly interpreter right then and there in the middle of the street.

Saint had always been crazy. He was bound to get himself killed one of these days. How many times had Major Matthews ripped him apart for tearing off his protective vest and weapons to run after an escaping target? Even now, the oft-repeated words rang through his mind.

"You *motherfucker!* You could've got yourself *killed!*"

"So? Let me be killed. We had to get that guy!" Mohammed was so damn stubborn.

"Damn it, Saint! You want to get yourself killed, at least wait until I'm back in the States!"

Apparently, he had not been able to wait that long.

Firas's bus was late. He had been attending a special-needs school for four years now, and this was the first time his bus had ever been so late. Mama called Baba, but he hadn't heard anything. An hour had gone by since the bus was supposed to arrive, and each passing minute brought her more fear and anxiety.

Everyone knew of at least one child who had been kidnapped on the way to or from school. Children were held for ransom, and were not always returned alive when it was paid. It was for this reason that fearful parents pulled their children from school, and now tens of thousands of children had lost out on years of primary education. But at least they were still alive.

Please Allah, please let Firas be okay.

Two hours passed, then three, and still no bus. Um Ali called everyone she knew, frantic, trying to find out what had happened. She was desperate. Her dear Firas wasn't like other children. He was at greater risk than most.

Terrorists had begun to kidnap those with Down Syndrome, strap them with bombs, and use their unwitting victims as suicide bombers. And now sweet, innocent Firas was out there somewhere in Baghdad, God only knew where, without anyone to protect him.

What's going on? Was I unconscious? Where am I?

The ringing was gradually fading from Mohammed's ears, and he wiped a hand under his runny nose in annoyance.

Then he stopped.

His hand was covered in blood. So were his clothes. A charred humvee sat in front of him, empty.

As clarity of thought gradually returned, Mohammed realized that he was lying in the shadows on the side of the road. But not just any road.

He was on Haifa Street, the most dangerous street in Baghdad, wearing a full American military uniform, complete with I.D., badge, radio, weapons and a Blackwater vest.

And he was all alone.

Mohammed couldn't wait in the shadows any longer. People had started to notice him, and the gathering of suspicious locals was slowly growing larger. He stumbled to his feet, still dizzy, knowing that he had only one option.

In full American gear and in the unforgiving light of day, Mohammed began to sprint the deadly mile to the Green Zone.

He pulled out his radio and switched it to his unit.

"Matthews, *they left me behind!*"

"*Saint?*"

"I've been left behind, you motherfuckers! I've been left behind!" Behind him, Mohammed heard footsteps quicken as people began to run after him.

"Saint! Stay where you are! I'm sending Quick Reaction Forces STAT!"

"What are you talking about? I'm already running! They're coming after me!" He picked up the pace.

He was a sight to see, a six-foot Iraqi in an American military uniform and black armor plated vest, loaded with two magazines, an army knife, a Glock in one hand and an AK-47 in the other, running for dear life as blood dripped down his face.

Behind him, terrorists had noticed and had started the chase.

Four hours late, the bus finally arrived. A bombing had occurred en route, and the bus had been forced to stop and wait for the area to be cleared. The important thing was that Firas was okay.

But the incident was enough. They had almost lost their youngest son and they wouldn't risk it again. Mama and Baba decided that from then on, Firas would stay home.

When he heard the first bullet fire, Mohammed didn't even turn around. It whizzed past his right side. Immediately, heart pounding, blood racing, he began running in a zigzag pattern, as more bullets flew around him.

He couldn't turn and shoot back at them. He'd be dead if he so much as slowed down.

He aimed his AK-47 at passing drivers and screamed in Arabic, "STOP! GET OUT OF THE CAR!" *If he could just steal a car...*

Drivers took one look at the armed and bloodied man and the terrorists who chased him, and shot past him with a squeal of their tires.

Mohammed was quickly tiring. Weighed down by heavy

weaponry and an agonizing, 25-pound Blackwater vest, all he could feel was the heat, the weight, and the burning in his lungs.

Bullets continued to fly around him, one nearly grazing his cheek.

Terror gripped his chest. His legs flew, but he urged them to fly faster.

He was sick, dizzy, bleeding, and tired under the weight of his gear. *But there was no adrenalin like the adrenalin of outrunning death.*

BANG! A bullet flew past his left shoulder.

He was going to die. There was no way he could make it.

"SOMEBODY COME GET ME! SOMEBODY COME GET ME!" His voice was high-pitched and breathless as he screamed into the radio. If there was a response, he didn't hear it.

BANG! BANG! Two more bullets exploded into the road around him.

Run. Just run. Death was chasing him.

He felt as though his lungs would burst. There was no air left. No oxygen. Somehow, his legs kept going without it. As if in a dream, he looked up to the see the gates of the Green Zone ahead of him. He was almost there, almost to the finish line. He willed himself to keep going, even as his vision grew fuzzy and dark.

He was vaguely aware of a short crossfire of bullets overhead, then it stopped abruptly. The insurgents couldn't open fire so close to the checkpoint without being shot at in return.

He reached the gate and collapsed.

The soldiers manning the checkpoint had watched him run, and as they realized who it was, their faces went white.

The last they'd heard, Saint was dead.

Mohammed was on his hands and knees in the extreme stages of hyperventilation. He tore off his vest, but it made no difference. It felt as though his lungs had squeezed shut, and with each attempt to inhale, there was only a shaky, high-pitched wheeze without relief. Tears were running from his eyes, though he didn't know why.

One of the soldiers threw water on his face, as others radioed for a medic and backup. Mohammed pulled out his radio one last time and switched it to be heard by the entire brigade, from the lowest private to the full-bird colonel.

"*To whoever fucking hears me,*" he screamed between breathless wheezing, "*You motherfuckers! You sons of bitches! You left me behind! I spent three days out there with you guys and you left me behind!*"

He let out a stream of curses as a medic placed an oxygen mask on his face.

Mohammed was still on the ground when Major Matthews arrived, livid with anger. He got out of the humvee, slamming the door so hard that the three-ton vehicle shook, and ran to kneel by Mohammed's side.

"Saint! Buddy, are you okay?"

"They left me behind!"

"I know. I'm going to work on it, I promise. But are you okay?"

"I don't know!" Physically, mentally, emotionally, nothing felt okay.

The medics worked quickly to remove his shirt, checking for bullet wounds. "He looks alright, but he'll have to be seen by the hospital to check for injuries caused by the bomb blast. He's in shock."

"How the hell could you leave me behind?" Mohammed wheezed.

"It wasn't me, I swear!" Matthews grabbed his hand. "I would never do that to you!"

In the end, the commander of the mission apologized to Mohammed in person, and the entire platoon was punished with Article 15. They had realized, after rushing back, that they had forgotten their volunteer interpreter. Someone had claimed him dead, perhaps because he truly thought him dead, perhaps to cover his own ass.

They would never forget him again.

FINAL DAYS

Kadhim had taken all of the usual precautions before leaving the base. He let his facial hair grow for a couple days. He wore a hat and sunglasses. He smeared his license plate with mud so that the *allasa* who waited outside the gate wouldn't be able to photograph it and track down his family. And he shot out of the gate like a bat out of hell, barreling down the empty highway at 95 miles per hour.

And yet there behind him, each seating four to five armed men, were two cars chasing him at top speed.

Fear of this kind was more than a tingling in the spine or a racing heart. It was something that gripped the entire body and soul. The veins in Kadhim's neck felt as though they were about to explode. His senses felt heightened. He pushed the gas pedal down as far as it would go.

Come on. Dear God, let this car go faster!

The Espero crept up to 100... 105...

A bullet to the head, perhaps a beheading, was right there behind him, lunging at his heels.

He kept his foot on the gas, and watched the speedometer continued to creep into red...115...125...140 miles per hour...

He was flying. The two cars behind him grew smaller in the distance, then gave up and stopped altogether. Still, breathless and shaky, Kadhim didn't ease his foot from the gas.

All this, just to get his paperwork in order.

When he applied for the Special Immigrant Visa to the U.S., they'd warned him that his name needed to be consistent on all of his documents, from the I.D. card and birth certificate, to his Iraqi passport and medical school transcript and degree.

This was a problem. Some documents used his tribal name, whereas others referred to him by first name, father's name, grandfather's name, and great grandfather's name, following the common Arabic naming system.

When it came to documents translated into English, the confusion was even worse. While his names were spelled accurately in Arabic, each official had chosen a different English spelling for each part of his name. It was a mess that would take months to straighten out, and Kadhim only had one day.

All the more reason to fly down these dangerous roads at 135 miles per hour. He started with a visit to the dean of Al Kindy Medical School, then drove across town to the Iraqi Nationality and Passport Directorate. After waiting for an hour in line, he was told that he was missing a document from his medical school, and was forced to make another trip to Al Kindy. New documents, stamps, verifications, and signatures, and for each one, a healthy bribe.

After numerous top-speed trips across Baghdad, Kadhim was finally down to the last and most important document when he noticed a smell coming from his car. He lifted the hood to find his oil nearly empty, and the engine completely overheated. It was time to call Ali.

"You might as well stop praying," Kadhim joked. "Even Allah can't find you a parking spot here."

Ali cursed at the cars that packed the marketplace of Bab Al-Sharji, and turned down another road. He had done what any good brother would do, leaving work to pick up Kadhim and help him complete what seemed like a bureaucratic mission impossible, and now there was nowhere left to park but Saadun garage.

It was an enormous garage, with one level stacked on top of another, and Ali preferred to avoid it at all costs. Pay ridiculously high rates for parking and then be forced to walk a mile before getting anywhere? No thank you.

Nevertheless, it was the only option. They pulled up to the third floor before finding an open spot, parked next to a little white Toyota, and got out of the car.

"What the hell *was* that?" Mohammed was nearby on one of the highest rooftops of Haifa Street when he heard the explosion and saw a thick black cloud of smoke billow into the air. His heart began to pound as he realized that it was in the Bab Al-Sharji marketplace, where Ali ran his business. What building was that? Was that... *Saadun garage?*

Immediately, Mohammed pulled out his cell phone and called Ali. There was no answer.

Surely he wouldn't have parked there. He never *parks there!*

He called again. No response.

Come on, Ali, pick up the phone!

He called Ali four or five times. Nothing. He called Kadhim, who had told him only half an hour earlier saying that he and Ali were on their way to the marketplace. Again nothing. With each minute that passed, his panic grew. By the time an hour had gone by, he was sure that they were dead.

Please, don't let this be the day that I learn of the death of my brothers. Not today.

He tried Mama and Baba; neither of them had heard from the two brothers. Half-formed plans started to take shape in his mind. *I'll have to leave the mission to go hunt for my brothers' bodies. I'll search the hospitals first, then join the long pitiful lines that form outside the morgues...*

Ring after unanswered ring sounded in his ear. Then, just as he was about to give up, a panicked and desperate voice answered the phone.

"It's gone! *It's all gone!*"

Kadhim and Ali had only been walking for ten minutes when they heard the sonic boom behind them. They didn't know where the explosion had occurred, but they were glad not to be in it.

Kadhim paid a $300 bribe for his new passport to be released in one hour instead of three months, and went to join Ali at his work, where he found his older brother in an agitated frenzy.

"It was Saadun garage! The explosion was in Saadun garage!"

"Shit. Well, let's go see the damage."

With any luck, it would be a relatively small car bomb that had charred the cars next to it. It was a huge garage, after all. Perhaps Ali's car would be okay.

They hurried down the street toward the garage, then slowed and stared in awe as the sight came into view.

Saadun garage had been completely flattened. Hundreds of cars were crushed inside, among them Ali's Mercedes. God only knew how many people had been inside as well. Kadhim and Ali themselves had escaped death by a mere ten minutes.

Ali shouted and cursed, and Kadhim put a hand on his brother's arm.

"It's alright, brother. Let that car be a sacrifice for you. Thank Allah it happened to the car and not to us."

"You don't understand!" Ali turned to Kadhim angrily. "I don't have to replace only my car! I left a huge sum of cash for the business in the car, and it's gone! All of it!"

It was a cool September day in 2008 when Kadhim entered Mohammed's trailer for the last time.

"I got my visa."

His older brother jumped up with huge grin and a congratulatory hug, then pulled a few beers out of his small fridge. "Here... to celebrate."

"Thanks." Kadhim accepted the offering, and the two sat down.

"So, how soon are you leaving?"

"I already bought my ticket. I leave in four days."

"*Four days?* What's the rush, *habibi*?"

"I'm ready to go, Mohammed. I'm serious—I'm done with this place. Besides, guess who called me in a rage the other day."

"Who?"

"Inas."

"Who's that?"

"I didn't tell you about her? She used to work with me as an interpreter, and there was something about the way she always asked personal questions that seemed fishy. Well, I said something to the Americans one day and they decided to check her out. Among her stuff they found a hard drive filled with the *real* names of all the interpreters on base. Including mine."

"Why the hell would you tell her your real name?"

"Are you kidding? I have *no idea* where she got all that information, but my gut tells me she was planning to sell it to terrorists... if she hasn't already." Kadhim took a swig of beer. "She's been in jail for a year and was just released yesterday."

"Why did they let her out?"

"Lack of evidence, apparently. That's the American justice system. Anyway, she called me and she was *pissed*. She made it very clear that she blames *me* for her year of imprisonment. She was cursing me to hell and wishing I would die. She wouldn't tell me how she got my name or why she had all those interpreters' personal information, but I did find out that her husband is big in the Mahdi Army. So I'm not going to stick around."

"I can't believe I never knew about this!"

Kadhim laughed. "What about you? When are you going to the United States? I've only been working with the Army for two years and you've been with them for six. Your visa should be approved any time now, right?"

"Yeah, I've been meaning to talk to you about that." Mohammed downed his beer and leaned back with an ironic half-laugh. "I think there's going to be a bit of a delay."

One look at his brother's face set off warning bells in Kadhim's mind. "What have you done now?"

"It's no big deal... I kind of got into a fight with one of the commanders."

"*What?* Are you *kidding?*"

"He insulted me, Kadhim! We were in a top-security meeting and he kept questioning why I was there, despite the fact that it was his *superior* who had brought me into the meeting! I was giving them insider information, really *valuable* information, and he questions why I'm there? I've risked my life with the Americans for six years, and *this* is the treatment I get?"

"So you *fight* him?"

"He kept insulting me under his breath in Arabic so the others couldn't understand. Don't come to *my* country and insult me! I held my cool as long as I could Kadhim, but when he started saying dirty things about our mother, I lost it."

"So what does this mean? Will you never get a visa?"

"Well, probably not as long as he's in the hospital."

"Holy shit, Mohammed! How long has he been in the hospital?"

"Only three months so far. But I have some good guys in my corner. Don't worry. They'll work it out."

"*Three months!*" Kadhim shook his head. "Brother, that temper has been getting you into trouble since the days of the Ba'ath regime. Why didn't you tell me?"

"I didn't want you to worry." Mohammed grinned. "It'll pass. Just don't tell anyone, because some of the commanders are working really hard to smooth this thing over, and the fewer who know, the better."

Kadhim laughed in disbelief. "You know, I have a strong feeling that all the stories we've shared with each other over the years are only the tip of the iceberg."

Four days later, Kadhim, Ali, and Mohammed headed to Baghdad airport. For Kadhim, it would be the last time. After years of rare visits home, Kadhim had spent two nights at his parents' house and was so excited, he'd been unable to sleep. At last, *at last*, the dream that he'd been told was impossible, the dream that he'd nearly given up on, was about to come true. True peace, true freedom, true *life*.

His excitement to finally leave the war behind and start his new life in the greatest country in the world was tempered only by the pain of saying goodbye to those he loved.

Mama, Baba, Firas, Salih, Ali... would he ever see them in person again? Would he ever eat grilled fish on the banks of the Tigris as the sun set behind the palm trees? Would he enjoy Mama's cooking? Would he one day return to proudly show off his grandfather's date farm to his children?

And Mohammed. How hard would it be to go to a new land without the man who was both his brother and his best friend?

The heartfelt goodbye was over before he knew it, and Kadhim boarded the plane. As he watched the city of Baghdad morph into a surreal scene of tiny cars and toy houses far below, Mohammed's promise rang in his ears.

"Arrive safely, *habibi*. And don't worry, brother, I'll join you soon."

EPILOGUE

AMERICA: LOVESICK

What did it mean to him, becoming an American citizen?

Kadhim had pondered the question all morning as he buttoned his shirt, straightened his tie, and pulled on his best suit. His nerves were afire—but good nerves, excited nerves—as he arrived at his destination and got out of the car. The weather was sunny and beautiful, perfect for a day five years in the making, and he entered, signed in, and took his seat among a pack of likewise enthusiastic immigrants.

Kadhim scanned the visitors' side of the room, searching anxiously for those who had come to support him.

Where were they?

He saw them at last, seated close to the aisle, and smiled with anticipation. They met his gaze with encouraging grins, and Kadhim relaxed. They were here. He could do this now. He could become an American citizen.

Upon landing in the United States, Kadhim had been greeted by a group of friends from the Ohio National Guard, the colonel the first among them. They had waited for him at the Columbus, Ohio airport until two o'clock in the morning, and to see their welcoming faces when he had expected no one was one of the greatest surprises of his life.

He was so thrilled to be in the United States that he didn't sleep at all the first night, browsing the internet instead in search of an apartment. By morning he had decided upon a place, and with the colonel's help he went there, explained his circumstances, and paid the entire six-month lease up front, in cash.

It made him laugh now to remember his first trip to an American grocery store. He had been amazed by the sheer enormity and variety of choices, and the self check-out had confounded him. He stood at the empty check-out counter for ages, all by himself, wondering what in the world he was supposed to do, before at last confessing to a surprised employee that it was his first day in America.

Kadhim missed his family and prayed for their safety, but after all he'd seen, he didn't miss Iraq. The bits of Iraq that he had known and loved in his youth—sharing Ramadan dinners, grilling fresh fish on the banks of the Tigris—were gone. All that was left were car bombs, murder, and a constant state of anxiety. He never wanted to go back.

It was as though someone had finally uncorked all the tension pent up inside him and he was free at last. Work and study fell to the wayside, as he went out and partied, laughed, and explored the country with friends old and new. He could breathe at last. He was free. He was alive.

Of all Iraqis, it was ironic that the first one Kadhim should meet in the States was Yum Yum. She had received her visa and her living situation wasn't working out, so at Mohammed's request, Kadhim allowed her to live with him rent-free until Mohammed came from Iraq.

"So what's the plan here?" Kadhim asked Mohammed one day over the phone. "Yum Yum keeps talking about her '*habibi* Mohammed' and says that you're going to come marry her."

"What?" His brother squealed with laughter. "She's crazy if she thinks I'm going to marry her! I'm just doing her a favor."

"*You're* doing her a favor? This woman is eating me out of house and home! You owe me big, brother. By the way, someone named Jumana keeps calling, asking for your number..."

"Juju? Do NOT give her my number!"

Mohammed finally landed in the United States, green card in hand, eight months after his younger brother, and joined him in Columbus. Kadhim, meanwhile, had long since blown through all of his savings, and his earnings from medical interpretation fluctuated too much to be reliable. It was time to get a real job.

Mohammed was greeted by Kadhim and the colonel at the airport and moved into Kadhim's second bedroom. Georgie had already immigrated to the United States, and as soon as he heard of his old friend's arrival, he joined the two brothers in Ohio. The three of them made the most of their freedom, reminiscing, enjoying the nightlife, and scaring Americans with their tales of Iraq. Georgie was in full form in the United States. He was slimmer, his English had vastly improved, and, no longer fearing for his life, he was free to pour all of his energy into thwarting Mohammed's efforts to get laid, which he did with gleeful abandon.

It was wonderful to be reunited with his brother and friend, and Mohammed soon proved to be just as adept with girls in the United States as he was with girls in Iraq. He relished the freedom and safety of his new home, and was grateful for his brother's presence, but the transition wasn't easy.

It was the quiet that was the hardest to get used to. He lay awake at night for months, just listening to the silence. Gone were the bombs, the mortars, Georgie's snores... *who would have thought I could miss things like that?* He didn't trust the calm. He longed for his gun and kept his doors locked constantly.

Mohammed had been forced to leave Iraq. His work had put not only him but his entire family at risk, and after Ali had been threatened twice by insurgents who noticed his resemblance to the interpreter, Mohammed had had no choice but to leave his country. He missed his family every day. He would have died to protect them, but the sad truth was that they were safest when he was far away.

And there was still the matter of Yum Yum. Now that she lived with them, Mohammed couldn't escape her. She was everywhere. Every time he, Kadhim and Georgie went out, Yum Yum insisted on tagging along, and to be honest, Mohammed had new fish to fry. Yum Yum had grown increasingly needy and depressed. She was bored, couldn't find work, had gained weight on an American diet and wanted Mohammed to commit.

"If you're not good to me," she threatened one day, "I'll move to California and live with my aunt!"

At last, an opportunity.

"You know Yum Yum, that might be good for you."

"What do you mean?"

"California's beautiful, and you'll be much happier with your relatives."

"You think so?"

"Absolutely. Plus it'll be easier for you to find work there."

"But what about us? We—"

Mohammed cut her off. "You should do what's right for *you*, Yum Yum. Go. Enjoy your life. You're miserable here."

"Are you sure? What about all my stuff?"

"Don't worry about that. Just visit your aunt, and if it's working out let me know and I'll send your stuff."

She bought a ticket to California, and before her flight had even landed Mohammed had packed all of her stuff and shipped it next day delivery to her aunt's address.

He breathed a sigh of relief.

Now *this* was freedom.

"Kadhim, meet Katriina. She volunteers with us a couple times a week. Katriina, Kadhim helps Arabic-speaking refugees find employment."

It was Kadhim's first week on the job at a local refugee resettlement agency and he was doing his best to keep everyone's names straight, but with one look at the young blonde in front of him, he knew that he would remember her.

"Nice to meet you, Katriina."

"*Tsharrafna*, Kadhim."

He raised his eyebrows. "You speak Arabic?"

She laughed, clearly having seen this reaction before. "*Eh, bahki 'arabi.*"

Her Arabic was fluent, and her accent—though not Iraqi—was flawless. They continued their conversation in Arabic.

"Are you Lebanese?"

"I'm American."

"I meant where are you from originally? Is your father Lebanese?"

"No."

"Your grandfather then?"

She just laughed.

"How do you speak Arabic?"

"It's not impossible to learn."

"I'm sorry, I've just never seen an American speak such fluent Arabic."

"I'm getting my degree in Arabic, and I've studied in the Middle East."

He scoured his mind for an excuse to keep talking to her, this fair-skinned American beauty with her mind-boggling Arabic, but he couldn't think of anything that didn't seem awkward or contrived. He had never met anyone like her, and all he could think was, *I need to get to know her.*

A week went by with no more than a few hellos between them, and then one afternoon Kadhim looked up to see Katriina standing at his cubicle.

"I'm arranging a trip for refugees to the state park, and I wanted to ask you a favor."

"Of course." His heart was pounding.

"I'm a volunteer and not on the company's insurance, so I was wondering if you'd like to come along and drive the van for us."

"I'd be happy to."

"You can bring your wife and kids, if you'd like," she added hurriedly.

Kadhim grinned. "I'm not married."

"Oh." She smiled and went a little red. "Well, here's the flyer. We'll see you Saturday."

It was the opportunity he'd been waiting for. A small group of Iraqi refugees had signed up for the trip, but by the time they made it to the park it was as though no one else existed. Kadhim spent the whole time talking to Katriina as they hiked the forest and explored the caves. She told him how warmly she'd been welcomed by Arabs while travelling in the Middle East, and how she wanted to extend the same welcome and helping hand to those coming to America. In the meantime, she had begun teaching Arabic at a nearby university. She was intelligent, had a quick wit, and conversation with her came naturally. They found a waterfall that ended in a small pool, and dipped their toes in the cool water while sunshine twinkled through the trees and highlighted gold strands in Katriina's hair.

Life was good. America was beautiful. Really beautiful.

By evening, Kadhim was hooked. He needed to see her more, talk to her, just be around her. He didn't have her number, so he decided to look her up on Facebook and send her a message. There was just one problem.

He didn't know her last name.

In fact, he barely knew how to spell her first name.

He toyed with the idea of asking a coworker but decided that it would be inappropriate to ask about the hot volunteer during his second week on the job. He'd have to look her up based on first name alone.

How many 'Katriinas' could there be on Facebook, after all?

Six mind-numbing hours later, he found her.

With nervous excitement, he wrote a message asking her to go on a date with him, reread it twenty times, and pushed send.

◇ ◇ ◇

In Iraq, Mohammed had been in his element. Hunting terrorists, saving lives, risking his own skin to work with the smartest, toughest and meanest while clearing the scum from his country... this was what thrilled him and gave his life meaning. In America, he struggled to find a career half as meaningful.

He had worked for a while acting as an "insurgent" in training exercises for those soon to be deployed. However, fewer soldiers were being sent to Iraq these days, and Mohammed was frustrated to realize that for all he had done in Iraq, he was no longer needed in the United States. At least, not as long as he wasn't a citizen.

After a stint in security, he jumped at a great job opportunity in Washington D.C., and soon he was leaving Ohio for the nation's capital.

Two agonizing days went by, and at last, a message appeared in Kadhim's inbox.

Kadhim, I will be honest with you. I would very much like to go out with you sometime. And I had thought of this even before you asked me out, although I never expected that you would actually ask.

But there are reasons why I hesitate as well -- one, things are a little complicated on my end right now, and two, we kind of work together (even though I only volunteer) and I love everything I do there. I wouldn't want anything to make us feel uncomfortable at the office.

So here is what it comes down to: I cannot say no, because truthfully the answer is yes, I would like to go out with you sometime, but can I ask you to wait? I want to make sure that this is something we both really want before jeopardizing other things that I care about. Could I also ask you to please not feel uncomfortable around me about any of this? I am very pleased and flattered that you would ask, and I hope sometime soon to take you up on your offer.

No number of reservations could lessen Kadhim's elation. He wrote back immediately, saying he understood and would give her all the time she needed to see that he was serious. As the weeks passed, their friendship grew. He began to teach her the Iraqi dialect and she took him to his first football game. Despite being from two different cultures, religions, and worlds, they seemed perfectly matched. He, an Americanized Arab and she, an American who understood Arabic and Arab culture; each a perfect mixture of East and West.

Katriina's presence brought Kadhim a strange but thrilling sense of internal calm, of being complete. She was healing him. He couldn't believe how quickly and how deeply he was falling for her. Within a few months, his feelings for her blew every feeling of love he'd ever had out of the water.

He thought of her constantly. The sound of her voice made him excited; seeing her made his heart pound. When he slept his mind was filled with dreams of her and thoughts of her filled the pages of his newly-purchased medical textbooks. It seemed recertifying his MD would have to wait. Although he tried to hold back, he was afraid he overwhelmed her. The truth was, he didn't know *how* to talk to her. She didn't want to be treated the way most Iraqi girls did, with poems and teddy bears. He'd never had any problem with girls before. In fact, he'd found that the less interested he was, the more they chased him. But with Katriina, his own feelings overwhelmed him.

Three months had passed when the two of them went out to celebrate his birthday with some drinks and a comedy show. High from the thrill of celebrating his birthday in America with a girl that he was crazy about, far from the bombs of Baghdad, he had reached out to kiss her, and she suddenly took a step back.

"Wait, Kadhim. The thing is, I just... I think... I don't feel *that way* about you."

His heart started to pound. "You mean you don't think there's a chance of us dating? Ever?"

She hesitated. "I don't think so. It's just... a little too much sometimes."

"I'm sorry." He didn't know what else to say. The strength of his feelings had been too much for her. He had messed it up.

He was devastated.

She first caught Mohammed's attention through a photograph. Amidst a group of people, she stood out to him, an attractive young woman in a well-cut gray suit and black headscarf. She looked as though she knew how to handle both herself and those around her.

"Who is that?"

"That?" Hisham glanced at the picture. "That's Maya. She's from an Iraqi family in Dearborn and heads the Michigan chapter of our club. She studied law and works as a prosecutor. She's smart, on top of things, and she's doing a great job of..."

"Look, I don't need to know all of this." Mohammed cut him off. "I need to know if she's single. *That's* why I asked."

Hisham looked at him and a conspiratorial smile slowly grew on his face. "You want me to arrange an introduction?"

At last, joining this Iraqi culture club was paying off.

It seemed as though Maya had seen through their guise. Mohammed was thrilled to see that she was even more beautiful in person than she had been in the picture. However, the look on her face had gone from surprise to skepticism as she took in the situation in the hotel lobby. An urgent meeting had been arranged, with the head of the club—Hisham—coming all the way from Washington D.C. But rather than a large group of people, it was only Hisham, his wife, and some tall guy that Maya had never seen before at any of the Michigan meetings. It felt oddly like a double date.

Mohammed watched in frustration as Maya flatly refused his invitation to go out to dinner and walked out the door. He had pulled out all of the stops, even taking off his jacket and not-so-subtly flexing his biceps. Rejection? Not he. Mohammed Al Baghdadi didn't get rejected. Challenge accepted.

Kadhim was miserable. A month had gone by without her, and every moment was agonizing. He ignored Katriina's phone calls and messages that she missed him and still wanted to be friends. The problem was that she didn't miss him the way he missed her. Kadhim *longed* for Katriina, ached for her bright smile and comforting laugh. He missed the thrill of hearing her incorporate bits of his native Iraqi dialect into her speech. When he opened a textbook, he found himself rereading the same lines again and again without comprehension, unable to focus without her next to him. He couldn't sleep, couldn't eat, and couldn't concentrate. He rarely saw her at work now that she had returned to school. Their few interactions were strained.

Mohammed was aware of the situation, but kindly refrained from saying anything. He knew better than to push the subject.

Kadhim had never been in so much anguish, not even in the worst days of Iraq. He worried about Katriina finding someone else, and the knowledge that she didn't want him tore away at his soul. The constant emotional torment made his heart ache and nauseated him. *How can it be, that I could survive the worst of Baghdad, but an unrequited love can bring me to my knees?* It was terrible, what love could do.

He was miserable without her.

Enough. I can't live like this. As much as the idea of her dating other men tormented him, Kadhim realized that he would rather be her friend than not have her in his life at all. He just needed to be near her.

"So your friend was shot while bringing his pregnant wife to the hospital to have a baby?" Katriina's eyes were full of sympathy as they sat talking in the car in the mall parking lot.

"Yes. That was when I left medicine. Well, after that and a year of facing corruption and death threats."

"Wait—*death threats?*" Her eyes went wide.

Kadhim rarely spoke of Iraq, but when he did dredge up the painful memories, he tried to spare her the details. They had returned to being friends and were closer than ever, but Kadhim let the friendship remain platonic. He didn't want to risk overwhelming her with feelings that he had learned to keep hidden. They sat in companionable silence for a while; then she turned to him.

"It amazes me, everything that you have lived through, Kadhim. I have to ask: how did you not go crazy?"

He smiled. "You *do* go crazy. You live only a moment at a time and never take anything for granted. You're constantly calling your family to check on them: 'Salih, did you make it to the university? Mohammed, did you go safely through the checkpoint? Ali, did you make it home okay?' Then at the end of the day you thank Allah that you and your family survived the day, only to wake up the next morning with the same fears as the morning before."

"But how did you *handle* that?"

"You do whatever you can just to try to forget what's going on outside. Alcohol, video games, girls... whatever it takes."

"I see..." She hesitated for a moment. "I guess what I'm asking about is... PTSD. I know people who've been through far less and handled it much worse. How can you be so... *normal?*"

Kadhim's hearty laugh broke the seriousness of the conversation. "Don't worry, I don't have PTSD. The sad truth is that Iraqis have been living with war our whole lives. We're used to it, used to seeing terrible things. Our media doesn't protect us from gruesome sights. Does war anger and disgust me? Yes. But I'm not shocked by it. All Iraqis have lost family members, but they have no choice but to continue living. You don't get time to grieve or recover, because the next tragedy is just around the corner and you're too busy trying to stay alive. It's about survival."

He stared ahead as the memories flooded back, and he didn't notice the way Katriina was looking at him.

It was as though she were seeing him for the first time.

It had become a matter of priority for Mohammed to make the trip from DC to attend all Michigan events of the Iraqi culture club, where he developed a professional relationship with Maya. They kept in touch casually, usually discussing work or weather, but occasionally Mohammed would suggest that they take their relationship to the next level. The answer was always no.

There would be no dating Maya. She came from a conservative family, and if he wanted to get to know her, then he would have to propose in true Iraqi fashion. And while he wasn't gung-ho about the idea of marriage, the thought of losing her to someone else was becoming increasingly difficult to stomach. The more he came to know Maya, the more he was attracted to her. She was beautiful, intelligent, and just as stubborn as he. And even as she rejected him, there was something hesitant in it, something not quite final. Their relationship never petered out, and his hope remained alive. However, after a year and a half of putting up with something that was never "yes" and never quite "no," Mohammed had had enough. For the first time in his life, he was the one demanding commitment.

And if she didn't want to commit, then it was time to walk away.

They hadn't spoken in months when Maya received his phone call.

"Is everything alright, Mohammed?" She assumed he had an urgent legal question.

"Yes, everything's fine. I just called because I want to get to know you better. Look, Maya, I really want to pursue this."

She hesitated. *Despite turning him down all this time, she had never quite been able to get him out of her mind. This was more consideration than she'd ever given any other man in her entire life. And while Mohammed was wrong for her in so many ways, there was just something about him... Maybe she should just give it a chance and see where it went...*

"Fine."

There it was. At last. But Mohammed wasn't finished yet.

"Okay, now give me your father's number, and I will call him and officially ask for your hand in marriage. And if at that point you decide to say no, then say no formally. No more beating around the bush and kind of saying no but not really. I'm tired of playing this game, Maya. If you want to reject me, do it so that you can't go back on it."

"Okay. That's fair." She gave him her father's number. There was something about the strength of his words that pleased her. "But first *I* have something to ask. Mohammed, you've pursued me for a year and a half. There are some men that need marriage because all they know is their mother's house and then their wife's house. But you? You clearly don't *need* marriage. You're thirty-five years old and doing just fine by yourself. So what is it that's making you pursue this relationship so much? I need to know what you're looking for from me."

"Honestly? I want someone I respect and care about, and who cares about me. And I want love. We can get engaged to appease your family so that we have a chance to properly get to know one another, but if you don't love me by the time we get married then I don't want to get married. I want to love you, and I want you to love me, and if that doesn't happen for us, then I'll stop seeing you, I'll stop talking to you, and that will be it."

It was, perhaps, the first time that he had ever spoken so honestly.

"Maya, I'm not looking for someone to cook and clean for me. I love food, but I've been doing just fine on my own for the past ten years. The only thing I'm missing is love and someone to grow old with. That's all I want."

"Well, there are some things you should know about me first, Mohammed. We've both been raised in a patriarchal society, but there isn't anything in the world that would get me to live my life with a man who feels he's entitled to tell me what to do or how to behave. I'm a grown woman, and I'm more than capable of determining my own behavior. I have a mind of my own, and if I want to work, I will work. If I need to go out for something, I'll go out. You can give suggestions, that is it."

Mohammed laughed. "That's fine by me." Her strength and stubbornness were the most beautiful things about her.

"Katriina, what's wrong?"

"I'm sorry, I don't want to talk about it, Kadhim." She looked at him with tears in her eyes and tried to smile. "Thanks for coming over. You're always there for me."

"Of course. Anything I can do to help..." Even with the tears, her eyes were beautiful, with an intriguing mixture of green, brown, blue and hazel that he had never seen before. She was usually so full of joy.

"Katriina, I just want to see you happy. Nothing and no one is worth your tears. You are beautiful."

And suddenly, without knowing why he was doing it and unable to stop himself, he put a hand on her slim waist and kissed her. She was startled, but she didn't pull away. His heart was pounding. He couldn't believe he was actually kissing her. *Finally.*

When he pulled away she stayed in his arms, looked up at him, and smiled. Nothing would ever be the same.

"I hereby declare, on oath, that I absolutely and entirely renounce and abjure all allegiance and fidelity to any foreign prince, potentate, state or sovereignty of whom or which I have heretofore been a subject or citizen..."

Iraq. There was so much about Iraq that made the brothers love the United States. The right to elect their president. The liberty to speak without fear and practice their religion without death threats. The freedom to build a future from their dreams.

"...that I will support and defend the Constitution and laws of the United States of America against all enemies, foreign and domestic..."

Iraq was still a mess, more than five years after they'd left it, but there had been some change for the better. Iraqis in Sunni areas such as Anbar and Fallujah had tired of the terrorists for whom they provided refuge. The *allasa* made their neighborhoods unsafe, demanded their daughters as temporary wives, and killed fathers who refused these requests. It was an insult to Iraqi honor—their daughters were not to be given away.

As the tribes realized the error of hosting this disease, they united and formed Awakening Councils whose main purpose was to rid their land of terrorists, and with the help of the Iraqi Army, the U.S. Forces and the Shiite-led government, they did so. At least for a time.

"...that I will bear true faith and allegiance to the United States of America..."

The United States had brought the brothers a life they had never dreamed of. Wild Mohammed had at last fallen in love with a woman who was a lioness in her own right, but there would be no wedding without the approval of Maya's father, who had decided to do his own research first. He took a picture of Mohammed to Baghdad and asked around in his old neighborhood. No one had seen Mohammed during the eight years he worked with the U.S. Forces, and it had been several more years since he'd landed in the States, so when old friends and neighbors looked at the picture, they saw not Mohammed, but his younger brother Salih. "Oh yes, he's a wonderful young man—conservative, well-behaved, and extremely shy."

Maya's father couldn't understand why they kept calling Mohammed by a different name, but he went home satisfied that his daughter's suitor was a religious, if somewhat bashful, gentleman. Mohammed and Maya's wedding was a spectacular, blow-out affair. The two brothers felt the absence of their parents and brothers, but otherwise it was a perfect day, and the colonel, Georgie, Katriina, and Kadhim were all there to share in Mohammed and Maya's happiness.

With Katriina by his side, Kadhim felt complete. Whole. At home. In her calming presence, he was at last able to return to studying medicine. When he left his job in order to study full-time, she and Mohammed worked harder in order to support him. The colonel, too, was a constant source of advice and support, becoming like a second father to him. It was fitting that he should be here on this day, considering how instrumental he had been in helping Kadhim reach this point. Kadhim passed the boards with flying colors, recertified his degree and obtained an American medical license. He was accepted into a surgical residency program and at last returned to practicing medicine. With Mohammed

415

and Katriina's help, he had accomplished the dream that had for so many years felt like an impossibility.

So what did getting his American citizenship mean to him?

It meant that the United States officially recognized what Kadhim had long felt to be true: that he—knowing what it was to live without them—loved more than anyone the values upon which the country had been built. He had been an American at heart long before taking this oath.

"...and that I take this obligation freely... so help me God."

Now, with his new status as an equal, Kadhim would return to the life he had built, a doctor in a free and beautiful country. Every day, he thanked God that he and Mohammed had made it safely out of Iraq. He thanked God that his family was alive and well, and looked forward to their impending arrival to the United States.

And he thanked God for the woman who made his every day a joy, his beloved wife Katriina. She approached him now, a proud smile on her face, and in her arms she gently cradled their cherished newborn son.

ABOUT THE AUTHOR

Tara Najim has a Masters degree in Arabic from the Ohio State University. She has lived and studied in the Middle East extensively, and specializes in the field of Middle Eastern refugee crises and resettlement.

Made in the USA
Middletown, DE
19 December 2015